FOOD and DRINK
IN AMERICA

Books by Richard J. Hooker

The Carolina Backcountry on the Eve of the Revolution: The Journal and Other Writings of Charles Woodmason, Anglican Itinerant (1953).
The American Revolution: The Search for Meaning (1970).
The Book of Chowder (1978).
Food and Drink in America: A History (1981).

FOOD and DRINK IN AMERICA

A HISTORY

Richard J. Hooker

THE BOBBS-MERRILL COMPANY, INC.
Indianapolis/New York

The author's special thanks to:

Molly Schwarz for permission to publish an excerpt from *The Journal of Mollie Dorsey Sanford,* ed. Donald F. Danger (Lincoln, Nebr.: University of Nebraska Press, 1959), p. 36.

The William and Mary Quarterly for permission to use portions of my article "The American Revolution Seen Through a Wine Glass," in the issue of January, 1954, pp. 52–77.

The Pleasures of Cooking for permission to adapt portions of my article "The Day of the Oyster," in the issue of October, 1978, pp. 40–47.

Published by The Bobbs-Merrill Company, Inc.
Indianapolis   New York

Library of Congress Cataloging in Publication Data

Hooker, Richard James, 1913-
  Food and drink in America.

  Bibliography: p.
  Includes index.
  1. Food habits — United States — History.
  2. Drinking customs — United States — History.
  I. Title.
GT2853.U5H66   394.1'2'0973   80–2733
ISBN 0–672–52681–6

Designed by Antler & Baldwin, Inc.
Manufactured in the United States of America

First Printing

To Nancy

Acknowledgments

In preparing this work I have become indebted to many people. I cannot repay these obligations by words, but I can gratefully acknowledge that they exist.

Through the years this book has been in preparation, friends have given me references and suggestions: Edna Florig, Frederick Schmidt, John S. Buchanan, Bernard A. Weisberger, Paul B. Johnson, David Miller, William Mares, Ruth Soloff, Virginia Latta, Jesse E. Harbison, Thomas Tarleau, Robert Diamant, Hortense Hoffman, Sybil Kitchel, Panos Anagnostopoulos, and Barbara Atwood. My warmest thanks go to them all.

On two separate occasions I received half-year research leaves from Roosevelt University to work on the book.

My wife, Nancy Harvison Hooker, to whom this work is dedicated, has helped me by reading the manuscript critically and by working with me in libraries.

And I am thankful to all who have written about American foods and beverages, whether travelers, the compilers of cookbooks, or the authors and editors of other works. Those writings I have used appear in the Notes to this work.

Like all who write nonfiction I owe a great deal to libraries and librarians. The staffs of the libraries in the following institutions were kind and helpful: The New York Public Library with its large holdings of American local history, cookbooks, and menus; the British Museum, especially for its fine collection of British and other travel accounts; the American Antiquarian Society and its outstanding collection of early American cookbooks; the Regenstein Library of the University of Chicago where much of the background research was done; the South Carolina Historical Society and the University of North Carolina Library (Chapel Hill) for manuscripts and early menus; the Lloyd Library, Cincinnati, for state agricultural publications; the Newberry Library for rare books; and the following, in roughly the order of their importance to my research, each for various works difficult to find elsewhere — regional and local histories or memoirs, rare local cookbooks, and some manuscripts: the Boston Public Library; the New Orleans Historical Society· the Chicago Historical Society; the New-York Historical Society; the

ACKNOWLEDGMENTS

Cincinnati Public Library; the Huntington Library; Dartmouth College; the Scottish National Library; Cornell University; the Library of Congress; the University of Texas (Austin); the Cincinnati Historical Society; the University of Washington; the Ross County (Ohio) Historical Society; the Eastern Washington State Historical Society; Arizona State Historical Society; the California State Historical Society; the Montana State Historical Society; and the University of Georgia (Athens).

Contents

CONTENTS

Contents

Introduction

This work attempts to describe American foods and beverages from the first English settlements in North America through the late twentieth century, together with information about the food habits of each of the principal peoples who came to America. There are background accounts of the major historical events and changes that have influenced the country's eating and drinking customs, together with discussions of the means by which foods and drinks have reached the people, and the public and private conditions under which they were consumed. Three topics have been touched only lightly: the nutritional value of foods and drinks, agriculture, and the technical and business aspects of the food industries. The emphasis, therefore, is on what foods and drinks have reached the table.

Research for this work has been difficult. Food has, except for health, agricultural, and dieting aspects, attracted little comment through the nearly four centuries of our country's history. American historians have rarely noticed the subject, and there have been only a few scholarly treatments such as Richard O. Cummings, *The American and His Food: A History of Food Habits in the United States* (Chicago, 1940), and Sam Bowers Hilliard, *Hog Meat and Hoecake: Food Supply in the Old South, 1840–1860* (Carbondale, Ill., 1972).

Fortunately, every part of America has been visited and described by travelers, some American and others foreign, who as strangers in new places have commented on the exotic foods and diets. Their writings are useful, although their unfamiliarity with the locale and the foods and beverages has at times handicapped their understanding and evaluation. Travel accounts, in short, must be used with discrimination.

Cookbooks are another valuable source. Printed ones of American cookery did not appear until 1796, but thereafter in an ascending volume they provided an index to trends and changes in direction of the foods and drinks of upper- and middle-class Americans. Some are of limited value, being nothing more than plagiarized compilations, but others are a sensitive, though lagging, guide to American creative cooking and to many of the less-known dishes of local use.

The fewest records exist, as is the case throughout human history, of the poor, the illiterate, the humble, and those without privileges. Though I have tried to discuss all levels of American society, it is quite possible that well-covered tables have been better described than near-empty ones.

⟡ 1 ⟡
The Beginnings

Bread, beer, and beef, yeoman's fare;
we have no kickshaws:
full dishes, whole bellyfuls.

Many forces have formed the American diet: the bounty of a soil-rich continent; the culinary habits and skills of people from throughout the world; the variety prompted by different geographical areas; a frontier experience that began at Jamestown and in time reached every part of the continent; and nearly every major social and economic change through the country's history, especially in transportation, the migration from farms to cities, a crescendo of food-related technical developments, and the pervasive powers of big business and large-scale marketing and agriculture.

It is in England that one finds the beginnings of American foods and beverages. Many foods have jockeyed for place on American tables and many kinds of cookery have bid for acceptance there, but the English contribution in both was first and has continued strong. As English law, government, language, literature, and economic thought made indelible impressions on Americans, so too did English social behavior.

The earliest American eating and drinking customs came from English homes of the sixteenth and seventeenth centuries, not from the mansions of rich and noble families whose cooks were frequently French — for few of the comfortable people came to the "howling wilderness" of America — but from the homes of yeomen and laborers who lived near the soil and whose traditions were Anglo-Saxon. The earliest English emigrants to America had grown to maturity during the reigns of Elizabeth I, the daughter of Henry VIII and monarch during one of England's greatest eras, and of James I and Charles I, the Stuart kings

1

whose behavior drove Puritans and haters of tyranny into rebellion. The foods and beverages in the time of these three monarchs were those first carried to America to endure as best they could in near-wilderness conditions.

By Elizabeth's reign the English were known as meat-eaters, one man admitting that "other Nations esteeme us gluttons and devourers of flesh," an opinion echoed a century later by a visitor from France who found that among the "middling" English there were ten or twelve sorts of meat which "infallibly" took their turns at the table.

It was beef, pork, mutton, and chicken that largely fed this reputation, though barnyards also held the makings of such dishes as Michaelmas goose, pigeon pie, roasted rabbit, roast kid or goat, and even roast peacock. Turkeys, an import from Spanish America, had been in England since the 1540s and were quite cheap in London markets by the 1570s. Fynes Moryson, an English traveler on the European continent during the late sixteenth century, found that English cooks were "most commended" for roasted meats. Roast beef was a great favorite, as were hearty meat pies flavored with onions and topped with a crust.

Whatever the meat, there was little waste. Without refrigeration, farmers slaughtered large animals only for festive occasions or to salt, smoke, and pickle. From the suet, scraps, and offal, housewives made puddings and, when any meat was boiled, saved the broth. For centuries in England and America, careful cooks placed both broth and pudding on the table to curb appetites before the meat appeared.[1]

Still more meat came from game and fish. The upper classes tried by law to reserve hunting for themselves, but some game was taken by all classes either legally or through poaching. Venison was made into steaks or pasties; hares and conies (a European type of rabbit) were roasted or boiled; blackbirds, rooks, larks, finches, sparrows, and thrushes among other small birds went into pies, as well as herons, bustards, swans, and even gulls, cranes, cormorants, and puffins.

Fishing rights on streams were privately held, though poaching was common. The eating of saltwater fish was widespread, for the government, to encourage shipbuilding and a supply of sailors for national defense, set aside "fish days" during the week and during Lent and fast days. Lobsters, shrimp, crabs, and prawns were also eaten, and by Elizabeth's reign the wealthy were importing pickled anchovies from the Mediterranean. From all these sources — domesticated animals, game, and fish — the English built a carnivorous diet, leading one Englishman to conclude that he had "just cause to cry with Socrates, God deliver mee from meats, that invite to eate beyond hunger."[2]

A filling but nourishing dish that grew in popularity during the seventeenth and eighteenth centuries was pudding. The varieties were without number and included those made with meat, the black puddings, and those without meat, the white puddings. Boiled suet pudding was a national dish. It was cooked in animal gut until the early seventeenth century when the pudding cloth came into use. Then such puddings could be part of the daily fare of nearly every class. Wrapped in pudding cloth, the dish could be simmered with the meat in a cauldron, thus allowing a single container to produce a two-course meal. To the suet were added such ingredients as flour, bread crumbs, sugar, eggs, currants, dates, plums, pepper, and warm milk. By the 1740s puddings were described as "so necessary a part of an Englishman's food" that with beef they were held "the victuals they most love."

Similar to puddings in content, but runnier and without suet, were the cereal pottages. These sweetened preparations were made directly over the fire as frumenty, gruel, pap, or milk pottage of barley, crumbled bread, rice, or sago. One, a thick bread and milk pottage, was made with boiled milk or cream to which were added bread crumbs and flour and enriched with butter, eggs, raisins or currants, spices, and sugar. This, brought to a second boil, was known as "pudding in haste" or "hasty pudding." Cereal pottages were usually a breakfast or supper dish.[3]

The eating of bread was probably most common among the poor, though all classes had it. Among the wealthy it could not compete with meat. A visitor to England in the 1690s met people who never ate bread, "and universally they [the English] eat very little."

During the sixteenth century and increasingly in the following one, wheat bread grew in favor. In London by the early seventeenth century wheat had become the most popular bread grain for all classes, and one man complained that "the poorer sort traversed the markets to find out the finest wheate, for none else

3

would now serve their use, though before they were glad of the coarser rye bread." Outside of London only the gentry knew wheat bread, other classes eating breads of barley, barley and peas, rye, and maslin, the last a combination of wheat and rye. A Yorkshire squire wrote that his household ate maslin or brown bread made of rye, peas, and barley, while his poorer neighbors ate bread that was four-fifths rye and one-fifth peas. The poor in rural districts made bread of whatever was at hand, including beans, buckwheat, and peas.[4]

All classes made lavish use of butter. The poor spread it on bread, and this with herbs sometimes made a country breakfast. Butter went into puddings and cereal pottages, on fish, and on all boiled foods. Among the rich the use of butter rose during the seventeenth and eighteenth centuries, and a visitor from France late in the seventeenth century was astonished at meals swimming in butter.[5] Americans were to continue the practice.

If meats, puddings, and pottages were popular, the same could not be said of vegetables, which one man described as "food more meet for hogs and savage beasts to feed upon, than mankind." An important change took place in the late sixteenth century when refugees from the disorders in Flanders arrived to settle in southeast England and East Anglia. The Flemish farmers brought herb and vegetable seeds, planted gardens, and sold the produce in neighboring towns and London, performing a role that German and Dutch immigrants would later play in America. The English upper classes were receptive; one man wrote that vegetables appeared "as daintie dishes at the tables of delicate merchants, gentlemen, and the nobilitie, who make their provision yearlie for new seeds out of strange countries." The less well-to-do had to be satisfied with melon and pumpkin patches, root gardens of turnips and parsnips, and plots of salad herbs and greens.

Vegetables were boiled, dressed with butter, and served with meats, or made into salads. "Boyled Sallets" comprised a boiled vegetable dressed with oil, vinegar, and pepper, or even currants. Or greens and herbs were mixed and dressed with oil and vinegar, butter and vinegar, or sugar and vinegar, and sometimes flavored with cinnamon, ginger, or pepper. Spinach was a prime favorite for these boiled salads, but also used were cauliflower, leeks, onions, asparagus, sorrel, endive, succory, and borage. Pickled vegetables were called preserved salads. In all these garlic was frowned upon, and a seventeenth-century authority on salads, John Evelyn, absolutely forbade "it entrance into our Salleting: by reason of its intolerable Rankness, and which made it so detested of old."[6]

The new interest in vegetables did not erase the ancient suspicion that they were unwholesome, especially when raw, and were safest when used as the foundation for soups and broths. The excessive boiling of vegetables by the English, and the Americans in turn, probably derived from just such fears.

Even greater misgivings extended to fruits. To prevent the further spread of a pestilence in London in 1569 the sale of fruit on the streets was forbidden, and during the terrors of the London plague in 1665 there was concern that cherries, melons, and gooseberries were related to the disease. Only raw fruits caused concern; fruit tarts, including the traditional harvest dessert, apple tart, were not involved.

Fruits peddled in London were too expensive for the city's poor, but rural dwellers had apple, pear, quince, or plum trees in their yards and currants, strawberries, raspberries, and gooseberries in their gardens. Currants were an immensely popular addition to puddings and cereal pottages. The rich had peaches, grapes, apricots, and medlars (a fruit that looked like a small, brown apple), and in Stuart times some grew orange and lemon trees in boxes which were set outside in summer.[7]

Among the English beverages, water was not a favorite. "Although Water be the most ancient drink . . . it is . . . in no wise agreeable," declared one man, expressing a widely held view. That water was often polluted and caused illness everyone knew, but where the contamination came from was a mystery. As a result all water was suspect. In cold countries, wrote one man in 1628, "it doth very greatly deject their appetite, destroy the natural heate, and overthrow the strength of the stomacke, and consequently, confounding the concoction, is the cause of crudities, fluctuations, and windiness in the body." Not suspected were whey, fresh milk, or milk and water, all consumed in large quantities, especially among the laboring classes of northern England and Scotland.

Wine, imported and expensive, together with beer, ale, cider, and perry, all largely homemade, were the usual beverages. Wines were brought in from Spain, Portugal, France, and the

German states and were widely used in spite of their cost; the poor students at Oxford University in 1556 were accused of insisting on their sack and malmsey whatever the expense. For beer and ale, each household was its own brewhouse, preparing malt beverages at least once a month. Until the late fifteenth century ale was the most popular home brew, but by 1598 a foreign visitor found beer to be the general drink. Both beer and ale were strong and were given such names as mad dog, father whoresonne, angels food, dragons milke, go by the wall, stride wide, and lift leg. In the West Country hard cider was common, and in many places perry was made from the fermented juice of pears. Throughout England two ancient beverages, mead and metheglin, were made from fermented honey.

There was little thought, even among the Puritans, that drinking was wrong, though there was some feeling against drunkenness, as George Gascoigne's *A Delicate Diet, for Daintie Mouthde Droonkardes* indicated in 1576. During Elizabeth's reign the problem was slight, because the English still favored the lighter drinks, wine, cider, and beer. But interest in stronger spirits grew: recipes appeared in the sixteenth century for distilled drinks; the Irish were making whiskey; and by the seventeenth century there were references to *aqua vitae,* a term loosely applied to many distilled spirits. The taste for stronger liquor would not be firmly established until the eighteenth century.[8]

The late sixteenth century saw the pattern of meals change. Breakfast became lighter or was omitted, one man writing that only travelers or the sick ate it. For everyone, the midday dinner was the most important meal. William Harrison in his *Description of England,* written during Elizabeth's reign, said that the nobles, gentry, and students dined around eleven in the morning; merchants and husbandmen ate at noon. The simple evening supper was taken between five and six by the upper classes and at seven or eight by the hard-working yeomen. The poor had no mealtimes, added Harrison, for they ate when they could.[9]

The poor also ate *what* they could. "Where fish is scant, and fruit of trees, Supplie that want with butter and cheese" was advice that the poor were often forced to follow almost daily. Breakfast was bread and cider. Some bacon or a thick broth added variety to the midday meal of bread, cheese, and beer. Supper was only bread and milk or oatmeal porridge. The poor ate little meat, and then usually pork or illegally acquired game. One dish the working class knew well was breeves, rye or barley bread soaked in pot liquor, an ancestor of the "pot likker" that Senator Huey Long was to tout three centuries later. In hard times the poor had even less: the barley or rye in their bread was diluted with peas, acorns, or beech mast; cheese was replaced by a porridge of dried beans, a vegetable considered fit "onely for plough-men, and such as are accustomed to an hard and coarse kinde of foode." English local records show malnutrition and starvation were frequent among the laboring people.[10]

The yeoman class, it was said, spent "seldome any money for any provision, but have it of their own as Beef, Mutton, Veal, Pork, Capons, Hens, Wild-fowl and Fish. They bake their own bread and brew their own drink." Wheat bread in which some of the bran remained was called yeoman's bread, although they also ate maslin and other brown bread mixtures. Butter, milk, and cheese were important, and each region had its special kind of cheese. Each locality also had its own puddings, among others Yorkshire pudding, Worcestershire black pudding, Devonshire whitepot, Gloucestershire bag pudding, and the Hampshire hasty pudding. Pies and tarts were popular desserts, with apple and mince pies highly rated.

The yeomen were said to have rejoiced in their hearty, plainly cooked meals: "no meat disguis'd with strange sauces; no straggling joynt of a sheep in the midst of a pasture of grasse; beset with sallads on every side, but solid substantial food." A play of the period was similarly nationalist and anti-Gallic, lauding the diet as "bread, beer, and beef, yeoman's fare; we have no kickshaws: full dishes, whole bellyfuls."[11]

Preference rather than economic need guided the gentry and nobility in the selection of food. Those who ate breakfast might have several poached eggs, wheat bread and butter, and a good draught of claret wine. Dinner included a greater variety of meats and vegetables than appeared on humbler tables. Foreign influences appeared in the wines and food preparation, since most nobles were said to have as cooks "musicall-headed Frenchmen and strangers." One Barnaby Googe, a Lincolnshire squire during the reign of James I, dined on an egg, a chicken, a piece of kid or veal, fish, butter, and sometimes a salad or fruit in season. Supper for the gentry was a lesser meal that could include a bite of pigeon pie, a little fish or cold meat, a salad, and wine or beer.[12]

Although to the north some citizens of Edinburgh ate well and even kept French cooks, most Scots had a diet that reflected the poverty of their country. Early in the seventeenth century the Scots were described as "living most on Corne and Rootes, not spending any great quantity of flesh," and others said that after the Reformation the Scots were raised on oatmeal porridge and the shorter catechism.[13] Their principal grains were oats and barley; the common vegetables were cabbage in the summer, kale in the winter.

Both lowland and highland Scots were united in an aversion to pork, a prejudice that Highlanders did not lose until after the mid-eighteenth century. Occasionally fresh beef was eaten, but most Scots relied on smoked, salted, or pickled mutton, geese, or fish. The Highlanders, isolated in their mountains, had poor land but a rich wilderness with salmon and trout in the streams and partridges, grouse, and small game on the heath. Their usual drink was the clear, cold water of the brook, but at times of celebration they turned to whiskey; the lowland Scots drank ale.[14]

Nearly all the British foods and drinks were taken to America to provide comfort to people far from home. Some food customs disappeared quickly, but others persisted through generations and even centuries: the large role given to meats, especially beef; a liking for fish; a heavy use of puddings; an addiction to cereal pottages; a love of wheat bread, tarts, and pies; the use of currants and raisins to flavor puddings and mushes; a dislike of garlic; liberal use of butter on meats and vegetables; a fear of raw fruits and lightly cooked vegetables; a generous use of cheese; the drinking of beer, ale, cider, milk, perry, mead, and metheglin; and light breakfasts and heavy noontime dinners.

An important, all-pervasive import to America was the English insistence, except by a small upper-class element, on foods simply prepared. Unlike the French, who combined ingredients to create subtle flavors, the English insisted on "honest" and "straightforward" cooking with the flavor of each food unimpaired. For them no "kickshaws." Any additional flavors were added in the form of catsups, butter, mustard, and so on. The overwhelming majority of Americans would remain true to the same credo.

The diet of emigrants to America began to change the day they set sail. Their voyage could be relatively fast and pleasant or unspeakably long and difficult, depending upon the number and condition of the passengers, the weather, the skill and humanity of the captain and crew, and the seaworthiness and comfort of the ship. When all went well the voyage was what a New England-bound clergyman in 1629 described as "healthful," "pleasurable," and "christian-like." But on vermin-infested ships, manned by callous crews, overcrowded, storm-tossed, and with inadequate food and drink, the emigrants found that their shipmates included hunger, disease, and death. A voyage in the seventeenth and eighteenth centuries could last from two months to twice that time. The Pilgrims needed sixty-five days to reach Plymouth, and the emigrants to Jamestown traveled for over four months by the southern route through the Azores and the West Indies. In the middle of the next century the average trip from England to Pennsylvania still lasted from seven to twelve weeks.[15]

For such long voyages the nature and amount of food and drink were prime problems. On the whole the emigrants ate the same kinds of foods that they had known at home during the winter months. Salted meats or fish and some kind of grain were the staples of most ship diets. Common supplements were butter and cheese, dried fruits, and root vegetables. Water was a necessity, and beer was carried for all. Those who could afford it also took some wine, brandy, and *aqua vitae*. In 1635 an emigrant to Massachusetts, Richard Mather, wrote that "we had no want of good and wholesome beer and bread; and as our land stomachs grew weary of ship diet, of salt fish and salt beef, and the like . . . we used bacon and buttered peas, sometimes buttered bag-pudding, made with currants and raisins; and sometimes drinked pottage of beer and oatmeal, and sometimes water pottage, well buttered."[16]

The lack of fresh food was a common complaint. Passengers of substance carried live fowl or livestock to be killed as needed. But most lived on what one disgruntled passenger called "terribly salty and stinking meat." Water, needed the more because of the salty fare, was often brackish or in short supply. When even this gave out the emigrants relied on rainwater which was "dipped from the deck tasted like tar and was full of rubbish," or on "no

9

drink but Salt-Water." Other complaints were of "beer as thick as puddle water or else salt," or bread "unfit to eat, gray and moldy."[17]

Matters were far worse when, through the greed or error of the captain or shipowner, there was little or no food. Five passengers who arrived in Pennsylvania in 1732 castigated the captain of their ship:

> Captain Lobb, a wicked murderer of souls, thought to starve us, not having provided provisions enough, according to agreement . . . for during the voyage of the last eight weeks, five persons were only allowed one pint of coarse meal per day, and a quart of water to each person. . . . To keep from starving, we had to eat rats and mice. We paid from eight pence to two shillings for a mouse; four pence for a quart of water.

A German who voyaged to Pennsylvania stated that on the ships specializing in carrying emigrants there was "terrible misery, stench, fumes, horror, vomiting, many kinds of sea-sickness, fever, dysentery, headache, heat, constipation, boils, scurvy, cancer, mouth-rot, and the like, all of which come from old and sharply salted food and meat, also from very bad and foul water, so that many die miserably." Actual starvation came to some. In the mid-eighteenth century a Boston newspaper recorded the arrival of a shipload of Irish: "They were so reduc'd as to eat up their Tallow, Candles, etc. And for some Time had fed upon the Flesh of the humane Bodies deceas'd." And a convict ship bound for Maryland in 1768 came to disaster when severe storms extended the voyage to over three months. The convicts were finally limited to three ounces of bread a day. Soon they ate the vermin which they picked off themselves, then their leather breeches, and eventually every shoe on board. Not until five convicts had died of starvation did the master of the ship open a 100-pound cask of cheese consigned to the wealthy Charles Carroll of Maryland.[18]

Although most emigrants did not endure such horrors, their food was often unpalatable, inadequate, and unhealthy. Even the pious and optimistic Reverend Francis Higginson of Massachusetts, reflecting on his shipboard fare, could find only one thing for which to thank God, that the voyage was "a method to cure me of a wonderful weake stomacke and continual payne of melancholly wynd from the splene."[19] Emigrants were probably ready, as they sighted land, to welcome almost anything that the New World had to offer in food and drink.

The settlers brought with them a conviction about the natural bounty of America. Through books, pamphlets, the theater, and the advertisements of trading companies promoting settlement, the New World was described as an Eden overflowing with things people craved. A character in an English play of 1605, *Eastward Hoe,* expressed the extravagant claims being made for Virginia:

> [It is as pleasant a country] as ever the sunne shind on: temperate and ful of all sorts of excellent viands; wilde bore is as common there, as our tamest Bacon is here: Venison, as Mutton. . . . There wee shall have no more Law than conscience, and not too much of eyther; serve God enough, eate and drink enough, and *enough is as good as a Feast.*[20]

While gold and gems, which many had hoped to find, were not discovered, those who dreamed of a wealth of natural foods found the size and quantity so astonishing that they feared their European friends would not credit their reports.

The waters of the bays, inlets, and rivers of the coastal plain teemed with seafood. There were bass, bluefish, smelts "in troops innumerable, which with a scoop or a bowl, or a piece of bark, a man may cast up upon the bank," alewives, eels, trout, shad, salmon, sturgeon, and giant cod weighing up to a hundred pounds. Lobsters in season were so numerous that "the very multitude of them cloys us." There were clams and mussels, and oysters up to a foot in length. Some "sober and well-advised persons, grew very angry when they were laughed at" for comparing one oyster to the large cabin of the ship *Discovery.*[21] This may have been the first American tall story.

The sky was a feast for hungry eyes, especially for a generation prepared to eat almost anything that flew. Eagles soared overhead; ducks, geese, and swans crowded the ponds and marshes; the shore harbored cranes, herons, and bitterns; and in season clouds of pigeons darkened the sky. Many small land birds were available for food, as were the swift-running turkeys and the more earthbound grouse.[22]

Of the wild life of the forests and fields, deer were the prime food source. Bears were numerous, and there was variety in elk, raccoons, rabbits, squirrels, muskrats, beavers, and even snakes.[23]

The land was a treasury of fruits, vegetables, and herbs. Along the coast grew raspberries, blackberries, gooseberries, and strawberries, the last immensely admired for their size and quantity. A settler in New Netherland found them so thick that "one can lie down and eat them." Another man spoke of "fields and Woods that are died red," and Roger Williams rated them the best of all the natural foods in Rhode Island. On cleared Indian land he had seen enough of them "within a few miles compasse" to fill a ship.[24] In the woods were trees of wild cherries, crabapples, persimmons, and plums among others, and in the southern regions peaches and figs that had spread from the early Spanish missions. The immigrants were excited by the varieties of grapes which they hoped to press for wine. Also highly valued were the chestnuts, walnuts, pecans, and other nuts.[25]

Some of the herbs of the woods and fields were familiar, but others were unknown until the Indians revealed their value. There were wild onions and leeks, cornsalad, violets, sorrel, purslane, and others. Of considerable food value were edible roots identified by the natives, including groundnuts, the tubers of a wild bean, and tuckahoes, an underground vegetable.[26]

The colonists in their fumbling approach to the wilderness would have suffered more had it not been for the foods already cultivated by the Indians. The coastal plains had been occupied for centuries by the descendants of East Asians who in prehistory had made their own migration through Siberia across a land bridge to Alaska and from there into all parts of both American continents. When the white men first arrived, the Indians throughout North America numbered no more than one to two million. The earliest contacts by the English settlers were with Algonquian tribes, whose way of life was based on the culture of corn, hunting, fishing, and gathering. They had no domesticated animals except the dog.

The Indians conformed to their physical environment and lived in harmony with nature. Through many generations they had come to know well the wild animals around them. They were skilled hunters, using such devices as the bow and arrow, the thrusting lance, clubs, snares, traps, and slings. But the Indians did not engage in senseless slaughter. They believed that animals, like men, had souls and that the use of slain animals should be governed by rules to prevent any offense to their souls. Deer was the most common game, bear was one of the most venerated, but all wild game was hunted. An early resident of New York noted that the natives did not scorn to eat skunks, possums, and turtles. Fishing in the freshwater lakes and rivers and along the coast was an important source of food, especially in New England where agriculture was less reliable than farther south.[27]

Gardening provided the Indians of the eastern areas with as much as half their food supply. Corn was the principal crop. This had probably been domesticated in central America five to seven centuries before the Christian era; it was the most important food discovered in the New World. The most common variety among the eastern Indians was flint corn, low growing with slender stalks, white cobs, and an eight-rowed ear.

The Indians had many uses for corn. Young ears, wrapped in leaves, were boiled or roasted. Corn was put into stews that might otherwise contain various combinations of meat, roots, beans, wild peas, squashes, mulberries, and other foods. Dried corn was pounded in a mortar, then formed into round cakes called pones which were boiled and then baked on hot stones. Coarser parts of the grain were boiled for hours to make a thick pottage whose name was translated as hominy. Corn kernels were parched and eaten whole, or corn flour was parched to make nocake, a standard nourishing food that kept well and was to be used constantly by both Indians and colonists. And everywhere corn was boiled with beans and sometimes other foods to make succotash. The great debt of the English was spelled out in their adoption of Indian words: pone, samp, hominy, suppawn, nocake, and succotash.[28]

Beans were second to corn as an Indian crop, and varieties — "too tedious" to list according to one settler — were grown, some being planted next to corn when it was high enough to serve as a pole. Squashes and pumpkins were planted between the corn hills, and separately the Indian gardens contained Jerusalem artichokes, sunflowers, and bottle gourds. From the fields and forests the women gathered fruits, nuts, greens, and herbs.[29]

The Indians were adept at preserving foods for times of scarcity and winter: berries, roots, nuts, beans, and pumpkins were dried; meat was cut into strips and smoked; fish and the meat of oysters, lobsters, and clams were dried on scaffolds over a slow fire. The chances of famine became small when to all these were added the fish and game.[30]

In theory, the American scene was not entirely forbidding to Europeans: there were vast stores of natural food and a native agriculture and cookery that waited adoption. The success or failure of the first settlements depended upon how well each seized the opportunities offered. In fact, the early years saw "civilized" Europeans dying of hunger while "savage" natives ate well, a grim illustration of how great an adjustment in living conditions these immigrants had to make.

⟳ 2 ⟲
The Difficulties
of Being First

Our drinke was water,
our lodgings, castles in the air.

The first small bands of immigrants who landed on the North
American continent could have feared the future. Behind them
lay a huge ocean and uncertain support from their home country.
Before them lay a wilderness that began at the beach line, inhab-
ited by Indians who might prove hostile. There was no certainty
that they could find food to supplement the few supplies they
carried with them, and all too soon they became aware of their
own limitations in garnering more. Coming from farms, villages,
and cities, they were not accustomed to the rigors of frontier life
nor did they know how to extract a living from a harsh new
world. Thus handicapped, hunger and starvation were to be their
lot. To be first was to suffer.

The greatest hardships came to the settlers of Virginia, men
more interested in easy wealth than in the grinding work of colony making. On April 26, 1607, the *Susan Constant,* the
Godspeed, and the *Discovery* sailed into Chesapeake Bay carrying
about a hundred men who were to make the first permanent English settlement. Their voyage by way of the West Indies had
taken over four months, and the "faire meddowes and goodly tall
trees" of Virginia were a welcome sight. One man described himself as "almost ravished" at the glimpse of the "fresh-waters running through the woods."[1]

For a few weeks the men searched for a place to settle. In
these sorties from the ships their introduction to American foods
began when they came upon a spot where the natives had been
roasting oysters and had left many, "very large and delicate in

15

taste," in the fire. The next day they found a place where mussels and oysters lay "thicke as stones" on the ground and then an area where there were "fine and beautiful Strawberries, foure times bigger and better than ours in England."

After many encounters with the Indians, who were at first hostile, then wary, the Europeans were at last welcomed to an Indian village and entertained with dancing, dining on "such dainties as they had, and of their bread which they make of their Maiz." Other meetings followed, and in late May, Captain Christopher Newport, one of the appointed leaders, led a small group up the James River to make contact with Powhatan, the head of the Algonquian confederation. They were greeted with a feast of strawberries, mulberries, corn bread, fish, roast venison, turtle, and boiled corn and beans. Powhatan and his companions were entertained in return with pork boiled with peas as a main dish and beer, *aqua vitae,* and sack to drink. Powhatan stood up well to the alcoholic beverages, but a local chief became ill, confessing later that the "hott Drynckes he thought caused his greefe."[2]

By late May a site had been chosen, the settlers landed, and a fort begun at Jamestown. As long as the ships remained, the colonists augmented their fare by trading for biscuits and other foods with the sailors, but in June 1607, Captain Newport and the ships returned to England, leaving provisions for only three to four months. These transplanted Englishmen, left behind, felt insecure. There existed, one of them noted, "neither taverne, beere-house, nor place of relife but the common kettell." And soon there was little to go into that. By fall their food was "but a small Can of Barlie sod in water, to five men a day. Our drinke, cold water taken out of the River; which was, at a floud, verie salt; at a low tide, full of slime and filth." As John Smith was to remember: "Had we beene as free from all sinnes as [we were from] gluttony and drunkenness, we might have bin canonized for Saints." It was a grievance that the president of the governing council, Edward-Maria Wingfield, reserved for himself "Otemeale, sacke, oile, aquavitae, beefe, egs, or what not," while the living conditions of the others were summed up in this way: "Our drinke was water; our lodgings, castles in the air." The men, weakened by the harsh life in Virginia, fell ill, and many died. "For the most part," one settler wrote, "they died of meere famine," and the same man was sure that without the supplies of corn, bread, fish, and game contributed by the Indians "wee had all perished." When Newport returned in January 1608 only thirty-eight men remained alive.[3]

The colony in Virginia perched precariously on the edge of wilderness and, during the years from 1607 to 1610, on the edge of disaster. The delicate balance was dependent on a number of critical factors, such as the attitude of the Indians, the weather, the incidence of disease, the bickering within the settlement, the supplies and instructions from England, the presence of natural foods and the colonists' ability to obtain them, and the success of domesticated animals and crops.

The Jamestown settlers had been supplied with horses, cattle, hogs, goats, sheep, and chickens. The hogs in particular flourished in the forest on roots, nuts, berries, and snakes and multiplied rapidly. At first the vegetable gardens probably did badly, for a large proportion of the earliest settlers were of the gentleman class, unaccustomed to farming and intent on making a fortune through the discovery of gold or silver or by trading with the Indians. As a result, one man noted, for three years the immigrants lived "chiefly of what this good countrie naturally affordeth."[4]

The colonists were overjoyed to find quantities of herring, shad, sturgeon, trout, bass, flounder, and other fish in the rivers or coastal waters, but through inept provisioning they lacked proper fishhooks or nets to take them. Two men described a day on Chesapeake Bay in 1608 when "the abundance of fish lying so thicke with their heads above the water" led them to attempt to land the fish with a frying pan, but they "found it a bad instrument to catch fish with." During the same expedition fish were seen lurking among the shore weeds. This time Captain John Smith led the assault "by nailing them to the ground with his sword." This unorthodox technique worked, and within an hour the men speared more than they could eat.[5]

Some familiar game animals and some "wild beasts unknowne" provided food, as did migratory birds, wild turkeys which ran "as swift as a Gray-hound," grouse, eagles, hawks, and what John Smith vaguely described as "diverse sorts of small birds, some red, some blew." Still, as Smith remarked, "Though there be fish in the sea, fowls in the air, and beasts in the woods, their bounds are so large, they so wild, and we so weak and ignorant, we cannot much trouble them."[6]

The wild plants of the fields and forests were an untended

garden of familiar fruits and berries and of strange oddities like the maracocks, the fruit of the American passion-flowers, or the scuppernong grapes, borne on huge vines which climbed high into the trees. At times the settlers ate tuberous roots that the Indians called tuckahoe, wild onions, and in the spring herbs "good for brothes and sallets, as Violets, Purslin [purslane], Sorrell, &c. Besides many we used whose names we know not."[7]

The wild foods were seasonal or elusive and gave no insurance against hunger. In the spring of 1609 the discovery that the stores of corn were rotted and eaten by thousands of rats sparked a crisis which came to be known as the Starving Period. John Smith, who had become president of the council, in an effort to improve matters dispersed the settlers to live as best they could by gathering, fishing, and hunting. One group of men was sent downriver to live on oysters; some tried to fish at Point Comfort; while still others went upriver to the falls where they found nothing but berries and acorns. At Jamestown only sturgeon were plentiful, and the "industrious" among the men dried and pounded these and mixed the powder with caviar, sorrel, and other herbs to make "bread" and "good meat."[8]

The food problem was still unsolved in late summer when a fleet of seven ships brought hundreds of new immigrants who found neither food nor housing to greet them. John Smith, who had maintained some discipline, forced idlers to work, and had largely directed the purchases of food from the Indians, returned to England after a serious injury. The settlers faced the winter with little food. The Indians were now hostile, and this prevented the colonists from hunting and gathering wild foods.

The full horrors of starvation came to the little colony. As the corn disappeared, men, women, and children subsisted on roots, herbs, acorns, walnuts, berries, and, at fortunate moments, a little fish. Soon worse fare had to serve. The skins of horses were consumed as well as, one man recalled, dogs, cats, rats, snakes, toadstools, and "what not." The "poorer sort" crept, for few had the strength to walk, out of the stockade and dug up an Indian who had been killed and ate the body. There were other incidents of cannibalism, and one man reportedly killed, salted, and ate part of his wife before he was discovered and executed.

In late May of 1610 Sir Thomas Gates, the advance agent and deputy of Lord De La Warr, the newly appointed governor,

arrived in Virginia with 175 more immigrants. He found Jamestown in ruins and but sixty survivors of the nearly 500 settlers who had been there the preceding fall. All the livestock had been killed by the Indians or eaten, and the seines for fishing were gone. It was decided to abandon the town and make for Newfoundland where, it was hoped, fishing boats would either give employment or passage to England. But as the colonists fell down the river they met the ships of Lord De La Warr and were ordered to return. So close did Virginia come to extinction.[9]

The hunger of Virginians did not end immediately, but never again were things so bad. Ships were sent to Bermuda for hogs and fish; the neglected cornfields and gardens were again tended; the new settlers were more inclined to work than earlier ones; and fresh supplies of cattle, chickens, goats, and sheep were imported.[10]

Far to the north of Jamestown and over a decade later, the little colony of Pilgrims at Plymouth was to know intense hunger. The *Mayflower* with its 101 passengers had been overcrowded and poorly provisioned; the brown and white biscuits, the smoked bacon, salt codfish, smoked herrings, root vegetables, grains, and dried peas did not make an ideal diet. Fortunately the Pilgrims had carried some of their own food. Beer for the voyage was brought in iron-bound casks watched over by John Alden, a cooper who came for that purpose.[11]

The *Mayflower* anchored off the tip of Cape Cod in the autumn of 1620, and an exploratory party set off to spy out the land and to find a permanent site for settlement. They found clear springs and drank their "first New England water with as much delight as ever we drunk drink in all our lives." They took note of partridges, geese, ducks, vines, an Indian store of dried strawberries, walnut trees, and Indian cornfields. They saw from a distance three bucks, "but we had rather have had one of them." Soon the scouts came across an Indian cache of corn and beans and, anticipating future centuries of American Indian policy, promptly stole both, the corn to be used for seed. During the following days other foods appeared: acorns, various fish, fine mussels, crabs, lobsters, and numerous herbs including wild leeks and onions.[12]

After all had landed at the place they named Plymouth, their troubles grew. Weak from scurvy and other shipboard-contracted

diseases, the Pilgrims badly needed nourishing foods. But the growing season was past, so there were no fresh wild fruits or greens. Game was around them, but their guns were the huge matchlocks, hard to load, with slow and noisy wicks, and so heavy that they had to be fired from stands. Though ineffective against deer, they did better when fired with "hayle shott" into flocks of wild fowl. As at Jamestown, fishing was nearly impossible for lack of small hooks.[13] Weakened by illnesses and the cold of their small makeshift huts, with inadequate food and a hard life, about half of the settlers died during the first winter.

The spring of 1621 brought hope. Aided by the friendly Indian Squanto, the Pilgrims planted corn and the seeds they had brought from England, and gradually improved in hunting and fishing. The Indians supplied them with game and taught them to recognize wild foods, including the valuable edible root called the groundnut, a tuber that grew in moist spots.

In the fall the corn harvest was adequate, but the wheat, barley, and peas all failed. Still, the food rations could be increased and, gratefully, the Pilgrims decided to observe a Thanksgiving holiday. The Indian Massasoit, invited to attend, came with ninety braves, so it was helpful that some of them went out and killed five deer. For three days the assembled crowd ate well of venison, roast duck, roast goose, roast turkey, shellfish, eels, corn bread, wheat bread, leeks, watercress and other "sallet" herbs, with dried berries and wild plums for dessert.

Misfortunes persisted. In November 1621 the ship *Fortune* unexpectedly brought thirty-five new mouths to feed, and rations were halved during the second winter. The 1622 harvest was poor, and in their hunger some settlers stole unripe corn and more after it was harvested. When sixty new colonists arrived in 1623, all they received in welcome was a bit of lobster or a piece of fish with a cup of spring water.[14] Poorly supplied by the English merchants who financed the colony, the food stores constantly depleted by new immigrants from England, and handicapped by a variety of disasters, Plymouth only narrowly escaped a starving time equal to Jamestown's. Aid given by the Indians certainly helped to keep the colony alive. "Oysters we have none near," wrote Governor Edward Winslow in 1621, "but can have them brought by the Indians when we will."[15]

All danger of starvation did not pass until 1624, and even

then there was no excess of food. Winslow mentioned that while there was an "abundance" of fowl, venison, and fish, these had to be taken, and that men unable to fare for themselves would do better to remain in England. "And can any be so simple," he asked in answer to critics of the colony, "as to conceive that the fountains should stream forth wine or beer, or the woods and rivers be like butchers' shops, or fishmongers' stalls, where they might have things taken to their hands?" New England was no place, he added, for "a dainty tooth, a beggar's purse, and an idle hand."[16]

During these early years it was largely food from the forest, the streams, and the ocean that kept the colonists alive. In the spring months eels, alewives, and smelts were caught in quantity, and from mid-May to September the bass and bluefish were in ample supply. Both clams and lobsters could be taken in the bay, the latter "so full of meat, and so plentiful in number as no more will believe that hath not seen." Wild fowl appeared in such numbers "that one man at six shoots hath killed 400."[17]

The civilized foods came slowly. By 1623 Plymouth had six goats, fifty pigs, and many hens, and the next year there were cows to provide milk and occasionally beef. Familiar vegetables were grown in household gardens. These, with the apple trees started from cuttings brought from England, must have given the Pilgrims the feeling that they were, however slowly, creating a more decent life in the "howling wilderness" they had chosen for their home.

In 1622 Thomas Weston, an old backer of the Pilgrims who had broken with them, tried to set up a rival colony on the southern shore of Massachusetts Bay, known as Wessagusset. The fifty men, immigrants from England led by Andrew Weston, failed to plant corn or to fish and hunt in preparation for the winter. As hunger became serious and a number died, some of the settlers became servants to the Indians, cutting their wood and hauling water in return for corn. Others stole from the Indians. Some men sold their bed coverings and clothes in return for food. All combed the beaches and woods for anything edible. One man looking for shellfish became stuck in the mud and died there, too weak to extricate himself. Soon the colony was abandoned.[18]

Starvation, like that in Virginia, Plymouth, and Wessagusset, was not repeated elsewhere. Although there were hard times,

21

food shortages, and malnutrition, later settlements had learned from these earlier disasters. Initial provisioning was more generous, and food could be obtained from the surpluses of already established colonies and from ships that called regularly at North American ports.

Maryland, carved out of Virginia, was fortunate in many ways. The first expedition of 1633, carrying between 200 and 300 people, stopped at Virginia where hogs, poultry, cows, and bulls were bought, all of which were to increase rapidly. In Maryland itself the immigrants found friendly Indians and arranged to occupy one of their former villages which had cleared lands. From the Indians they purchased so much corn that they shipped 1,000 bushels of it to New England in exchange for salt fish and other goods. In their own forests and streams, guided by the natives, they had a rich supply of wild fowl, fish, deer, and other game. Soon the Marylanders were enjoying a quantity and variety of foods greater than many of them had known in England.[19]

Massachusetts, settled in 1630, lacked the long growing season of Maryland and had no near source of food other than the always poor colony of Plymouth. Livestock brought from England fared badly: wolves made havoc among the hogs, many cattle died during the first years, and there was not enough pasture for the sheep. Even corn yields were small, for until plows were imported the settlers had to plant corn in hills after the Indian manner.

The early colonists, wrote one man, "in the misse" of beer drank water, and in the absence of bread ate fish. Each day at low tide the women went to the beaches to gather mussels and clams for the daily meal. The settlers collected wild greens and fruits and bartered with the Indians for venison and raccoons. Goats, which flourished and multiplied where other livestock failed, provided both milk and meat during the early years and made it possible to retain the increase of cattle for sale to newcomers. Pumpkins were another staple food. Some time later one man wrote: "And let no man make a jest at Pumpkins, for with this fruit the Lord was pleased to feed his people to their good content, till Corne and Cattell were raised."

The general contentment with this diet was questionable, for the lack of wheat, barley, and rye was a "sore affliction" to some. When ships arrived from England, settlers of even "good rank and quality" would beg the masters to accept gold, silver, cloth-

ing, "or whatever precious" for bread. Diet deficiencies bred scurvy and other diseases from which as many as 200 may have died. A general recovery from scurvy took place in January 1631, when a ship came into Boston harbor carrying lemon juice.[20]

Of the settlements begun in the first half of the seventeenth century, Connecticut, New Netherland, and New Sweden also lacked food. During the migration from Massachusetts in 1636 the first settlers of Connecticut, led by Thomas Hooker, lived in great part on the milk from their cows, and emigrants to the Connecticut River valley from Dorchester were reported to have lost most of their cattle and to have existed for a time on acorns, malt, and grain.[21] The Dutch in New Netherland in 1624 failed in the four succeeding years to have a good harvest and lacked "proper sustenance." And on the Delaware River in 1638 the Swedish settlers had food shortages for some years which were said to have caused many deaths in 1643.[22]

By the 1660s, when Charles II began his huge land grants that led to the founding of New Jersey, Pennsylvania, and the Carolinas, there was little danger of starvation. For a time the early settlers of New Jersey turned to fish when their powder and shot for hunting gave out, but they could still buy corn, venison, and pork from the Indians. The first settlers on the Ashley River in Carolina had some trouble. Governor Sayle, in the first summer, reported that their daily rations were a pint of peas per person, "the Country affording us nothing," and not until March 1673 could the colonists report that they had "quite mastered the want of victuals." Immigrants to Pennsylvania, nine years later, bought corn and beef from the Swedes in Delaware and other foods from New York and New England. William Penn thought too much salt meat was the "greatest hardship," but by eating fish in summer, poultry in winter, and other meats when available, matters had become "very passable."[23]

Hunger, malnutrition, and even starvation did not disappear from the American scene. All, instead, receded from open view into the bodies of the anonymous poor where they would lurk for centuries to come. Urban and rural laborers, both slave and free, those marooned in economic backwaters, newly arrived immigrants, and frontiersmen were to suffer from lack of food. At times they would attract attention and even compassion, but it was not until the 1960s that hunger and malnutrition were to be seen finally as a large-scale and persistent part of American life.

⚜ 3 ⚜
The Seventeenth Century

While Pon and Milk, with Mush well stoar'd,
In wooden Dishes grac'd the Board.

English culture put down deep roots in America during the first century of colonization. Not only were English settlers the most numerous, but they also maintained close ties with the mother country. English thought and customs proved so strong that when later waves of non-English immigrants reached America, they often found it easier to accept the adjustments made by the English majority than to attempt new ones.

The pattern of settlement in the colonies perpetuated the ties with England. Nearly everyone lived on or near the coast or the larger rivers flowing into the ocean. All the early cities were seaports. Boston was the largest, but Newport, New York, Philadelphia, and Charleston had strategic locations and showed promise of coming importance.

Even by the century's end few people lived in cities. Most colonists were farmers or small planters, working hard to make their holdings profitable, staying close to home the year around, and knowing only their near neighbors. Travel was discouraged by roads so poor as to be nearly impassable. Nearly all families consumed only what they raised on the land, shot or collected in the forest, took from the nearby waters, or purchased on infrequent visits to the nearest town.

Life gradually became more secure and comfortable. The crude dugouts and bark huts which had been the first New England shelters were replaced by wood-framed, clapboard-sheathed houses. The Dutch in New Amsterdam built stepped-gable brick houses in imitation of those in Holland. And less than a decade after the landing at Jamestown, some Virginians owned houses of framed timber like those in England. Small farms were cleared from the virgin forests, familiar livestock was imported, and vegetables and fruits from Europe were raised alongside native plants.

For most Americans the kitchen was a focal point of family life. That it was the source of every meal, cooked in the great fireplace or adjacent oven, gave the room much of its importance. The same fireplace provided heat in cold weather and was the principal source of light after sundown. Families spent their indoor waking hours in the kitchen, for here meals were eaten, books read, accounts kept, and conversations exchanged. Often it was where guns were racked and the family's library kept, and in small houses it held both beds and storage chests. The kitchen, in short, was the soul of the house where warmth and light, the fragrance of cooking, and social contacts all met and mingled. Among the wealthy, whose kitchens were staffed with servants, it played a lesser role. And in the South, concern about summer heat led to the removal of the kitchen from living areas, at first into the basement and then to a separate building.

As families rose above frontier conditions, the quantity and quality of the kitchen equipment increased. The simple benches and tables made by putting planks on trestles were replaced with carpenter-made tables and chairs, dressers, and storage chests. Around the walls, cupboards and shelves held knives and choppers, pastry equipment, mortars and pestles, skimmers, skewers, and colanders. In the kitchen, or its extensions, room was found for pots and pans in many sizes and shapes and for less-used pieces such as salamanders, spit toasters, and pot pushers. There were also tools for preserving foods, like the powdering troughs in which food was salted down, and dairy equipment such as milk pails, a butter churn, a cheese press, strainers, butter paddles, and various containers.

One wall of the kitchen was dominated by the large brick or stone fireplace. High in its chimney, hidden from view, was the lug pole, a bar, usually of iron, set in the masonry, on which pothangers or trammels of varying lengths were hung to hold the cooking kettles. In time the lug pole would be replaced or supplemented by cranes, movable iron rods which swung out from the back or sides of the fireplace. On the hearth sat the andirons with circles or hooks to hold spits.

Fireplace cooking was an art that was to remain little

changed for over two centuries. In the fireplace the cook must keep one or more fires or beds of coals alive. Over these, great and small kettles suspended from trammels had to be raised, lowered, or removed. In preparing a meal a variety of iron implements were marshaled and moved in relation to the fire — pots, skillets, trivets, frying pans, griddles, toasters, spits, toasting forks, and tongs. A cook needed to manage both small and large fires, to reduce a fire with water or increase it with bellows, kindle it from coals carried in iron boxes, or begin it with a tinderbox.[1]

Five ancient cooking methods were used: boiling, roasting, broiling, frying, and baking. Of these, boiling was the most versatile, and into the kettle went fish, fowl, meat, or vegetables. The broths, a by-product of meat boiling, were eaten at once or kept to make gravies and sauces. Gruels, porridges, and pottages were boiled as well as numerous puddings. Vegetables were overboiled and fruit was stewed. Some of the iron, copper, or brass boiling vessels were small, while others were vast like those in the South which were hung outside to cook at one time all the food for servants and slaves.

A seventeenth-century writer described English cooks as "most commended for roasted meates." Cooking before an open fire required attention to the heat of the coals, turning the spit, and proper basting. A well-equipped kitchen needed spits of various shapes, weights, and lengths to skewer meat, fowl, fish, or even vegetables. Turning the spit was frequently the task of a child, though later well-to-do households had contrivances called smokejacks or clockjacks.[2]

Broiling, a less-used cooking method, was done on rectangular or circular grids mounted on short legs and moved by a long handle. Steaks, chops, small fowl, and birds were broiled on these over the open fire.

Frying became so general that through the centuries foreign visitors were to identify it as the typical American method of preparing food. In part this attachment to the frying pan was due to the addiction to pork which provided fat in which other foods could be cooked. Frying was also promoted by the frontier experience through which successive generations passed. A frying pan was portable and versatile, advantages where traveling light was necessary.

Baking, or cooking with dried heat in an enclosed space, was done in the fireplace or an oven. The simplest means was to place food directly on the hot hearth, invert a pot over it, and pile coals onto and around the pot. A more common way was to use an iron bake-kettle with legs, in time to be known as a Dutch oven. This was placed over coals while other coals were put on the inverted lid.

Oven baking was done either inside or outside the home in brick, stone, or clay chambers which were heated by fires built within them. When the oven became hot, the coals and ashes were removed. Then the cook, using a long-handled wooden or iron peel, placed in the oven a week's supply of bread, pies, tarts, puddings, and sometimes meat or beans. Seventeenth-century ovens were put at the rear of the fireplace, but later at one side of the fireplace opening. Outdoor baking ovens were common to reduce the danger of fire and, in the South, to cut down household heat.[3]

Except for those wealthy enough to have a dining room, meals were eaten at a table in the kitchen. Such foods as mush, porridge, or stew were served in wooden bowls from which all ate directly with spoons of wood, horn, or a gourd. In later years the more prosperous colonists replaced wooden dishes with those of earthenware, pewter, or even silver. The rich also had sharply pointed knives to spear food, but forks were long a curiosity. Governor John Winthrop brought a fork to Boston in 1633 which he kept in a leather case with a knife and bodkin.

All but the poorest families used napkins and a board cloth of homespun and home-woven linen. A saltcellar was the centerpiece, marking the line between honored guests who sat above it toward the host, and the less important below it.[4]

The settlers were fortunate that both England and the colonies had temperate climates that eased the transfer of all grains, vegetables, fruits, and livestock. As much as anything, this similarity of climates made it possible to shape the American wilderness into a semblance of England.

As confirmed meat-eaters, the English wanted a good supply in America. Since few were skilled hunters, they imported livestock as quickly as possible, but it was soon clear that each variety of domestic animal had its own problems of adjustment.

Monuments are not usually raised to the goat, but this animal played a remarkable role in the early settlements. Although those first taken to Jamestown were eaten during the Starving Period, they were replaced and multiplied so that in 1634 it was said that pork and kid were the only red meats at the "better houses." As late as mid-century goats were listed with cattle, hogs, and fowl as making up the colony's livestock.[5]

In Massachusetts, goats provided the settlers with milk and meat for over a decade. In 1628 there were about ninety each of cows and goats, while six years later there were 4,000 goats but only 1,500 head of cattle. The difference indicated no preference, however, for when beef became cheaper in the 1640s the keeping of goats declined. In 1650 it was said that goats in Lynn, once common, had "almost vanished."[6]

Unhappily for the beef-eating English, cattle herds grew slowly. Virginia was poorly stocked until mid-century and there, as in Maryland, most cattle lived in the woods and became wild.[7] In New England heavy immigrations kept prices for breeding cattle high so that little was eaten. When the English Civil War began in 1642, however, the Puritan element could fight rather than emigrate. This hurt the market for cattle in New England and with this "fall of the cow," beef increasingly replaced goat meat on tables there.[8]

The English also liked mutton and lamb, but the imported sheep fared badly. In Virginia and Maryland they lacked grasslands and attracted wolves to the plantations.[9] The same problems existed in New England and the Middle Colonies, but in time these barriers were overcome.[10]

The lowly pigs had the greatest success. These matched goats in their ability to live off the land, to multiply, and to endure frontier hardships, and pork had the further advantages of being easily preserved and of providing both lard and meat. As corn became the leading grain and a food mainstay, so pork rose to first place among the meats. The two together were to serve as the great American staples for centuries.

Pigs carried by Columbus to the West Indies were reputedly the ancestors of those taken by explorers and conquistadors to Mexico, New Mexico, and Florida. Then in 1608 three sows and a boar were carried from England to Jamestown where within eighteen months they had increased to about sixty pigs. Allowed to fend for themselves, the pigs ran wild in the woods, little bothered by the mild winters and thriving on the forest foods. Well before the century's end both Virginia and Maryland were exporting pork and becoming famous for fine hams.[11]

In spite of wolves and severe winters, hogs also flourished in New England. A livestock census in Massachusetts in 1635 gave definite figures for all kinds except swine which were simply listed as "innumerable." The Dutch in New Netherland bought their first pigs from the English, while early settlers of New Jersey purchased theirs from Indians who had probably found them running wild near other English settlements.[12]

With no refrigeration, the killing of any large animal posed problems. Sometimes the carcass was shared with neighbors in the expectation that they would some day reciprocate. More often what could not be quickly eaten was dried, smoked, or salted. Venison was sliced and dried on latticework grills over fires in the Indian manner. Large slabs of beef were salted and then soaked in brine for some weeks before being hung to dry. Pork was salted and smoked, the last most simply by hanging the meat in the chimney of the great kitchen fireplace. Some houses had attic smoke ovens or basement smoke furnaces, and in the South especially the smokehouse was a separate structure. Pigs' feet were pickled, and cooked meats were preserved in pots sealed with butter or lard.[13]

In an age of large families (ten to fifteen children were not uncommon) barnyard fowls presented no problems of storage or preservation. This advantage, together with the desire for eggs, made the keeping of chickens general. Though much harder to raise, some domestic turkeys were also kept. By the end of the century they were in all the colonies. In Massachusetts some wild turkeys were domesticated when, by the 1660s, they became scarce in the woods.[14]

The European vegetables fared much better than livestock. Carrots, beets, turnips, onions, peas, and cabbages among others were quickly planted, and both English and Dutch settlers rejoiced that the virgin soil produced "garden fruit" superior to any they had known in Europe.[15]

Careful housewives could serve vegetables throughout the year. Successive plantings gave harvests during the spring, summer, and early fall; partially cooked vegetables were sealed by fat in crocks for winter use; peas and beans were sun-dried; and root vegetables and cabbages were stored in dry cellars or in straw and sand. In the fall pickles, sauces, and catsups were prepared to give variety in color, texture, and taste to the winter table.

Salads were also enjoyed by settlers of the middle and upper classes, and friends in England who planned to emigrate were advised to bring with them "for comfort" vinegar and either butter or oil for dressing. Kitchen gardens were planted to lettuce, leeks, succory, cresses, endive, shallots, spinach, garlic, chives, and cucumbers, and some people combed the fields for wild greens.[16] An active interest in vegetables, however, was probably limited to the middle and upper classes. For most Americans the frontier experience, to be repeated in time across the continent, would discourage all but potatoes, pumpkins, cabbages, and a few root crops.

Both sweet and white potatoes made their appearance during the century. Some sweet potatoes were found being grown by Indians of northern Florida and eastern Carolina, and other varieties were imported from the Caribbean islands to Virginia and Maryland. Bermuda even shipped a cargo of sweet potatoes to Massachusetts in 1636.[17]

It was by a devious route that the white, or Irish, potato reached the colonies. Spanish conquistadors had found it growing among the Peruvian Incas and had taken it to Spain from whence it spread into Italy and then northern Europe. From there it came to the English colonies. In 1674 Lord Shaftesbury, a proprietor of the newly created colony of Carolina, ordered settlers on the Edisto River to grow white potatoes. They may or may not have done so, but a decade later they were grown in gardens of southern Carolina. By 1680 the Dutch on the Mohawk River in New York had them, and five years later they grew in Pennsylvania.[18] But the tuber had no immediate success; it was to be a century before it became an everyday food in the colonies.

Fruits, like vegetables, throve when shifted to the new continent. By 1629 Massachusetts had received the seeds and stones of peaches, pomegranates, plums, cherries, pears, quinces, and apples, as well as currant plants, and all but the first two did well there. Young fruit trees were also imported and by 1631 Dorchester was said to have had large orchards.[19] As soon as the trees bore, much of the fruit was put up for year-round use. "Quinces, Cherries, and Damsins set the Dames a-work" wrote the seventeenth-century writer John Josselyn of Massachusetts, noting that in every house he found marmalades and preserved Damson plums. Fruits were not only dried, but candied, preserved in syrup, made into jams, or pressed to make sweet wines.[20]

In the Middle Colonies the quality and quantity of peaches, apples, and pears astounded travelers from abroad. Accustomed to seeing fruits treated as precious and expensive commodities, one visitor was amazed to see Americans taking carts into the orchards to gather peaches.[21] In Pennsylvania the huge fruit surpluses were used to fatten hogs, accounting, some thought, for the superior flavor of the pork there.[22]

The English found peaches and figs along the South Atlantic coast. The figs were probably native, but the peaches had been carried to St. Augustine, Florida, by Spanish adventurers under Menendez in 1565 and from there taken throughout the South by Indians. The Virginia-Maryland region, planted to other fruits, was soon described as "full of gallant orchards" with fruits "more lucious and delightful" than those of England.[23]

Grains were less easy to transfer to America. The early Massachusetts settlers felt sharply the lack of the "English grains" — wheat, rye, barley, and oats — and bought any they could from English ships.[24] It was a disappointment, too, to find that wheat grew poorly in eastern New England, though in time the "rye and Injun" bread became accepted and even popular.[25]

In the Middle Colonies wheat and rye grew so well for the Dutch, Germans, Swedes, and English that in time the region would be called the "bread colonies," supplying the other English settlements and the West Indies as well. South of Pennsylvania little wheat was grown until the late eighteenth century.[26]

Oats provided the early immigrants with food for the voyage and the early years on shore until other crops were grown. Settlers in Massachusetts, Maryland, and Virginia planted oats, and the Spanish spy Molina mentioned it as the only grain eaten in Jamestown in 1614. Soon, however, it was grown mainly by immigrants from northern England and Scotland for their cakes and porridges.[27]

Of vastly greater importance than the imported grains was

what the English, fumbling for a name, called Turkish wheat, Indian wheat, and finally Indian corn. This grain grew on nearly all soils from Maine to Florida; it was easily planted and cared for; it provided food for man and beast; it yielded more to the acre than European grains, and it was easily harvested and stored. It quickly found its way into the food patterns of all levels of society and in all regions. For centuries it was to be the great staple, the keystone of the American diet.

The Algonquian Indians in Virginia showed the Jamestown settlers how to plant corn in 1607, and by 1614 the colony had about 500 acres of it. Soon almost all the planters of Virginia and Maryland grew corn, and the inhabitants of the Chesapeake Bay region were describing the grain as "the thing most necessary to sustaine man" and "the main staffe of life." A visitor to Maryland in 1679 found that corn bread and water alone were the customary food of slaves and indentured servants. The bread, wrote a contemporary, was kneaded without "leaven or yeast, salt or grease, and came from the oven heavy, moist, and barely holding together." A generation later it was said that corn pone was the "constant" bread of the poor and the choice of some planters.[28]

New Englanders used corn in their "rye and Injun" bread, the rye keeping the loaf from drying too quickly. Corn was also made into suppawn, a thick cornmeal and milk porridge, and into samp, corn pounded to a coarse powder and then boiled and eaten with milk and butter. Both were common New England dishes.[29]

The Dutch in New Netherland also learned to make cornmeal in a hollowed-out tree stump, mix it with water, and form it into cakes to be wrapped in vine or corn leaves and baked in hot ashes. They also made suppawn and their own version of samp, a hotchpot of coarsely powdered corn mixed with root vegetables and salt meat and boiled in a huge kettle to provide food for many days.[30]

Dairy products nearly matched grains in importance, for these were in the traditional diets of the English, Germans, Dutch, and Swedes. For a time in New England and Virginia goat's milk had to suffice, but by 1634 all the "better" plantations of Virginia were said to have plenty of milk, butter, and cheese, and throughout New England milk was drunk, made into cheese, or eaten with samp, suppawn, fruits, and baked pumpkins.

Everywhere curds and cream, a mixture of coagulated milk and cream, was rated a delicacy.[31]

What was to become a characteristic of the American diet — an addiction to sweet dishes — also appeared in the seventeenth century and was nourished by an ever-expanding supply of low-priced sweeteners. In their first years New Englanders bought cane sugar from Holland and Madeira, but then the rapid expansion of sugar planting in Barbados and throughout the West Indies gave the mainland colonists a cheaper supply than Europeans had. Emigrants were advised to defer their sugar purchases until they reached the colonies.[32] Far less expensive than sugar was West Indian molasses. This became the common sweetener of the poor everywhere in America and found its way into the cooking of all classes. Not only would it sweeten cookies, cakes, and puddings, but it would be used to flavor milk dishes, vegetables, and meats, especially pork.

Maple sugar did not become important during the seventeenth century. It is a moot point whether it was first made by the Indians, who before trade with the Europeans lacked vessels that could be placed over direct high heat, or by the colonists.[33] In any case it remained little more than a curiosity to the European settlers until well into the following century.

A low-cost source of sweetness appeared during the 1630s and 1640s when both the Dutch and the English imported bees from Europe. The "English flies," as the Indians called them, multiplied rapidly and a description of New York in 1670 claimed that "you shall scarce see a house, but the South side is begirt with Hives of Bees." Pennsylvania was similarly described shortly afterward, and choice honey sold in Philadelphia for five cents a pound.[34]

Easy access to sweeteners gave the colonists a liking for desserts that would characterize their descendants as well. In New England the pumpkin pies of the first years were soon followed by apple, pear, and quince pies. Late in the century Samuel Sewall, the Puritan judge, diarist, and condemner of witches, enjoyed apple and mince pies, tarts, curds and cream, sugared almonds, honey, gingerbread, and plum cake among other delicacies. New Englanders liked the native blueberries. These were commonly picked, sun-dried, and sold by the bushel by the Indians. The settlers found them a good substitute for the currants and raisins so much used in English cookery, and put them into boiled and baked puddings, in water gruel, or ate them with milk and flavored with sugar and spices.[35]

The Dutch in New Netherland loved cakes and cookies, and they contributed the words cookie and cruller to the American language. A common Dutch cake was the olykoek (oil cake), a rich battercake that was boiled or fried in oil, and another favorite was the izer cookie, a tea cake made in long-handled wafer-irons.[36] These and other Dutch dishes would persist long after the English seized the colony in 1664.

For baking, pickling, preserving, and general cooking, the well-to-do imported spices. In 1629 the Massachusetts Bay Company dispersed from its warehouse pepper, nutmegs, cloves, saffron, mace, and cinnamon. The common herbs were easily available, some from the fields and woods. Such "English seeds" as parsley, hysop, thyme, and marjoram did well in American gardens.[37]

More important was salt, needed by every household to preserve meats and by the New England fisheries to preserve their catches. Domestic salt-making was never adequate so that imports were made from England, France, Spain, the Canary Islands, and, increasingly, the West Indies. Although any salt could be used at the table, the "bay salt" from southern Europe was preferred for curing meat and fish.[38]

Foreign trade brought more than salt. Once established on land the colonists had built ships and begun to export their surpluses of fish, grain, meat, tobacco, hides, furs, and naval stores. From other colonies and foreign places they brought back both staple foods and luxuries.

It was not long before food surpluses led to intercolonial trade and, consequently, to greater variety in each colony's diet. The first Maryland settlers sent a corn surplus, bought from the Indians, to New England, taking in return salt fish and other things. The Dutch in New Netherland, a few years before England conquered it in 1664, were buying beef, pork, wheat, and butter from Long Island, beef, pork, and fruits from Virginia, and beef, wheat, flour, biscuits, salt, fish, butter, and cider apples from New England. The South Atlantic coast region came to depend upon the northern colonies for beef, cider, flour, biscuits, onions, apples, hops, and dried fish.[39]

Luxuries came from farther afield. Ships from New England and the Middle Colonies carried meats, fish, and grains to the West Indies and returned with "roots and herbs," sweet potatoes, oranges, rum, pimiento, chocolate, molasses, coconuts, sugar, and ginger. From France, Spain, and the Canary Islands came fruits, olive oil, lemons, lime juice, spices, sugar, and wines.[40] With such delicacies the Virginia planters or Massachusetts merchants could indulge themselves or entertain their friends in a show of elegance and refinement.

The first arrivals in America had reason to worry as the stocks of beer, ale, and wine that they brought with them ran out. They were not used to drinking water and looked upon it as a sorry beverage that, in England, was frequently polluted.

Thirst, the scarcity of any alternative, the extreme heat of American summers, and the presence of cold, bubbling springs all played a part in making water acceptable. The Pilgrims came to appreciate it quickly. Their landing party on Cape Cod discovered some spring water which in their "great thirst" was as "pleasant unto them as wine or beer had been in foretimes." William Bradford, their historian and for long governor, in time bravely decided that while the water was not so wholesome as the beer and wine of London, it was as good water as any in the world and "wholesome enough to us that can be content therewith." Others agreed, one rating New England water better than "Bad Beare, Wheay, or Buttermilk." A Massachusetts man in 1630 reminisced about the preceding year when "it was not accounted a strange thing in those days to drink water."[41]

Even when more popular drinks were available, water, plain or mixed with something else, was widely drunk, especially by the poor. The English colonists used the name "beverage" for a number of drinks that were heavily diluted with water and intended only to quench thirst. A beverage could consist of spiced cider mixed with water, water flavored with ginger and molasses, or even ciderkin, which was made by soaking in water the crushed apples that had been used to make cider. Early settlers in Charleston, South Carolina, made their "common drink" of molasses and water. And late in the century a Virginia historian listed the small drinks of that colony as "wine and water, Beer, Milk and Water, or Water alone."[42]

Anxious to have their customary beer, the early emigrants

brought malt with them and searched for ingredients to brew. Poorer Virginians used persimmons, cornstalks, pumpkins, and Jerusalem artichokes, and for a time Pennsylvanians used molasses, well boiled and flavored with sassafras or pine.[43] Wealthy colonists imported beer, the Virginia planters buying from both England and Holland.[44]

Colonial breweries appeared very early; by 1629 Virginia had two brewhouses, and Massachusetts licensed its first in 1637.[45] The local brews were well received. A resident of New Amsterdam thought that the colony's beer equaled that in "our Fatherland."[46] And at the century's end a Philadelphian described the beer there as half ale and half stout, strong as London beer and bringing a higher price than English beer in Barbados.[47]

By mid-century cider eclipsed beer in New England and rivaled it in many colonies to the southward. Each fall a great part of the apple crop was crushed in wooden mortars, the pumice pressed in baskets, and the juice fermented. Some was good enough to be compared with the famous cider of Herefordshire, England.

Throughout New England cider became the general drink, served at every meal, carried to workers in the fields, and drunk by young and old on every social occasion. President Holyoke of Harvard College needed thirty or more barrels a year for his entertainments, and some Virginians stored as much in their cellars. South of Virginia, where apples grew poorly, the planters and merchants imported cider from the northern colonies.[48]

Where pears were plentiful the settlers made perry, a beverage whose English roots were as ancient as those of cider. The naturalist John Lawson found both cider and perry in North Carolina, but he preferred a "Wine, or Liquor" made there out of quinces that was called quince-drink.[49]

Many of the displaced Europeans, however, wanted wine. The expectations for viniculture were extravagant and led to determined efforts. The first arrivals in Virginia saw wild vines loaded with grapes and were delighted by the promise they held. But during the first years in Jamestown only about twenty gallons of wine were made. In Massachusetts, Governor John Winthrop tried unsuccessfully to start a vineyard, and other New Englanders did no better.[50] The first, enthusiastic attempts to produce wines in all the other colonies made only local and brief gains before failure was admitted. Endemic plant diseases, the high cost of labor, the unsatisfactory taste of the wines, competition from more easily produced beverages, and the greater money to be made from other crops all blighted wine-making attempts.

The demand for European wines was heavy, and early emigrants to Maryland were advised to bring some with them to trade for cattle. More and more ships arrived in American ports with wines from Spain and Portugal and their possessions, as well as lesser amounts from France and Germany. On the whole the colonists followed the English in preferring the heavier, sweeter wines, among which the favorites were Madeira, Canary, Malaga, Fayal, Sherry, and Muscadine.[51]

As large-scale trade developed between the colonies and the West Indies a new drink appeared. Although it was known as early as 1651 as kill-devil, it was soon after called "rumbullion" or "rumme." Rum was made cheaply in the West Indies and became increasingly popular among the poor. When cheap molasses became available from the French West Indies, New England began to distill its own rum, the first Boston distillery being founded in 1657.

Guardians of public morality became alarmed as rum spread among the poor. When the Reverend Increase Mather, president of Harvard College, lectured a criminal awaiting execution in 1686, he lamented that it was "an unhappy thing that in later years a kind of strong drink called Rum has been common amongst us, which the poorer sort of people, both in town and country, can make themselves drunk with. They that are poor and wicked too, can for a penny or two make themselves drunk."[52] The identification of rum with poverty was to continue for two centuries and more.

Their uninhibited pleasure in drinking led the colonists to make still other beverages. In New England and the Middle Colonies apple brandy was a by-product of cider making. Sometimes it was distilled, but an easier way was to expose cider to freezing weather, then remove the surface ice as it formed, leaving the remainder of higher alcoholic content. Pennsylvanians specialized in peach brandy, but they also distilled corn, cherries, grapes, and wild plums. By 1682, Carolinians had macerated corn, fermented it, and distilled "a strong spirit like Brandy." Two other drinks, mead and metheglin, were made throughout the colonies. These fermented, honey-based beverages came from a distant Anglo-Saxon past.[53]

The American liking for mixed drinks appeared early, some of them combining cider and rum, cider and brandy, or cider and mead. Very popular was flip which existed as early as 1690. Flip was beer sweetened with sugar, molasses, or dried pumpkin and strengthened with some spirit, usually rum. Into this mixture a red-hot iron was thrust which made the liquor foam and gave it a burned, bitter flavor. Although flip may have been of English origin, by the War of Independence it became so thoroughly Americanized that John Trumbull, the poet, hailed it as the symbol of the revolutionary spirit:

While briskly to each patriot lip
Walks eager round the inspiring flip:
Delicious draught! whose powers inherit
The quintessence of public spirit.[54]

Punch was probably the most popular mixed drink. The word was used loosely, for William Penn mentioned a "punch" of rum and water as rivaling beer in Pennsylvania. Usually punch was an upper-class beverage made by combining wine, brandy, or rum with citrus fruits and water. The heavy importations of orange, lemon, and lime juices into the colonies were certainly to provide major ingredients of punch.[55]

Everywhere in the colonies there was worry about excessive drinking. Governor William Bradford of Plymouth complained in 1646 of "the excess and the abuse of wine," and Massachusetts set up a tight control over wine sellers. Director Peter Stuyvesant of New Netherland asserted in 1648 that nearly a fourth of the buildings in New Amsterdam were "Brandy shops, Tobacco or Beer houses." In Virginia there was alarm over drunkenness as early as 1619, and in 1638 the governor stated that half the colony's gain from tobacco planting was wasted on wines and "strong waters." A visitor to Maryland in 1679 criticized the settlers there who drank "so abominably together" when ships arrived with wine and brandy that their supplies were soon exhausted.[56] But widespread concern did not prompt action. To prohibit alcoholic liquors was unthinkable, and even the idea of temperance, except as a matter of individual choice, would not be urged until the following century.

The poor in the colonies — the black slaves, the white indentured servants, and many of the wage laborers — did not worry about excessive use of either food or drink. The indentured servants were those needy who had sold their labor, usually for four or five years, in return for passage to America. They were semislaves during their indenture, for although they had some legal rights they were seldom able to enforce them before a law court. Consequently, what shelter, clothing, food, kindness, cruelty, or punishments might be meted out to them depended on the character and circumstances of those who bought their indentures.

The indentured servants were rarely well fed. A traveler in Pennsylvania claimed that those there lived on nothing but corn and water. In 1679 it was said that the Maryland servants had for their "usual food" only "maize bread to eat, and water to drink, which sometimes is not very good and scarcely enough for life." Such a diet was less startling when compared to that which Ebenezer Cook, a poet, found in a Maryland planter's home:

> While Pon and Milk, with Mush well stoar'd,
> In wooden Dishes grac'd the Board;
>   With Homine and Syder-pap,
>   (Which scarce a hungry Dog wou'd lap)
> Well stuff'd with Fat, from Bacon fry'd,
> Or with Molossus dulcify'd.[57]

The food of the black slaves was probably like that of the white indentured servants. Indeed, the earliest blacks were sold as indentured servants, but without a terminal date on their indentures so that their status became that of slaves. During the seventeenth century they remained few in number. The first, fourteen in all, were sold in Virginia in 1619, but as late as 1670 there were but 2,000 slaves in the colony's population of 40,000.

If but few were slaves, so but few were wealthy. The average American lived on his own acres with a standard of living well above that of his social equals in Europe. As yet only a few benefited from the enterprise, luck, or cupidity that in the next century would raise a minority to great wealth and power.

As class stratification was slight, so too were regional differences. Still, three major sections were emerging — New England, the Middle Colonies, and the southern colonies. Each had its own soils, climate, topography, natural resources, and peculiar mixtures of nationalities. Regional differences in food and drink were inevitable.

The New England diet reflected the English origins of most of the people, the limited fertility of the soil, the short growing season, and the richly endowed coastal waters. Game of all kinds, corn, pork, beef, fish, shellfish, root vegetables, beans, pumpkins, squashes, milk, cheese, apples, cranberries, and blueberries were prepared with a mingling of English traditions, Indian examples, and American invention. Puritanism did not inhibit the settlers from as full an enjoyment of foods and drinks as their circumstances allowed.

The typical New England breakfast was hasty pudding, to be known in time as cornmeal mush, eaten with milk or molasses. The main meal at noon was more hasty pudding, or pea or bean porridge, or fresh or salt meat with vegetables, or a stew of meat and vegetables. Along the coast fish often replaced meat. Very often the meats, whether salt pork or corned beef, were made into hashes, ragoûts, thick stews, or a hotchpot of chopped meats and vegetables which eased the task of forkless diners.[58] Supper was like breakfast. Everywhere hogs were kept for meat and lard, chickens for their meat and eggs, and cows for milk and cheese.

The Middle Colonies had less bounty from the sea than New England, but were blessed with more fertile land and a longer growing season. Rich with food surpluses, these colonies provided all immigrants the foods they craved. The unique food habits of the section came originally from the Dutch in New Netherland and the Germans who accepted William Penn's invitation to live in Pennsylvania.

The Dutch never emigrated in great numbers, but their cultural impact was strong. Although Holland shared many eating and drinking habits with the English and Germanic countries, the Dutch had a unique culinary heritage. In Holland they took great stores of fish from the North Sea, while the farmers made the land flourish with fruits, flowers, and vegetables. Late in the sixteenth century a much-traveled Englishman, Fynes Moryson, commented on Dutch fare. "Butter is the first and last dish at the Table," he wrote, "whereof they make all sawces, especially for fish, and thereupon by strangers they are merrily called Buttermouths." The other "white meats" were popular. Milk was drunk regularly, and cheeses were traded from city to city. It was a common sight, wrote Moryson, to see the Dutch sitting at their doors lunching on cheese with bread and butter.

When meat was eaten, most commonly pork, it was baked or made into a hotchpot which combined flesh, root vegetables, and fat. This dish was served day after day with fresh ingredients added as needed. The Dutch ate many vegetables, oysters, and fresh and salt fish. Mushrooms and frogs' legs were delicacies. Since wine was heavily taxed in Holland, beer was the common drink.[59] Moryson could also have mentioned that the Dutch were adept at making cakes, cookies, wafers, and crullers.

The Dutch who emigrated to New Netherland between 1624 and England's seizure of the colony forty years later in large part continued the diet they had known in Holland. In America they ate little meat, preferring milk, butter, and cheese. The hotchpot was the main dish in many homes, accompanied by cabbage salads and beer. Cakes, cookies, and other pastries of Dutch kitchens flourished in America because of the availability of low-cost sugars.

The Germans, like the Dutch, easily maintained their traditional diet in the moderate climate and the rich soils of the Middle Colonies. In Germany, pork and veal were the favored meats, and great meat puddings were so well liked that they figured in the proverbial German wish for short sermons and long puddings. Although few Germans had access to seafoods, they did use the fish from their ponds and rivers. Their bread was of rye, and gingerbread was a favorite cake. Skilled farmers and gardeners, they raised many vegetables, of which cabbage was the most common and was regularly served as "crawt." Moryson was impressed by the prodigious German thirst for beer. Wine was served as a "dainty," and there were different kinds of *aqua vitae*.[60] All these preferences were carried to Pennsylvania and other colonies. Since spasmodic emigrations from Germany to America continued over several centuries, the long-term effect on American eating habits was considerable, probably second only to the English.

In the southern colonies, as in New England, the English influence was dominant. The emphasis on a few staple crops — tobacco in Maryland and Virginia and rice in Carolina — prevented the diversified farming that might have produced greater variety. As it was, corn and pork became the basic foods of the South, supplemented by fish and shellfish in coastal areas, by game everywhere, and by peaches, persimmons, rice, sweet potatoes, root vegetables, and greens. The lack of good pastures and refrigeration discouraged the eating of meat except for salt pork, game, and barnyard fowls. Although wealthy planters could buy and produce a range of foods, even they, in their liking for corn bread and ham, reflected the strength of regional forces.

❧ 4 ❧
The Eighteenth Century I

Pork upon pork and again pork upon that.

During the eighteenth century everything in the American colonies seemed to be expanding explosively: through immigration and a high birthrate the population increased from a quarter of a million people in 1700 to more than five million a century later; prosperity followed access to the rich, untapped supply of natural resources; and the span of England's possessions in America grew immensely through a series of wars against France. The colonists equated growth with progress and reached the satisfying conclusion that America, under God's guidance, was leading mankind toward ultimate perfection.

Since England, unlike Spain and France, did not restrict who could settle in its colonies, its American possessions became the home of people of different races, national origins, social ranks, religious affiliations, and political convictions. A traveler of the mid-1700s who took the long, even dangerous trip by land from Georgia to northern New England would experience the excitement of a journey through strange, foreign countries. Slow passages through deep forests were broken only barely by the cleared lands of some of the few million inhabitants. Roads were often little more than footpaths or twin ruts, better suited to travel by horse than by wagon or coach. Small rivers were forded and the larger crossed by ferries. Inns were few and crude; in the South, especially, travelers had to rely on private homes for food and lodging.

In Georgia, founded in 1732 mainly as a buffer to protect wealthy South Carolina from the hostile Spanish in Florida and the Indians, the few thousand inhabitants included English, Scot Highlanders, and Germans, the latter largely Lutherans, Salzburgers and Moravians who had fled German oppression. Until the

43

War of Independence the colony remained a lightly populated and militarily weak frontier.

Along the coast of South Carolina were rice plantations worked by great numbers of black slaves. In Charleston, the only large southern city, planters, lawyers, and merchants lived in beautiful houses and held fortunes made from rice, indigo, and trade. To the north and west was a backcountry of small farms owned by Scotch-Irish, Germans, Swiss, Welsh, English, and other nationalities, all expected to protect the low country from Indian attacks.

North Carolina, thickly forested and without good harbors, was nearly isolated from the rest of the colonial world. With few slaves and planters, the population of English, Scotch-Irish, and Germans, among others, farmed or, with British subsidies, produced tar, pitch, and turpentine from the tidewater pine barrens.

In Virginia and Maryland there was again a planter-dominated society whose wealth came from the tobacco tended by slaves. Virginia was large, populous, and rich, and its fine plantation houses sheltered families that monopolized all positions of power from justice of the peace to seats in the House of Burgesses.

Pennsylvania had large areas of productive soil worked by settlers of English descent, including many Quakers, and by perhaps 70,000 Germans. The latter made Pennsylvania bilingual and their farms were the envy of all who saw their fine herds, bulging barns, and neatly cultivated fields. Cosmopolitan Philadelphia was the largest and most important city in the colonies. On the Pennsylvania frontier were great numbers of Scotch-Irish, the descendants of Scots who had colonized northern Ireland until the economic, political, and religious discriminations of the English forced them to look for a better life in America.

New Jersey also had a mixture of religions and nationalities, including English Quakers, Dutch, and Germans. Without a good harbor or an important city, New Jersey was economically and culturally dependent on New York City to the north and Philadelphia to the south.

New York City had the most polyglot population and the most magnificent harbor on the Atlantic coast. The descendants of the Dutch founders mingled with English, French-speaking Wal-

44

loons, Welsh, Irish, Swedes, Jews, French Huguenots, Germans, Scots, Scotch-Irish, and Africans. Along the Hudson River were huge estates of powerful families that controlled factions of the colony's representative assembly.

Throughout New England place names, manners, and local government all revealed the strong English influence. Boston and other coastal towns had wealthy merchants and professional men, but generally New England was a region of small farmers and of considerable economic and social democracy. Through their town meetings they even enjoyed a high degree of self-government.

Although the larger colonies from New York to Georgia mapped their lands far to the west, settlement there had been discouraged by fear of the French and their Indian allies. France claimed the entire Mississippi Valley and Canada, and its fur traders, trappers, priests, officials, and soldiers had thinly occupied these regions. Beginning in 1689 the English and French colonists supported their mother countries in four wars, the last of which was the French and Indian War of 1754 to 1763, a conflict that began in western Pennsylvania and expanded into Europe's Seven Years' War.

The results of this war in America were immense: England took from France all of Canada and clear title to the lands that lay between the Appalachians and the Mississippi River, and Spain received from France all the land between the Mississippi River and the Rocky Mountains. With the French menace removed, lessening the need for British military support, the colonists could indulge their burgeoning nationalism and defy what they termed the tyranny of Great Britain. The following twelve years saw a series of crises between England and its colonies that ended in the War of Independence.

This war, which lasted from 1775 to 1783, did more than create a new nation. British restraints upon American manufacturing and overseas trade ceased. Social and cultural ties between England and America were weakened at the same time as the 1778 alliance with France opened Americans to a Gallic influence that was strengthened at first by the presence of French troops in America and then by the arrival in the United States of refugees from revolutionary France. Independence also forced the new nation to undertake a series of experiments in government that led in 1787 to the framing of the Constitution.

What Americans ate and drank during the eighteenth century was affected by these and still other changes — immigrations, economic developments, internal and overseas commerce, class stratification, and the movement of people to cities and westward. Change came most quickly to the middle and upper classes. Least touched were the poor who, as always, knew only the cheaper foods and those that could be taken from the water, the sky, and the forest around them.

Most Americans were farmers and largely self-sufficient, but in the small cities markets were needed. These probably began as gatherings of wagons and crude stalls, but by the early eighteenth century sheds or buildings were constructed. In 1722 Charleston, South Carolina, built a market on Tradd Street at the Bay, and during the next decade others opened in Philadelphia, Boston, Newport, and New York. Philadelphia's became by far the most famous, lauded by all for its cleanliness, orderliness, the neatness and beauty of its goods, and the stunning variety of fruits, vegetables, seafoods, meats, and game that it displayed. New York City, by the century's end, had four markets, but though highly rated for their fish, one traveler thought them below those of Philadelphia for meats and vegetables.[1]

Among foods corn was the "grand product of the country,"[2] and all families used it daily. Cornmeal mush was the ordinary breakfast and supper dish, served with milk and flavored according to what was available with molasses, maple syrup, sugar, currants, raisins, blueberries, or, in frontier regions, bear's oil or venison grease.[3]

In the South, where wheat was scarce, corn was universally used in breads, cakes, mush, and hominy. It was a major food of poor whites and black slaves, and the wealthy Virginia planter William Byrd noted that a boatwright was "affronted that I gave him pone instead of English bread for breakfast." However, Robert Beverley, the eighteenth-century historian of Virginia, found that though rich planters had wheat bread, some of them "rather choose the Pone."[4]

Corn bread was most simply made from cornmeal, salt, and water and called pone, johnny cake, corn dodger, or hoecake.[5] Since corn bread was best when fresh and hot, this may have led to the American preference for hot breads. An English visitor in the early 1720s found that Virginians daily baked breads, "eating

46

too much hot and new bread, which cannot be wholsom," a criticism that other Europeans would echo for two centuries.[6]

The colonists also liked hot buttered toast, and the toasting fork or more elaborate wrought-iron toaster were common. Although toast was not an American invention, eating it hot was another example of the colonists' liking for hot breads. The English toast rack would not find a home in America.

Hominy, like corn bread, was part of the daily diet in the South, and together they spanned the centuries. The man who wrote soon after Maryland was settled that "their ordinary diet is Poane and Omine" would be echoed by a traveler two centuries later who found that "corn-cake and 'big hominy' is the universal provender" of the South.

Great hominy was made by scalding shelled corn in a kettle of water and wood ashes until the hulls separated, then winnowing and drying the grains. After washing and soaking, the corn was boiled and came from the pot soft, plump, and white. Small-grained hominy, in time to be called grits, was often made into a kind of hasty pudding or dried for winter use. Hominy was served in many ways. In Virginia and Maryland it was boiled with beans and milk until the whole mass became firm, after which it could be eaten hot or cold with bacon or other meat. In some places "hog and hominy," hominy fried with pork, was a standard dish. At times hominy was fried in venison grease or combined with bear's grease and sugar.[7]

Everywhere in the colonies fall marked the season of "roasting ears." This, like all corn dishes, was adopted from the Indians and consisted of boiling the young ears of field corn or baking them in ashes and dressing them with salt and butter. In cities, toward the century's end, it was sold in the streets to cries of "Hot corn, hot corn!"[8]

The middle and upper classes of the country showed a growing preference for wheat bread, and this grain was largely grown in the Middle Colonies. In coastal South Carolina and Georgia, however, rice was the principal grain. This had been planted in South Carolina near the end of the seventeenth century and soon became the colony's principal crop.[9] The breads, cakes, and cookies of the lowlands were largely made with rice flour.

Some colonists preferred dark breads. The Germans in Pennsylvania ate rye bread partly through custom and partly in order to sell the more profitable wheat, and eastern New Englanders, unable to grow wheat, became attached to their "rye and Injun."[10]

Vegetables, unlike the grains and meats, were not assigned a large role in American meals. The frontier experience, which every part of the colonies had known, together with the easy access to meat, had tended to eliminate from common use all but a few of the hardier vegetables. Israel Acrelius, a Swedish visitor to Delaware at mid-century, said that while "almost every home" had a vegetable garden, they grew only several varieties of beans, the common root vegetables, and a few kinds of lettuce, all other vegetables being "regarded as a rarity."[11] According to Benjamin Rush, the noted doctor, Philadelphians ate few vegetables other than turnips and cabbages until a number of German gardeners settled near the city, after which "the tables of all classes of citizens have been covered with a variety of vegetables in every season of the year."[12] Plant diseases and poor gardening probably limited the use of many vegetables. The wealthy Virginia planter, Landon Carter, bemoaned twenty years of difficulties with turnips and more recent troubles with carrots, field cabbages, and broccoli.[13]

The easily grown pumpkin remained in use, especially in New England. Colonists there ate them roasted and served with butter, boiled, and boiled and mashed. Pumpkin pulp was mixed with corn and other flours and baked into bread and cakes or used to make puddings, pies, tarts, and even pancakes. Imitating the Indians, the colonists dried long slices of pumpkin before the fire or in the sun. These kept for years and were eaten with meats as needed. By long boiling, even pumpkin molasses could be made. Sarah Knight, a doughty lady who journeyed from Boston to New York City and back in 1704, met pumpkin in several forms. At Stratford Ferry, Connecticut, the "pumpkin and Indian mixt Bred" in a poor family's home had "such an Aspect" that she refused it. On her return through Connecticut an inn served her "Rost Beef and pumpkin sause" for supper.[14]

The Jerusalem artichoke was also widely grown. This tuber, somewhat like a small, starchless potato, was a relative of the sunflower and probably originated west of the Mississippi River. It had been carried to Europe early in the seventeenth century where it was called an artichoke because of its taste and Jerusalem from a corruption of the Italian word *girasole,* the sunflower.[15]

In the Middle Colonies the cabbage stood high in importance. The Dutch in New Netherland often included a "great salad" as part of their dinners, very likely the "koolslaa" that would spread throughout the country. The Germans of New Jersey and Pennsylvania not only liked fresh cabbages but converted them into sauerkraut which was kept in vast crocks from which it was taken as needed. A German indentured servant in New Jersey found his master's family served pieces of boiled beef from one kettle and entire heads of cabbage and whole turnips from another.[16] Where cabbages grew poorly, as in the South, they brought high prices in the markets.[17]

Turnips were important everywhere. Although they were a plebeian food, even prosperous people ate them with mutton.[18] In New England they were raised as a filling food, much as potatoes would be later. And though Landon Carter failed to grow them successfully in Virginia, in time they would become an important southern food.

Peas and beans, both fresh and dried, played very large roles. Amelia Simmons in her 1796 cookbook listed nine varieties of beans, nearly all adopted from the Indians, and seven kinds of peas. Both peas and beans were mixed with corn, other vegetables, and sometimes meat to make succotash or other filling dishes. Lima beans, though of American origin, were seldom mentioned, though some existed in a Cincinnati garden by the century's end.[19]

Green peas were a great delicacy. These were no mere "sauce," but a food worthy of special mention, especially in the spring or early summer when, after a long winter of salted meats and root vegetables, they came as a delicious, early sign of better times. Neighbors competed to have the first. One Philadelphia woman planted some six weeks too early, her husband thought, "from an anxiety" of having them before their neighbors. Thomas Jefferson at Monticello won the local contest so regularly that he once told his daughter to let a neighbor believe that he had won. Also proud were those who gathered peas as late as September.[20]

Only slowly did the Irish potato become known and popular. In March of 1699 the Steward of Harvard College bought three-fourths of a pound of them for one pound one shilling, and eight years later some were served at a dinner celebrating the installation of a president of the same school.[21] Were these imported or locally grown? An early historian stated that the potato had been introduced into New England by Scotch-Irish immigrants who planted some in Andover, Massachusetts, in 1719.[22]

The potato was not immediately successful in New England, possibly because it was identified with the Scotch-Irish, who were the object of prejudice. More likely it was because the kind of potato grown, as one man remembered, had "so rank a taste that it was scarcely eatable." Although two better varieties were obtained soon after 1740, potatoes remained uncommon in New England until shortly before the War of Independence.[23]

The growing of potatoes in the Middle Colonies was no doubt encouraged by the presence there of Dutch, Germans, and Scotch-Irish. By the mid-1730s potatoes were in the upper Hudson River valley and just before the War of Independence heavy crops were reported in New York. In Pennsylvania and Delaware a small, knotty, bright yellow variety existed by the 1720s, and the potato made few friends in those colonies until about 1770 when several better kinds were imported from New England.[24]

Throughout the Tidewater South the Irish potato not only grew poorly but had to compete with hominy, sweet potatoes, yams, and rice. Although such wealthy planters as Washington, Jefferson, and Landon Carter raised white potatoes, most planters who desired them depended upon imports from northern colonies.

As yet only a few uses of the potato were known. It was certainly fried, as were so many things, as well as boiled, roasted, and mashed. People of English descent liked potatoes with roast beef, and the Germans enjoyed the potato soup which they introduced to America.[25]

Sweet potatoes remained popular in the South, especially in the Carolinas and Georgia.[26] Yams were less common, though the botanist William Bartram found them in Mobile, Alabama, in 1733. A visitor to Benjamin Franklin's home in Philadelphia in 1749 was served yams, and a Charleston, South Carolina, manuscript cookbook of 1770 gave a recipe for yam pudding.[27]

Some vegetables were scarce. A German traveler found fine cauliflowers in Bethlehem, Pennsylvania, in 1783 but thought they grew badly in New York and Philadelphia. Salsify, rhubarb, and eggplant were rare everywhere. It was said that Hessian mercenaries of the English introduced kohlrabi, broccoli, and the black radish during the War of Independence, but Jefferson had grown broccoli at Monticello as early as 1767, and then or soon afterward celery, asparagus, artichokes, endive, garlic, and salsify as well. Others grew shallots, and late in the century rutabaga came from Europe. Leeks, though much grown in the British Isles, were rare in the colonies. Settlers on the Virginia frontier in spring ate the wild pokeweed for greens, as did Southerners elsewhere.[28]

The artichoke, though grown in Virginia as early as the 1720s, came late to New England. A few years before the War of Independence a Boston resident said she had never seen one. They probably arrived with America's French allies, for a few years after the war a French traveler claimed that artichokes grew well in Massachusetts but only as a "curiosity" for "no one eats them."[29] In time they would be called French artichokes.

It is not known where and when okra first appeared in the colonies. It possibly came on slave ships either directly from Africa or by way of the West Indies. In 1748 it was grown in Pennsylvania gardens for use in soup and was said to have been liked especially by blacks. Jefferson listed okra among the vegetables grown in Virginia gardens in 1781.[30]

The eating of mushrooms was probably discouraged by the lack of any reliable method of distinguishing the edible from the poisonous. Landon Carter and Jefferson both ate mushrooms, and they were advertised for sale in the *South Carolina Gazette*. They were not only stewed, but used to make mushroom catsup, one of the popular sauces of the time.[31]

Momentous to the future was the coming of the tomato. This fruit, a native of tropical America, had been carried to Europe by Spanish explorers in the sixteenth century. It was first grown as an ornament, but by the eighteenth century it was an important food in both Italy and France.

Charleston, South Carolina, knew the tomato as early as 1770, and eleven years later Jefferson mentioned that they were in Virginia gardens.[32] Thereafter their use grew slowly but steadily until the early nineteenth century when they began a steep rise in popular favor.

51

From fields and gardens the middle and upper classes continued to gather greens for salads. A French traveler noticed that northern New Englanders favored beet greens for salads. The dressings varied. The Landon Carter family in Virginia complained that the melted butter in theirs was rank; a visitor to North Carolina endured "raw salad" at an inn that lacked vinegar; and a guest at Washington's home at Mount Vernon was served a salad without oil. Olive oil, he decided, was more common in northern than in southern states.[33]

It was still meat that played the central role in the American diet. Even more than the English, Americans had become meat-eaters. Released from the scarcities of Europe and in the midst of an immense store of animals, birds, and fish, they set flesh-laden tables.

Nearly everyone still lived near the ocean or the major rivers flowing into it, and fish and shellfish naturally made part of the daily meals. The supplies seemed limitless. Stories were told of men becoming physically tired from pulling fish from the rivers, of catches with hooks of 600 sturgeon, and of immense takes on the rivers with seines, eelpots, weirs, and fish pots. Sturgeon was everyday food for many Southerners, fresh in summer or pickled in winter. Each spring schools of herring filled the Potomac, and north of Chesapeake Bay and the Delaware River the shad came by the millions to every river, one man reporting over 5,000 being taken at a single haul of the seine.[34]

Innumerable seafoods were offered in the New York City markets near the century's end: sixty-three kinds of fish in addition to oysters, lobsters, freshwater and saltwater crabs, crawfish, prawns, eight other kinds of shellfish, and turtles. The Boston market matched or exceeded this variety.[35] Even those who lived in the interior found streams filled with trout, immense catfish in the larger rivers, and ponds and lakes alive with perch, pike, sunfish, chubs, bass, suckers, and other fish.[36]

To have fish for Saturday dinner was a custom in New England that continued until the Civil War. The practice dated from Elizabethan England when, to encourage the fisheries and indirectly strengthen the country's naval power, Parliament had decreed that fish should be eaten certain days each week.[37] The importance of New England's fisheries gave sanction to its own version of the custom.

Shellfish varied in popularity. Lobsters, larger and different from those of Europe, were eaten in New England but did not yet rate as a delicacy. Although the Dutch had had lobsters in New Netherland, they must at some time have disappeared. Later, it was said, a ship carrying some from New England broke into pieces about ten miles from New York City, dropping its live cargo into the sea. By mid-century lobsters were reported to be numerous near New York. Fishermen claimed that cannon fire and the noise of ships' anchors made them rare again during the War of Independence, but after the war they returned.[38]

Mussels were little eaten in the northern colonies, but clams were much relished. Dr. Alexander Hamilton, a Maryland physician, ate his first fried clams when he visited Staten Island in 1744.[39] In New Jersey, late in the century, peddlers sold clams as well as oysters and fish, and Flemington had a clam-buying club whose members went in turn to New Brunswick for supplies.[40]

Shrimp were found and eaten along both the south Atlantic and Gulf coasts, and crabs were the special delicacy of Chesapeake Bay.[41] Landon Carter rejoiced that the rivers and creeks of Virginia provided not only crabs but the finest prawns he had ever seen.[42]

Oysters, taken in immense quantities from New England to Florida, were vastly more popular than any other seafood. By the last decades of the century oysters had become the best-loved food of coastal America. "Americans have almost a passion for oysters," wrote Moreau de Saint Méry, a French refugee, "which they eat at all hours, even in the streets." Oysters were peddled from barrows by the dozens and hundreds, he added, "to the accompaniment of mournful cries."[43] For long, the New York City supply came from Oyster Island in the bay between New York City and Elizabethtown, New Jersey. By the early 1780s, however, the most and best oysters, some eight to ten inches long, were coming from Blue Point on the southern coast of Long Island.[44]

Whatever their source, the city's oysters were so cheap and plentiful that by the late eighteenth century they had become a principal food of the city's poor. One traveler said they sustained "a great part" of the poor, while another man stated that in the city "very many poor families have no other subsistence than oysters and bread."[45]

Not for the poor were the huge sea turtles that were caught in the ocean off the southern colonies or were brought by ships from the tropics to various ports. Late in the century the mayor of Philadelphia commented that the United States wouldn't change places with any country in the world, for here one could have venison, turtle, and wine.[46]

A few people sensed limits to the seafood supply. Peter Kalm, a Swedish botanist, talked to aged Philadelphians who remembered far larger catches of fish in their youth. They blamed the change on riverside mills which prevented fish from going upriver to spawn and on the many commercial fisheries along the rivers. George Washington and other Virginia planters used weirs to take shad and herring for their slaves and to be salted and sold to the West Indies for the slaves there.[47]

There was also less game on land. Deer were still shot in most rural areas and venison sold cheaply in cities, but a few years before the War of Independence Marylanders found deer "exceedingly diminished" from earlier times. On the trans-Appalachian frontier game remained plentiful. For a time elk and buffalo were shot. No one praised elk meat, but the buffalo was highly rated. The tongues, hump, and udders were especially liked, and the tallow, which kept well in hot weather, served frontiersmen as a substitute for butter or lard. By the 1770s, however, the buffalo had disappeared from western Georgia, and it was soon gone from all lands east of the Mississippi.[48]

The wild turkey was also disappearing. In western Massachusetts the cost of dressed turkeys rose from one and a half cents a pound in the 1730s to four cents a pound by the end of the century, by which time they had almost disappeared east of the Connecticut River. They still existed in upstate New York, western Pennsylvania, and most of the South.[49]

Wild carrier pigeons provided a seemingly inexhaustible source of food. They wintered along the southern coasts where they were taken at night by torchlight, beaten from their low roosts and placed in sacks while confused by the sudden light. Their migrations were the occasion for tremendous killings in which anyone wielding a club could participate. A woman in Albany, New York, said these migrations "occasioned . . . a total relaxation from all employments, and a kind of drunken gaiety, though it was rather slaughter than sport; and, for above a fortnight, pigeons in pies and soups, and every way they could be dressed, were the food of the inhabitants." A traveler in Rhode Island found pigeons at such a time almost the sole food at taverns, and the "common people" were said to be living almost entirely on them.[50]

An astonishing range of other wild birds were eaten. A botanist in 1739 listed the game birds of Virginia:

> Wild turkeys were numerous, partridges, wild geese, swans, brants, cormorants, teal, duck and mallard, black ducks and another sort we call summer ducks, plover 2 or 3 sorts, soris [sora] (a delicious eating bird in shape and way of living like y'r water rails), heath fowls (called here improperly pheasants) 2 sorts, wild pidgeons in prodigious great flocks, fieldfares (robins), woodcocks . . . snipes, herons, bitterns, eagles, larkes 2 sorts. . . .

William Byrd, the Virginia planter, spoke highly of crows, turtledoves, parrots, thrushes, catbirds, Baltimore orioles, warblers, whippoorwills, and cranes, but found the fish crows unpleasant and the cormorants inedible.[51]

But the edible birds were declining. Peter Kalm wrote in 1748 that all the American-born Swedes and English he questioned said that the birds had decreased markedly since they were children, and even their fathers had complained of this. Where sixty or seventy years earlier a person could kill eighty ducks in a morning, he might now wait in vain for one. Some elderly Swedes remembered when incredible numbers of cranes had been killed every spring, but by mid-century only a few men lived who as youths had eaten cranes.[52]

Few animals escaped being shot for food, for men at times ate foxes, panthers, otters, muskrats, minks, porcupines, and skunks, the last being described as delicious. Bears were highly prized. The Moravians in North Carolina rated the meat as "very wholesome" and thought that bear's fat was as good as olive oil with salads. Philadelphians considered leg of bear a "great delicacy."[53]

The growing number of Americans who depended upon livestock for their meat ate such great quantities as to astound travelers from Europe. The German traveler Johann D. Schoepf, in 1783, concluded that Americans, like the English, consumed more meat than vegetables, while Moreau de Saint Méry, a decade later, estimated that Americans ate seven or eight times as much meat as bread.[54]

Meats varied greatly in quantity, quality, and kind from place to place. Good ones of every kind could be bought in the great public markets of Boston, New York, or Philadelphia. But a visitor to the Newport, Rhode Island, market in 1788 saw only a "few chunks of second-grade meat which awaited nonexistent buyers." It was explained to him that Newporters lived on fish they caught themselves.[55] While this may have been true for most of that city, it was not the whole story. The Reverend Ezra Stiles of Newport fared better. Stiles kept a cow both for milk and to enable him to slaughter a calf every spring. In winter he might buy up to 500 pounds of beef and put a round of it up the chimney to be smoked. Every December he would have a hog or two butchered which he had either fattened himself or purchased, and at times he bought mutton, lamb, fish, or fowl.[56]

Throughout the colonies the English preference for beef had taken firm root. Beefsteaks were especially well liked. Travelers met with them at the principal inns, and in 1744 in Philadelphia a "Beef-Stake Club," probably imitative of its London predecessor begun in 1738, met at Tunn Tavern every Saturday. Visitors to some Philadelphia taverns late in the century could order one of the combinations for which they had a reputation: beefsteaks and shad, or beefsteaks and oysters.[57]

Although sheep were raised in New England and the Middle Colonies to provide not only wool but mutton and lamb, there was widespread prejudice against both meats. This may have been because neither could be successfully preserved by salting or smoking, or because their taste could be easily damaged by poor slaughtering methods.[58]

Pork remained the basic meat everywhere. Pigs were easily raised and provided not only meat but flavoring for many dishes and the lard that served as cooking fat for others.

A traveler in New England in 1740 found all meats good, but "as to their pork, they challenge all the world." The Dutch and Germans everywhere favored pork. The Germans used every part of the pig, making pig stomach, filled souse, sausages, pork with dumplings, and scrapple. The autumn pig-killing and sausage-making, or *metzel,* included the dispatch of heaping dishes of sausage to close family friends who, if they lived nearby, sent delicacies to the family engaged in butchering.[59]

Southerners gloried in their pork, and Virginians lauded their hams as superior in flavor to "any in the world." The salted hog meat of Smithfield, Virginia, and vicinity was already famous.[60]

Ham figured large in the Virginia diet. Ham and eggs with coffee were often "the sole entertainment" in Virginia ordinaries, and no landlord thought he could do business without ham and pork. A clergyman noted that in the polite circles of Williamsburg "it is the custom to have a plate of cold ham upon the table; and there is scarcely a Virginian lady who breakfasts without it."[61]

North Carolinians also raised pigs. When the Virginia planter William Byrd visited there early in the century he found the settlers very fond of pork which, for lack of salt, they ate fresh. He described his own meals there as "pork upon pork and again pork upon that." The colony swarmed with hogs and, after the War of Independence, ten to twelve thousand were driven yearly to South Carolina or Virginia. North Carolinians used the expression, "We make pork."[62]

Back from the coast, pork competed with game for table space. On the South Carolina frontier the Reverend Charles Woodmason, an Anglican itinerant, found little beef or mutton. When there was beef the inhabitants "jerk it and dry it in the Sun — So that You may as well eat a Deal Board." The settlers generally ate pork in winter and bacon in summer.[63]

Poultry was cheap and plentiful everywhere. Chickens were fried, roasted, boiled, or put into a pie, a favorite fall dish in New England. Turkeys were boiled, hashed, made into pie, or roasted, and a goose was roasted and served with an onion sauce.[64] By the War of Independence, guinea hens were numerous in Long Island, New Jersey, and Pennsylvania and occasionally peacocks were eaten.[65]

With meats easily available, there was little need of dairy products as substitutes. But milk, butter, and cheese were in the traditions of the English, Germans, Dutch, Swedes, Swiss, and other immigrants who enjoyed them all for their own sakes.

New Englanders probably drank the most milk. In the usual village each householder could keep a cow or two in a nearby field. In the larger towns milk was vended by men who carried large pails of it suspended by shoulder straps.[66] Both the Dutch and Germans in the Middle Colonies were fond of dairy products, and the Scotch-Irish of western Pennsylvania and the southern backcountry converted milk into the sour thick product that they called bonny clabber.[67]

There was less dairying in the South. Since milk spoiled quickly there, it was often converted into butter, and buttermilk, a by-product, became a favorite beverage. Some milk reached the slaves. Landon Carter mentioned that slaves in Virginia were given buttermilk for supper when they were engaged in mowing, and on some plantations skimmed milk was included several times a week in the slave rations.[68] At the other end of the social scale, William Byrd of Westover noted in his diary that he "ate" milk for breakfast, drank it between meals, had milk and barley, milk tea, hot pone and milk, milk and strawberries, milk and apples, milk and rhubarb and, when sick, warm milk.[69]

The wealthy everywhere made rich desserts of milk and cream. When John Adams visited the Continental Congress in Philadelphia in 1775 he was invited to "sinful feasts" that included curds and cream, fools, trifles, floating islands, and whipped syllabubs, none of which accorded with his wish to diet.[70] Syllabub, frothed cream or rich milk flavored with wine and spices, was a cherished dessert from England.

Cheese was eaten regularly throughout the North. The family of Ezra Stiles in Rhode Island used about a pound daily. In Albany, the Dutch ate cheese at both breakfast and dinner, rasping it to resemble coarse flour "which they pretend adds to the good taste." The Germans in New Jersey and Pennsylvania also enjoyed cheese daily.[71]

Southerners had less cheese. A Charlestonian in 1733 noted that newly arrived Swiss settlers made both cheese and butter, "which the people did not have before." Southern planters bought cheese from England, Rhode Island, and Windham and Litchfield counties in Connecticut.[72]

English cheeses, especially Cheshire, were imported for sale in all the colonies. Even after independence, when Congress placed heavy duties on foreign cheeses, men of means imported them. Brissot de Warville, the French revolutionary leader who traveled in the United States, thought this was through habit, for some American cheeses compared favorably with the English Cheshire and French Roquefort. But others might not have pleased him. Amelia Simmons warned against such "deceits" as salt-petering the outside of cheeses, or coloring them with hemlock, "cocumberries," or saffron.[73]

The universal growing of fruits that had begun in the preceding century continued unabated. Except in the southern Tidewater every farmer planted an orchard as a matter of course, usually of apples, pears, cherries, and, in the Middle Colonies and parts of the southern Piedmont, peaches.

Apples were by far the leading fruit in the North. A woman who lived near Boston even decided that "Hay and Apples [are] the chief produce of the Land." During the year, she estimated, "Have made 90 Barrels of Cyder. . . and at same time consumed 100 Bushils of Apples in the Family. The Children almost Live upon 'em when ripe."[74]

Little of the fruit would be considered marketable today. Orchards were rarely tended and soon became infested with plant diseases. A foreign traveler decided that the American "cared little for what does not grow of itself, and is satisfied with the great yields of his cherry, apple, and peach trees." Apples grew poorly in the Tidewater South. Washington raised some adequate for cider and brandy, but in 1762 he ordered three barrels from New York for eating purposes. Other planters also bought from the North.[75]

Pears were grown in New England and New York both to eat and to convert into perry. They were of the European type, and in 1780 a blight appeared in the Hudson River valley which spread and in time destroyed pear trees everywhere. Not until about 1840 were hardy Asiatic pears introduced into the United States. Later still, disease-resistant hybrids of the European and Asiatic types were planted.[76]

Peach trees did well in the Middle and southern colonies. William Byrd mentioned the "unbelievable" amounts that were crushed to a paste and dried in Virginia and used to make bread, fancy cakes, beer, and other items as occasions demanded. For a time farmers in the Ohio Valley raised peaches both to eat and for the popular peach brandy.[77]

Melons and watermelons were favorite fruits and sold heavily in city markets. A description of New Jersey in 1770 mentioned fields of watermelons from which farmers ate at any time of day as laborers in England would drink ale or small beer.[78]

Wild fruits added to a family's store of food, and gathering them made a summertime party. An Albany woman mentioned these summer festivals in which each person went forth with "very pretty light baskets made by the Indians with lids and handles, which hung over the arm, and were adorned with various colors." So many berries were to be found in the woods, she added, that no one cultivated them. Scottish settlers on Cape Fear, North Carolina, were pleased to find wild mulberries, persimmons, plums, cherries, raspberries, Spanish figs, and blue and white grapes.[79]

Tropical and semitropical fruits reached many colonists. Oranges, figs, nectarines, and pomegranates grew on the coastal plain from South Carolina to Florida. Northern cities received shipments of oranges, lemons, limes, pineapples, and figs from West Indian islands, and tropical fruits were said to be nearly as cheap in New York as in their native lands. They came to the table fresh and preserved and in puddings and tarts.[80]

By the middle of the eighteenth century, then, only the poorest Americans worried about inadequate food, and even they probably ate well compared to their European counterparts. Most colonists were pleased with the produce of their lands, the foods from the forests and ocean, and the luxuries from abroad.

❧ 5 ❧
The Eighteenth Century II

Let us eat potatoes and drink water. . . rather than submit.

Although most American meals were simple and unpretentious, suited to hard-working farm families, some wealthy and sophisticated people, both rural and urban, had a more complicated diet. This minority used herbs, spices, and wine to flavor dishes, imported foods through intercolonial and international trade, and at times adopted foreign methods of cooking. As there had been a gulf between the food of the court and that of the yeoman in Elizabethan England, so in America there were few similarities between the meals of rich planters or merchants and those of farmers or laborers.

Class differences were revealed in the flavoring of foods, for spices were expensive and the use of herbs required some sophistication. Amelia Simmons, in her New England cookbook, found thyme the "most useful and best approved" of the herbs, especially for soups and stuffings; sweet marjoram was best for turkeys, and savory for sausages, salted beef, turkeys, and legs of pork. Sage flavored both cheese and pork but wasn't "generally approved." Parsley she liked for soups, to garnish roast beef, and with bread and butter in the spring. For spices, Miss Simmons relied heavily on cinnamon, mace, nutmeg, and, less often, coriander seeds, allspice, and caraway seeds. At times she used rose water, orange water, fennel, and ginger.[1]

Butter and other fats flavored the dishes of all classes. Melted butter, served in a cup or boat, was put on both meats and vegetables.[2] A foreigner who had visited many wealthy Americans noted that all dishes were heavily buttered.[3] Another traveler concluded that the only American sauce, even for roast beef, was melted butter and that "their turnips and potatoes swim in hog's lard, butter or fat."[4] Pork routinely flavored baked beans, chow-

61

der, porridge, vegetables, and even puddings and pies. This was especially true in the South where there was less butter. On the frontiers, bear's oil and venison grease served the same purpose.

More knowledgeable cooks made both white and brown sauces, and sweet sauces for puddings. The upper classes also used catsups, usually of walnuts or mushrooms, condiments that had existed in England since at least 1690. Meals were given variety through preserved fruits and pickles made of cucumbers, onions, peppers, or other vegetables.[5] Currants and raisins, and in New England blueberries, went into many dishes, including puddings and breakfast and supper porridges and mushes.

There were several sweeteners for food and beverages. From the West Indies came the expensive refined sugar, sold in the form of large white cones, called loaves, weighing from eight to ten pounds. A sugar loaf was locked up to be taken out as needed and cut, carefully and sparingly, with sugar shears.[6] A family might use one loaf a year, but at the Carter plantation in Virginia a loaf lasted only three weeks.[7] Coastal cities got sugar relatively cheaply from the West Indies, but inland the price rose steeply. As late as 1788 it was estimated that the average annual consumption was only five pounds per person.[8]

From the West Indies, too, came molasses, a low-cost and satisfying means for the poor, especially, to sweeten nearly all foods, including mush, puddings, meats, and vegetables. Madame Knight stopped at a small farmhouse in 1704 to find that the only food was boiled milk with molasses. An English traveler credited the bad teeth he saw everywhere to the use of molasses at every meal, "even eating it with greasy pork."[9]

Honey was another important sweetener, and farmers north and south kept bees. In western settlements, where honey was often the only sweet flavoring, wild honey was collected in the forest, each tree providing from fifty to seventy-five pounds.[10]

The use of maple sugar and maple syrup grew slowly. In 1664 a British official mentioned sugar from trees in Massachusetts, but he did not state whether it was made by Indians or English settlers. A 1723 description of maple sugaring in Massachusetts, however, made it clear that it was done by the colonists. Commercial production came later. In 1765 the London *Annual Register* mentioned that one man in New England had made over 600 pounds of maple sugar during the preceding year and that some towns in northern and western Massachusetts had sent several hundred pounds of sugar to be sold in Boston.[11]

Following independence from England a small boom in maple sugar production occurred, a movement promoted by a desire to strike at slavery in the West Indian sugar plantations. In September 1789, seventy-two subscribers, mostly Philadelphians, agreed to buy each year for three years a given amount of maple sugar at fixed prices. Quakers especially urged the use of maple sugar to "reduce by that much the lashings the Negroes have to endure to grow cane sugar to satisfy our gluttony."[12] Almanacs in the spring urged readers to make maple sugar: "Sugar made at home must possess a sweeter flavor to an independent American of the north, than that which is mingled with the groans and tears of slavery."[13]

Sweeteners of some kind were needed for the flood of pies, tarts, puddings, cookies, and cakes that poured from American kitchens. The addiction to desserts was universal and without class distinctions. The Dutch women of New York and New Jersey were known for their pastries, and Anne Grant, a resident in the Albany area, wrote that with the great abundance of fruit and with sugar cheap from the West Indies "the quantity of these articles used in families, otherwise plain and frugal, was astonishing."[14]

Everywhere pies were popular, made of cherries, apples, and peaches and of less usual ingredients such as cranberries, marmalade, grapes, or currants. Apple pie was a universal favorite. In the fall the Germans of Pennsylvania made them in deep earthenware pie plates, and in Delaware apple pie was the evening meal of children. Country people there, one traveler found, called it "house pie" and made it from apples "neither peeled nor freed from their cores, and its crust is not broken if a wagon-wheel goes over it."[15]

Gingerbread, a traditional European pastry, appeared throughout America as cakes and cookies. It was originally made of dough rolled thin and cut into shapes of gingerbread men or other imaginative shapes, but in time a soft, cakelike gingerbread appeared for which Amelia Simmons gave a recipe late in the century. William Byrd in 1711 "ate gingerbread all day long" while watching the Virginia governor train the militia. Also popular were the Shrewsbury cake, plum cake, pound cake, and, for weddings, a bride's cake. All were single layer, for multilayered cakes were to be well in the future.[16]

Pancakes were also eaten everywhere and an American word appeared for them. In her 1796 cookbook Amelia Simmons called them Indian slapjacks.[17] In Virginia and elsewhere the English custom was observed of eating pancakes on Shrove Tuesday, or Pancake Day.

In the Middle Atlantic area, especially western Pennsylvania and New Jersey, buckwheat cakes were a nearly universal winter breakfast dish. An English woman in Hunterdon County, New Jersey, wrote of workmen at breakfast: "[W]hen the cake plate is empty of Buckwheat then they will take pye to their coffee."[18]

The Germans and Dutch imported the eating of waffles, but few other colonists knew them. Thomas Jefferson, always curious about foods, bought a waffle iron when he visited the Netherlands in 1788.[19] These long-handled irons, held in the fireplace, made small square or rectangular waffles which were eaten hot with butter.

Ices and ice creams, though known in Europe from the late seventeenth century, must have been new in the colonies in 1744 when a Virginian was entertained at the governor's mansion in Annapolis, Maryland. He was fascinated by a "curious" dessert: "Among the Rarities of which it was compos'd, was some fine Ice Cream which, with the Strawberries and Milk, eat most Deliciously." Shortly before the War of Independence immigrant caterers introduced ices and ice creams to some city dwellers, and a few wealthy planters made their own. In 1784 George Washington bought an ice-cream freezer to use at Mount Vernon, and in 1789 Jefferson brought with him an ice-cream recipe from France.[20]

While many enjoyed rich desserts and full tables, some lacked enough of anything to eat. Black slaves, indentured servants, and other underprivileged groups did not participate in America's bounty and their hardships were increased from time to time by war or bad harvests. The recurrent Anglo-French wars in America caused severe food scarcities that hit hardest at the poor. In 1713, toward the end of Queen Anne's War, about 200 impoverished Bostonians rioted while searching for corn, and for some years thereafter the selectmen of Boston purchased corn and stored it during the winter months to sell to the needy.

Hunger appeared in South Carolina in 1715 during the Yamessee War when Indian attacks drove the settlers into Charleston and made farming difficult. A planter wrote in 1717 that "we are ready to eat up one another for want of provisions, and what we get is very bad." The cost of food, especially meat, rose beyond the reach of the poor, and even the wealthy found it nearly impossible to find corn.[21]

The food given to slaves was often insufficient. Allotments differed according to the intelligence and humanity of slave owners, the wealth of the area, and the foods available. One man, describing Virginia in 1724, said that the slaves depended upon corn in the form of bread, cakes, mush, and hominy, with sweet potatoes, various roots, and pulse making up the rest.[22] In South Carolina, during the 1730s and 1740s, a diet for the slaves inferior to that of the whites was given official sanction. In public accounts food for blacks was budgeted separately at half to three quarters that given to whites, and in time it became accepted that the slaves needed only smaller amounts of cheaper foods with minimal quantities of meat. Private owners of slaves often did no better. George Washington, according to a Polish visitor to Mount Vernon in 1797, allowed his slaves to keep a few chickens and tend a small vegetable garden but not to keep ducks, geese, or pigs. Their rations were a peck of corn each week for the adults, half that for children, and twenty salt herring a month. At harvest time the field hands received some salt meat.[23]

Whatever the contents of eighteenth-century meals, they were not necessarily clean. Cooking and eating took place at times in such primitive conditions as to explain why a Philadelphia lady of the period, having a "weak stomach," always took off her spectacles when she ate at sea "that she might not see anything disgusting in her food."[24] Without screens, food everywhere was at the mercy of flies that swarmed from nearby hog pens, stables, and privies. A traveler from France near the end of the century wrote: "At table and above all at dessert they light upon and befoul all food, all drinks. They taste everything they see. One's eyes are revolted by them; one's appetite destroyed."[25]

In other ways meals could arouse disgust. Dr. Alexander Hamilton, on his trip from Maryland to New England, observed a ferry-keeper and his wife who, without a tablecloth, napkins, knives, forks, spoons, or plates, took fish from a trencher with their hands without bothering to separate the skin and bones.[26] An English prisoner, billeted with a Low Dutch family at Flatbush, Long Island, in 1777, described his daily food:

A sorry wash, made up of a sprinkling of bohea [black tea], and the darkest sugar on the verge of fluidity, with half baked bread, fuel being among the scarcest articles at Flatbush, and a little stale butter, constituted our breakfast. At our first coming, a small piece of pickled beef was occasionally boiled for dinner, but, to the beef, which was soon consumed, succeeded *clippers* or clams, and our unvaried supper was *supon* or mush, sometimes with skimmed milk, but more generally with buttermilk blended with molasses, which was kept for weeks in a churn, as swill is saved for hogs. I found it, however, after a little use, very eatable; and supper soon became my best meal.[27]

These were not typical meals, for many enjoyed clean, plentiful, and appetizing food. French visitors to America after the War of Independence referred often and approvingly to the cleanliness of the kitchens in upper-class homes.[28]

The preservation of food during summer months was a problem. Dairy products were kept in the relative coolness of the cellar or hung down the well. Some farms had springhouses where the cold spring water was used to cool dairy foods, wine, and other liquors. Even so, milk and cream soon soured, giving rise to sour milk biscuits, pancakes, waffles, and other delicacies. Late in the century the icehouse, a square pit usually below ground and roofed with boards or sod, appeared in Virginia, Maryland, and Pennsylvania. Washington had one built at Mount Vernon in 1785.[29] The influence of ice on American food and drink had begun, a development of immense importance that was to expand in the following century.

For cooking instructions the colonial housewife depended mainly upon what she learned from her mother and other women in the household, recipes obtained from friends and neighbors, and a few printed works. English cookbooks — *The British Housewife, Hannah Glasse's Art of Cookery,* and others — were mentioned in wills or other inventories or were advertised for sale in newspapers. In 1742 an English work, *The Compleat Housewife* by E. Smith, was published in Williamsburg, Virginia. This differed from the English edition by omitting ingredients not available in America. An American cookbook containing American recipes did not appear until 1796 when Amelia Simmons published, at Hartford, Connecticut, her *American Cookery, or the Art of Dressing Viands, Fish, Poultry and Vegetables, and the Best Modes of Making Pastes, Puffs, Pies, Tarts, Puddings, Custards and Preserves, and All Kinds of Cakes, from the Imperial Plumb to Plain Cake, Adapted to this Country and All Grades of Life.* This slight book used American foods like Indian corn, pumpkins, squashes, and Jerusalem artichokes, together with recipes that would have been strange to English cooks, such as roast turkey with cranberry sauce, watermelon pickles, and johnnycake.[30]

Many of the foods and recipes in Amelia Simmons's work were known throughout the colonies, and these, notably corn and pork, minimized regional differences. A lively coastal trade did so also, making rice available to New Englanders and apples to Georgians. Still, as the colonists moved away from frontier simplicities, sectional differences became clearer.

Most New Englanders had a simple diet, their soils and climate allowing only limited varieties of fruits and vegetables. In 1728 the *Boston News Letter* estimated the food needs of a middle-class "genteel" family. Breakfast was bread and milk. Dinner consisted of pudding, followed by bread, meat, roots, pickles, vinegar, salt, and cheese. Supper was the same as breakfast. Each family also needed raisins, currants, suet, flour, eggs, cranberries, apples, and, where there were children, food for "intermeal eatings." Small beer was the beverage, and molasses for brewing and flavoring was needed. Butter, spices, sugar, and sweetmeats were luxuries, as were coffee, tea, chocolate, and alcoholic beverages other than beer.[31]

Shortly after the War of Independence the College of Rhode Island, the future Brown University, listed what it proposed to give its teenage students. Breakfast would be tea or coffee with buttered white bread or toasted and buttered brown bread. An alternative was chocolate or milk with white bread without butter. The college's dinners for a week were as follows:

> Two meals of salt beef and pork, with peas, beans, greens, roots, etc., and puddings. For drink, good small beer and cider.

Two meals of fresh meat, roasted, baked, broiled, or fried, with proper sauce or vegetables.
One meal of soup and fragments.
One meal of boiled fresh meat with proper sauce and broth.
One meal of salt or fresh fish, with brown bread.

Suppers were of hasty pudding, rice, samp, white bread, or milk porridge, with tea, coffee, or chocolate. Meals, especially dinner, would be varied during the week by the addition of puddings, apple pies, dumplings, or cheese as often "as may be convenient and suitable."[32]

Even simpler meals were described by an English officer paroled in 1777 in a home outside of Boston. His breakfast was "pretty substantial" and consisted of bread and milk or boiled cornmeal mush with butter and molasses spread over it. Noontime dinner was of salt pork and "sauce (the name they gave to roots and greens)." Fresh meat was served only when a fox was frightened into releasing a chicken it had seized. Supper was bread and milk. Equally austere was the food of a large family on Nantucket Island as seen, late in the century, by the French author St. Jean de Crèvecoeur. Clams, oysters, and Indian dumplings made up their daily and "most substantial" food, he wrote. But there was also a good supply of smoked bacon, and larger fish, when caught, were "a source of dainties."[33]

Breakfasts and suppers in New England were always light and plain. When John Adams attended Harvard College, he normally received bread, biscuit, and milk in the morning.[34] A resident of Ipswich, Massachusetts, claimed that during the seventeenth and eighteenth centuries both morning and evening meals there were of pea and bean porridge or, more commonly, broth "made of liquor of boiled salt meat and pork, and mixed with meal, and sometimes hasty pudding and milk."[35]

More varied were the meals of the Middle Atlantic colonies, reflecting the better soil and warmer climate and the diversity of the settlers. The Germans and the Dutch, in particular, influenced the eating habits of the other colonists. Both these groups liked dairy products, fruits, and vegetables. Bread, butter, milk, buttermilk, cheese, cottage cheese, salads, apples, and vegetables appeared frequently on their tables. A visitor among the Dutch in Albany, New York, reported that they ate wheat bread with butter or milk as part of every meal. When they combined bread, buttermilk, and sugar, the visitor noted, "then it is a delicious dish for them."[36]

The Germans of Pennsylvania ate less meat than other colonists, though they had numerous recipes for pork, but they did consume large quantities of vegetables, especially turnips, onions, cabbages, and salad greens. Apples were eaten fresh, dried for winter use, or converted into applesauce or apple butter. Other favorite dishes were potato or noodle soup, sauerkraut, cottage cheese, fritters, souse, scrapple, sausage, liver pudding, filled pig's stomach, pork and dumplings, and a variety of pies and cakes.[37]

Israel Acrelius from Sweden who spent time in Delaware wrote a full account of the meals of town and country people in that colony. In part, at least, he was describing the descendants of the original Swedish settlers who had come there over a century earlier.

During the summer months the breakfast of the town dwellers, wrote Acrelius, was tea or coffee, bread, and thin slices of smoked beef. In winter they ate either toasted bread soaked in milk and butter or light buckwheat pancakes. Dinner consisted of a meat, and Acrelius listed as choices ham, beef, roast beef, beefsteak, tongue, roast mutton and mutton chops, veal and veal cutlets, fowl, turkey, goose, chicken pie, partridges, or lamb, together with potatoes or turnips and another vegetable such as peas or beans. The second course was apple, peach, cherry, or cranberry pie. Cheese, butter, and, presumably, bread completed the dinner. An afternoon meal known as the "four o'clock piece" was usually the same as breakfast. If an evening supper were taken, it was most commonly chocolate made with water.

Country folk had simpler, and probably heartier, meals. A summer breakfast, Acrelius found, was made from one or more of the following: cold milk and bread, rice, milk pudding, cheese, butter, or cold meat. In winter cornmeal mush and milk, milk-porridge, or hominy and milk could be substituted. The noon dinner often included *såppa*, a thin meat broth in which bread was crumbled, and a fresh, dried, or salted meat accompanied by fruits, such as apples, or vegetables like cabbages, potatoes, beans, or squashes. Other possibilities for dinner were boiled or baked puddings, dumplings, bacon and eggs, fruit pies, and during the winter months a hominy soup cooked with salt beef and bacon, or lamb and chicken pies, or wheat and buckwheat pancakes. Suppers, if eaten, were the same as breakfast.[38]

Another large immigration in the eighteenth century was of the Scotch-Irish, those Scots who had settled in northern Ireland and their descendants. Though many of the Scotch-Irish went to New England and upstate New York, a far greater number moved to the frontiers of Pennsylvania and the southern colonies. Their diet for many years was that of the frontier, dependent on the gathering of wild fruits and greens and on fishing and hunting. The common meats were bear, venison, elk, rabbit, squirrel, woodchuck, and turkey. Wild birds were shot, and sometimes flocks of wild turkeys were driven into log-pen traps. As soon as some land was cleared, corn, rye, and buckwheat were planted, as well as the coarser vegetables like sweet potatoes and turnips. Pigs were raised, and a cow was much prized on the frontier, for its milk could be eaten with the corn and rye mush. Without cow's milk the mush was combined with molasses, honey, or meat gravy. Pone was the usual bread for breakfast and dinner, and porridge or mush was eaten for supper.[39]

On the southern frontier food supplies were precarious and variety limited. When Charles Woodmason, an itinerant Anglican minister, visited the South Carolina backcountry in 1767 he found "no Eggs, Butter, Flour, Milk, or anything, but fat rusty Bacon, and fair Water, with Indian Corn Bread." He later discovered bacon and eggs in some places, but only rarely milk, fresh meat, or fowl. In late June when the backcountry settlers reaped their wheat and barley, bread was available, "but hundreds have not a Mouthful of Meat — But are reduc'd to the sad Necessity of gathering Apples Peaches &c. green from the Trees, and boiling them for food." Woodmason learned to carry with him biscuits, cheese, rum, sugar, chocolate, and tea, together with cups and a knife, spoon, and plate. After a year on the frontier he tried to summarize his eating experiences: "Where I am, is neither Beef or Mutton — Nor Beer, Cyder, or anything better than Water — These People eat twice a day, only. Their Bread, of Indian Corn, Pork in Winter and Bacon in Summer."[40]

Throughout the more heavily populated coastal parts of the South the staples were pork, game, corn, seafood, and rice. Fewer fruits and vegetables were grown than in the Middle Colonies, and dairying was discouraged by the lack of refrigeration and good pastures. Fish and shellfish throve in coastal waters, however, especially in Chesapeake Bay, and the well-to-do could import fruits, wheat, cheese, salted meats, and other foods from northern colonies.

Generalizations about southern food customs are difficult, for geographical differences and class stratification divided the section. A poor woman in South Carolina described her diet to a friend in England. The most plentiful food, she noted, was Indian corn ground upon a steel mill, boiled stiff, and eaten with milk. There was much salt beef, but very little mutton or any fresh meat, and water was the usual drink.[41]

The planters of tobacco, rice, and indigo fared much better. They breakfasted on bread and butter, with thin slices of ham, beef, or venison, and tea or coffee. Dinner, at three o'clock, might include fish, fowl, and ham with cabbage or greens, puddings, cheese, and beverages. Harriott Horry, the daughter of Eliza Lucas Pinckney, compiled in 1770 a cookbook that included numerous beef, veal, and seafood dishes, puddings of oranges, yams, carrots, apple, and ratafia (a variety of cherry), Shrewsbury and cheese cakes, pickles, marmalades, rusks, gingerbread, almond cream, and sweetmeat and strawberry jellies among other delicacies. Well-to-do South Carolinians might also have afternoon tea and an evening supper of milk and fruit. The middle and lower classes had simpler breakfasts and dinners and commonly omitted supper.[42]

Social occasions were often informal. Anne Grant, in Albany, described children's birthday parties when the parents were "bound" to leave home, directing a servant to give the children tea, chocolate, preserved fruits, nuts, cakes, and cider or syllabub. Picnics required a cool weak punch and perhaps some cold pastry, leaving the main dishes to the men and boys who caught fish or hunted fowl or other game. At other times each guest brought something: one wine for negus (a beverage of hot, sweetened wine and water flavored with lemon and spice), another tea and coffee, a third a pigeon pie, and so on. Or a rural excursion could be a "roast," and for this it was thought only mischievous to steal a pig or fat turkey since all farmers had many of both.[43]

Barbecues and fish feasts were popular in Virginia, differing only in the food served. The barbecue may have come from the

West Indies, for the word itself is Haitian. Landon Carter, shortly before the War of Independence, regretted that the "old method" of having each family bring its own dish had died out, for that was more private and less expensive. The new way was for subscriptions to be sold with the result that some brought five or six to eat at the same price as one. Rather than a gathering of friends, Carter lamented, many now attended "only for the sake of getting a good dinner and a belly full of drink." Huge barbecues accompanied important occasions, as when the cornerstone of the Capitol was laid in Washington on September 18, 1793.[44]

Weddings occasioned lavish displays of food and drink. In Pennsylvania about 1735 a marriage of English settlers involved a "sumptuous" feast at the bride's house and the sending of cakes, meat, punch, and other things to all neighbors, rich and poor. A guest at a Mennonite wedding in Pennsylvania in 1780 found a "German repast" where everything was boiled and roasted "to rags." After four hours of games came dinner, a "profusion" of soups, meats, pies, and other foods adequate for " a Reg[imen]t of soldiers."[45]

An upper-class Philadelphia wedding at the end of the century entailed protracted food rites. After the ceremony the guests were given cake and wine, at two o'clock an elaborate dinner, then conversation until tea time in the late afternoon, and, finally, soon after, supper. For the three following days the bride served punch and cold meats to friends and for three more days she gave evening teas for friends and acquaintances.[46]

The traditional holidays had food customs. New Year's Day was celebrated by special cakes and an open house for friends. Twelfth Night was marked by southern planters with a dinner and a "twelfth cake," and Shrove Tuesday by pancake eating. During Easter holidays in the South young men and women dyed boiled eggs and engraved on them various devices before exchanging them as love tokens.[47]

After independence, July 4 was celebrated. In 1778 the delegates to the Continental Congress in Philadelphia and "other Gentlemen" met at the City Tavern and dined to the music of an orchestra. The meal featured a large baked pudding in which were implanted a flag and various symbols and figures.[48] Although New England Congregationalists still abhorred Christmas as a "papist" day, others, especially Anglicans, feasted on the day and William Byrd, the wealthy Virginia planter, gave his slaves rum and cider.[49]

There were numerous local and seasonal celebrations, such as the annual Melon Frolic that took place late in the century at the Red Lion Inn near Philadelphia. Here, in August, people gathered to eat melons and to dance.[50]

In rural areas there was a round of cooperative labors: log rollings, house raisings, harvesting, or even work on the roads. In the fall women met at each other's houses to peel, quarter, and core apples to dry for the winter supply and, when the work was done, to join their husbands for refreshments and dancing. Reaping and mowing were also often done cooperatively, the hard labor being followed by a hearty dinner. At harvest time in the trans-Appalachian West meat pies, called pot pies, were a standard dish. Into these went a half dozen kinds of meat from both domestic animals and game. Flour and water were added to make gravy, sage and red pepper to heighten the flavor, and a crust formed on the sides and bottom.[51]

Most social meetings took place without any special occasion being involved. Often the loneliness of rural life was enough to justify "visiting." During the winter, an entire family might go to a neighbor's house in the evening to talk, eat gingerbread, and drink cider until bedtime.[52]

In coastal cities turtle feasts were popular among the "gentry." A Philadelphia family which had received two green turtles in 1786 was inspired to have a grand family dinner:

> We had a black woman to cook and an elegant entertainment it was — having three tureens of soup, the two shells baked besides several dishes of stew, with boned turkey, roast ducks, veal and beef. After these were served the table was filled with two kinds of jellies and various kinds of puddings, pies, and preserves; and then almonds, raisins, nuts, apples, and oranges. Twenty four sat down at the table. I admired the activity of the lusty cook, who prepared everything herself, and charged for a day and a half but three dollars.[53]

Good weather in New York City brought groups of men and women to one of several houses on the East River to spend the day enjoying a turtle feast, fishing, and drinking tea. In Boston when a ship arrived from tropical waters with a turtle, a large party would be organized to go to Goat Island for a feast lasting until late at night. Bostonians could hear the party singing as it sailed back across the harbor and walked home.[54]

In northern cities winter was the time for sleighing parties. Groups of thirty or forty would leave Boston around seven o'clock at night, go by sleigh to an inn about twenty miles away, drink and "carouse" until dawn, and then awaken the sleeping citizens of Boston on their return with singing and sleigh bells. A participant in such a party in New York City in 1768 said the sleighs were preceded by fiddlers on horseback, and the company went to a country inn "where we danced, sung, romped and eat and drank and kicked away care from morning till night." In Philadelphia the socialite Nancy Shippen attended a more sedate sleighing party in 1784, the group going only three miles out of town to enjoy mulled cider and biscuits.[55]

Many men, including a growing number of travelers, enjoyed eating at the taverns, ordinaries, and inns of the cities. Early in the century Boston had the Blue Anchor, the Rose and Crown, and the Royal Exchange, all reputable taverns where merchants, officials, and professional men met for conversation and food. New York City had good "victualling" houses, and Charleston, South Carolina, had the tavern of Henry Gignilliat on Broad Street which served meals and, when requested, banquets of "about 40 Dishes."[56]

As cities grew in wealth and size, they supported more pretentious eating places. Dr. Alexander Hamilton visited New York City in 1744 and ate an "elegant supper" at a place called the Hungarian Club and again at Todd's where he had veal, beefsteaks, green peas, and raspberries. In the same city, later in the century, the highly rated Tontine House served from twelve to sixteen dishes each day, including bear steak, venison, wild turkey, wild ducks, lobster, terrapin, oysters, wild pigeons, and other game in addition to more common foods. Shortly after the War of Independence the French refugee Brissot de Warville had the most expensive dinner he had ever eaten anywhere in a tavern in Cambridge, Massachusetts.

Philadelphia had some outstanding places to eat, including Moyston Tavern which Brissot de Warville pronounced excellent. In the same city were the so-called fishing companies, private clubs for men which existed as early as 1732 and whose members met at principal taverns to converse over large meals. A prominent one was the "Beef-Stake Clubb" which gathered weekly at Peg Mullen's Beefsteak House. A by-product of these clubs was the famous Fish House Punch, a strong mixture that usually combined rum, brandy, lemon juice, sugar, and water.[57]

Those who traveled the countryside ran far greater risks in eating, as Sarah Knight discovered when she arrived at a post stage in Rhode Island on October 3, 1704:

> Here, having called for something to eat, the woman bro't in a twisted thing like a cable, but something whiter; and laying it on the bord, tugg'd for life to bring it into a capacity to spread; which having with great pains accomplished, shee serv'd in a dish of Pork and Cabage, I suppose the remains of Dinner. The sause was of a deep Purple, which I tho't was boil'd in her dye Kettle; the bread was Indian, and every thing on the Table service agreeable to these. I, being hungry, gott a little down; but my stomach was soon cloy'd, and what cabbage I swallowed serv'd me for a Cudd the whole day after.[58]

Forty years later Dr. Alexander Hamilton, traveling in the Middle Colonies, was unevenly served. He breakfasted on some "dirty chocolate" near Baltimore, supped upon "very fine" pickled oysters in Brunswick, New Jersey, was given fried clams with rye bread and butter at the Narrows Ferry on Staten Island, and at Jamaica, Long Island, breakfasted at an inn upon bread and moldy cheese, stale beer, and sour cider.[59]

When Johann D. Schoepf toured the United States in 1783 he found the provisions at public taverns quite limited. In Virginia the ordinaries, as taverns were usually called in that state, admitted only gentlemen and normally gave them coffee, ham and eggs. Teamsters carried their own provisions and slept and ate "in the bush." In the "woods-hotels" of the Pennsylvania mountains Schoepf generally received meals of bacon, ham and eggs, fresh or dried venison, coffee, tea, butter, milk, cheese, rum, corn whiskey or brandy, and cider. In Edenton, North Carolina, he spent four days at a tavern where he got nothing but old geese, suckling pigs, and raw salad. But the South had better taverns, of which one, the Eagle Tavern at Richmond, gained some fame.[60]

Most travelers in the South stayed at private homes. Moreau de Saint Méry generalized that between Massachusetts and

Maryland travel was heavy, inns were numerous, and the people were not very hospitable. From Maryland to South Carolina, however, the inns were scarce and expensive but the people were "hospitable even to generosity."[61]

When the War of Independence began in the spring of 1775 food supplies were threatened. Most deprived were troops in the field. Often farmers preferred British gold for their crops to the rapidly depreciating paper money of the Continental Congress. As early as 1777 General Washington told a committee of Congress that some supply agents were incompetent and that the soldiers had "scarcely sufficient" vinegar, drink, and soap. Two years later the army was without bread and was on half-allowance of rice. At times during 1780 and 1781 the soldiers lacked both meat and flour. In September 1781 the militiamen between the James and York rivers in Virginia were living on four ears of corn per man per day.[62]

Civilians, especially those on fixed incomes, also knew food shortages. As trade slowed and the Continental Congress issued great quantities of paper money, the prices of all foods soared, including such basic items as salt, coffee, tea, sugar, wheat, and rye. The war may have promoted the growing of Irish potatoes which became a staple food in the North for both armies and civilians. John Adams, in a patriotic effusion to his wife Abigail, wrote: "Let us eat potatoes and drink water . . . rather than submit." She, not too seriously, proposed that if supplies gave out they could "live on whortleberries and milk from their cows," although at that moment their only shortages were of coffee, sugar, and pepper. Several years later they were without sugar, molasses, rum, coffee, chocolate, and wine.[63] Less fortunate Americans lacked far more important foods as a result of inflated prices.

As the center of the war moved southward to its final stage at Yorktown, most of the country began to repair the damages from the conflict and to return to the normal condition of food surpluses. A visitor in Philadelphia at the war's end found "no sign of want" but rather the "same exuberant plenty" as always. It was hard to find a family, he wrote, that did not daily enjoy fine wheat, good meat, bread, fowl, cider, beer, and fish.[64]

As the scarcities ended, another influence of the war upon American food habits was only beginning. Due to the Franco-American alliance of 1778, Americans came into direct contact with the well-defined and highly cultivated French cuisine.

Prior to this time the French impact on American eating habits had come from a small immigration of French Huguenots or had reached the colonies in diluted form through upper-class English or Scots of sophisticated tastes. When France deprived its Protestants of toleration in 1685, some fled to the American colonies, settling mainly in coastal cities. Many found a home in Charleston, South Carolina, where in spite of near-frontier conditions they must have influenced the cookery of the colony.

During nearly two-thirds of the eighteenth century Roman Catholic France, its American possessions, and Indian allies were the perennial enemies of Protestant England and its colonies. The fears and hatreds aroused by this struggle would have made any public recognition of Gallic culinary art appear treasonable.

The outbreak of the War of Independence changed things. Americans at war with their mother country were less inclined to look to London for social or gastronomic guidance. Then the alliance of the United States with France in 1778 brought hundreds of adventurous French officers and numerous French troops into the country. This began an infiltration of French customs, including culinary ones, that has never ceased. The French influence was felt most at the upper levels of society which had long imitated European, primarily English, manners and customs. To the extent that French cookery would affect American eating habits, the process would be one of gradual, and often incomplete, percolation, beginning among wealthy sophisticates and moving slowly and imperfectly into lower levels of society.

The English had long recognized a basic difference between their own cooking and the more contrived French dishes. Gervase Markham, an English writer whose life bridged the sixteenth and seventeenth centuries, made the distinction in his work, *The English House-Wife,* when he referred to "banquetting and made dishes, with other conceits and secrets." The term "made dishes" was carried to America and used there into the twentieth century. It is still used in England. A definition appeared in Scotland early in the nineteenth century:

What is technically called a *made-dish,* presupposes either a more elaborate mode of cookery than plain broiling or roasting, or else some combination of those elementary processes, — as for example half roasting and finishing in the stew-pan, which is a very common way of dressing a *ragout.*

All dishes called French dishes are of this class, such as fricasses and ragouts, meat braised, larded, &c. as well as hashes, curries, and generally all viands that are re-dressed. To dress a made-dish properly requires rather judgment and contrivance than manual dexterity. *Made-dishes* are valued by the gourmand, for their seasonings and piquancy, but they are equally esteemed by the economist from the circumstance of a much less quantity of material than would suffice for a boil or roast . . . while, by various modes of re-dressing, every thing cold is turned to good account.

An American cookbook of 1838 gave the popular Anglo-American reaction to such foreign fripperies: "What has generally been understood by a 'made dish' is, something too rich, and too highly seasoned, to be wholesome, and too expensive to be available for a family dinner."[65]

For the great majority of Americans, whose cooking was simple, direct, and hearty, the world of "made dishes" would remain strange and incomprehensible. The gap between the croissant and corn bread was not easily bridged. Only in Creole Louisiana were the French and Anglo-Saxon modes of cookery to mix with still other influences to result in something quite new but basically French.

The reorientation of the upper classes that followed the alliance was expressed by John Adams who visited France in 1778 on a diplomatic mission. Not long after his arrival he reported that "the cookery and manner of living here, which you know Americans were taught by their former masters [the English] to dislike, is more agreeable to me than you can imagine."[66]

A few weeks after George Washington was inaugurated as the first president in 1789, the French Revolution began. Soon a small stream of refugees arrived in the United States as kaleidoscopic changes in the French revolutionary governments made life hazardous for the aristocracy. Among the refugees were chefs and pastrycooks, too close to their aristocratic patrons to feel comfortable when the Reign of Terror began. In America they opened cafés, boardinghouses, inns, and restaurants. The word restaurant was itself a new French import.

An early arrival was Jean Baptiste Jullien, formerly cook for the archbishop of Bordeaux, who in 1794 opened a restaurant called Jullien's Restarator in Boston. Another refugee was

Anthelme Brillat-Savarin, the great French gastronomist, who later wrote the *Physiologie de Goût*. Brillat-Savarin, who remained in the United States for three years, visited Jullien:

> While I was in *Boston*, I taught the restaurateur *Jullien* the secret of broiling eggs with cheese. The dish was new to the *Americans*, and became so much the rage that *Jullien*, in recognition of his indebtedness to me, sent me, in *New York*, the back of one of those delicious little roe-deer.[67]

In New York City a French pastrycook named de Singeron opened a shop in which he sold gilt gingerbreads made in the figures of the French king and queen and New Year's cakes with cupids surrounded by garlands of roses.[68] And in several American cities French immigrants gave an impetus to the novel dish ice cream. Two French-owned places in Philadelphia sold the confection, as did a third run by a Creole from San Domingo. Similar ice-cream shops appeared in New York City, one of which was mentioned by Brillat-Savarin:

> *Captain Collet* was another who grew rich in *New York* in 1794 and 1795, on the proceeds of the ices which he made for the folk of that mercantile community. Women in particular found so novel a taste irresistible, and nothing could be more amusing than the little grimaces they made when eating them. They were utterly at a loss to conceive how a substance could be kept so cold in a temperature of ninety degrees.[69]

After revolutionary France declared war on England in 1793, Americans became increasingly divided into the pro-French followers of Thomas Jefferson and the pro-English Federalists led by Alexander Hamilton. As politics grew bitterly partisan, a man's views often decided the restaurant he attended. Thus in Boston the Republican element gathered at the "Sign of the Alliance" kept by one Tahon where the cooking was thoroughly French.[70]

Before the immigration of the French refugees there had been few references to soup. The neglect of soup was an inheritance from England where it was felt that soups were French and not quite honest. A *Satyr agst. the French,* published in 1691, mentioned French dishes "which few Mankind know beside; With Soops and Fricasies, Ragou's, Pottage." And Jonathan Swift about forty years later noted contemptuously:

She sent her priest in wooden shoes
From haughty *Gaul* to make ragooes:
Instead of wholesome bread and cheese,
To dress their soops and fricassees.

But if soups were disdained, broths were not, and both the English and their American descendants regularly used these by-products of boiled meats. Near the century's end a French visitor described American dinners as having broth but no soup.[71]

Soups were not unknown. Turtle soup was a frequent excuse for a party, and Brillat-Savarin often went to a café-tavern in New York where that delicacy was served of a morning. As early as 1770 tomato soup was made in Charleston, possibly introduced there by French Huguenots, and among the Pennsylvania Germans potato soup and meal soup were favorites. But most Americans ignored the dish. Gottlieb Mittelberger, a German visitor to America in mid-century, concluded that the "English know little or nothing of soup eating."[72]

The French refugees encouraged the affluent, at least, to use soups. Jullien, in Boston, became known as the Prince of Soups, the words "bouillon" and "consommé" entered the American language, and when Brissot de Warville ate at the home of a wealthy Philadelphia Quaker the meal included two soups.[73] But it would still be another century before soups became even slightly popular.

During and after the War of Independence formal dinners in Philadelphia became imitative of the French in style and cookery.[74] Diplomats who knew France contributed to this, notably Jefferson who returned in 1789 after eight years in France to become Washington's secretary of state. Jefferson delighted in French cooking and was probably the foremost American student of European foods and wines. In France, as elsewhere on the Continent, he had jotted down recipes for dishes he found new and outstanding. He introduced vanilla and macaroni to his own country and wrote to ask a colleague, about to leave France, to bring him Parmesan cheese, Marseilles figs, nectarines, raisins, almonds, mustard, estragon vinegar, olive oil, and anchovies.[75] As president, early in the following century, he would delight guests at the White House by the culinary marvels prepared by his French chef.

❧ 6 ❧
Eighteenth-Century Drink

*Now will come on their
Season of Festivity and Drunkenness.*

Bracketed between the necessary asceticism of the seventeenth century and the blossoming temperance of the nineteenth century, the eighteenth century in America was one in which alcohol flowed freely and unashamedly everywhere.

Neither the churches nor the general public had yet decided that drink was evil. At the ordination of a minister in New England in 1785 the eighty people present drank thirty bowls of alcoholic punch before the ceremony, and the sixty-eight who remained for dinner disposed of an additional forty-four bowls of punch, eighteen bottles of wine, eight bowls of brandy, and some cherry rum.[1] An equal dedication to drink was shown at fashionable dinners. A French visitor to America wrote that the entrée was accompanied by Bordeaux or Madeira which "they keep drinking right through desserts." After dinner the women withdrew and "the bottles go the round continuously, each man pouring for himself. Toasts are drunk, cigars are lighted, diners run to the corners of the room hunting night tables and vases which will enable them to hold a greater amount of liquor."[2]

Although the idea of temperance hardly existed and the concept of prohibition was unthinkable, a basis for both was being created by the widespread drinking of water. Even newly arrived immigrants were likely to adopt the custom. The clear, cold, unpolluted springs which were numerous throughout New England, the Middle Atlantic colonies, and the southern Appalachians invited the use of water. The heat of American summers, the large consumption of salt meats, and the expense of beer and wine also helped to make water a common beverage. A Virginian described it as "the general drink of abundance; not so much out of necessity, as choice."[3] And a German immigrant ranked the "delicious and healthy water" as the first beverage of Pennsylvania. As population moved from coastal areas where alcoholic drinks were easier to obtain, the importance of water increased. A surveyor near the frontier in the early 1720s recorded wistfully: "All we drink here is water and sometimes rum, but that is very dear and very little money to buy it."[4]

In cities and villages the water was not always good. In Charleston, South Carolina, it contained sand or earth, while in Albany it had an acid taste. A traveler reported that New York City had no good water but that some distance out of town there was a large spring to which New Yorkers went to get water for their tea. By the 1790s spring water, called tea-water, was distributed in the city by horse-drawn carts, and in 1799 the state legislature created a company which was supposed to provide the city with good water.[5] Old wives' tales about the dangers of water still lingered. During hot weather, a French traveler noted late in the century, thirst was so irresistible that several people died each year from drinking cold pump water while they were overheated. Handbills advised the addition of alcohol to the water and suggested cold water in the face or even bleeding for victims of excessive water drinking.[6]

Beer and ale retained a large following, although they had to compete with cider and watered rum throughout the northern colonies. In the South the use of malted drinks was kept to a minimum both by the lack of grains and by the dispersed population which would have required each planter to build his own brewhouse.[7]

Still, many Americans both north and south continued to brew their own beer. The ingredients were legion. According to St. John de Crèvecoeur, a French surveyor and author who lived in Pennsylvania and upper New York from 1760 to 1774, rural families made their beer from pine chips, pine buds, hemlock, fir needles, roasted corn, dried apple skins, sassafras roots, and bran. These made pleasant beverages, he thought, with some hops and a little malt added. There was also a "health-beer" of some seventeen or so ingredients.[8] The upper classes did not scorn such beers. Eliza Lucas Pinckney of South Carolina in 1756 recorded a recipe for beer that combined spruce or common pine tops, chinaroot, sassafras, corn, molasses, yeast, and water. New Englanders commonly used the bark or twigs of sassafras, birch, or spruce trees mixed with molasses and water or maple sap. Some boiled pumpkin and apple parings with water, malt, and roots.[9]

Spruce beer was so widely used that after the War of Independence began the troops surrounding the British in Boston were given a quart of either spruce or malt beer with their daily rations, and the Continental Congress in November 1775 ruled that all soldiers should receive daily a quart of either cider or spruce beer.[10]

Until the war both southern planters and northern merchants imported York and Bristol beers and Dorchester, London, or Taunton ales from England in both casks and bottles. Bristol beer, consumed in "vast quantities" in Virginia, was even thought to improve during the sea crossing.[11]

Early in the eighteenth century porter, a mixture of beer, ale, and small beer, originated in England. This dark, bitter, and hearty beverage, named for its popularity with London porters, became known in the colonies about 1740, and a brewery near Philadelphia began to make it shortly before the War of Independence.[12]

The large German population of Philadelphia made that city a major brewing center. Although other beers of the Middle Colonies were described in mid-century as "brown, thick, and unpalatable," a visitor to Philadelphia found a "delicious, strong, sweet beer." Philadelphia breweries increased after the war, and by 1788 there were fourteen.[13]

In New England and the Middle Colonies, as had long been the case in England's West Country, cider was drunk more than beer. It was cheap, easily made, and although alcoholic, was thought suitable for the entire family. Huge amounts were pressed each fall for home use and, in New England, for sale to the South. Its wide use is well documented: a man traveling between New York and Philadelphia saw a cider press at every farmhouse he visited; a visitor to New Jersey was told that cider was the usual winter drink, as water mixed with rum was the summer drink; and in 1767 it was estimated that 1.14 barrels of cider per capita were drunk in Massachusetts.[14]

Rural New Englanders may have drunk more cider than water. It appeared on the table thrice daily, and when Brillat-Savarin visited a Connecticut farmhouse he saw at each end of the dining table "vast" jugs of it, "so excellent that I could have gone on drinking it for ever." Farmers carried jugs of it to the fields in summer and to the woods in winter, and cider was automatically offered to every visitor. John Adams drank a large tankard of cider every morning before breakfast throughout much of his life.[15]

The quality of cider varied. A traveler in Maine described it as purified by frost, colored with corn, and with the appearance and taste of Madeira. A British visitor to Virginia rated the cider there above any he had ever had in England: "It is genuine and unadulterated, and will keep good to the age of twelve years and more." Moreau de Saint Méry decided that Newark cider deserved its reputation as the country's best, with Philadelphia's close behind. But Israel Acrelius criticized cider in Delaware as made of good and bad apples, drunk too fresh and too soon, and as generally unwholesome.[16]

Cider was given many forms. Diluted with water and flavored with nutmeg, it was a summer drink. Ciderkin was for children, made by adding water to the solid dregs after cider had been pressed, and then pressing them again. Cider royal resulted from several treatments: greatly reducing cider by boiling; fortifying cider with brandy and sugar; or cider and mead fermented together. Cider mixed with rum was called "stone-wall," and in Pennsylvania the Germans sometimes drank their cider hot and sweetened.[17]

Commercial viniculture succeeded no better than in the preceding century. Imported vines succumbed to disease, and the market for wines made from native grapes was too small to justify their production. Farmers made easier profits through grain or cattle.[18] Only in the home did wine-making flourish, for there all the fruits of the orchard and the fields were gathered to make sweet wines. William Byrd praised the "splendid" quince wine in Virginia.[19]

Most wine drinkers, however, looked to Europe. Because of the close trade relations of England with Spain and Portugal, most imported wines in America came from those countries and their possessions, especially the island of Madeira.

Americans loved Madeira wine. Not being a product of Europe, it could be shipped to the colonies directly without breaking the Acts of Trade. This promoted its use in America by reducing its cost. Its popularity began during the eighteenth century and reached its height in the following one. It was consumed during dinner in fashionable circles and was the wine most used for toasts, including the first toast to the king. According to Adam Smith, in his *Wealth of Nations*, British officers who went to the colonies in 1755, at the beginning of the Seven Years' War, developed a liking for Madeira wine which they carried home to England where it had not been "much in fashion."[20]

The white wines of Spain and the Canary Islands, given the collective name of sack, were also favored in the colonies. Samuel Sewall, the Puritan judge of Massachusetts, enjoyed both sack and sack-posset, a mixture of sack and ale thickened with eggs and cream. William Byrd of Virginia had sack and toast for a morning snack and once joined his wife in combining sack, lemons, and Madeira brandy to make a punch. Sherry and port were also popular wines, as were Fayal, Cape, Teneriffe, Lisbon, and the more loosely named Sidonia wines.[21]

Almost continuous hostility between England and France had kept the importation of French wines to a minimum, but as the century progressed they became more common, and rapidly so after the French alliance of 1778. References to claret, by which was meant usually any red Bordeaux, appeared during the century as did, less frequently, mentions of Burgundy and Champagne.[22]

German Rhine wines were often called hock in America from the German Hockheimer. These were plentiful in Pennsylvania taverns, presumably meeting the demand of the German settlers. They may have been too dry for the taste of some Americans; William Byrd noted on one occasion that he and others drank "some Rhenish wine and sugar."[23]

The sweeter wines of Spain and Portugal were sometimes used for syllabub, a mixture of wine with milk or cream, sugar, and sometimes spices, all brought to a frothy state. One technique was to milk directly from the cow onto a shallow pan which contained the other ingredients. Syllabub was usually a drink, but a "solid" syllabub was also served as a dessert. Samuel Sewall made his syllabub with cider to which was added sugar, nutmeg, and thick cream.[24]

The most radical change in American drinking habits was in the use of dark New England rum. As poor men everywhere developed a taste for this cheap beverage, the number of New England distilleries multiplied, especially in Massachusetts and Rhode Island. By 1763 there were 159 distilleries making rum in New England, and about five-sixths of the molasses they processed came from the French West Indies. Some of the rum was shipped to Africa to be exchanged for slaves, and large quantities were sold to the Middle Colonies and the South.[25]

Some men drank rum straight, but most mixed it with water. A sling was rum and water in equal parts, while grog was three parts water to one of rum. William Byrd found New England rum in northern North Carolina that was bad enough to merit its name of "kill-devil." North Carolinians, he added, entertained with bowls of Bombo, named after an admiral "Bombo" [probably the English Admiral John Benbow] and made of equal parts of rum and water flavored with New England molasses.

Rum was a basis for other mixed drinks: with cherry juice it made a cherry bounce, with bilberries a bilberry dram, and with warmed cider a "Sampson." Fresh milk and rum was a doctor, and egg yolks beaten with sugar and rum and thinned to taste with water made an egg toddy. In Delaware and Pennsylvania hot rum, sweetened and flavored with spice or juniper berries, was served at funerals.[26]

In the South rum was used to fight the widespread malarial chills and fevers. The use of spirits as medicine had been imported from England where, during the eighteenth century, Highland "bitters," made by infusing spices and herbs into whiskey, had been taken as a stomachic before meals, especially breakfast.[27] In America, Southerners adopted the custom less to encourage good digestion than to ward off the endemic malaria. In some places this morning potion was known as a julep, a mint julep when flavored with mint leaves. When rum, brandy, whiskey, or Madeira wine was flavored with the bitter bark of certain shrubs or trees, the concoction was called a morning bitters.[28] It was also to be the immediate ancestor of the modern cocktail.

Although rum might find a place in any household, it became primarily known as the drink of the lower classes and of laboring men, the reapers and mowers, fishermen, lumbermen, and shipyard workers of New England. William Byrd described the Carolina County courthouse in Virginia as having an ordinary with wine and "other polite liquors" for the Bench and a "rum ordinary" for those of "a more vulgar taste." One traveler decided that the heavy consumption of rum was due to its low price, the lack of other similar drinks, and the belief that "in great heat, in great cold, and during severe work, this heart-strengthener is indispensable." Israel Acrelius wrote that at harvest time the laborers would often take a drink of rum followed by one of water, "from which the body performs its work more easily and perspires better than when rye whiskey or malt liquors are used."[29] In New England country stores and taverns stood casks of black-strap, a mixture of rum and molasses, with a salted codfish hung nearby to promote thirst.[30]

About mid-century a potential rival to rum appeared on the frontiers of Pennsylvania and the southern colonies where the Scotch-Irish had settled. By the 1760s the backcountry settlers of South Carolina were distilling whiskey.[31] Soon there were stills in hundreds of frontier areas, including Kentucky and Tennessee, always where transportation costs made rum expensive and the shipment of corn to eastern markets impossible. Frontiersmen came to look upon whiskey distilling as a natural by-product of farming, and the beverage became so common as to be a medium of exchange. In Maryland and Pennsylvania, whiskey was often distilled from rye, and the so-called Monongahela rye of Pennsylvania was highly esteemed.[32]

The federal excise tax on whiskey of 1791 aroused a storm of protest among frontier whiskey makers, armed resistance to the tax collectors, and in 1794 the Whiskey Rebellion in western Pennsylvania. President Washington finally called out 15,000 militiamen to suppress this small frontier protest,[33] an act that deeply angered the frontiersmen but hardly slowed their whiskey-making activities.

Brandy was another form of strong drink which people of wealth imported from France while others were satisfied with the apple and peach brandies distilled in the home. Apple brandy was widely made in New England, competed with peach brandy in the Middle Colonies, and gave way to peach brandy in the South. Some cherry brandy was made in New York, as was persimmon brandy in the Middle Colonies and the upper South. A visitor to Germantown, Pennsylvania, in 1748 described these homemade brandies as not for those of "more refined taste," but rather for "the common kind of people, such as workmen and the like." No snobbish distinctions disturbed the South Carolina frontier where the Anglican itinerant Charles Woodmason described the fall season: "Now will come on their Season of Festivity and Drunkenness — the Stills will be soon at Work for to make Whiskey and Peach Brandy — In this Article, both Presbyterians and Episcopals very charitably agree (Viz.) That of getting Drunk."[34]

The fruit brandies were not always coarse drinks. An English traveler who visited Nansemonde County, Virginia, on the border of the Dismal Swamp, discovered that the peach brandy made there, when properly matured, was an "excellent liquor, much esteemed," and had a delicious flavor from the "infusing" of diced pears in it.[35]

Among upper-class Americans no beverage was so popular as punch. This drink had existed for 2,000 years in India, its name derived from the Hindu word for "five" in reference to spirits, sugar, citron juice, water, and aromatic flavorings. East Indian merchants had introduced it to Britain whence it was carried to the colonies. Although in America it could be made with any alcoholic liquor, it also needed the juice of lemons, limes, oranges, or pineapples, the "sowrings," and these, imported in demijohns, were rather costly. J. Crosby, "Lemon Trader," advertised in the *Salem Gazette* of Massachusetts in 1741 that he had fine orange juice "which some of the very best Punch Tasters prefer to Lemmon, at one dollar a gallon. Also very good Lime Juice and Shrub to put into Punch."[36]

Punch could be made with rum, preferably a strong Jamaican, or with brandy, wine, cider, whiskey, or any combination of these. Citrus juices, sugar, spices, and sometimes ice were added by choice. When Sarah Knight stopped in Connecticut at Stratford Ferry on the New Haven road, she was offered a "Barelegg'd Punch" but thought it had "so awkerd or Awfull a sound" that she refused it.[37] Sangaree, the name corrupted from the Spanish *sangria*, came from the West Indies and was commonly made of red wine, water, sugar, citrus fruit juices, and spices.[38]

Any special occasion was excuse enough to serve punch: college graduations, funerals, ordinations, baptisms, weddings, the governor's birthday, a political meeting, or before and after a dinner party.[39] The frequency with which punch and other alcoholic drinks could be served in a wealthy home was recorded in the diary of a man who visited a Philadelphia family in 1744. Cider and punch were served for lunch; rum and brandy were drunk before dinner; during dinner punch, Madeira, port, and sherry were offered, followed by punch and liqueurs with the ladies; and then wine, spirits, and punch were served until bedtime. The punch, he noticed, was served in bowls "big enough for a goose to swim in."[40] Following the War of Independence, if not before, it was the custom at elegant dinners, when it was time for the toasts, to pass around a "great bowl" of punch from which each guest drank in turn. One such bowl in New York held enough for forty people.[41] In winter a hot punch might be prepared, and in 1774 an Italian in Virginia, Filippi Mazzei, observed that both hot and cold punch were served before a dinner.[42]

Heavy drinking was encouraged by the practice of toasting, a custom known to all levels of society. Whenever men took glasses of wine, rum, or beer in hand they found it natural, and certainly convivial, to ask their companions to join them in symbolic obeisance to a person, an institution, or an idea. During private dinners it was expected that the guests, women included, would be prepared to offer toasts.[43] And when men met to dine and spend the evening together, conversations and toasts would mingle and supplement each other, as when John Adams recorded a supper during the First Continental Congress where "we drank sentiments till eleven o'clock."[44]

The most impressive toasts were those offered at public celebrations and banquets that honored the king's or queen's birthdays, Saint George's Day, or, during the revolutionary period, March 18, the day of the Stamp Act repeal. Two to five hundred celebrants might meet to eat together, often outdoors, and after a "handsome collation," the toasts, which had been carefully prepared in advance, would be offered by a toastmaster, "president," or "master of the feast." Impressive ceremonies accompanied each toast: the booming of cannon fire, volleys from small arms, music, and cheering.[45] When Portsmouth, New Hampshire, celebrated the Stamp Act repeal in 1766, the twenty toasts were highlighted by the discharge of many cannon, a display of flags, and the music of trumpets, French horns, and drums, together with bonfires and illuminations.[46]

During the eighteenth century the first signs appeared of what would become the large-scale temperance movement of the following century. When Georgia was founded in 1732, its English trustees banned spirits in the settlement to "prevent the pernicious effects of drinking Rum." But soon Savannah was full of illegal taverns, and the inhabitants successfully petitioned for legal spirits both to purify the water and to make Georgia's fur traders competitive with those from South Carolina in dealing with the Indians. Elsewhere in the colonies worry about strong drink, especially as it affected the working classes, grew. Opposition to excessive drinking was expressed both by Philadelphia Quakers and American Methodists.[47] The anti-rum element was cheered by the loss of trade with the British West Indies as a result of the War of Independence and the consequent steep rise in rum prices. Since rum was most used by the poorer classes, whose drinking caused the greatest concern, this change was doubly welcomed. In 1788 a son-in-law of James Madison argued that it had been proven that spirituous liquors were not necessary for reapers and other laborers and that people were both healthier and happier drinking beer, cider, and molasses and water.[48]

Advocates of temperance should have been pleased that a growing number of Americans were becoming devoted to three nonalcoholic beverages — tea, chocolate, and coffee. All had appeared in the colonies during the seventeenth century, but it was in the succeeding one that they became entrenched in favor.

Tea remained rare during the first few decades of the century. Byrd, the Virginia planter, drank afternoon tea as early as 1710, and during the following decade the Dutch in Albany, New York, began to drink tea for breakfast, taking it without milk and placing a small lump of sugar in their mouths to add sweetness. Both then and later, probably three-fourths of the tea in America was brought in by Dutch smugglers who, since they did not pay the English tax, were a major factor in keeping American prices low.[49]

Tea had its greatest success between about 1720, when it began to be sold commercially, and 1767, when it became embroiled in Anglo-American controversy. By the revolutionary period it was so well established a habit that many Americans gave it up reluctantly.

More than coffee or chocolate, tea became a social drink. Although it appeared at breakfast and supper tables, it found its unique place as the beverage of an afternoon moment of self-indulgence or a party. An English visitor to New England in 1740 discovered that tea had become the "darling" of the women there and that nearly every tradesman's wife sipped tea for an hour or more in the morning and again in the afternoon. Only china dishes would satisfy them, he reported, and some spent thirty or forty shillings on a "tea equipage" that included a silver spoon, silver tongs, and other instruments. In New Jersey, eight years later, it was said that the drinking of hot tea in the morning was so general "that there is hardly a farmer's wife, or a poor woman," who abstained.[50]

Not all drank tea. The Germans in Pennsylvania showed little interest in it, and it was quite unknown throughout the western settlements. Charles Woodmason found that neither tea or coffee existed in backcountry South Carolina, and a man who lived in Ohio late in the century remembered that there had been a prevalent idea that tea was "only for people of quality, who do not labor, or the sick. A genuine backwoodsman would have thought himself disgraced by showing a fondness for those slops."[51] There were some, throughout the colonies, who by preference or to save money used tea substitutes. Samuel Sewall in Massachusetts drank sage tea. In North Carolina a substitute was made from a shrub called Japan, later corrupted to Yapon, which not only was drunk in place of Bohea tea, but was used to treat "almost every kind of sickness" and to purify water. In western Pennsylvania a tea was made of "red-root," and elsewhere sassafras tea had followers.[52]

In 1767 tea became a political issue when the British Parliament placed a duty upon it and some other items imported into the colonies. The colonists struck back with nonimportation agreements, but Dutch smugglers saw to it that tea was still available and cheap. Still, not to drink tea became patriotic. Its use, especially in public, declined, and "Liberty teas" of all the old, and some new, substitutes appeared.[53] Personal battles were fought between duty to country and addiction to tea. John Adams, who dearly loved the brew, once at a Falmouth tavern begged a cup of tea "provided it has been honestly smuggled or paid no duties," but was refused by the patriotic landlady who offered him coffee instead. "I must be weaned," he wrote his wife Abigail, "and the sooner the better."[54] In 1773 England subsidized the export of tea to America while retaining the duty, and the consequent Boston Tea Party touched off a series of crises that culminated in the War of Independence.

After the war, tea drinking again became fashionable, especially at aristocratic tea parties in the cities or at public places like the Florida Gardens or the "pretty" garden of one Mr. Cummings in New York City.[55] The feminine penchant for tea remained strong. A French visitor complained of too much tea with the ladies and too much Madeira with the men.[56]

Chocolate, a beverage of American origin, never approached the popularity of tea. When Cortez maneuvered the seizure of Mexico in 1519, he discovered that the Mexican Indians were drinking "chocolatl." It was introduced into Spain, by 1657 was known in England, and soon afterward found its way into the English colonies from the West Indies. In 1670 Dorothy Jones was licensed by Boston to sell "cuchaletto," and the drink soon joined tea and coffee as standard offerings in Boston public houses. Sarah Knight in 1704 carried chocolate with her from Connecticut to New York City and back and asked her hostesses to prepare it for her with milk. And when Dr. Alexander Hamilton journeyed from Maryland to New England in 1744, he frequently took chocolate for breakfast both at inns and at private houses. Four years later a traveler listed tea, coffee, and chocolate as "even the country people's daily breakfast."[57]

Coffee succeeded more rapidly than tea or chocolate. It had appeared in Europe early in the seventeenth century, but the first reference to it in the colonies may have been in the 1670 advertisement of the enterprising Dorothy Jones in Boston. Only six years later the Boston Selectmen licensed the first American coffeehouse, an institution that like its predecessors in England became an important meeting place for merchants and men of affairs. By 1690 Boston had two coffeehouses and others appeared in New York City, Philadelphia, and Charleston. Some of these followed the London custom of serving only coffee and chocolate (was tea considered too effeminate?) while several of those in New York City provided food and lodging as well.[58]

Coffee, unlike tea or chocolate, was served with meals. The Marquis of Chastellux, a general with the French troops in America during the last years of the War of Independence, pronounced himself at last "perfectly accustomed" to the American habit of drinking coffee with meat, vegetables, or other food. Coffee with milk, at breakfast or otherwise, also astonished visiting Europeans. Only at fashionable dinners was the European custom followed of offering coffee only at the end of the meal.[59]

During the war coffee became scarce when trade with Martinique, Santo Domingo, and Surinam was curtailed, and substitutes of burned rye, parched beets, peas, or potatoes were tried. After the war the import of coffee rose enormously, more than sevenfold by the 1790s.[60] This was but a token of the future.

It was apparent, by the late eighteenth century, that the United States would not be a beer-drinking or a wine-drinking country but rather, due to the mixture of ethnic groups and the great range of climates, a nation of many beverages.

❦ 7 ❦
The Early Nineteenth Century, 1800-1860, I

The dairy, the poultry-yard,
the forest, the river, and the ocean,
all contributed their spoil.

The sixty years between the elections of Thomas Jefferson and Abraham Lincoln to the presidency saw the United States grow from a weak and lightly settled country to a strong and populous one. In 1800 the 5,300,000 inhabitants lived mostly along the East Coast. During the following sixty years the population increased to about 35,000,000, the western half of the Mississippi Valley was bought from France, Spain was intimidated into selling Florida, Texas and the lands westward to the Pacific Ocean were wrenched from a weak neighbor, Mexico, and a portion of Oregon was acquired by treaty with Great Britain. In most cases exploration and a thin settlement had preceded the formal acquisitions. At times there was war: the War of 1812 with England, war with Mexico, and after Lincoln's election a Civil War.

The English tradition in thought and manners was increasingly diluted by other immigrations. The largest inflow was from southern Ireland where the potato crop failures that began in 1845 brought appalling suffering and starvation. About the same time many Germans came as refugees from poverty and repressive governments.

There were also large movements of people within the country. The demand for cotton by the northern states and Europe quickly created an immense Cotton Kingdom in the South extending from the Atlantic coast to Texas and Arkansas, everywhere controlled by a planter class that used black slaves for labor. At the same time the rich soils of the upper Mississippi Valley brought emigrants from both free and slave areas of the older states.

Another stream of population migrated from rural areas to the cities where business and manufacturing, especially in the Northeast, gave a livelihood to growing numbers. These city dwellers were largely dependent on others for food supplies, and the panics and depressions of 1819, 1837–1840, and 1857–1860 brought hunger and malnutrition to the cities with little relief beyond a few soup kitchens. During the depression of 1837 Horace Greeley, then a young New York writer and publisher, saw children burrowing in a cellar, a "prey to famine on the one hand and to vermin and cutaneous maladies on the other."[1] Again in 1857 there was acute suffering in New York City. Bakers' wagons were sometimes looted on the streets, and the Common Council was forced to distribute food to the poor to prevent rioting.[2] The country had acquired a proletarian class, its numbers swollen by indigent immigrants from Europe. These wage earners joined the black slaves and the poor whites in rural areas everywhere as humans who ate badly in a country where the more fortunate looked on prosperity and material progress as the natural order of things.

New tools enabled those with money to promote their own and the nation's welfare. Some of these were agricultural, and one of the most important was a plow which scoured and polished itself, developed in 1837 by a young blacksmith in Vermont, John Deere. This made it possible to convert the western prairies into vast fields of corn and wheat. About the same time a Virginian, Cyrus Hall McCormick, invented and then improved the reaper, a tool of immense consequence to American agriculture.

Another change early in the century was hardly less revolutionary, affecting the lives of most women. This was the improvement and large-scale manufacture of the cast-iron stove, an object whose importance has received only slight notice in a male-dominated world.

Since primitive times cooking, save for baking, had been over the open fire. Through the centuries little had been done to relieve women from the back-breaking, dangerous, and inefficient task of fireplace-cooking. Swinging cranes, various pothooks, and spits powered by servants, children, dogs, or mechanical devices had only slightly lessened the housewife's daily chores of bending before the fire, of maneuvering heavy pots and kettles away from or over it, of controlling fire, coals, ashes, soot, and smoke, of regulating the heat, and of adding to or subtracting from the ingredients that went into the cooking vessels. Wrenched backs, blistered hands, smoked eyes, singed hair, and scorched clothes were normal accompaniments of fireplace-cooking.

Only a few people owned iron stoves at the beginning of the century. In 1815 the James cookstove was patented in Troy, New York, winning a certain popularity, and others followed. Stoves were rare until the 1830s when they began to replace fireplaces in the homes of the well-to-do. But fireplace cookery remained "in universal use" in Virginia as late as the 1850s, and in some rural parts of the country until well after the Civil War.[3]

The stoves normally burned wood, though coal was employed later where it was easily available. In either case, women could now stand upright to cook, more easily control and change the temperature under pots and pans, prepare food in smaller amounts, and carry out with relative ease such maneuvers as adding ingredients, mixing, stirring, tasting, and watching, all of which had been difficult in fireplace cooking. For the first time in history it was possible to keep from the food such things as soot, ashes, and other fireplace debris. But there were losses, too. Some thought that the iron stoves did not bake bread and pastries as well as the old brick ovens, and roasted and broiled meats almost disappeared. Today's "roasting" is, of course, really baking.[4]

Compared to the later gas or electric stoves, the wood-burning stove was a crude and cumbersome thing, but contrasted with the open fire at floor level it was a major release and delight for the housewife. The flowers, arabesques, and wreaths that decorated the stoves can be looked upon as celebrative symbols.

A lesser refinement of the time removed the dining table from the kitchen into a room all its own. The dining room in middle class homes was largely a nineteenth-century development in American domestic architecture. Only then did it become general; by 1850 it was included in the plan books for all but farm cottages. In the great plantation houses of the South or in the fine houses of wealthy Northerners, a dining room that would seat at least twenty persons was usual.[5]

As Americans took to dining in rooms made for the purpose, increasing attention was paid to the table settings. The wooden trenchers, eating bowls, spoons, noggins, and tankards were more and more put aside in favor of pewter, glass, or china dishes. Beginning in the 1820s machinery to press glass appeared, and by the 1840s glass factories throughout the country were turning out masses of low-cost dishes in many patterns, allowing housewives to make displays of goblets, plates, compotes, sauce and honey dishes, and celery containers. About 1790 large quantities of blue English Staffordshire china with English and American scenes were sold to those who did not wish to buy the hand-painted china sets of the time.

Tableware was also changing. By the late eighteenth century knives and forks had become common. The forks were but two sharp prongs on a handle and were held in the left hand to keep the meat in place while it was cut with the knife held in the right hand. The fork, still in the left hand, then carried pieces of meat to the mouth while the knife, flat, broad, and with rounded ends, was used by the right hand as the principal eating instrument. An immigrant knifesmith from Strasbourg, Germany, who had brought with him a large stock of tableware, discovered that his pointed knives could not sell in America.[6] Eating with the knife was not considered inelegant except by visitors from abroad; rather, it was virtually universal. Frances Trollope, the English novelist, spoke of the "frightful manner of feeding with their knives, till the whole blade seemed to enter into the mouth,"[7] and another English visitor cited dinner parties in Washington where the guests, almost all senators and government officials, "plunged into their mouths enormous wedges of meat and pounds of vegetables, perched on the ends of their knives."[8]

Early in the nineteenth century the two-tined fork gave way to one with three tines. Then the Tremont House in Boston introduced the four-tined fork, derisively called by some the "split spoon." As this became fashionable the two- and three-pronged forks receded into rural and western areas, as Captain Frederick Marryat, the English sailor and novelist, noticed. "When you stop at humble inns you must expect to eat peas with a two-pronged fork."[9]

Armed with the four-tined fork, able to lift any food, American society worked out a unique method of eating. It was known that polite Europeans ate with a fork held in the left hand. To eat with a fork was now feasible, but the American habit of holding the eating instrument in the right hand was deeply entrenched. As the four-tined fork became common, therefore, Americans continued to use it in the left hand to hold the meat while it was cut and then, bowing slightly to etiquette's demands, laid down the knife, transferred the fork to the right hand, and used it to eat everything. A compromise had emerged between fashion and custom.[10]

If table manners caused problems, this was not the case in the purchasing of food. Urban dwellers went basket in hand to the city markets to confront either the producers or the small middlemen who handled meats, fish, vegetables, fruits, imports, herbs, and confections. These markets were a source of local pride, a site to be shown visiting travelers, and a ready gauge of the region's foods. In them chicanery and subterfuge were kept to a minimum, both by city regulations and policing and by the need of sellers to satisfy their daily customers. And the customers included everyone, according to a poetic description of the New York market in 1814 as

The place where no distinctions are,
All sects and colors mingle there,
Long folks and short, black folks and grey,
With common bawds and folks that pray
Rich folks and poor, both old and young. . . .

Contemporary descriptions of markets were usually favorable. Thus a visitor to Boston's Faneuil Hall Market in 1838 found it divided into 128 stalls of which fourteen were for mutton, lamb, veal, and poultry; two were for poultry and venison; four for butter and cheese; nineteen for vegetables; twenty for fish; with still more for fruits, other meats, and so on. The visitor was "struck and delighted" with the cleanliness of the stalls, especially of the meat benches.[11]

In New York City the markets offered an "immense" variety of fish, a "great proportion" of which were kept in tubs of seawater to be sold alive. These live fish were brought to the city, as they had been since before the Revolution, in smacks, fishing boats originally invented by the Dutch which were provided with "fish wells" placed in the center of the vessel by which seawater could flow in and out. In addition to fish there were good pork and beef, according to one man, but inferior mutton and veal. A visitor in 1825 was critical that there were no stalls for vegetables which were "scattered about" and that the "neatness and order" fell below that of the Philadelphia market. As in other cities, sales were regulated, butchers licensed, unwholesome food forbidden, and the quality of the butter watched.[12]

The Philadelphia market continued to astonish and delight all who saw it. One person who went there in 1818 thought that it probably displayed the greatest quantity of fruits and vegetables in the world. The market began on the banks of the Delaware River and continued for a mile. Boats on the river, wagons from nearby farms and the interior, and ships from distant points all brought goods. Fish came by light carts from New York and Burlington, New Jersey. "The dairy, the poultry-yard, the forest, the river, and the ocean," wrote Frances Trollope, "all contributed their spoil." She, like others, found the market immaculate and even beautiful. All was fresh and fragrant; the stalls were spread with snow-white napkins; everything was tastefully exhibited; there was nothing disagreeable to see or smell; and the sales-people were polite and extremely clean. "If a speck is to be seen on the white apron of the butcher," one man wrote, "it may be inferred that it came there on the same morning." Another claimed that the white linen frocks of the butchers "might vie with a lady's wedding dress."[13]

The Baltimore market in 1826 was described as pleasing, with low prices and great variety: "Here an old woman sitting with a table spread with nice bread and butter, veal cutlet, sausages and coffee; there another, with a table bending under the weight of candy, sweet cakes, oranges and apples; another with choice vegetables; another with fowls, as fat as corn would make them." A slaughterhouse "in an airy situation" just outside the city provided the Baltimore markets with fresh meat daily.[14]

The markets of Washington, a social leader of that city wrote in the 1850s, afforded "every luxury of earth and sea, and that at a price which gives the owner of even a moderate purse a leaning towards epicureanism."[15] At the "remarkably neat and clean" market of nearby Alexandria a visitor found "exquisite" fish, oysters, crabs, and foreign fruits, wild ducks, small and poor vegetables, potatoes of poor taste, and "indifferent" fowls, lamb, and veal.[16]

In the markets of Charleston and Savannah the seafoods were outstanding, but good fresh meats were few. Venison, pork, opossums, and squirrels were seen in the Charleston market, with great quantities of corned beef and salt pork imported from northern states. The few local vegetables were expensive, but an "immense" quantity of onions, cabbages "&c." were brought from northern states. Fish were generally sold alive. Visitors were pleased to find oranges from Florida and pistachios and pineapples from Cuba.[17]

All who saw the French Market in New Orleans were fascinated. Along the levee as far as the eye could reach were ranged two rows of market people. Some had stalls, but most put their wares on the ground: "innumerable wild ducks, oysters, poultry of all kinds, fish, bananas, piles of oranges, sugar cane, sweet and Irish potatoes, corn in the ear and husked, apples, carrots, and all sorts of other roots, eggs. . . ." One man rated the fish as large and excellent but the beef "wretched." Fredrika Bremer, a Swedish novelist, thought the fruit stalls were "gorgeous." The market was filled with people of all nationalities and races. Sunday was an important market day, for this was when the slaves could sell anything they desired.[18]

Among interior cities, Cincinnati had an outstanding market. When Frances Trollope lived there in the late 1820s there were bakeries, but otherwise all foods had to be purchased at the market. She found the quality of foods varied greatly: beef and poultry were excellent, but mutton and veal inferior. Eggs, butter, and nearly all vegetables were excellent, but except for watermelons all the fruits were "miserable." By 1851 Cincinnati had six market houses and meats and vegetables were also sold from stands, wagons, and carts outside the buildings. Fish came largely by rail from Lake Erie, oysters from Baltimore, and game from the prairies. The city was famous for its pork and beef, and a few days before Christmas the industry and the holiday were jointly celebrated. A parade of beef cattle wound through the city's streets, the animals decorated and escorted by bands and marching infantry. After the parade the cattle were slaughtered to be sold on Christmas Day.[19]

City dwellers had other sources of food. Many homes had gardens and chicken yards, and the streets were daily filled with vendors, each with his or her particular cry. In New York City about 1816 the street sellers included those with oysters, fish, clams, buns, hot spiced gingerbread, yeast, tea rusk, and hot corn. The baker's boy with a basket of tea rusk would cry "Tea ruk, ruk, ruk, tea ruk." During the late summer and fall a black woman called "Hot corn, hot corn, here's your lily white hot corn," while another would shout "Baked pears, baked pears, fresh baked, baked pears!" From a horse-drawn cart the clam man cried out:

Here's clams, here's clams, here's clams to-day,
They lately came from Rockaway;
They're good to roast, they're good to fry,
They're good to make a clam pot-pie.
Here they go![20]

Both the markets and the street vendors bent to seasonal forces. Winter was the time for fowls, fresh meat, and root vegetables; spring brought veal, shad and herrings from the rivers, and the first greens from the fields; summer saw a crescendo of garden produce, but milk soured quickly and fresh meat became scarce; and fall brought the harvest outpouring of fruits and vegetables.

An increasing use of ice in the early nineteenth century began to blur the edges of this seasonal pattern and at the same time to improve the condition of perishable foods in the home. Icehouses on farms and plantations, already numerous in the late eighteenth century, increased. Even southern cities began to get ice. In 1799 a hotelkeeper in Charleston, South Carolina, set up an ice depot and soon both Savannah and New Orleans had theirs. Ships and, in the country's interior, flatboats took ice to other southern locations from northern ponds and lakes.[21]

By the first decades of the century city dwellers had crude iceboxes, and at least by 1827 the streets of New York City were traveled by wagons carrying the word "ICE" in large letters. A few years later Frances Trollope, visiting there, could not imagine that a house in the city lacked "the luxury of a piece of ice to cool the water, and harden the butter."[22]

Wherever transportation allowed it, ice became general, and was soon in all public eating places, saloons, restaurants, confectioneries, and passenger ships. An English visitor of 1850 decided that every hotel and boardinghouse, "down to the lowest tavern in the bye streets," of New York City had plenty of ice. "Ice," stated a writer in *De Bow's Review* five years later, "is an American institution — the use of it an American luxury — the abuse of it an American failing."[23]

Although iceboxes would remain crude and inefficient throughout the century, the use of ice in the home made for profound changes in American eating and drinking habits. Larger quantities of perishable foods could be purchased at a time, and housewives were able to plan meals further in advance and to learn the problems of cooking with leftovers. Long hot summers were relieved by cold drinks, while ice cream and other cold desserts flourished.

At least equally important was the use of ice in the storage and movement of foods, especially fish. After the Erie Canal was completed in 1825, fish packed in ice was taken by canal boats to upstate New York. As early as 1837 ice-packed fish was shipped inland by rail from Boston, and by the 1840s large shipments of cod, haddock, and halibut reached Albany, New York City, and Philadelphia. Gloucester, Massachusetts, became a large shipper of fish when the railroad reached it in 1846.[24] City markets also benefited from the use of ice. A visitor to New York City's in 1855 saw no fresh provisions on display, only to learn that they were stored in hundreds of ice chests.[25]

A less pleasant development was the growing adulteration of foods. The problem was not solely an American one, for an English book of 1820 lamented that tea, coffee, bread, beer, wine, distilled liquors, salad oil, pepper, vinegar, mustard, cream, confitures, and catsups were commonly "sophisticated" and that some substances were scarcely ever to be found otherwise.[26] In the United States, Eliza Leslie, a writer of cookbooks, complained in 1857 that it was hard to find sugar not mixed with flour or ground starch, vinegar not concocted of "pernicious drugs," bread and cakes not made unpalatable by hartshorn, and pickles not containing dangerous drugs. "Which of our American doctors," she asked, "will write a book on 'culinary poisons'?" Adulterers of food should be legally punished, she added, and there were so many foods adulterated that "it would indeed be well if we could make at home, as far as possible, every thing we eat and drink."[27]

Others worried about what their countrymen ate and drank, for this was a time of aggressive reform. During the 1830s many

Americans, New Englanders in particular, came to believe that all humans could be lifted to a new, more perfect status. In this crusade all wrongs were addressed — the plight of imprisoned debtors, the mistreatment of the insane, the low status of women, slavery, the horrors of prison life, the use of snuff and tobacco, flogging in the navy, and war itself, among others. Earnest efforts were made to solve these problems through education and remedial laws with human perfection the ultimate goal. Intemperance and the need of a wholesome diet were not overlooked. The various movements overlapped. Those who opposed slavery, which by degrees became the greatest cause, might also favor temperance and vegetarianism and wish to abolish smoking.

Food reform became prominent during the 1830s and was in part a reaction to the grossness of the American diet, the excessive use of meat, the prevalence of fried foods, and the huge dinners that followed men from farms to city desks. One individual proposed a Society for the Suppression of Eating, though his goal was actually to eliminate gluttony.

Most food reformers argued that many, if not most, of the world's ills had come from flesh eating and that vegetarianism would bring health, happiness, beauty, and general good for mankind. Sylvester Graham, who had begun his career in 1830 as a temperance lecturer, turned to food reform and spoke to large crowds in New York and New England. His talks and publications appealed strongly to women, and "Ladies' Physiological Reform Societies" were formed to discuss the theories of Grahamism and to work for the cause. Graham boardinghouses appeared in cities where the believers could follow their leader's injunctions, including hot baths three times a week, Graham bread, and well-chewed, meatless meals.

Vegetarianism won prominent converts. Joseph Smith, founder of the Mormons, became a follower, as did the great Presbyterian revivalist Charles Grandison Finney, and the author of *Walden*, Henry Thoreau. A vegetarian commune, Fruitlands, was begun in Massachusetts in 1843, and the Oneida Community, founded in upstate New York by John Humphrey Noyes, practiced vegetarianism for both health and ethical reasons. Bronson Alcott, the visionary educator and father of the author Louisa May Alcott, raised his famous daughters on a diet that excluded meat, cheese, butter, milk, and tea, giving them meals that might have only porridge, fruit, vegetables, bread, and water. Thoreau tried to live for eight months almost entirely off the beans he raised and what he could find in the forest, spending less than nine dollars for food during the whole period. At times he ate meat, but never without the uneasy feeling that it was unclean.[28]

To a great degree the temperance and vegetarian movements mingled. In 1845 a horticultural show in Boston was the setting of a temperance dinner where the menu, shunning meat and alcohol, featured cakes, fruits, ices, tea, milk, and whey. And in 1853 a banquet of the New York Vegetarian Society offered the guests two soups, nine breads of which the first was Graham bread, sweet potatoes, squashes, fruit pies, pumpkin pie, six fruits, baked apples, plum jellies, coconut custard, fruited ice cream, and "Pure Cold Water."[29]

The food reform movement, most successful in New England and elsewhere in the North, began to decline in the 1850s. It had added to the American diet Graham flour, Graham crackers, and Graham bread and converted thousands to vegetarianism. Perhaps most important, the country had seen a public debate on the nature of its diet, with sensible commentary appearing side by side with foolish dogma.

The wealthy and adventurous continued to toy with French cooking. It fascinated some who tried it, was poorly imitated by those who knew too little of it, and was by some highly rated only because it reputedly saved money by using foods often discarded. Thomas Jefferson remained the best-known student of the French cuisine in America. He brought to the White House in 1801 a fine collection of French wines and a French chef whose excellence and superior skill, wrote one man, were acknowledged, for never had such wines or dinners been offered by a president. Political friends and foes went happy with anticipation to dine on such exotic foods as macaroni, Parmesan cheese, meringues, and vanilla-flavored desserts.[30] At about the same time interest in French cooking was stimulated by refugees from the slave revolts in Haiti who as chefs and confectioners took up residence in Baltimore and other parts of the South.[31]

The French influence sometimes met resistance. Amelia Simmons in her *American Cookery* dismissed garlic as something "used by the French" but "better adapted to the uses of medicine than cookery."[32] In 1828 appeared a Philadelphia edition of Louis

Eustache Ude, *The French Cook,* and four years later Eliza Leslie of Philadelphia published *Domestic French Cookery, Chiefly Translated from Sulpice Barné.* In her preface Miss Leslie explained that the American edition omitted many dishes "as useless in a country where provisions are abundant" where "all persons in a respectable life can obtain better articles of food than sheeps' tails, calves ears, &c."[33] In a later cookbook of her own, Miss Leslie praised the French custom of cooking vegetables in very little water, found the French *pot-au-feu* laudable, but concluded that French cooks were incapable of making good mint sauce. Equally condemned were the "delicate" French soups: "In such a country as America, where good things are abundant, there is no necessity of imbibing the flatulency of weak, washy soups."[34]

Sometimes French cooking was admired more for its practicality than for its quality. The editor of one cookbook wrote that "it is generally admitted that the French excel in the economy of their cooking. By studying the appropriate flavors for every dish they contrive to dress all the broken pieces of meats, and make a variety of dishes from vegetables at small expense."[35] Hotel cooks who adopted the economies but lacked the art aroused the scorn of Eliza Leslie. She attacked those "public tables" where leftovers were made into "indescribable messes, with ridiculous French names, and passed off as French dishes, by the so-called French cook, who is frequently an Irishman." She denied that good French cooks, "as is generally supposed," customarily made dishes "from the refuse of the table."[36] An English traveler, highly critical of American cooking, also condemned immigrant hotel cooks, charging that "every broken-down barber, or disappointed dancing-master, French, German, or Italian, sets up as cook," and that the greatest evil was "the odious attempts at *la cuisine française.*"[37]

Mainly due to the French influence, soup was being accepted, but only by the well-to-do. Among the mass of Americans it remained a dish almost unknown. A Swiss who joined his fellow immigrants in preparing their own food on the American ship *Xenophon* wrote: "Americans want nothing to do with soup, and the sailors and officers almost die laughing when they see us prepare our soup every day."[38] But on shore fashionable people felt otherwise. When Boston's Tremont House opened in October

1829, both terrapin and julienne soups were served with the fish course.[39] American cookbooks told how to make soups with peas, oysters, clams, tomatoes, cabbage, macaroni, mushrooms, corn, and various fish.[40]

The prestige of French cooking was reflected in the American language. Not only did words like restaurant, café, and menu become common, but what one man labeled the "à la" dishes appeared on menus — often incorrectly, with French and English words combined in extraordinary ways. A visitor to Chicago in the 1830s found that hotel menus there were at times very limited, and on one occasion only a single dish was listed, "*Pomme de terre au naturel.*"[41] At better-stocked restaurants words like blanquette, à la jardinière, croquette, filet, escalope, piquante, meringue, fricassée, and sauté were used frequently enough on menus for the wealthy and worldly to become familiar with them. By 1842 the menu of the City Hotel in New York City gave all its dishes in French.[42] French words were brought into the home when, during the 1850s, some wealthy families employed French chefs. This source of contact with the French cuisine was to expand greatly after the Civil War.

If French cooking appealed to the upper classes, the German influence was felt mainly by those of the middle classes. Although most German immigrants were peasants, there were also thousands of artisans and intellectuals, political refugees from the revolutions of 1830 and 1848. Many Germans formed colonies in Baltimore, New York, Cincinnati, St. Louis, Chicago, and Milwaukee or acquired farmland in such states as Missouri and Wisconsin. Since the Germans usually emigrated as families, far fewer became domestics than was the case with the Irish. Still, by the mid-1850s, Germans made up perhaps 15 percent of the domestics in New York City and, as kitchen help, influenced the eating habits of their employers.[43]

German participation in the food industry was remarkable. In addition to those who became brewers, Germans owned taverns, beer gardens, hotels, boardinghouses, and groceries, all becoming centers of German influence. By 1855 there were 1,500 German bakers in New York City, far outnumbering the Scots and Irish who had earlier dominated the industry. Other Germans became sugar refiners and wholesalers of chocolate, coffee, and German-style mustard. Increasingly, importers and dealers in European delicacies stocked such items as Magdeburg sauerkraut, Göttingen wurst, German poppy oil, lentils, Westphalian hams, and German wines. During the 1850s immigrants from the lower Rhine valley took over a great part of the corner groceries of New York and other cities and German cooks, aided by the prestige of European cooking in general, found work in restaurants and hotels.[44]

The German foods and drinks brought numerous new words into the American language, but unlike comparable French words, few of them were restricted to a sophisticated minority. Words like sauerkraut, noodle, and pretzel were probably used by Americans before the War of Independence, and others came after the immigrations of the nineteenth century: pumpernickel, lager beer, beer garden, wienerwurst, bock beer, sauerbraten, schnitzel, leberwurst (sometimes half-translated to liverwurst), zwieback, hamburger, and delicatessen.[45]

The number of Irish in America rose sharply following the potato famine that began in Ireland in 1845. Quickly the eastern cities of the United States became ringed with the shanty huts of poor Irish who had fled poverty and starvation only to meet religious and social prejudice. They were feared as Roman Catholics in a country that was strongly Protestant, and they were accused of being impulsive, turbulent, and too addicted to strong drink.

Although signs reading "No Irish need apply" were nailed on factory doors, there were other openings. Americans have never let prejudice stand in the way of a bargain in domestic service, a work usually shunned by the native-born as demeaning. Because this work was available, a high proportion of Irish immigrants were single girls and women. In New York City in 1846 it was estimated that between seven and eight thousand of the ten to twelve thousand domestic servants were Irish.[46] Many of them cooked, especially when they were the only menial in a household, but how much they shaped the American diet is unclear.

Their own adjustment to American eating habits was not always easy. In Ireland the poor depended overwhelmingly on the potato. Oatmeal, buttermilk, and vegetables made up much of the remainder of their food, for few could afford meat. Accustomed to potatoes, the Irish sometimes refused other foods. Captains of emigrant ships saw Irish passengers throw cheese, chocolate, and other "strange" foods overboard, while the children cried for potatoes.[47]

There was some contempt of the Irish for their limited range of foods and inadequate cooking. They were described as unable even to boil potatoes when they sent half-boiled ones to the table. An American traveler in Ireland discovered the reason. A potato only partly cooked retained a hard center, or "bone," which was indigestible and gave hungry people the impression that their stomachs were better filled than was actually the case.[48] One man accused the Irish of eating overmuch in America of what they had earlier considered luxuries, including meat "three times a day rudely cooked and in large quantities." And a German immigrant bewailed the plight of any German in America who married an Irish woman: "And what will she cook for you! Sauerkraut and Bratwurst? Your very obedient servant — tough beefsteak or stewed fish."[49]

On the whole the authors of American cookbooks were friendly, rather than hostile, to foreign influences. One stated in her preface that "as our Republic is made up from the people of all lands, so we have gathered the best receipts from . . . the different nations of the Old World."[50] England had been a conduit for Indian dishes since the eighteenth century, and cookbooks carried these as well as recipes from Spain, Turkey, Persia, the West Indies, and elsewhere.[51] Eliza Leslie's *New Cookery Book* of 1857 not only gave French recipes, but others for mutton kabob, "much approved by those who have eaten it in Turkey or India," an Irish stew, an East Indian pickle, veal kabob ("a Turkish dish, and is much liked"), Country Captain, two recipes for curry powder and three curried dishes, pork Italian style, Scotch cake (a shortbread), sauerkraut (a French recipe), and a West Indian cake.[52]

As yet such foreign conceits touched only lightly the lives of a few adventurous Americans. To most people, hog and hominy or roast beef and potatoes were more meaningful than omelettes and meringues, and that the French used for food what others might waste was more comprehensible than the subtleties of their culinary art.

⚜ 8 ⚜
The Early
Nineteenth Century,
1800-1860, II

*You shall find a sparkling jelly to your
dessert where you sighed in vain
for so simple a luxury as a well-cooked potato.*

Many families suffered dietary shocks as they moved west. Those
who left the Chesapeake Bay region for the trans-Appalachian
West would have missed the crabs, oysters, and saltwater fish
they had enjoyed since childhood. In the same fashion New Englanders who moved into the upper Mississippi Valley would
yearn for fish cakes, chowder, cranberry sauce, and rye and Injun
bread. Not all suffered from the change. Many a New Englander
left a small rocky farm for lands in Indiana or Illinois that gave
wildly of their bounty.

One change in the food supply, the decline of game, was felt
by everyone east of the Mississippi. The indiscriminate and unrestricted slaughter decimated many species. The buffalo was
soon found only on the Great Plains, while by 1820 the wild turkey and the bear had retreated into southern and western areas
where the human population was small.

In the eastern cities most kinds of game could still be purchased. A visitor to the New York City game market in the 1830s
found not only 300 head of deer, but quantities of bear, raccoons,
wild turkeys, geese, ducks, and "every variety of bird in countless
profusion."[1] Presumably not everything was fresh, for there were
complaints that some venison sold in winter was "hard, dry, and
black, and decomposing," requiring spices, wine, currant jelly,
and other additions to make it *"eatable,* not *wholesome."*[2]

Among men, game dinners on festive or important occasions were still possible. During the mid-century years an annual Thanksgiving dinner was given at the Fremont House in Chicago for leading businessmen. Through eight courses the diners ate trout, black bass, a choice of several salads, and seventy kinds of game which included mountain sheep, the choice parts of the buffalo, jackrabbit, black and cinnamon bears, elk, sandhill cranes, butterball ducks, redwings, marsh birds, antelope, wild goose liver, and spotted grouse, as well as more ordinary birds and mammals.[3]

Venison was cheap enough in cities to provide variety in homes, and in hotels and restaurants to be served as a luxury, fashionably cooked at the table. A Briton wrote that a "high-flavored, but half-starved, fatless kind of venison, is considered a dainty" and was always presented "disgustingly underdone" on pewter or tin plates and placed over burners so that each person could cook it in a "thick gravy according to his fancy."[4]

In the South game was eaten throughout the year, but fall and winter were the best hunting seasons. During the coldest months, when poultry and eggs were scarce, wild turkeys, rabbits, partridges, and squirrels were shot. Opossums, which could be caught with dogs, were eaten both by black slaves and whites,[5] and there were those who ate raccoons, porcupines, rattlesnakes, and frogs' legs. A man visiting Florida was given "gopher" steaks cut from land tortoises and served with sourings, which was pounded corn soured by baking in the sun.[6]

Through the rural parts of the trans-Appalachian West venison, bear, wild turkey, and squirrel remained staple foods for some generations. When a family first settled a wilderness area and lacked both grain and vegetables, the breasts of wild turkeys and lean venison were called "bread," while bear's flesh was "meat," a subterfuge that did not prevent children from becoming sick on the limited diet.[7] Squirrels, both black and gray, provided soup and meat, but the bear was more important. Although bear meat was sometimes strongly flavored and stringy, it was relished. It also provided a grease that served as a shortening, and a frontier cabin normally contained a deerskin bag of bear's oil. Like venison, bear's meat could be jerked to keep for long periods.[8]

Wild passenger pigeons remained numerous. Migrating in

the spring and fall, they flew in immense clouds up to a mile or more in length, and where they lighted people had what one man called "good sport," shooting or netting them or using poles to knock them from trees where they roosted. A man in western Virginia remembered that in 1853 he and a few others with shotguns killed enough between sunset and midnight, using torches for light, to fill a light wagon. The pigeons were eaten fresh, dried, and pickled, made a cheap food for servants and slaves, and were used to fatten hogs.[9]

The guns of both professional and amateur hunters kept up a steady barrage at other birdlife. The canvasback duck, which fed on the wild celery bordering Chesapeake Bay, was shipped from both Baltimore and Norfolk to all the principal cities of the country and even sent on ice to Europe.[10] Wild geese, brants, and swans were killed in large numbers as were snipes, woodcocks, quail, prairie chickens, partridges, sandhill cranes, ruffed grouse, and plovers. The demand for small birds, both for homes and restaurants, continued unabated and included reed birds, curlews, marsh birds, doughbirds, and robins.[11]

Given such a general and unrestricted slaughter, it is understandable why as time passed an ever larger proportion of the population had to depend upon domestic meats. The amount eaten astounded visitors from Europe. The Americans, wrote Frances Trollope, "consume an extraordinary quantity of bacon. Ham and beefsteaks appear morning, noon, and night."[12] One American decided that the vegetarian movement led by Graham and others was a reaction to the excessive use of meat.[13]

As in earlier centuries the lack of refrigeration meant that most meat was smoked, salted, pickled, or dried. Fresh meat was usually a wintertime food except in cities with slaughterhouses or among families which shared with their neighbors. As American cities grew in size, supplying meat to them became a problem. One solution was to drive animals from the hinterland. Since hogs lost weight and quality during a drive, this traffic was mainly in cattle and sheep. A second source of supply was the midwestern packing houses, where meat was salted or smoked and shipped in barrels. Cincinnati, close to salt supplies, became a center of hog packing, and by the 1850s Chicago was becoming the major packer of grass-fed beef.[14]

On farms it was still the custom to slaughter and prepare

one's own meat. Where the winters were cold, a slaughtered animal might be frozen and hung in a shed or attic to protect it from marauding animals. When a piece was wanted, it was hacked off with an axe. During warmer seasons and throughout the South it made good sense to share slaughtered animals with neighbors in rotation. In one South Carolina community early in the century, eight families would join to divide a calf, and those whose calf was killed received the head and loin and by custom entertained all the villagers with calf's head soup. Four families shared a lamb or pig, and eight or sixteen divided a cow.[15] Among the Pennsylvania Germans butchering was a fête day. It took place late in November, and neighbors of both sexes were invited. They arrived about four o'clock in the morning to find huge log fires already burning and the hogs and beef cattle butchered, scalded, and hung up. The day's work consisted of cutting up the meat, rendering the lard, making sausages and scrapple, and smoking the hams and bacon over fires of green hickory chips. All returned home at night with as much sausage and fresh meat as they needed.[16]

The ascendancy of pork throughout the country was impressive, though its dominance was greatest in the South and West. In many places "meat" meant pork; Kentucky was known as the land of pork and whiskey; and in Tennessee bacon was called familiarly "Old Ned." A doctor in Columbus, Georgia, struck out sharply at the excessive use of pork:

> The United States of America might properly be called the great Hog-eating Confederacy, or the Republic of Porkdom . . . . [In the South and the West] it is fat bacon and pork, fat bacon and pork only, and that continually morning, noon, and night, for all classes, sexes, ages, and conditions; and, except the boiled bacon and collards at dinner, the meat is generally fried, and thus supersaturated with grease in the form of hogs' lard. But the frying is not confined to the meat alone; for we have fried vegetables of all kinds, fried fritters and pancakes often, fried bread not infrequently, and indeed fried everything that is fryable, or that will stick together long enough to undergo the delightful process.[17]

In eastern cities, where many meats were available, a more restrained use of pork appeared. Eliza Leslie, whose Philadelphia-based cookbooks contain a running commentary on what was or was not proper, said that roast pork should always be served with applesauce; pork spareribs were rarely seen on "good" American tables; and the practice of splitting a young pig and removing the brains to enrich the gravy was condemned. The pig, stated Miss Leslie, should be served whole: "We have always thought it a most unfeminine fancy for a lady to enjoy eating the head of any thing, and the brain particularly."[18]

Throughout the country beef ranked second to pork, and it was especially popular in the Northeast and northern urban areas. Much of the beef was corned and was served fried, stewed, or boiled with carrots, cabbage, potatoes, or parsnips. Fresh beef was often stewed or a round of beef was converted into "beef à la mode," a dish of English origin, by cutting incisions in it which were stuffed with a mixture of bread crumbs, onions, spices, herbs, and butter, covered with water, and cooked in a stew pan. Fried beefsteaks were eaten everywhere, and in the northern states might appear on the table for every meal, breakfast included. Eliza Leslie, in the 1850s, claimed that the English custom of eating them rare or underdone "is now becoming obsolete." To ladies, especially, she wrote, any red or bloody-looking food was disgusting, and doctors had discovered that nothing was wholesome unless well cooked: "The introduction of French cookery has done that much good."[19] In Charleston, South Carolina, beefsteaks were apparently a masculine dish. It was a local custom, at least, for steaks to be served to the men at supper parties after the women had left the table.[20]

Both lamb and mutton met considerable prejudice, even in New England where they were most used. Throughout the South and West and even in the Northeast there was a widespread dislike for these meats. Opposition in the South was not universal, for many planters used them. But a visitor to Illinois in 1819 reported a strong opposition to mutton there among settlers who had come from the South. It was held, he wrote, "in the utmost contempt, and I have heard them say, people who eat it belong to the family of wolves." Many, he added, when short of pork in summer would live on corn bread for a month rather than eat an ounce of mutton, veal, rabbit, goose, or duck: "Their dislike arises from prejudice, as many of them have never tasted these things." Some people admitted they liked mutton, but would never buy it because of the "scoffs" of their neighbors.[21]

Despite Eliza Leslie's genteel qualms about pig's brains or

rare steaks, the period was not a squeamish one. Calf's head was stewed or used for soup and calf's feet for jelly. Tripe, tongues, pigs' feet, calf's liver and brains, sweetbreads, and beef heart were all quite common, though a New England woman said that liver was "much despised." Cookbooks rarely mentioned kidneys, but they were eaten sometimes as a breakfast dish.[22]

Fish or shellfish appeared often on the tables of those who lived near the ocean or the larger rivers that flowed into it. In the Hudson and other principal rivers sturgeon were common, and sometimes huge. Though New Yorkers and Philadelphians reportedly held the sturgeon in low regard, Virginians were said to have been "better judges." Of all fish it was the many-boned shad that aroused the greatest excitement when it arrived each spring. A resident of Washington, D. C., remembered that in the 1850s the banks of the Potomac were "alive with gay sightseers" each year during the shad-seining season.[23] Delaware River shad were a Philadelphia delicacy and were often cooked on oak or hickory planks, a method also used at riverside fishing parties.[24] From interior places men came hundreds of miles to take back wagonloads of shad or herring to sell, but by the 1840s and 1850s the decreasing quantity of both caused worry in North Carolina.[25]

One seafood dish became immensely popular. Chowder may have first existed in French seaside villages where fish were cooked in a large cauldron known as a *chaudière*.[26] But the English knew chowder by the mid-eighteenth century and it was very likely by then prepared on ships throughout the Atlantic world. Sailors, possibly Breton fishermen, may have carried it to Newfoundland, Nova Scotia, and New England during the early eighteenth century.

For about a century American chowder was made of fish, onions, biscuits, and water, and was a stew rather than a soup. The earliest reference to it was in 1732 when a New Englander noted in his diary that he had dined on a "fine chowdered cod."[27] Nineteen years later a recipe for chowder, flavored with spices, herbs, and wine, appeared in rhyme in the *Boston Evening Post*.[28]

Chowder took various forms. Amelia Simmons, in the second edition of her *American Cookery* in 1800, gave a recipe in which the fish, pork, and crackers were fried.[29] Soon chowders were made along the entire Atlantic coast, with clams sometimes replacing fish and with flavorings that included lemon, cider, tomato catsup, or curry powder. In New England, regional differences appeared. On Nantucket Island neither crackers nor potatoes were used, while in Massachusetts and Maine a little heated milk or cream was put in. In Rhode Island, Connecticut, and states farther south tomatoes were sometimes added to clam, and occasionally fish, chowders.[30]

Even greater popularity came to the country's oysters. These had been eaten since the founding of the colonies, but it was during the first half of the nineteenth century that their universal appeal left foreign visitors dumbfounded. Captain Marryat in 1837 decided that three things were in great demand among male Americans of every class: "to wit, oysters, spirits, and tobacco."[31] Charles Mackay, an English traveler about twenty years later, concluded that "the rich consume oysters and Champaigne; the poorer classes consume oysters and *lager bier*, and that is one of the principal social differences between the two sections of the community."[32] One cosmopolitan American thought that oysters and ice cream were aspects of American life which English readers could never understand nor English tourists appreciate.[33]

The size of American oysters caused astonishment. William Makepeace Thackeray, visiting America, said that after trying his first oyster he felt "as if he had swallowed a baby." Others mentioned oysters of cheese-plate size, so large that four to six made a respectable meal, and those that needed to be cut into three pieces before eating.[34]

In coastal cities and towns oystermen pushed wheelbarrows of oysters or carried pailfuls on each arm as they made their rounds. The Boston oystermen, about 1830, cried out "Oys! Oys! Oys! — Here's your fine, fresh Oys! Come, buy!" In homes the oyster supper was a frequent event, and on cold winter evenings thoughts of a steaming-hot oyster stew made the oysterman welcome.[35]

The consumption of oysters was awe-inspiring: The oysters eaten yearly in Savannah provided shells for a mile of road; the Revere House in Boston used 100 gallons each week; and a Britisher found that New York City consumed daily £3,500 worth.[36] In Philadelphia oysters were little eaten in 1810, but their use rose rapidly until by 1840 over 4,000 tons destined for the city passed through the Delaware Canal from Chesapeake

Bay between October 8 and December 16. Ships also took oysters from Chesapeake Bay to be transplanted at Egg Harbor and Long Island for the New York City markets.[37]

The craze for oysters was countrywide. Before railroads were built, express stagecoach wagons of The Oyster Line carried oysters from Baltimore westward as far as western Virginia and Ohio. After the Erie Canal opened in 1825, canal boats took oysters to Buffalo and other lake towns where they were fed on salt water and cornmeal until purchased.[38] Oysters from South Norwalk, New Haven, and Stamford, Connecticut were packed in kegs or saddlebags and taken on horseback to interior towns. Soon oysters and fish were taken by spring wagons to Hartford, Springfield, and even northern New York and Vermont.[39] During the winter of 1837–38 the Lake House in Chicago served some happy customers, at "fabulous" prices, with the first fresh oysters to reach that city. They were said to have been brought by sleigh from New Haven, Connecticut.[40]

During the 1840s an enterprising man in Baltimore began to can oysters, and the bivalve — fresh, canned, and pickled — soon was sold throughout the continent, transported by the growing network of railroads. In the early 1840s Chicago restaurants had both fresh and pickled oysters; fresh and canned oysters were in Kansas and Nebraska by the 1850s; and by 1856 St. Louis received "hermetically sealed" oysters daily by express from the seaboard.[41]

Although oysters on the half shell was the favorite form, there were countless other means of preparation. One man recorded that "at breakfast they are stewed, broiled, or fried. At dinner you have oyster soup, oyster sauces for the fish, fried oysters, scalloped oysters, oyster pies, and when the boiled turkey is cut into, it is found stuffed with oysters."[42]

Inhabitants of the country's interior also hungered for other seafoods. During the 1840s New Brunswick and Maine began to can salmon and lobsters,[43] and as railroad lines were extended both these and fresh fish were carried far inland. By 1851 Chicago was receiving ice-packed fish only three days from the sea.[44] Salt fish packed in kegs and boxes went from New England and the Chesapeake Bay region to every part of the country,[45] providing displaced New Englanders with the makings of codfish cakes and creamed codfish.[46]

Inlanders also took fish from their own streams and lakes. Southern rivers held catfish, and the Great Lakes contained quantities of whitefish, soon to be accepted as a major delicacy, as well as lake trout, sturgeon, pickerel, and other fish. Smaller lakes and rivers held such fish as bass, trout, perch, and pike. It was said that from some streams the fish could be taken with pitchforks, and a man in Grant County, Wisconsin, claimed that with a seine he took a wagonload of fish in thirty minutes.[47]

Compared to meat, the role of vegetables was negligible. In winter, few were eaten. A pharmacist remembered of the region around Indianapolis before the Civil War that from February until about June 1 people lived on eggs, bread, and meat, with potatoes the only vegetable. With spring there was a frantic search for anything green, including dandelion greens and lettuce an inch high. The swift change of diet brought epidemics of diarrhea.

Many Americans hardly touched vegetables. Frances Trollope found farmers in Maryland who had no gardens and lived on pork, salt fish, and corn bread. A Missourian who grew up near the Iowa border said he had been raised on "meat, gravy, bread, potatoes, milk, butter and pie, with green corn, watermelons, and wild blackberries and plums in season." "Gardens were not common in my youth," he added, and his family did not eat salads.[48]

In the South some planters kept good gardens, but the average southern family had little more than sweet potatoes, cabbages, okra, turnips, collards, pumpkins, cowpeas, and in the spring the pokeweed to supplement the corn and pork. Many Northerners did little better. The editor of a gardening magazine in 1835 said that people of means in smaller towns and villages would become dissatisfied with their winter turnips and potatoes if they could see the vegetables and fruits in the markets of Boston, New York, and Philadelphia.

As railroads extended their lines, those who lived in large cities benefited even more. By the 1840s trains brought to New York City fresh peas and strawberries, and during the following years the northern cities received a growing number of fresh fruits and vegetables from southern states, greatly extending the seasons for such items as strawberries, peaches, grapes, and tomatoes.[49]

The ancient fear of vegetables continued, probably kept alive by the fact that they were sometimes washed in polluted streams or eaten in summer months when epidemics were common. Long cooking was thought necessary, as were such precautions as cutting cucumbers very thin and dropping each slice in cold water. The water in which potatoes were boiled was thought unwholesome, and cooks were warned to soak potatoes in salt and water before adding them to stews.[50]

Still the white potato was widely accepted throughout the North and the upper South, and often appeared in gardens of the lower South. Eliza Leslie in 1837 called it a "part of every dinner," and William Alcott rated it a "principal food" in much of the country despite a tendency among the fashionable to regard it as "somewhat vulgar." Farmers in New England's interior, it was said, sometimes supped chiefly on cold potatoes and turnips.[51] The quality varied greatly. A Swiss immigrant in Pennsylvania found them bad tasting, while a visitor to Albany found "very superior" ones.[52]

Potatoes were fried, boiled, roasted, baked, mashed, and made into cakes, puddings, and soup. By the 1860s some restaurants offered French fried potatoes. New Englanders and the Dutch in New York liked to mash boiled turnips and potatoes together to be eaten with a sauce or butter.[53]

In 1853, according to a quite credible account, a new potato recipe was born at Moon's Lake House, a hotel near the spa and horse-racing center of Saratoga Springs, New York. Here the cook, insulted by a patron's request that the fried potatoes be cut thinner, angrily made paper-thin slices which were dropped into boiling fat. The result pleased him and others, leading the hotel owner's wife to put some into paper cornucopias for guests. Popular immediately, the novelty, known first as Saratoga potatoes and later as Saratoga chips, spread through the country.[54]

The tomato continued to be rare and to be thought possibly dangerous: an Italian painter reportedly introduced some in Salem, Massachusetts, in 1802 but could get no one to eat them; in 1814 a recipe for stewed tomatoes appeared in a New York cookbook; in 1821 "Love Apples or Tomatas" were said to be growing in New England gardens; and in that year they provided the base for a Philadelphia recipe of a catsuplike preparation. In the same decade a Virginia cookbook carried recipes for tomato marmalade, tomato catsup, and tomatoes with okra and eggs, and in 1828 Frances Trollope found tomatoes of the "highest perfection" in the Cincinnati market and proclaimed the fruit "the great luxury of the American table in the opinion of most Europeans."[55] Though a Massachusetts cookbook in 1838 said that the tomato was "chiefly" used as a sauce or condiment, recipes existed for tomatoes pickled, scalloped, stewed, broiled, steamed, stuffed, used in soups, or sliced with an oil and vinegar dressing. Popularity came swiftly, and an English traveler in the early 1850s decided, of tomatoes, that "its very name I now perfectly dread — so constantly, so regularly, does it come up every day, prepared in every imaginable way."[56]

Though some might know the pleasure of sliced tomatoes with a dressing, salads in general were neglected. Some cookbooks gave no salads, while others acknowledged those made with lettuce, cucumber, cabbage, or tomatoes. An orange salad in 1861 anticipated a future deluge of fruit salads. Chicken salad kept its high popularity as a party dish.[57]

Of the grains, corn remained king. Everywhere cornmeal was made into gruels, stirabouts, or mushes to be eaten with milk or molasses for breakfast and supper. Hominy and grits were also daily fare, especially in the South. A visitor to Jacksonville, Florida, from Connecticut in 1855 wrote that "I eat more Rice and Hominy at one meal than all that is eat in Hartford for a week."[58] Corn breads remained common everywhere, not only the simple combinations of meal, salt, and water that made hoecakes, ashcakes, pones, and corn dodgers, but innumerable variations using such ingredients as milk, buttermilk, eggs, wheat flour, rice flour, and sweet potatoes.

Sweet corn, due to be a major delicacy, came late to the American table. Some had been found growing in 1779 in an Indian village on the banks of the Susquehanna, but it remained nearly unknown for decades. By 1820 it was grown in New Haven, Connecticut, and soon after it was advertised in seed catalogs. Thereafter, it was quickly adopted. In 1850 Fredrika Bremer described it as a "standing dish" at American tables in the fall, served boiled with butter. Some people, she added, took the "whole stem" to gnaw with the teeth.[59]

In the upper Mississippi Valley wheat became the grain of the future. Beginning in the 1840s immigrants from northern Europe and native-born Americans pushed into Iowa, Wisconsin, Kansas, Nebraska, and Minnesota to grow both corn and wheat on the rich lands.

For long the lack of a reliable rising discouraged baking with wheat flour. Homemade yeasts or combinations of milk with baking soda often failed to generate the gases needed to raise the dough. The country's doctors generally agreed that health was endangered by eating hot, heavily buttered biscuits that were yellow with imperfectly neutralized baking soda. It was a major relief to all cooks and an encouragement to the use of wheat flour when an accurately formulated baking powder appeared in 1850s, combining acid and base in dry form.[60]

With the increasing use of wheat bread came the first, tentative appearances of the sandwich. Although the sandwich in its modern form had existed in England since about 1760, supposedly invented as a means to allow the Earl of Sandwich to eat while gambling, there were no references to it in North America until long afterward. An English cookbook reprinted in New York mentioned it in 1817 as a supper dish to accompany more important foods, and twenty years later Eliza Leslie in her *Directions for Cookery* suggested ham sandwiches as a supper dish, rolled up or laid flat on plates. As an afterthought she added that shredded or grated cold smoked tongue could be substituted for ham.[61] By the late 1850s Miss Leslie's ideas of sandwiches had changed only slightly. Sandwiches of ham or tongue could be seasoned with French mustard, or sandwiches could be made of the *"lean of cold beef* (roast or boiled) cut very thin." The sandwiches should be rolled up "nicely," and there existed silver cases made to contain them for travelers. About the same time another cookbook author proposed anchovies as a filler[62] — a small but daring step toward a wildly imaginative future.

Simplicity characterized not only sandwiches but other foods on American tables, their appeal depending more on natural flavors than on art. Depth and subtlety of taste were conscious goals only in a few leading restaurants, among certain of the well-to-do, both north and south, and in New Orleans. The average housewife turned for flavoring to butter, pork, molasses, salt, catsup, and pepper.

The numerous herbs and spices known to the first settlers were now largely ignored. A New York cookbook of 1823 said basil, savory, knotted marjoram, or thyme could be used where needed, "but with discretion." Eliza Leslie thought cloves and allspice "coarse" and unsuited for "good" tables. Mace, nutmeg, ginger, and cinnamon, among spices, were alone proper for "nice" cookery, and of these mace and nutmeg went well with meat or poultry. Harriet Beecher Stowe, the famous author, complained that spices in "made" dishes were used to excess: "In living a year in France I forgot the taste of nutmeg, clove, and allspice, which had met me in so many dishes in America."[63]

A few sauces and condiments were used by knowledgeable cooks. In addition to the catsups — and tomato catsup grew increasingly in favor — the white, or cream, sauce was known, as well as a brown sauce for cooked celery or lettuce, applesauce for bear or pork, currant jelly for venison, a capers sauce for mutton, a mushroom sauce for beef, and an oyster sauce for boiled turkey or chicken. Eliza Leslie liked sweet sauces made from fruits for roasted meats or cranberry sauce for poultry.[64]

Mayonnaise, a gift of the French, was urged for cold meats and lettuce. Other sauces were of English origin. A popular one was named Soy and was made of anchovies, mushroom catsup, walnut pickle, Madeira wine, and mustard seed — all boiled, bottled, and sealed for ten days. For fish and game there were imported bottled English sauces such as Kitchiner's, Quin's, Harvey's, or Soyter's, and Eliza Leslie gave recipes to reproduce each of them. By the 1860s Worcestershire sauce had also appeared.[65]

Although few families used more than the commonplace apple or cranberry sauces or a catsup, many added taste and color to meals with pickles. A conscientious cook could make pickles from peaches, cabbages, peppers, tomatoes, walnuts, artichokes, mushrooms, cauliflowers, beets, cucumbers, onions, eggs, plums, butternuts, nasturtium seeds, mangoes, and indeed almost any fruit, nut, or vegetable,[66] although one cookbook editor argued that since all pickles had "nearly" the same taste, a few of the best should satisfy any table.[67] Her advice probably went unheeded. Pickles added dash and interest to the winter table, and making them was a satisfying experience for cooks both north and south. Harriet Martineau, visiting a planter's home in Montgomery, Alabama, saw "an extraordinary variety" of pickles at lunch.[68]

The American liking for sugar-based dishes continued. It had long been nurtured by cheap sugar and molasses from the West Indies and Louisiana, maple sugar from northern states, and honey from domestic and wild bees. Frances Trollope found Americans, particularly the women, "extravagantly fond" of puddings, pies, and all kinds of "sweets." And Harriet Beecher Stowe thought American women better able to cook confections than anything else: "There are more women who know how to make good cake than good bread, — more who can furnish you with a good ice-cream than a well-cooked mutton-chop; a fair charlotte russe is easier to come by than a perfect cup of coffee, and you shall find a sparkling jelly to your dessert where you sighed in vain for so simple a luxury as a well-cooked potato."[69]

The quantity of sweet dishes was sometimes overwhelming. An English traveler found that the second course, in eastern cities, was followed by "a wilderness of sweets,"[70] and at a Baltimore banquet of 1857 guests chose among twenty-four different desserts.[71]

Sweet dishes might appear in any course or meal. New Englanders served both pies and puddings at breakfast, though by 1820 it was said that this practice was receding from "genteel" houses to farms and small country taverns.[72] Many New England homes also followed the English custom of serving the pudding first, before the meat, giving rise to the expression "I came in season — in pudding time." The poet Joel Barlow wrote of

The pudding of the bag, whose quivering breast,
With suet lin'd, leads on the Yankee feast.

A visitor to the home of John Adams in 1817 noticed that a form of Indian pudding was the first course, followed by meats and vegetables.[73]

Increasingly, such first-course puddings, originally intended to check the appetite for meat, were replaced by sweet puddings that followed the meat and vegetables. Certain of these were very common: potato pudding, rice pudding, tapioca pudding, molasses pudding, brown Betty (called apple pandowdy in the North), lemon pudding, and those made with other fruits. The lemon-flavored Marlborough pudding was a favorite. Plum puddings were commonly eaten and appeared even in unpretentious restaurants.[74] Bread puddings flavored with raisins and spices and served with milk or cream offered an economical use for stale bread. Pudding sauces were usually made from combinations of sugar, butter, wine or brandy, oranges and lemons, and spices.

Pies could make part of any New England meal and of dinners and suppers elsewhere. They were made of every fruit, both fresh and dried, as well as rhubarb, already called "pie plant," pumpkins, squashes, sweet potatoes, mincemeat, custard, coconut, and cranberries. Fruit pies were usually made with two crusts, though the "genteel" element might omit the upper one. As for mince pies, Eliza Leslie rebuked all silly men and exposed coy women: "The foolish custom of setting the pies on fire after they come to the table, and causing a blue blaze to issue from the liquor that is in them, is now obsolete, and considered ungenteel and tavern-like. If this practice originated in a polite desire to *frighten the ladies*, its purpose is already a failure, for the ladies are not frightened; that is, not really."[75]

As sugar became less expensive, cakes were made in profusion. Parties were celebrated with jelly cakes, pound cakes, plum cakes, or lady cakes, and notable visitors to the United States were honored with cakes named after them: the Jenny Lind cake for the "Swedish nightingale" whose tour under P. T. Barnum's auspices was a continuous ovation in 1850–51; the Lafayette cake to honor the revolutionary hero who revisited the United States in 1824–25; or the Kossuth cake, a Baltimore specialty named after the Hungarian patriot Louis Kossuth who arrived in 1851.[76]

Cookies also poured from kitchens of the day, though this word of Dutch origin was used for only one or two kinds. A sugar cookie flavored with nutmeg or cinnamon was so named, but other small, sweet baked items were called wafers, kisses, drops, jumbles, snaps, macaroons, ginger crackers, or gingerbread. There were also "fried cakes" such as crullers, doughnuts, and fried biscuits.[77] Doughnuts were eaten throughout the country and may have been of German origin.[78] Whatever their background they were made in such shapes as ovals, diamonds, and squares. The day of the circular doughnut with a hole had not yet arrived.

When the affluent gave parties or banquets, complicated and beautiful desserts were customary — charlottes, creams, meringues, jellies, blanc manges, tarts, syllabubs, soufflés, and special ice creams. While most of these were of English or French origin, they were sometimes transformed by American ingredients and modifications. Some, however, were too difficult for the average cook. For an omelette soufflé, Eliza Leslie advised, "It is safest for an inexperienced housewife to engage a French cook to come to the house with his own ingredients and utensils, and make and bake the omelette soufflé while there."[79]

At times the desserts were made by cooks whose sophistication exceeded that of the guests. A belle of the 1850s in Washington, D.C., often saw men distinguished for their aplomb look hopelessly at dishes set before them, uncertain about the correct approach. On one occasion she was at a party where parallelograms of paper were served with accompanying silver trowels. She gratefully imitated a foreign guest who used the trowel to remove a *glace* from the package but noticed that other guests were quite lost as to how to proceed.[80]

Syllabub, a rich milk dessert of English origin, was popular. One could pour milk into a dish from a height, whip cream with a whisk, or shake the concoction in a wide-mouthed bottle.[81] Jellied desserts made with port, Madeira, champagne, or a liqueur or cordial were for special occasions. "We do not recommend them," wrote a cookbook author, "except as some exhileration to the fatigue of a party."[82]

As ice became available throughout the United States, so too did ice cream. From the expensive delicacy that it had been in the late eighteenth century, it became by Andrew Jackson's administration of 1829–1837 a democratic dish enjoyed by nearly all levels of society.

When a cookbook offered a recipe for pineapple ice cream in 1814, probably only a few individuals had the ice, equipment, and pineapple to attempt it.[83] But ice cream could be purchased. A New Yorker remembered that about 1816 there were ice cream parlors with rows of "boxes," whitewashed or green-painted, each with a plain bare table running through the center and bare board seats on the sides, lighted by a dimly burning wick. Here waiters served vanilla and lemon ice creams, and strawberry in season.[84]

During the next two decades ice cream was seized upon by an eager public. In the 1830s the English traveler and author Captain Frederick Marryat found it "universal and very cheap." He was in one ice cream parlor in New York City "when about a dozen black swarthy fellows, employed at the iron-foundry close at hand, with their dirty shirt-sleeves tucked up, and without their coats and waistcoats, came in, and sitting down, called for ice-creams."[85] An American a decade later mentioned ice cream as "the most universal luxury." It was served, he wrote, in public gardens, in saloons that held a thousand people, at the large confectioners, and on steamboats at the uniform price of six cents, and generally of excellent quality. He suspected that more was sold in New York City alone than in all of Europe.[86]

Ice cream followed ice into distant parts. Harriet Martineau while in Kentucky in 1835 enjoyed the luxury of "daily piles" of strawberries and "towers" of ice cream.[87] Chicago got the confection in 1835 with the first large drugstore, followed during the next decade by a succession of ice cream "saloons."[88] A visitor to St. Louis found waiters at his hotel offering slices of ice cream "which suggest the resemblance of small prairies."[89]

Ice cream was served in many ways. Boston put it in glasses, but Albany thought this "ungenteel." Some devotees made huge pillars, or pyramids "rivalling those of Egypt." At times it was made in molds of dolphins, doves, and baskets of fruit. "We have seen ice cream," wrote Eliza Leslie, "in the shape of a curly lapdog, and very well represented."[90]

Fruits were often served for dessert. Some were available everywhere while others, like the pawpaw or the persimmon, were found only in parts of the South or lower North. Throughout most of the South the peach had become the favorite fruit.[91] Wherever found, all fruits were still suspect. The *New York Mirror* in 1830 warned that fresh fruits should be forbidden to everyone, especially children, and two years later city councils forbade their sale because of the cholera epidemic. William Alcott, who compiled a cookbook in Massachusetts, criticized the "general prejudice" which prevailed in regard to fruits about the time of summer and autumn diseases. He denied also the "ancient idea" that fruits were unwholesome in the morning. The prejudice against fruits, he claimed, was not confined to the "more ignorant," for during a cholera epidemic "not a few" doctors had forbidden the use of summer fruits.[92]

No fears kept some fruits from becoming highly popular. During the early nineteenth century horticulturists gave the strawberry more attention than any fruit but grapes, and about mid-century the public joined in what became known as the strawberry fever. The Massachusetts Horticultural Society held the first strawberry exhibition in 1848, and a decade later the first Strawberry Festival was held in Belmont, Massachusetts. The custom of serving strawberries and cream at festivals spread through the country, as did that of giving strawberry parties. A rush into strawberry raising led to overproduction that brought a sharp reaction after the Civil War.[93]

There was a slow but steady increase in the quantity of tropical fruits in American markets. Oranges had probably been introduced into Florida by Ponce de Leon when he discovered it in 1513, but it was not until after 1821, when the United States acquired the land from Spain, that the groves in the St. Augustine area were rapidly expanded, together with others along the St. Johns River south of Jacksonville.[94] Oranges, pineapples, and other tropical fruits were hawked about most eastern cities by the 1830s, and even in Chicago by 1840 the Great Western Fruit Store was selling oranges, lemons, and other exotic fruits.[95]

Small amounts of bananas had reached New York City early in the century, and about 1843 well-established shipments began. By 1850 clipper ships brought both red and yellow varieties to be sold for from ten to twenty-five cents each in New York, Philadelphia, and Baltimore. Railroads carried some into the interior, a number reaching even Wisconsin during the 1850s.[96] For a time there was uncertainty how to treat the fruit. Eliza Leslie listed bananas among the vegetables in her 1857 cookbook and gave a recipe for frying them.[97] Fredrika Bremer, the Swedish novelist, tried bananas, "which people here are so fond of," in Charleston in 1850 and disliked them. She persisted, however, and within the year decided that "bananas, negroes, and negro songs are the greatest refreshments of the mind, according to my experience, which I found in the United States."[98]

ᨠᨠ 9 ᨠᨠ
Drink, 1800-1860

Stranger, will you drink or fight?

A striking and pervasive development of the early nineteenth century was the temperance movement. The few tentative steps in
this direction during the preceding century were now superseded
by a drive against excessive drinking that had momentum and
mass support and whose spokesmen were strident and demand-
ing, cowing legislators and laying down new rules for human behavior.

To some extent the crusade against liquor was part of an effort by the old order.to maintain control over the common man
who was beginning to assert his rights and to question the powers of his employers and political leaders. In New England the
orthodox Calvinist clergy and the conservative Federalists advocated temperance, and employers were more likely than employees to see merit in the movement. A temperance society founded
in Moreau, New York, in 1808 argued that a limit on drinking
would increase the efficiency of laborers.

The temperance movement grew rapidly, especially in the
northeastern states. In 1833 the local, state, and regional organizations formed the American Temperance Union, which within a
few years claimed 8,000 chapters and 1½ million members. By
this time the armed forces allowed the substitution of cash or
coffee for the traditional rations of rum or whiskey, many New
England merchant ships and whalers had gone dry, and it was
said that 4,000 distilleries had been forced to close.

During the 1830s the teetotalers gained control of the
movement, particularly in New England where the idea of community responsibility was strong. In 1841 Maine took the radical
step of banning the sale of alcoholic beverages, a law, reinforced
in 1846, which was to become a model for other states. Soon

about a dozen northern states adopted the Maine law, but the move toward prohibition was checked when Governor Horatio Seymour in 1854 vetoed a New York bill as unconstitutional. Within a few years all the state laws had been repealed or eliminated by court action except in Massachusetts and Vermont. During the entire temperance and prohibition movement the South stood aside. An early stirring of interest there in the 1820s had died when the northern temperance supporters joined forces with antislavery advocates.[1]

Temperance advocates made life unpleasant for drinkers. Their crusade used sermons, books, tracts, hymns, plays, revival-like mass meetings, and cartoons. Orators like John B. Gough drew large crowds, and two temperance plays were huge successes. *The Drunkard*, which opened in Boston in 1844 under the auspices of P. T. Barnum, showed an honest man degraded by drink, then rescued from it and reunited with his wife and daughter. The reception was even more enthusiastic for *Seven Nights in a Bar-Room*, based on the tract of Timothy Shay Arthur, *Ten Nights in a Bar-Room*. During this play little Mary was hit by a glass thrown in a tavern while she was singing "Father dear Father, Come Home with Me Now," a song that itself became a national success. Later Mary died on stage from the blow, as her father renounced drink forever. During the finale the entire cast proposed to destroy all the liquor in the town and to vote for the Maine law.[2]

Although the temperance movement made public drinking less acceptable and restricted access to liquor in many states, it nowhere cut off determined drinkers from their accustomed rounds. A visitor to Portland, Maine, was told at one hotel that a thirsty man need only descend the stairs to the bar and ask to see the "striped pig" or "Dusty Ben" to get wine or spirits respectively. At other towns the key word was sarsaparilla. And when Congress banned the sale of spirits in the Capitol building, the lawmakers soon arranged it so that in the basement oyster shop and refectory a request for pale sherry produced gin, for brown sherry, brandy, and for Madeira, whiskey.[3]

The availability of good water, and increasingly of iced water, eased the work of temperance reformers. Temperance literature not only praised water extravagantly, but more often than not paid tribute to *cold* water. At temperance dinners the guests sang:

Though Alcohol has had his day
And great has been his slaughter,
He's now retreating in dismay
And victory crowns cold water.

Or, to the tune of *Auld Lang Syne:*

Shall e'er cold water be forgot,
When we sit down to dine?
O no, my friends for is it not
Pour'd out by hands divine?[4]

The temperance movement gave water a near monopoly of public tables. Foreign visitors were astonished to see only ice water where eighty to 100 people were dining. "If people will drink," one traveler concluded, "they must do it secretly. They must retreat to the bar-room, or inhale their sherry cobbler behind the folding-door." An English woman found the "temperate, tea-drinking, water-drinking habits" remarkable. Iced water, she noted, appeared in railroad cars, hotels, waiting rooms, steamers, and stores.[5]

The quality of water varied. An English visitor in 1848 found Mississippi River water healthful but "slightly cathartic to the novice." New Yorkers had poor and brackish water which some mixed with brandy or gin. In schools and factories molasses or elixir of vitriol might be added.

New Yorkers welcomed wildly the new Croton Reservoirs opened on July 4, 1842. As water flowed through the mains it was celebrated by parades, fireworks, band concerts, spouting fountains in City Hall Park and Union Square, and a banquet for the city leaders. Philip Hone, a former mayor, found the universal joy astounding, especially in view of the enormous expense involved.[6]

Temperance probably encouraged the drinking of milk. Fredrika Bremer found it, cooled by ice, popular in Charleston in 1849 and other Europeans saw it, watered and iced, taken with meals.[7] But well before mid-century the purity of milk was questioned. By the 1830s some 18,000 cows in New York City and Brooklyn were kept in dairies run by breweries, crowded into crude stables which they never left and fed fermented mash. The breweries added water to the milk for volume, chalk for color, and molasses to give body, adulterations that caused *Leslie's Illustrated Newspaper* in 1858 to write of "milk murder."[8]

In the South the hot weather and scarcity of refrigeration led to the conversion of milk into butter and this promoted the use of both buttermilk and sour milk. Buttermilk was widely drunk and used to make innumerable breads, pies, ice creams, and candies. Missourians who sold food and drink to westward-moving emigrants found that Southerners bought buttermilk while Northerners and Easterners rarely did.[9]

Tea and coffee, like milk, gained from the shadow over alcohol. The rise of coffee was meteoric. Imports climbed from nearly 12 million pounds in 1821 to almost three times as much in 1832. Then the Tariff of 1833 admitted coffee free of duty, and by 1844 about 150 million pounds were imported. In the thirty years after 1821 the average yearly consumption per person rose from one pound four ounces to 6¼ pounds.[10] Everywhere, as earlier, coffee was both an occasional drink and one to accompany meals.

Coffee substitutes were numerous. A Philadelphia newspaper in 1815 stated that coffee, which "a few years back, was looked upon as unnecessary," was now "one of the necessaries of life." But, the writer continued, its high price made substitutes useful, and he praised one made from potatoes. Others used parched rye, peas, or pumpkins as well as other plants and grains.[11]

In the more settled parts of the country tea remained popular, especially for supper, with green tea exceeding black tea by about ten to one. In the trans-Appalachian West tea was considered effeminate and expensive, but there were those who drank it or substitutes like sassafras, dittany, spicewood, mint, or sage.[12]

In the East the afternoon tea continued, varying from formal parties with elaborate refreshments to family teas which often substituted for the daily supper. For small afternoon teas which were neither parties nor suppers the "never-failing" accompaniments, according to Frances Trollope, were hung beef "chipped up" raw, and "sundry sweetmeats of brown sugar hue and flavour."[13]

The heat of American summers and the ease of obtaining ice created a new category of drinks. Soft drinks, though the term came much later, began to appear in American cities during the late eighteenth century. In New York City the Tontine Coffee House at the corner of Wall and Water streets opened fountains of Ballston, Soda, and Seltzer waters in 1794. By 1809 soda water was sometimes served with wine and sugar added, and shortly

130

after ginger pop was sold. In New York City vendors, beneath signs which showed a bottle with liquid pouring into a tumbler, offered ginger pop, spruce beer, mead, and cakes. Those who sold only ginger pop had a sign picturing two men dueling with bottles from which corks had been ejected by streams of liquor. The word "pop" seems to have been taken from the sound produced when the cork was removed from the bottle.

A visitor to Philadelphia in 1819 claimed that "the first thing every American who can afford five cents . . . takes, on rising in the morning, is a glass of soda water." In the same year a traveler in New York City noticed that ice-chilled soda water was sold "on every street corner" as a "pleasant and healthful drink" in summertime. In 1819 a patent for carbonated mead was issued, and five years later one was given for sarsaparilla mead. By 1830 the preferred flavors were lemon, long to be the leader for both soda water and ice cream, together with strawberry, pineapple, vanilla, and ginger. By the 1850s a beverage called root beer was also sold.[14]

The temperance movement, buttressed by water, milk, coffee, tea, and carbonated drinks, slowly checked the open use of alcoholic beverages. In public dining rooms the presence of women made ice water dominant on the tables, and there was a similar movement away from alcohol in homes.

Cider, although increasingly hurt by temperance, remained in widespread use throughout the North and in parts of the South. In New England and upper New York cider drinking started at breakfast and continued all day both during and between meals. A New England farmer, it was said, felt insecure without twenty to thirty barrels of hard cider lining his cellar as winter approached. So much was it the usual drink of New Englanders, rich and poor alike, that it was considered a breach of manners not to offer some to any visitor or traveler. Reports of its use revealed a nationwide appeal: In New York City cider was reportedly the common drink after water; the Pennsylvania Germans continued to use it freely; it appeared at dance frolics in North Carolina; it was sold in Kentucky taverns when beer was unavailable; and Harriet Martineau noticed that it was often served in Montgomery, Alabama.[15]

The widespread use of cider must have reduced the home brewing of beer and ale. The number of commercial breweries, however, increased. Those owned by German families in Philadelphia continued to be the most reputable, and across the Appalachians other German breweries appeared in Pittsburgh as early as 1806 and Cincinnati in 1812. Those in Cincinnati made draft beer as well as bottled ale and porter "in the best Philadelphia manner," selling to merchants, innkeepers, and the "river trade," some of their product going into the South by flatboats on the Ohio and Mississippi rivers.[16]

It was about 1840 that a revolution started in American beer drinking. It that year John Wagner, who had a small brewery behind his house on St. John Street in Philadelphia, began to make lager beer. This beer was a reflection of German tastes and was brewed by a German method, unlike the earlier malt beverages which had been made according to British preferences and techniques. Lager beer was made with a yeast that fermented to the bottom, rather than the top, of the vat and had to be kept cool during fermentation and quite cold during storage. Sparkling and effervescent and with a rather low alcoholic content, lager marked a whole new direction in the American beer industry.[17]

A wider market for lager beer was opened by the German immigrations that followed the 1848 revolutions. A restraining factor in its dispersal throughout the country was the need to keep it cold during storage. In the South, where German settlement was slight and the problem of refrigeration greater, lager beer was for some time rarely seen. A southern planter might offer his guests imported London porter or Allsop's India ale, while the poorer folk made beer out of persimmons or sweet potatoes.[18] Lager beer faced still another handicap both north and south: the native middle classes looked down on beer as alien and lower class, attributes that were to cling to it well into the twentieth century.

A pleasant result of the German immigration of the 1840s was the beer gardens that appeared in every city of any size. These were sometimes outdoor gardens, but more often they were buildings with large halls that were decorated in the manner of gardens. Some of those in New York City were huge and able to contain anywhere from 400 to 1,200 guests. One of the largest, and a favorite, was the Atlantic Garden on the Bowery. Here men and women gathered to drink beer, talk, listen to the orchestra, waltz, or amuse themselves at the Garden's bowling alleys, billiard tables, or shooting gallery.[19]

Wine, even more than beer and ale, had a limited following. The wealthy and worldly drank wine, but the average American turned to it only on festive occasions, if then. Visitors to the United States were astonished at how few people drank wine at hotels or restaurants or even in the homes of the rich when no guests were present.[20]

Well-to-do Easterners still preferred the heavy, sweeter wines of Spain, Portugal, the Canary Islands, and Madeira. As a rule only small amounts of the lighter and drier French and Rhenish wines were laid by in conscientiously kept cellars. Port was used medicinally and at times was brought out to please English visitors. Sherry had some appeal, but it was Madeira, as during the preceding century, that made up the largest and choicest part of the private cellars.[21]

Families prided themselves on their collections of Madeira and paid up to forty dollars a bottle for the rarest, a fantastic price for the time. True experts were familiar with the outstanding vintages which usually took their names from the ships in which they were brought to American ports: The famous New York Madeiras included The Marsh and Benson, 1809, The Coles Madeira, The Stuyvesant, The Clark, and The Eliza; the outstanding Boston Madeiras were The Kirby, The Amory 1800 and 1811, The Eclipse, and The Otis; while The Burler, 16 was highly thought of in Philadelphia. In Charleston and Savannah, Madeira worship took place at wine parties. Guests would be invited for five o'clock, following the three o'clock dinner, to find a table set with finger bowls and four pipe-stem glasses at each place. The table also held olives, parched peanuts and almonds, and half a dozen bottles of Madeira. For an hour or more the guests would sit, tasting and commenting on the wines as they were served.[22]

In some parts of the South the dry red wines of France were extensively used. A visitor to New Orleans shortly after the Louisiana Purchase of 1803 found that the French there drank the wines of Bordeaux and the southern coast of France, the Americans chose Madeira, and the Spanish preferred Malaga but were increasingly accepting the French wines. Two decades later it was said of New Orleans that "every family is provided with Claret, as we at the North are with cider." Virginians and Carolinians reportedly drank Madeira in winter and claret in summer, and in 1835 Harriet Martineau found claret "the most common drink" in Alabama. Southern wine drinking was probably encouraged by the belief that it was an antidote to "marsh-fevers."[23]

For festive occasions the country chose champagne. By 1820 the consumption was large and in 1838 Captain Marryat thought it "enormous." Champagne refreshed feasting diners between the first and second courses, and it was a favorite accompaniment to oysters. "An American who means to do the thing handsomely," wrote one man, "takes champagne. No other wine is worth his drinking."[24]

Not all that bubbled was champagne. About 1818 a foreign visitor thought the cider in Newark, New Jersey, tasted like champagne. Others must have too and by the 1840s, one man remarked, Newark was making most of the best champagne "which we import." Described as made from cider or from a mixture of turnip juice, brandy, and honey, Newark's "champagne" was rated by some a good imitation of the original.[25]

Other men practiced even greater chicanery. The landlord of a Philadelphia inn met all orders for expensive wines with the same low-cost wine at a high price, and other inns were accused of acting similarly. And for twenty dollars, it was said, anyone could buy from a New York source instructions on how to make wines and brandies from whiskey or neutral spirits and artificial flavorings.[26]

Two centuries of repeated failures did not stop efforts to use European grapes in commercial viniculture, but in each case endemic diseases brought failure. With native grapes there were some successes. In the early 1800s the red Alexander grape was widely planted in Pennsylvania, Ohio, and Indiana, and during the next fifty years still better native varieties were developed.

The most important native grape was the famous Catawba. German vintners from the Rhine Valley used the Catawba to make wine on the islands of Lake Erie and in the Ohio Valley. Nicholas Longworth, a Cincinnati lawyer, proved most successful. In 1825 he bought some Catawba cuttings and three years later tasted the first wine from his plantings. He promptly gave up law in favor of viniculture, and by 1842 he had 1,200 acres planted, and at the present site of Eden Park in Cincinnati made the country's first champagne. By the late 1850s Ohio was the leading wine state, with numerous vineyards extending up the Ohio valley for forty miles above Cincinnati. But disaster came shortly before the Civil War when the vines were destroyed by disease.[27]

California had made wines before the Gold Rush, but the demand by miners and new settlers brought a large increase in commercial viniculture which continued until the 1870s when the dreaded phylloxera disease joined with worldwide depression to bring about a temporary setback.[28]

Home wine-making probably flourished everywhere. The Pennsylvania Dutch made wines from wild plums, wild cherries, elderberries, dandelions, white clover, and wild grapes, and a cookbook of 1861 listed thirty-nine wines, including such exotics as apricot, ginger, gooseberry, peach, and tomato.[29]

Among the "hard" liquors, rum faced the greatest difficulties. Independence from England had ended the free flow of sugar and molasses from the British West Indies to New England distilleries, and of rum to the United States. Later, Anglo-French warfare, accompanied by maritime restrictions on American neutral rights, cut down trade between the West Indies and North America, as did the ensuing War of 1812. Even the abolition of the slave trade by the United States in 1808 had a similar effect, for this trade had taken American slave-trading ships to Africa and then to the West Indies where humans were exchanged for sugar and molasses.[30]

Nevertheless, rum remained relatively cheap and very popular along the East Coast. In New England "a pint of rum to a pound of pork" was a common measure for a worker's food and drink early in the century. Yankee rum dominated the stock of dram houses in New York City. And in far-off New Orleans a dozen or more distilleries made rum and tafia, the latter a low-grade rum sold both locally and upriver.[31]

For those of little means, stills throughout the country made simple, strong brandies from apples and peaches, while the moneyed element imported expensive French brandies, the quantity rising fourfold and more between 1830 and 1839. Home distilling was common. Apple brandy was a household product in New England as were so-called rums made from molasses, maple sap, and potatoes.[32]

In the new western states and territories nothing stemmed the flow of whiskey. So ardently did Kentucky embrace whiskey that by 1811 there were an estimated 2,000 distillers there. Efforts to improve distilling practices were made by Dr. James C. Crow who came to Kentucky in 1823 and reputedly introduced the "sour mash" process among other innovations. Exactly when Bourbon whiskey first appeared is not known, but this blend of corn and rye made with limestone water and aged in new, charred, white oak barrels existed as early as 1846 and took its name from Bourbon County, Kentucky.[33]

Neighboring Ohio also became a center for the distilling and distribution of whiskey. A man who spent his boyhood during the early 1820s in southern Ohio remembered that within two miles of his home there were three distilleries. When the family's whiskey jug was empty, a boy would be sent to one of these with a bag of grain to exchange for a gallon of whiskey. Men of that area drank whiskey regularly, and women took it sweetened and reduced to a toddy. On social occasions it served as "an invigorator and a sign of hospitality."[34]

Although as late as 1816 whiskey was little known in New York City and other eastern centers, within a decade it had won a following. Some men drank it straight, while others took it with water or in whiskey punch, a mixture of whiskey, sugar, and water with a bit of lemon.

Whiskey came to be even cheaper than rum. In Maryland, wrote Frances Trollope, it flowed everywhere "at the same fatally cheap rate of twenty cents the gallon," and a settler in Princeton, Illinois, in 1842, wrote that "whisky is about ten cents per gallon, it is so cheap that it ant worth drinking."[35]

The low cost promoted chicanery. Grog-shop owners colored it with oak juice to make "first rate Cognac brandy" or sold it as gin, Monongahela whiskey, or schnapps. Southern grog-shop owners sometimes "improved" whiskey with logwood, juniper berries, dog-leg tobacco, and even strychnine. Whiskey was commonly watered, and in Mississippi some "genuine Old Rye" was said to have frozen during a cold snap.[36]

Unlike rum, whiskey carried no class distinctions. In its better forms it pleased discriminating drinkers, while its cheapness made it the daily drink of farmers, laborers, soldiers and sailors, and even prisoners in jails. Whiskey and rum were sold secretly to slaves at high prices, and store boats on the Ohio carried stills to make peach and apple brandies and rye whiskey for sale to slaves and poor whites.[37]

The multiplication of mixed drinks continued, aided by the southern custom of taking morning bitters. The French *savant* Constantin Volney, visiting the United States in the late 1790s, reported that South Carolinians and other Southerners took what they called bitters, "of which brandy, rum, or Madeira wine is the basis," to ward off the "annual fevers." Such drinks, made by pouring the liquor over wild cherries, wormwood, or certain barks or herbs, became a daily pre-breakfast rite in western Pennsylvania and throughout the South.[38]

The mint julep began as such a morning potion and was met with as early as 1797 by a traveler near Petersburg, Virginia. In 1809 the barkeeper in Opelousas, Louisiana, was expected each morning to fill a long shelf against the side of the tavern with glasses containing mint, sugar, and a spoon. Here, upon rising, all the young men of the village gathered to take their "morning bitters" after rum, whiskey, or brandy was presumably added to the glasses. The glasses must have been small, for the "usual allowance" was reportedly ten to twelve glasses before breakfast. By 1816 New Yorkers had heard of the mint julep as a southern preventive against malaria.[39]

In time the mint julep attracted round-the-clock followers who spoke with deep gratitude of the relief the drink provided during hot weather. Frances Trollope became one of its captives:

It would, I truly believe, be utterly impossible for the art of man to administer anything so likely to restore them from the overwhelming effects of heat and fatigue, as a large glass filled to the brim with the fragrant leaves of nerve restoring mint, as many solid lumps of delicately pellucid, crystal-looking ice, as it can conveniently contain, a proper proportion of fine, white sugar, (not beet-root), and then — I would whisper it gently, if I knew how — a whole wine-glass full of whiskey poured over it, to find its insinuating way among the crystal rocks, and the verdant leaves, till by gentle degrees, a beverage is produced, that must create a delicious sensation of coolness, under a tropical sun, and a revival of strength, where strength seemed gone for ever.[40]

Cultists of the mint julep were invariably lyrical, but divided as to the exact shape of the deity. A decade after Trollope's description, Captain Marryat appraised the julep. He found it "one of the most delightful and insinuating potations" ever invented. Of the many recipes made with claret, Madeira, and so on, he wrote, the "real" mint julep consisted of a tumbler containing mint leaves, a spoonful of white sugar, and equal proportions of peach and common brandy and filled with rasped or pounded ice. "Epicures rub the lips of the tumbler with a piece of fresh pineapple, and the tumbler itself is very often incrusted outside with stactities [sic] of ice." Whether it originated in Virginia or not, the mint julep varied from place to place. One traveler mentioned it as an "acrid and scorching mixture" in northern taverns.[41]

However made, the mint julep flourished in the North for decades. When New York City celebrated the Fourth of July in 1837 it was sold at booths that lined Broadway, and when Boston observed the same day in 1849 an English traveler anticipated that the sun that day would rise on "seas of sherry-cobblers and cataracts of mint-juleps."[42]

The sherry cobbler — a combination of lemon juice, sugar, sherry, and fine ice sipped through a straw — was close behind the mint julep in popularity. A bewildering variety of other mixed drinks had names like apple toddy, gin sling, whiskey skin, Connecticut eye-opener, Alabama fog-cutter, lightning smash, thunderbolt cocktail, streak of lightning, rum salad, brandy smash, gin flip, stone fence, and timber doodle. Mobile, Alabama, was proud of a drink named Lisbon bitter, a strong and bitter mixture of brandy, "tonic roots," and sugar.[43]

Some of these mixed drinks were cocktails. The earliest known use of the word, and a definition, appeared in the spring of 1806 in a magazine published at Hudson, New York: "*Cock tail* then, is a stimulating liquor, composed of *spirits* of any kind, *sugar, water,* and *bitters* — it is vulgarly called *bittered sling.*" There is some evidence that many early cocktails were made with gin. An English passenger on a Mississippi River steamboat in 1831 noticed that the crowded bar served mint juleps and apple toddies to the "refined" while the "lesser" elements drank gin slings and cocktails. The same man, passing a bar in Louisville, Kentucky, heard the following exchange: "Have you got any good gin, sir?" — "Yes, sir, Hollands" — "Well mix me a cocktail — I want to wet up." But what really distinguished a cocktail was the presence of bitters. Four men, cruising the New England coast in

138

1858, went ashore at Provincetown to buy cocktails. They discovered that the only man in town with something to drink was an apothecary and he had never heard of a cocktail. After the drink was described, however, he found a bottle of sherry bitters and, since the "other requisite materials" were on board the sloop, success was assured. Jerry Thomas, whose work *The Bar-Tenders' Guide* appeared in 1862, gave cocktail recipes, each made with bitters. The cocktail, Thomas noted, "is a modern invention, and is generally used on fishing and other sporting parties, though some *patients* insist that it is good in the morning as a tonic."[44] This remark ties the cocktail to the pre-breakfast morning bitters.

Except for a few universal favorites, mixed drinks were usually made by professional barkeepers. And bars multiplied across the country. Although not yet looked upon as disreputable, they were exclusively male and served as places of refuge from the storm of temperance agitation.

The earliest bars in New York City were said to have appeared in corner grocery stores, at first owned by Irish and then gradually taken over by Germans. The Irish next established "saloons," separate from groceries, as did the Germans when lager beer became popular.[45] Soon all but the smallest hotels across the country found room for a bar, and some in the greater hotels were labeled "splendid," "magnificent," and even "palace-like." The typical hotel bar was hardly so grand. It was described in 1838 as a large room in the basement with a long counter behind which were two or three barkeepers: "Here the eye reposes on masses of pure crystal ice, large bunches of mint, decanters of every sort of wine, every variety of spirits, lemons, sugar, bitters, cigars and tobacco. . . . Here you meet everybody and everybody meets you."[46]

The bars of New Orleans were famous. A visitor from Illinois in the late 1840s was dazzled by the ground-floor barroom of the St. Charles Hotel: "At ten o'clock at night you behold it in its glory. At least a thousand men, speaking all languages, habited in all costumes, representing all nationalities, were engaged in laughing, talking, betting, quarreling, chewing, smoking, and drinking." During the day the major bars of New Orleans were centers of commerce and information with news bulletins, the latest telegrams, and the daily newspapers all at hand. They were meeting places for transactions in sugar, tobacco, corn, and cotton, and the scene of auctions of ships, steamboats, real estate, stocks, and slaves. The bars were also famous for their free lunches which daily included soups, fish, roast joints, fowls, salads, bread, and cheese, all paid for with the dime that bought a mint julep, a whiskey punch, a sling, or some other drink.[47]

A free and easy exchange of both drinks and conversation took place in these all-masculine centers, and a barroom vocabulary developed. By the late 1820s a saloon in New York City could be called a gin mill. A patron stopped to "liquor up" or to "wet up." A morning drink was an "eye opener," while a small drink was called a smile. A strong drink could be named a phlegm disperser, a steadier, a gum tickler, an antifogmatic, a phlegmcutter, or a gall breaker. Barroom manners were informal. Captain Marryat found that in a bar anything was an excuse for a drink and that it was so common to begin an acquaintance with one that to refuse was a serious offense. In the South and West, he concluded, it was literally: "Stranger, will you drink or fight?"[48]

❧ 10 ❧
Dining Out, 1800-1860

*The crash of the crockery
and the clash of the steel.*

Although nearly all American meals were created in home kitchens, more and more people found it necessary, convenient, or pleasurable to "eat out." A number of reasons took people from their homes at mealtimes: businessmen traveling for their companies; the distance of urban business centers from residential districts; a growing affluence that made eating at restaurants less extravagant; and large-scale migrations, especially from east to west.

The most luxurious dining, though not always the best, was found in the large hotels of a few major cities. The modern hotel came to America with the opening of the City Hotel in New York City in 1794. The seventy-three rooms of this building set it apart from the earlier and smaller inns. During the next few decades other large hotels were built in New York, Boston, Philadelphia, Baltimore, and Washington, but the era of the luxury hotel did not begin until 1829 when the Tremont House opened in Boston. With its granite facade, 170 bedrooms, ten large public rooms with marble floors, and other innovations, the Tremont House set a new and high standard. One of its imitators in elegance, the vast Astor House in New York City, palatial and gaslit, was built during the 1830s and became famous throughout the country.[1]

For some time the hotels continued the custom of the earlier inns by giving everyone set meals, all paid for by the guests whether eaten or not, and served at long tables at fixed hours. The entire meal was placed on the tables at once, and the guests helped themselves. Not until the 1830s did the larger eastern hotels bring some degree of order and pace by offering their table d'hôte meals in courses. The Tremont House, which began this, also drilled its waiters to serve each course with elaborate military precision. Other hotels adopted the practice and made the serving of their meals a memorable event. A British army officer in America during the late 1830s decided that the Astor House waiters were drilled as regularly as his regiment.[2] A visitor to a large hotel in Newport, Rhode Island, described the maneuvers of the waiters there under the command of a leader,

> at the wave of whose hand they put on and take off the dishes, marching in a row, orderly and erect. But the most unaccountable thing that they do, is, at the epoch of the pudding, cheese and dessert, (all of which come on at the same time, and form one course), when they first march down the room, bearing the dishes aloft and, clustering round their leader, form themselves into the figure of a star — then up the room, and form into some other kind of figure — then up and down and round each other, with marvellous rapidity and precision — and while you are still wondering where in the world all those melons and pineapples and oranges are to go — Whiz! at the well-known signal, they are popped down beside you, and off march the waiters, empty-handed and in double file.[3]

The waiters at the International Hotel in Niagara Falls went through their marching and "distracting evolutions" to the music of a full band: "There is a march for them to enter; a three-four movement for soup; a pisicato [sic] passage for fish; the covers come off to a crash of trombones, cymbals, and gongs; and so the whole dinner goes off to appropriate music, with an accompaniment of champagne corks like the firing of skirmishers."[4]

Some of the larger hotels discarded the fixed courses in favor of menus from which each guest ordered separately. The first menus appeared in the 1830s and became general at the major hotels by the 1850s. Such menus made it possible to substitute small tables for the long tables, but they also doomed the ceremonious march of the waiters. Only a feeble remnant of the custom would carry into the twentieth century when at some large banquets the lights would dim while a dessert, each tray or cart illuminated, was brought in by a procession of waiters. Still another step toward modern practices occurred in 1844 when the New York Hotel adopted what in time would be called the European Plan by which guests paid only for the meals they ate rather than for all. Other hotels soon adopted the arrangement.[5]

Some hotels won limited fame as gastronomic centers. In New York City the Astor House, the New York Hotel, the Globe Hotel, the St. Nicholas Hotel, and the Metropolitan Hotel all had French chefs and lavish menus. The Tremont Hotel in Boston was famed for its French cooking, and the Parker House there maintained high culinary standards. The St. Charles Hotel in New Orleans served excellent Creole meals in that city of fine cooking.[6]

The hotel menus of the 1850s reveal a large choice, but only rarely were the dishes elaborate. The foods were listed in courses under such categories as soup, boiled meats, cold dishes, side dishes, roast meats, puddings and pastry, and fruit. Near the Atlantic coast a fish course followed the soup course. The soups were very limited. A few hotels gave a choice of several kinds, but frequently only vermicelli soup was listed. Not many vegetables were offered, and salads were nearly always omitted. Pies usually led the list of desserts, followed by such favorite dishes as blanc mange, Bavarian cream, tapioca pudding, raspberry puffs, ice cream, and fruit.[7]

A number of hotels were openly American in their offerings. The Revere House in Boston during the 1850s retained the New England tradition with only occasional nods to alien influences. A traveler noted one day's menu: The first course was chowder, the fish was baked cod, and the boiled dishes included mutton with caper sauce, turkey and oysters, chicken, pork, corned beef and cabbage, ham, and tongue. There were several cold meats and "side dishes" that included mutton cutlets with Madeira sauce, baked macaroni, chicken curry, rice croquettes, ducks with turnips, pigs' feet with piquant sauce, and hominy. The "roast" course contained various fowls, mutton, veal, beef, and ham with champagne sauce. There followed apple, squash, and quince pies, jelly puffs, cabinet pudding, macaroons, and damson meringues. Dessert consisted of lemon ice cream, apples, almonds, raisins, and English walnuts.[8]

Some city restaurants equaled or excelled the great hotels as centers of good cooking. Two in New York City, Taylor's and Delmonico's, created a certain awe among all but the most sophisticated. The first flourished during the 1850s and was magnificent in appearance. On Broadway Avenue, it was "ablaze" with decorations and had rows of fluted and polished marble pillars and a marble floor. An alcove at one end was filled with orange trees, while a crystal fountain cooled the air. One viewer spoke of "a complete maze of fresco, mirrors, gilding and marble." One could go to Taylor's day or night for an ice served from "large reservoirs, shining like polished silver," or could order a meal that included ham boiled in champagne or woodcocks stewed with truffles and crawfish.[9]

Less ostentatious but more concerned with good cooking was Delmonico's, a restaurant that for almost exactly a century was to be a great example of culinary excellence. In 1827 John and Peter Delmonico, Swiss immigrant brothers, opened a café and pastry shop where at six pine tables they served wines, liquors, fancy ices, bonbons, orgeats (a non-alcoholic drink flavored with the juice of almonds and other essences), pastries, coffee, and chocolate to immigrants from Europe. In 1831 they opened the first Delmonico's restaurant, and in the same year a nephew, Lorenzo Delmonico, in time to become a famous teacher of gastronomy, arrived from Switzerland to help. After the great fire of 1835 destroyed their restaurant the brothers opened a much more imposing one with a large menu that included salads and vegetables prepared in the French manner.[10]

Others spread the French influence in New York City. Many French and Swiss immigrants became cooks, confectioners, or proprietors not only of restaurants but of chocolate shops, bakeries, and cafés. In 1815 Francis Guerin opened a confectionery and later an adjoining ladies' lunchroom. From a small bakery Louis Curtillet offered to the public meat pies, plum puddings, confections de crème glacées, and punch à la Romaine. In the 1840s J. Pinteux made his Café de Mille Colonnes a lavishly furnished meeting place for the wealthy. In 1848 this was taken over by Ferdinand Palmo, an Italian impressario, who renamed it Café de la Republique.[11]

Other cities had outstanding restaurants. In Washington, D.C., immigrant chefs competed with each other both in their restaurants and at private homes where they catered. The early Creole restaurants of New Orleans — Antoine's, Moreau's, Victor's, Miguel's — began to win recognition as did others on Lake Pontchartrain where there was rivalry among both chefs and cellars. A visitor to New Orleans in 1832 decided that one restaurant there (which he did not identify) was the best in the country.[12]

A growing number of city restaurants sprang up to serve midday meals to businessmen. Most provided a "quick lunch." The idea was not new, for rural America had not treated meals as a time for relaxation and conversation.

On May 21, 1827, an English traveler, Captain Basil Hall, was taken by friends to the Plate House, a quick-lunch place in the center of New York City's business district. He entered a long, narrow, and rather dark room fitted up with two rows of boxes, each box holding four persons. Small boys took the orders, bawled out their content and the box number, and almost within seconds waiters brought the dishes. During the twenty minutes in the restaurant, he noted, two sets of diners were served.[13]

Both businessmen and others ate in the numerous oyster saloons or oyster cellars that existed in all the principal towns and cities. Those in New York City were below street level, their presence marked by "balloons" of red or red-and-white striped muslin stretched over bare frames and lighted at night by candles within. Often, too, the words "Oyster Saloon" were printed in large letters on the basement story.[14]

Most oyster cellars were about twenty-five by 100 feet. Some were resplendent with gilding, plate-glass mirrors, and pictures. Curtains provided clients with privacy in their boxes. At such places, wrote an English tourist, gathered judges, generals, and parsons, all enjoying excellent oysters. At less ornate cellars there was a long counter where two or three men, frequently blacks, opened oysters which were swallowed by customers "with astonishing relish and rapidity." Family groups went to tables in a gaslit room at the rear.[15]

Some of New York City's less expensive oyster cellars served on the "Canal-Street Plan," named after the wide street that crossed Broadway. The plan consisted of providing as many oysters as the customer wished for sixpence. Having paid, the client ate oysters as they were opened for him until he said "Enough!" An overgreedy customer, it was said, might in time be given an inedible oyster.

Still lower in cost were the small wagons that sold oysters in the streets. These provided pedestrians with oysters, biscuits, pepper, and ginger beer. For a few pennies, wrote an observer,

145

"the carter or mechanic has a whet which might satisfy even a gourmand."

Most patrons of oyster bars were men. But there were some fashionable oyster saloons at ground level which were described as being "as large as the great music halls in London, and . . . frequented day and night by ladies as well as gentlemen."[16]

Outside the big cities travelers by horseback or stagecoach were entertained at inns along all the principal highways. The landlords of New England and New York were described by one traveler as "topping men," field officers of militia, with good farms attached to their taverns. One man characterized them as men who felt themselves "on an equality with senators, and who not infrequently become senators," and who took pride in entertaining their guests: "They sit at the head of the table, and invite the President, the Governor of the State or distinguished foreigners, to take wine with them. They have the manners, not of a head-waiter, but of a gentleman of fortune dispensing the hospitalities of his mansion." The wife of the host sat at the foot of the table, and at smaller inns the daughter of the household not only officiated at both breakfast and supper but waited table at dinner. "Their behavior," one man noted, "is reserved in the extreme, but it enables them to serve as domesticks, without losing their rank of equality with those on whom they attend."[17] Meals were served at one or more long tables. These, enlarged versions of the farmhouse dining table or the long tables erected outdoors at rural frolics, had appeared at inns in the late eighteenth century and became general during the early decades of the following one.

In some western inns the guise of family hospitality was not apparent and mealtime could be rude and competitive. A warning bell brought all diners to the dining room, and a second bell indicated the opening of its doors. In a description that was similar to those of many other witnesses, an English tourist pictured the scene at a Nashville, Tennessee, inn in 1831:

The door was unlocked, and we all rushed into a long hall, like a squadron . . . charging the enemy, and found tables covered with meat, vegetables, preserved fruit, tea, coffee, and bread, both of maize and wheat, and soft hoe and waffel cakes. Down the company sat in a hurry — noses were blown to one side — cotton handkerchiefs were spread on the knees — cuffs were turned back, and then commenced "the crash of the crockery and the clash of the steel." No ceremony was used; each man helped himself with his own knife and fork, and reached across his neighbor to secure a fancied *morceau*. Bones were picked with both hands; knives were drawn through the teeth with the edge to the lips; the scalding mocha and souchong were poured into saucers to expedite the cooling, and cup deposited in a saucerette on the right. Beefsteaks, apple tart and fish, were seen on the same plate the one moment, and had disappeared the next. . . .

I was rather bewildered, and could not eat for some minutes, when I saw first one man get up, and then another, and walk out of the room wiping their mouths with the heel of their hand. . . . The rest continued to eat as if it was their last meal, or as if they intended to choke themselves, and disappeared so suddenly that it seemed as if they had finished by eating one another; but on going into the bar I found them all alive and well, lounging about with their hands in their pockets, balancing themselves on the chairs, taking a quid from their "bacco-box," or receiving a stiff glass of sling from the bar-keeper.[18]

Behavior was sometimes unseemly. A foreign visitor at an inn in Louisville asked someone to pass the chicken; the man cut out the entire body for himself, then handed over the dish with the legs. But the haste with which everyone ate was not confined to one region. A traveler remarked on the "inconceivable rapidity" with which people in Maine ate, and at the Virginia Hotel in St. Louis he discovered that of the 250 who sat down to dinner only twenty remained longer than ten minutes. An Englishwoman believed that the competition for what was on the table led men to "heap everything eatable on their plates at once."[19]

West of the Appalachians the quality of food and lodging was a matter of chance except in the larger cities where the inns or hotels might maintain high standards. A composite description of a country tavern in Ohio during the 1818–1820 period stated that it would be a log, frame, or brick house, often with a wooden piazza in front. From a tall post hung a signboard on which was painted a picture of Washington, Andrew Jackson, or some other admired figure, but each hero was identifiable only by the name beneath. A small bell on top of the house summoned travelers and boarders to the table where a state governor or a general of the militia might be sitting beside a wagoner. The meals were simple but bountiful, with beef, pork, and game together with vegetables, preserved fruits, and wheat and corn breads. When stopping at such an inn, wrote Marryat a decade later, "you must expect . . . to set down to meals with people whose exterior is anything but agreeable."[20]

Simple foods and crude eating conditions met all who approached the frontier. Witness the adventures of Mrs. John Test who, as her daughter told it, arrived with her children in Brookville, Indiana, about 1810 and decided to go to the "hotel" for dinner:

When our faces were all washed up, and clean aprons put on, and hair combed, we sallied forth with all the courage of children, whose appetites have been sharpened by a wearesome journey. Enquiries were continually made as we passed, nay scrambled over logs, stumps, and often intercepted by briers, of where is the village? and where is the hotel? . . . But finally after many a scratch upon our hands, and many a rent in our dresses and white aprons . . . we reached and stopped at a small cabin surrounded by a rough worm fence, which we all were instructed to climb, to make our entrance into the cabin hotel. This hotel contained four large feather beds, made up with nice quilts, but something in the form of graves, a corner cupboard, with dishes all arranged for show, a table and several split bottomed chairs, and a looking glass. . . .

The meal that followed, however, was cleanly prepared and served and consisted of "deliciously" cooked fried squirrel, wild turkey, corn bread, potatoes, bacon, and eggs.[21] Isabella Bishop, an Englishwoman, visited Davenport, Iowa, in mid-century where in a woodshed she was given a breakfast of johnnycake, squirrels, buffalo hump, corn bread, buckwheat, tea, and whiskey.[22]

Travelers in the Mississippi Valley would come to houses that bore signs reading "Corn bread and common doings," which in translation meant corn bread and fat pork. At some taverns there was the more expensive "chicken fixings" or "wheat-bread and

148

chicken fixings," a meal which included ham, veal cutlets, sausages, steaks, and other items to accompany the fried chicken. Near Alton, Illinois, a house bore the sign, "Stranger, here's your chicken fixings," while at Cairo, Illinois, a "Shanty Hotel" offered a breakfast of "pig and coffee." When Frederick Law Olmsted, the great landscape architect, ate at a small and unattractive inn in Kentucky in the mid-1850s he partook "innocent and unsuspicious" of corn bread and bacon, "without a thought that for the next six months I should actually see *nothing else*," except for "vile coffee" as he journeyed through Kentucky, Tennessee, and Texas.[23]

At times the sanitary conditions were revolting. Filthy table settings were among the more obvious problems. One man was awakened early because the landlord wanted his sheets to use as tablecloths; another man saw his landlady take the tablecloth from under her sick husband's bedclothes. Flies were everywhere and on everything. Food preparation was sometimes so unsanitary that people newly arrived in the West could not bring themselves to eat. When a clergyman took his wife by stagecoach across Illinois, they stopped at a small tavern where she saw her first western meal prepared: "The chickens were killed, picked and cleaned, cooked and served before our eyes, and the leaden biscuits and half raw corn bread were kneaded and baked under our inspection." Her conclusion was that "eyes . . . were very much in the *way* of people who proposed to travel 'out West.'" A traveler who visited Michigan in 1841 would probably have agreed, having mentioned not only "dirty taverns" but "dirty meals and dirty women" as well.[24]

Those who were forced to accept the hospitality of private individuals were sometimes fortunate. One Colonel James Creecy, caught by nightfall in the wilderness of central Mississippi, was given refuge and a meal at a frontier cabin. The husband had just killed a deer, and the wife cut at least four pounds of the venison into slices, washed, salted, and drained them:

She then took from a keg about a half gallon of meal, sifted it, poured boiling water on it, threw in a little salt, made it up into small pones, wrapping each very carefully in the inner shucks of corn, fresh from the ear, scraped away the embers

149

from one corner of the ample fire-place, laid them down and covered them over deeply, with hot ashes and embers. . . . The venison was then quickly and artistically broiled, on an old (but *clean*) gridiron that had seen trouble, then left near the fire to keep warm in a deep plate; and in a very short time the corn cakes were drawn from the ashes and unrolled — done to a turn — the bowls were filled with milk, and all of this was accomplished speedily, without "noise or confusion." . . . There was a meal that Heliogabalus never dreamed of![25]

Much of the travel was by new conveyances, both on land and water. In 1817 New York State began to construct the Erie Canal, a project that was completed in 1825 and that became a major means of travel into the upper Mississippi Valley. During the next several decades other canals were built, but only a few were really successful. Also in 1817 a steamboat pushed upriver from New Orleans to Cincinnati, and within a few years there were steamboats on all the large tributaries of the Mississippi River system. The railroad came soon after the canals and steamboats. The Baltimore and Ohio Railroad, begun in 1828, was but one among a number that by the 1840s were connecting eastern cities with each other and with the trans-Appalachian West.

Food and drink on the canal boats differed greatly according to the time and place. The meals were served on long trestle tables that were set up three times a day in the main cabin where the men slept at night and in the women's cabin where the women and children slept. Everything was placed on the tables at once. One traveler to Buffalo over the Erie Canal wondered how such ample meals of roast turkey, chicken, beef, ham, vegetables, pies, and puddings could be prepared in "the little closet aft." Equally bountiful were the meals served Charles Dickens, the English novelist, in 1842 on Pennsylvania canal boats. Breakfast and supper consisted of tea, coffee, bread, butter, salmon, shad, liver, steaks, potatoes, pickles, lamb chops, black puddings, and sausages. The midday dinner was the same, but without tea and coffee. A passenger on a Wabash and Erie boat in 1854, however, spoke of breakfast beefsteaks that were dry, small, and much underdone. The captain, furthermore, "looked very black" if anyone asked for a second helping.[26]

On steamboats, too, the meals were not always good, especially during the early years. In 1820 a family that took a week's trip on a Mississippi boat received nothing for dinner but salt beef, pork and gray beans, and two "stinking turkies weighing about 30 lb." Protests to the captain accomplished nothing, and he would not even allow them to put their own provisions on the table, saying it would be an "insult" to him.[27] A passenger on an Illinois River steamboat listed the dinner fare as "the never eaten roast beef, roast pig and sole-leather pudding; and for breakfast and tea, a dark colored witch's broth."[28]

Such experiences led well-to-do families to bring along a slave or servant to prepare special dishes. With this in mind they carried not only foods but especially the wines and liquors to which they were accustomed. When any of these were put on the long tables in the saloon, others had to be warned at times that a particular bottle or dish was "private."[29]

As steamboating matured the best of the floating palaces of gleaming white paint and shining brass served meals that were greatly admired, especially by those to whom the whole represented a magnificence and luxury for which their rural backgrounds had not prepared them. Even a sophisticated Englishwoman thought the dinner she ate on a Hudson River steamboat was "the best and the most neatly served that I have ever seen in any hotel in this country."[30] The cooks on the crack Mississippi boats bought fresh poultry, vegetables, fruits, and meats in towns where the boats docked, and the rivers provided fish. Often elaborate menus on these boats listed Creole dishes from New Orleans together with choice game from the northern forests and plains.[31]

However uncertain the cooking, there was abundance and variety. A traveler from St. Louis to Louisville in 1833 mentioned thirty-one different dishes put before twenty-two passengers at a meal, while another spoke of a steamboat's table as "literally covered with dishes, wedged together as closely as a battalion of infantry in solid square." Meats were likely to dominate. One traveler kept a record of typical meals on a trip in the early thirties up the river from New Orleans. Breakfast included beefsteaks, fowls, pigeon or chicken fricassee, ragoût, plates of cold ham and other meats, and coffee and tea. Dinner consisted of great platters of beefsteaks, baked pork or turkey, smaller quantities of ducks,

151

chicken or other fowl, various cold sliced meats, potatoes, rice, corn, puddings, tarts, and rum and water. Supper was very similar to breakfast.

Both foreigners and Americans criticized the table manners of steamboat passengers. A Cincinnati editor, in an account of one voyage, declared that at least half the passengers were unused to the elaborate fare put before them but were determined to get their money's worth from the prepaid meals. He saw one man begin his dinner by swallowing a beautifully molded dish of blanc mange, while others also did not wait for the hot dishes but began on tarts, pies, and jellies.[32]

Far different was the lot of the deck passengers. These, except for a stove that served both for heating and cooking, were left to their own resources. They brought their own food and utensils and prepared their own meals. Often they misjudged the length of the voyage, and actual want and suffering could result, for the opportunities to purchase goods along the way were rare and the prices were sometimes excessive. Provisions were chosen with convenience and the problem of spoilage in mind, and dried herring, bologna sausage, crackers, cheese, and a bottle of whiskey were the most common items.[33]

The railroads were slow in finding a satisfactory means of feeding their passengers. Some early trains would stop at mealtime and wait while their passengers picnicked in the fields with their own provisions. Captain Marryat in 1838 described a different method that, in isolated places, persisted into the twentieth century. About every fifteen miles there were "refreshment rooms" where "the cars stop, all the doors are thrown open, and out rush the passengers like boys out of school, and crowd round the tables to solace themselves with pies, patties, cakes, hard-boiled eggs, ham, custards, and a variety of railroad luxuries too numerous to mention." Soon, too, "young gentlemen" began to carry trays through the cars selling gum drops, lemon drops, tobacco, apples, and cakes.[34]

Railway food remained of uncertain quality. The complaint was made in 1856 that once away from New England the meals were not worth the standard charge of fifty cents, or even a dime. The train would stop after an all-night ride, the conductor would call out "Twenty minutes for breakfast," but it was hard to enter the restaurant because of the crowd and to get a seat was even more difficult. Those who were successful could buy weak coffee, a piece of tough fried beefsteak, some fried potatoes, and a heavy sour biscuit. Two muscular men were posted at the door to collect payment, and the passengers were often indignant.[35]

⊸❦ 11 ❦⊸
Parties, Frolics, Bees, and Celebrations, 1800-1860

Six miles of roast pig!

Whether Northerners or Southerners, farmers or city dwellers, rich or poor, Americans of the early nineteenth century entertained themselves with an enthusiasm that would have astounded their forebears. The lightheartedness of the era no doubt owed much to the country's growing wealth and to the general peace that was interrupted only by brief wars against England and Mexico.

Food and drink almost invariably played a part in the entertainments of the time. Sometimes food was the reason for a party, and people got together to enjoy a feast or a special delicacy. At other times food and drink were only incidental. When the French chef of the New York Hotel suggested in 1844 that the hotel offer à la carte room service in place of public dining, a journalist admonished him: "Tell a country lady in these times that when she comes to New York she must eat and pass the evening in a room by herself and she would rather stay home. The going to the Astor and dining with two hundred well dressed people and sitting in full dress in a splendid drawing room with plenty of company is the charm of going to the city."[1]

Wealthy traders and merchants in the Northeast and planters in the South were able to give dinner parties that were impressive, even ostentatious, but not always joyous. A Bostonian remembered that early in the century a dinner party had two courses, each a full dinner and so large that the tablecloth was

154

barely visible. A first course might include the head and shoulders of a large codfish, a dish then fashionable both in England and Boston, pea soup, venison, roast chickens, boiled ham, beef collops, potatoes, celery, parsnips, jelly, pies, and marrow pudding. A second course would be young turkeys, scalloped oysters, roast rabbits, wild ducks, lamb, smelts, a mutton ragoût, several vegetables, cherry tarts, and stewed pippins. Finally, and by itself as was proper for such a delicacy, came ice cream. Wine was in decanters so that each guest could serve himself, and toasts were offered to individuals and to popular ideas.[2] A French traveler in Boston in the 1830s recorded that he had "never anywhere seen dinners more sumptuous."[3]

Fredrika Bremer denounced similar dinners in New York City as wearisome, dismal, intolerable, indigestible, stupefying, and designed to kill both body and soul. They began at five-thirty or six, she complained, and continued to nine with repeated courses being eaten in almost complete silence.[4]

Lavish display existed also in the South. A New England visitor to the Carter family's great Virginia plantation, Shirley, was tremendously impressed to discover that the service was entirely of silver, that one drank porter out of silver goblets, and that the dinner table was furnished with the finest Virginia hams, saddle of mutton, turkey, canvasback ducks, beef, oysters, the choicest celery, sparkling champagne, desserts of plum pudding, tarts, ice cream, peaches preserved in brandy, figs, almonds, raisins, the richest Madeira, the best port, the softest Malmsey, and innumerable other delicacies. A traveler in Natchez, Mississippi, in 1806 dined at several places where the dinner consisted of three courses and a dessert, "where the service was of solid plate, where a negro, magnificently dressed, stood behind every chair."[5] In New Orleans wealth and superior cooking joined to produce impressive parties. When Bernhard, Duke of Saxe-Weimar-Eisenach, visited the city in 1825 he was given a dinner by John Randolph Grymes, a Virginian who had come to New Orleans a few years earlier. After the second course, large folding doors opened and the guests beheld another dining room with a table set with dessert. The guests moved from one room to the other, keeping the same order at table.[6]

Less formal were the balls at the great plantation houses. A woman who lived on a Louisiana plantation recalled one given there. The staircase of the big house was garlanded with roses for three full flights, fragrant flowers were in many places, and the women wore gorgeous lace dresses with jewels and plumes:

On the menu, the cold meats, salads, *salmis, galantines* quaking in jellied seclusion, and an infinite variety of *à las,* were served from side tables, leaving the huge expanse of carved oak, besilvered, belinened and belaced, for flowers trailing from the tall silver *épergne* in the center to the corsage bouquet at each place; fruits, cakes in pyramids or layers or only solid deliciousness, iced and ornamented; custards, pies, jellies, creams, Charlotte Russes or home-concocted sponge cake spread with raspberry jam encircling a veritable Mont Blanc of whipped cream dotted with red cherry stars; towers of nougat or caramel, sorbets and ice creams served in little baskets woven of candied orange peel and topped with sugared rose leaves or violets. . . . Various wines in cut glass decanters, each with its name carved in the silver grapeleaf suspended from its neck, iced champagne, deftly poured by the waiters into gold-trace or Bohemian glasses. . . .

Candles in candelabras and chandeliers illuminated the room. Supper was followed by dancing until dawn. Just before the guests left, they were given plates of hot gumbo and cups of strong coffee in preparation for the often long carriage ride to their own plantations.[7]

Even a reception could involve great effort and expense. On March 4, 1851, the Ridgely family of Hampton, a short distance north of Baltimore, gave one which their records show was no small affair. Twenty-four chickens were bought for a salad, as well as twenty-nine partridges, five pheasants, ten turkeys, a twenty-five pound round of spiced beef, two boxes of mushrooms, twelve sweetbreads, twelve gallons of opened oysters for stewing, four bushels of oysters for pickling, five dozen terrapins, twenty dozen rolls, four dozen loaves of bread, four salted tongues, three boiled hams, and twelve heads of lettuce. For dessert the hosts provided four Charlotte Russes, two Russian creams, two "swans," six "swans" in meringue, twenty-four quarts of ice cream and water ice, five gallons of punch, twelve pounds of cakes, eight pounds of grapes, a box of oranges, and a box of lemons. To drink, in addition to the punch, there were seven dozen bottles of champagne, six bottles of Madeira, six of brandy, and six of whiskey. The total bill, including the payment of servants, came to $328.86, a huge sum for the day.[8]

The quality of the cooking at the great entertainments was often high because of the widespread use of caterers or cooks hired for the occasion. Philip Hone in New York City lamented in 1829 the death of "the celebrated cook Simon" who had long been the fashionable cook in the city and whose loss would "be felt on all occasions of large dinners and evening parties."[9]

Although it was still uncommon, some parties were given at restaurants. Ward McAllister, the wealthy, epicurean leader of New York society, organized a series of successful cotillion dinners at Delmonico's, each limited to less than 100 people. It was after one of these that the Earl of Rosebery, who on his first visit to New York had been the guest in many great mansions, commented that "you Americans have made a mistake, your emblematic bird should have been a canvasback, not an eagle."[10]

Not all entertainments of the rich involved a surfeit of food and drink. William Douglas, a wealthy New Yorker, gave a number of parties during Andrew Jackson's administration that were called *"déjeuners à la fourchette."* To Philip Hone they seemed an island of good taste and elegance in the sea of vulgarity sweeping the country. The guests came at one o'clock in the afternoon and stayed until four enjoying music, dancing, and a two o'clock "breakfast" of coffee and chocolate, light dishes of meat, ice cream, confectionery, lemonade, and French and German wines.[11]

The tea parties which had appeared during the eighteenth century continued. A tea might be no more than the steaming pot and biscuits or, as Frances Trollope discovered in Cincinnati, there could be tea or coffee together with hot cakes, custards, hoe-cake, johnnycake, waffle cake, dodger cake, pickled peaches, preserved cucumbers, ham, turkey, hung beef, applesauce, and pickled oysters.[12] Sometimes a tea party substituted for supper and was followed by songs, instrumental music, and a "sprightly" dance. In 1855 a visitor in Jacksonville, Florida, from Connecticut was intrigued by the use of small card tables to which slaves brought tea, milk, sugar, oysters, and cake among other things.

In Charlottesville, Virginia, however, afternoon teas disappeared by the 1840s and callers were given a small glass of Madeira and plain cake, iced cake being allowed only in the evening.[13]

As during the eighteenth century, city dwellers took gay excursions into the countryside to enjoy particular foods. New Yorkers, thirty or forty men and women together, would go to the East River to dine at a tavern, drink tea in the afternoon, fish, and otherwise enjoy themselves until evening. Then, in pairs, they returned to the city in Italian chaises, each man giving his companion an appropriate salute at the Kissing Bridge about three miles from the city.[14] Turtle feasts pleased all among the well-to-do. In Newport a slave named Cuffy Cockroach was rated the best cook for these and was rented for the purpose.[15]

Some fine restaurants and taverns at Roxbury, Brighton, and Cambridge were goals for Bostonians throughout the year. During the snow season, sleighing parties were organized. If the party was a large one, it took a huge sleigh bearing a name like Cleopatra's Galley or The Mayflower. Each held up to forty persons and was lined with black bearskins and carried rugs and wrappers to keep everyone warm. The summer traffic to the same places was described by an English traveler as "the great equestrian feature of New England . . . the gaiety of the carriages, the caparison of the horses, the hilarity of the company, their natural tendency towards the good things of this life, with the fullest determination to assail them — the high-road race, the side-road inn, the strife and the shout, the victory and the defeat." The dinner at the end of the trip could be incidental or the real goal. When on January 14, 1853, twenty men went to a dinner at Taft's Hotel in West Roxbury, they ate venison with grape and currant jelly and eighteen kinds of birds, including, if the menu is to be believed, wild turkey and grouse from Illinois, brant from Delaware, spruce partridge from Canada, sprig-tail ducks from Georgia, mallard ducks from North Carolina, together with wild geese, canvasback ducks, and other varieties of duck, teal, quail, and partridge.[16]

Each city had its favorite sites for rural outings. Citizens of Washington, Alexandria, and Georgetown went to the falls of the Potomac River for picnics, sometimes on a hired canal boat, while the young people of Charleston, South Carolina, took their baskets to Sullivan's Island. A summer pastime of Philadelphians was to go to a country tavern for a catfish supper, and Cincinnatians took carriages to a garden about three miles from the city where they were served strawberries and cream.[17]

In the South, particularly, the barbecue remained popular. It was usually given by an individual or group, and invitations might go to selected families or an entire neighborhood. In Virginia, according to one man, early on the selected day slaves were sent to an oak grove with a wagonload of young pigs, several lambs, some fine old whiskey, a supply of wine, tablecloths, plates, knives, forks, and bread. Pits were dug, fires started, cooking begun, and a place cleared for dancing. When the guests arrived, with the women dressed in white with scarlet shawls, games were played and the feast eaten. Then followed hours of dancing the Virginia reel, until the weary older guests departed, leaving the younger ones to return home by moonlight. The slaves, with what was left of the barbecue, went to a nearby grove where with fiddle and banjo they enjoyed their own party.[18]

There were also political barbecues, announced by placards which listed the speakers and invited all to come. When these took place in the fall, cider was the common drink, but otherwise beer was usual. Such a barbecue could be huge, as that held in Joneswood, New York, in 1860 on behalf of Stephen A. Douglas, candidate for president against Lincoln, Bell, and Breckenridge, where a crowd estimated at from 20,000 to 30,000 gathered. This was far too many for the whole roasted steer, sheep, calf, and pig and the 500 barrels of beer. A foreign visitor reported a "veritable wallow of food on which the famished mob leaped like a pack of wild animals," and the New York *Times* told of a "pulling and hauling at greasy bones and gravy-soaked fibre, a melee over the rind of pork, a tossing of crackers and bread and meat hither and thither, and the barbecue was ended."[19]

Another kind of picnic that was popular in coastal areas, especially in New England, was the chowder party. By the 1820s such parties were common in the Boston area and were held at least as far south as Virginia. Boston harbor was a popular place for "a chowder," and the guests would catch fish, collect shellfish, and make the chowder and other dishes on the spot.[20] Like the barbecue, the chowder party was sometimes a political affair, as in Rhode Island in 1848 when 10,000 people gathered for one.[21]

Food was also a focus of entertainment throughout the farming and frontier parts of America. The loneliness of rural life made any coming together of people pleasurable, and the hospitality that has always been strong among country people was expressed in food and drink.

Much of the social life of this farm world was tied up with the cooperative labor that was both efficient and pleasant. The variety of such gatherings was as great as the number of large-scale, difficult, or monotonous tasks of a rural community or farm.

The corn shucking or husking party was one of the most common of these work-play bees. For this fall task farm families gathered at each other's homes in rotation. They sat among the gathered corn in the barn and husked the ears, all the time singing, gossiping, exchanging information, engaging in repartee, and carrying on flirtations. The finder of a red ear might claim a kiss from a girl but, one Ohioan remembered, "I never knew it to be necessary to produce a red ear to secure a kiss where there was a disposition to give or take one." In Illinois, a red ear gave the discoverer a long pull at the whiskey jug, which circulated continuously anyway, though it was held disgraceful to drink too much. After the husking was completed, the host gave a dinner — which in Kentucky would include a burgoo stew, a highly seasoned thick stew of various meats and vegetables — after which the company danced and talked. The meals were always hearty, not only because the hostess's generosity and skill were on display, but because the fall season meant the chickens were plump, the pigs were fat, and a number of fresh vegetables were at hand.[22]

On the larger plantations of the South there were corn huskings for the slaves alone. These were grostesque perversions of the event, for they induced the slaves to work during hours when they would otherwise have had leisure. The huskings took place at night, and the slaves, singing while they worked, husked the corn and then went to the plantation kitchen where a special meal awaited them. A song of the slaves revealed an anticipation of food and fun, and possibly an attempt to influence the planter:

All dem purty gals will be dar,
  Shuck dat corn before you eat,
Dey will fix it fer us rare,
  Shuck dat corn before you eat,

160

I know dat supper will be big,
  Shuck dat corn before you eat,
I think I smell a fine roast pig,
  Shuck dat corn before you eat,
I hope dey'll have some whisky dar,
  Shuck dat corn before you eat,
I think I'll fill my pockets full,
  Shuck dat corn before you eat.[23]

One witness to a slave husking "feast" mentioned only thick soup and limited amounts of whiskey and peach brandy. The supper was followed by a dance.[24]

Innumerable other rural frolics or bees linked work and the pleasures of food and drink: logrolling, hog-killing, stump pulling, house-raising, flax pulling, reaping, sap collecting, sugaring-off, wood chopping, apple-butter "biling," plowing contests, races among mowers, cradlers, or hacklers, road clearings, and new-road building. Women gathered to sew, make quilts, or spin. The upper Mississippi Valley knew walnut cracks, and throughout the northern states there were bees where women pared, quartered, cored, and strung apples to be hung to dry for the winter supply. These apple bees declined as hand-cranked apple-paring machines multiplied during the 1840s and 1850s.

At all of these bees the work was usually followed by a meal, or at least substantial refreshments, provided by the host family, though at house-raisings the guests might bring the food if the family being aided was newly arrived and without provisions.[25]

Church bees helped many an underpaid clergyman feed his family. Women of one church took over the parsonage on a given day and prepared a feast for the congregation of doughnuts, floating islands, piles of cheese, loads of rich cakes and bread, "oceans" of cream, plates of frizzled beef, smoked turkey, fried oysters, roast chicken, butter, brandied peaches, preserved plums, ginger, strawberries, tea, coffee, and iced water. As they departed, the "friendly invaders" left behind for the minister's family a side of bacon, a cask of butter, some fine cheeses, a load or two of flour, a bag of buckwheat and another of cornmeal, a barrel of sugar, a chest of tea, and a cask of molasses.[26]

Among the more picturesque country gatherings were the sugaring-off parties of New England, upper New York, and Ohio.

During the early spring the sap of the sugar maples was gathered and boiled in great kettles at night in forest groves. Spruce boughs provided couches in the snow for the young men and women who waited until the sap boiled down to the sugaring-off point when it could be placed on the snow to harden into sugar.[27] In the Catskill Mountains descendants of the Dutch invited the entire neighborhood to these parties. A "sumptuous feast" was followed by dancing to the music of a fiddle, and whiskey and maple sugar kept the dancers going until after sunrise.[28]

Throughout the country most social events were small, unpublicized, and so anonymous that the eraser of time has left only glimpses of them. A New Yorker remembered that as of about 1816 visiting during the evening hours was general. In the winter families would meet together for quilting parties and entertainments where hickory nuts, apples, new cider, and doughnuts were served, and sometimes a whiskey punch that had been sweetened with guava jelly. At evening parties for the young there were doughnuts, crullers, apples, hickory nuts, and cider. Boiling and pulling molasses candy was part of the fun.[29] Parties of the young were often called, appropriately, "kissing parties." At these, dancing was interspersed with games at each of which every girl would be kissed at least once.[30]

When young people got together in North Carolina refreshments might be only persimmon beer and roasted sweet potatoes or, at dances, cider, blackberry acid, and mint slings for the women and whiskey or brandy for the men.[31] In the Louisiana delta the Acadians of the early nineteenth century loved to dance and, it was said, needed only several fiddles for music, four candles for light, and some wooden benches to sit on. Tafia, a low-quality rum diluted with water, was drunk and a gumbo served for food.[32]

Marriages invariably included food and drink for the guests. Among the middle and upper classes the wedding cake, usually covered with icing, was a tradition. At times it resembled a fruit cake. When Margaret Bayard Smith, a socially prominent Philadelphia girl, married in September 1800, she did not serve what remained of her wedding cake until the following November at a tea. Often a pound cake was used for weddings, though by the late 1850s the lady cake, which was a white cake, and plum cake were becoming more common. In New England, at least, each guest at the wedding was given a piece of the cake to take home: "The young ladies, it is said, place this cake under their pillows, and then dream of their future lovers."[33]

Country weddings sometimes involved great efforts on the part of the bride's family, and the preparation of the wedding dinner might take days. In Ohio or Indiana long tables of boards supported by wooden horses, placed outdoors if the weather permitted, sagged under the weight of roast beef, pork, turkey, cakes, pies, crullers, numerous vegetables, pickles, preserves, and sauces. An immense pot pie which might contain six hens, two roosters, four pullets, and a half-peck of onions dominated the table. A dance followed the dinner. On the day after the wedding the "infare" would be held at the groom's house where the same guests would enjoy more food and dancing.[34]

On some southern plantations the marriage of slaves was followed by a dinner. An Episcopalian minister married six slave couples at a plantation on the Santee River, South Carolina, in 1843, after which the bridal party had a dinner of venison, wild ducks, ham and rice, pound cakes, custards and coffee, while at a distance the other slaves were given venison and rice.[35]

Holidays also called for special foods. In New England states when the governor took his seat "with pomp and rejoicing" all the housewives competed in making Election cakes. At town meeting time in March in New England, both housewives and bakeries made "Meetin' cakes," each about the size of a pancake.[36]

The Fourth of July was celebrated nationally. On some southern plantations even the slaves were given a barbecue to mark this day of freedom. In the larger cities the populace turned out on the streets. A Bostonian remembered that about 1830 Boston Common would be surrounded by every kind of booth on July 4, "where were sold all manner of abominable and indigestible concoctions, to eat and to drink, and everybody seemed to buy them." About twenty years later a visitor to the same city wrote that on Independence Day the Bostonians drank cobblers and juleps and were faced with "wildernesses of crackers, pyramids of edibles, mountains of lollypops."[37] The celebration of the day was similar in New York City, as Captain Marryat observed in 1837:

On each side of the whole length of Broadway were ranged booths and stands, similar to those at an English fair, and on which were displayed small plates of oysters, with a fork stuck in the board opposite to each plate; clams sweltering in the hot sun; pineapples, boiled hams, pies, puddings, barley-sugar, and many other indescribables. But what was remarkable, Broadway being three miles long, and the booths lining each side of it, in every booth there was a roast pig, large or small, as the centre attraction. Six miles of roast pig! and that in New York City alone; and roast pig in every other city, town, hamlet, and village in the Union. What association can there be between roast pig and independence? Let it not be supposed that there was any deficiency in the very necessary articles of potation on this auspicious day: no! the booths were loaded with porter, ale, cider, mead, brandy, wine, ginger-beer, mint juleps, besides many other compounds, to name which nothing but the luxuriance of American-English could invent a word.[38]

New Year's Day was another secular holiday that was observed nationwide. In New York City, early in the century, the mayor and other city officials had held open house on January 1 and generally, as one man noted, "All the complimentary visits, fun, and merriment of the season seem to be reserved for this day."[39] In time the "complimentary visits" played the principal role in the day's activities, at least among all who had social pretensions. The women remained at home to entertain, while the men went forth on foot, by carriage, or by sleigh if there was snow, to visit as many homes of friends and acquaintances as possible. At each house the women, dressed in their best, received the visitors and offered them wine, cake, and such delicacies as chicken salads, lobster salads, and pickled oysters. The visits were a time to heal personal differences, the day being one of "kindness and reconciliation" in which small quarrels were to be forgotten and trifling injuries forgiven.[40] Throughout the city the bakers made New Year's cakes with raised figures, very popular with children, while the bars offered free drinks to steady customers. By night, one man noticed, the city's streets "offer a slightly Bacchic and eccentric spectacle."[41]

Similar New Year's customs existed throughout the country. In cities everywhere women stayed at home to receive the peripatetic men. In the South the eggnog was the principal refreshment. Guests in St. Louis, however, received small crunchy pastries called *croquignoles* and glasses of cordial, reflecting the city's French origins. In far-off San Francisco the women received in ball gowns, and tables were loaded with terrapin, chicken salads, sandwiches, eggnogs, wines, and coffee. The homes of the social leaders from the South were especially festive.[42]

The observance of Christmas was not universal. In New England, only the Episcopalians and some Roman Catholics paid any attention to it. Among Congregationalists the Puritan disdain for this "papist" holiday persisted, and not only were the schools kept open but most Protestants ostentatiously went about their usual business on Christmas.[43]

Elsewhere, special foods marked the day. Those of Dutch or German origin or descent made cookies with recipes long handed down. Some were fashioned with tin cookie cutters to resemble animals, and those who had springerle boards made cookies representing a deer, a rose, a castle, and so on. The Pennsylvania Dutch might make paper-thin sand tarts, the *lebkuchen,* a chewy, citron-flavored cookie, and even macaroons.[44] Some Pennsylvanians of British descent gave goose pies as Christmas presents. These, probably descendants of the famous Yorkshire Christmas pie, had a standing crust and contained goose, chicken, pigeon, and various other things. By 1857, however, Eliza Leslie labeled the custom "old-fashioned" and "obsolete."[45]

Throughout the South the planters celebrated Christmas with a large dinner. Such a feast in South Carolina in 1839 was described by a young Episcopalian minister who was invited to a plantation between Charleston and Beaufort:

> About 4 P.M. — about 20 sat down to a table groaning under a Load of Beef, Venison, Ham, Ducks, Turkey, Chickens, Oyster pie, Hog, hominy, rice and sweet potatoes — wine — Brandy — Cordial and Gin — The Cloth was removed (except the Liquers) and a 2d. course came on, plum pudding, mince, coconut and various other descriptions of pies, whips, custards, jellies of a great variety — with other good things to match. After this came the 3d course of viands, cake and various liquers — wine and cordials.[46]

Hotels gave Christmas Day dinners of equally stupefying proportions. Any guest at Louisville's Galt House on Christmas in 1856 could choose from saddle of venison, rib of bear "with fancy sause," wild turkey, stuffed red-head duck, wood duck with hunter's sauce, wild goose, bridge of buffalo tongue, arcade of pheasants, four soups, two fishes, fifteen vegetables, and a surfeit of desserts including Charlotte Russe, all for a charge of fifty cents.[47]

The slaves were not overlooked at Christmas. Many were given from four to six days' relief from the ban on visiting other plantations, and a large feast was prepared for them on Christmas Day. On the large plantations whole steers, hogs, or sheep were cooked, and the slaves were given such treats as peach cobbler or apple dumplings and often enough liquor to get drunk if they chose. During the holidays there might be both dances and athletic competitions.[48]

While most New Englanders ignored Christmas, they made up for it by their celebration of Thanksgiving, a custom that was carried across the country by westward-moving emigrants. It was a day set aside by individual state governors until 1863 when President Lincoln proclaimed it a national holiday.

When Fredrika Bremer visited New England in 1849 she tried to discover the origins of Thanksgiving and was told that early in the history of Massachusetts, when hunger existed, five ships had arrived from England with wheat. It became the custom on that day, she was told, to place five grains of corn on the dinner plate of each person to commemorate the event, a practice that was said to continue still in certain parts of the state at the time of her visit.[49]

Like the Christmas dinners, those on Thanksgiving Day were lavish, with an emphasis on meats and desserts, the season preventing any great variety of vegetables. A Thanksgiving dinner in a private home in Geneva, New York, in 1831 contained five different meats and eleven desserts, but otherwise only potatoes, yams, succotash, and pickles.[50]

Shaped by the season and tradition, Thanksgiving dinner began to take on a definite form. Fredrika Bremer found that roast turkey and pumpkin "pudding" were the two indispensable dishes for the day.[51] Nearly as obligatory as turkey was chicken pie, a fall dish that would long remain popular in New England when winter approached and food for chickens became a problem. Harriet Beecher Stowe remembered her childhood Thanksgivings of about 1820 in Litchfield, Connecticut, as the "king and high priest of all festivals." For up to a week in advance the children would be put to chopping mince for pies and pounding cinnamon, allspice, and cloves in the great mortar. Pie making, not only for Thanksgiving but for the entire winter, took place at this time, and dozens, if not hundreds, of pies were put into a cold storehouse. The dinner itself saw the turkey, chickens, chicken pies, and an "endless" variety of vegetables all put on the table at once. "There was much carving and laughing and talking and eating, and all showed that cheerful ability to despatch the provisions which was the ruling spirit of the hour." Then came the plum puddings and finally the overpowering array of pies. Edward Everett Hale, the author, remembered that there were always four kinds of pie, including a lemon-flavored Marlborough pie, and each housekeeper was convinced that her grandmother had left the best possible recipe for this. To have introduced ice creams or sherbets "or any other kickshaws of that variety" into the Thanksgiving dinner, he added, was unthinkable.[52]

With few changes the Thanksgiving dinners of this time would continue for a century or more to come.

⚜ 12 ⚜
The Regions, 1800-1860

I sat down to a dinner of hog, hominy, rice and sweet potatoes.

By the middle years of the nineteenth century regionalism in the diet stood out more clearly than would ever again be the case. There were several reasons for this. Settlement eastward of the Great Plains was mature enough for soils, climates, and populations to have interacted into unique sectional patterns. Too, the railroads and refrigeration had not yet given national distribution to fresh foods, nor had the sale of prepared foods under brand names become large. In 1850 most Americans depended upon local sources for their foods and prepared them much as their parents had done before.

A great part of the regional cooking of the time was of native origin, for foreign influences were relatively weak at this moment of history: The War of Independence and the War of 1812 had loosened ties with England; only a few wealthy and worldly people yet felt the influence of the French cuisine; the heavy influx of Irish and Germans in the 1840s was too recent to have carried great weight; and the other immigrations from Europe and Asia were still slight.

In New England many lived close to the sea and ate from it. Few places matched the Try Pots Inn of Nantucket in Herman Melville's *Moby Dick* where it was chowder for breakfast, chowder for dinner, and chowder for supper, but many families ate fish for Saturday dinner with the leftovers for Sunday breakfast and others ate fish nearly every day. A description of a Cape Codder's meals listed "at breakfast, fish; at dinner, fish — fish fried, broiled, boiled, baked, and chowdered!"[1] Fish cakes, fish balls, and fish hash, all combining fish and potatoes, and creamed codfish were familiar dishes.

New Englanders betrayed their British heritage by eating heavily of beef, lamb, and mutton and the broths from boiling each of them. Although the use of pork declined, it was still salted for winter fare and used to flavor such dishes as baked beans, chowder, fried fish, boiled fowls, leg of mutton, dried peas, mush, some pies and cakes, and various vegetables, as well as making part of the "pork and 'lasses" combination.

Dried peas, dried beans, and corn all gave bulk to New England meals in the form of mush, samp, pork and beans ("very popular" wrote Eliza Leslie), succotash, and various porridges. These were not always simple dishes. A bean porridge made in northern New Hampshire early in the century consisted of corned beef, white beans, cornmeal, hulled corn, and salt and pepper. Succotash made in Plymouth, Massachusetts, for the annual "Forefathers' Day" dinner combined salt pork, corned beef, chicken, turnips, potatoes, white beans, and hulled corn.[2]

New Englanders ate many boiled dishes, perhaps because for several stoveless centuries they had needed fires in their fireplaces during seven to nine months of the year, providing a daylong heat for the great iron pots. The boiled dinner, a full meal in itself, was a New England institution and consisted of meat in a boiling pot to which a number of vegetables were added in sequence so that all might mingle their flavors and be done at the same time.

For flavoring, New Englanders used not only butter, maple sugar, and pork, but molasses which still flowed into their port cities from the West Indies. Cranberry sauce might appear in any dinner but was especially liked with fowl. Apples, both fresh and dried, went into many dishes, including puddings and pies.

The New England breads reflected the environment. Harriet Beecher Stowe, who sprang to fame in 1852 by writing *Uncle Tom's Cabin*, characterized the "rye 'n injun" bread of New England as the result of what grew best on the hard and stony soil, "but I can inform all whom it may concern that rye and Indian bread smoking hot, on a cold winter morning, together with savory sausages, pork, and beans, formed a breakfast fit for a king, if the king had earned it by getting up in a cold room, washing in ice-water, tumbling through snow-drifts, and foddering cattle."[3] Another writer described the same bread as dark, glutinous, and heavy but added that it was still preferred over the best wheat loaves, and not by "plain people" only.[4]

Both light and dark rye breads were widely used in New England, and William Alcott claimed that rye bread was eaten by thousands of people including distinguished literary men. Another common bread, known as "the third bread," consisted of wheat, rye, and corn, a third part of each. Corn was used by itself in some breads, as well as in pancakes. Among the latter was the Rhode Island jonnycake (the local spelling) which was made of water-ground white cornmeal, salt, boiling water, and milk.[5]

The Middle Atlantic states — New York, New Jersey, Pennsylvania, and Delaware — were so diverse in population and geography that they did not comprise a unified culinary region. They did share a longer growing season and better soils than New England, and through much of the area wheat and rye grew well as did most vegetables, fruits, and all forms of livestock.

The most distinctive and persistent pattern of cooking in the Middle Atlantic states was that of the so-called Pennsylvania Dutch. These were the Amish, the Dunkards, Mennonites, and other Protestant sects, most of which were descended from the German Anabaptists. Unlike the majority of the Pennsylvania Germans who were assimilated into the general population, these sects largely cut off contacts with the outside world and lived among themselves. One result of this self-imposed isolation was that their eating habits persisted with little change from one generation to the next.

On the whole the foods of the Pennsylvania Dutch were those of farm people who lived isolated and self-sustaining lives. As in all rural areas they depended in winter on preserved and pickled foods, dried and smoked meats, and provisions which could be stored.[6] Their meals showed a passionate love of pork and tended to be heavy with numerous fried foods and doughy dishes such as dumplings in dozens of forms. Like their German forebears, they considered soup a main dish. They made puddings from scraps of pork, liver, and sometimes beef. As byproducts of their slaughtering they made an assortment of sausages, as well as scrapple, aspic, pepperpot, headcheese, souse, and pickled pigs' feet. Among the vegetables, fresh cabbage and the sauerkraut made from it were frequently on the table. They employed more Jerusalem artichokes than did other ethnic groups, and white potatoes were used in soups, salads, pretzels, fritters, and bread.

When they extended hospitality to guests, a lavish number of side dishes appeared in conformity with the centuries-old tradition of "seven sweets and seven sours." These included such things as ginger pears, jams, honeys, apple butter, marmalade, sweet watermelon pickle, chowchow, and pickled oysters.[7] Apple butter was made yearly in huge quantities and eaten as part of every meal. A traveler found that in summer cottage cheese, or smearcase, which was cottage cheese thinned with cream and seasoned, "must not be absent from a table."[8]

The Pennsylvania Dutch housewives were indefatigable bakers. They had more recipes for cakes than for any other category of food, and they cultivated the art of pie-making, using deep earthenware pie plates. Their coffee cakes and breakfast cakes included the cinnamon bun, the potato bun, the shoofly pie, and the Moravian bun.[9] A woman who visited a Pennsylvania Dutch home in the 1820s reported that "they can prepare all manner of baked goods, *Lebkuchen,* pastry, and cake: in short, everything which belongs in the realm of delicate gluttony they understand well."[10]

Still different food and drink habits appeared in the South Atlantic states. Contemporaries attempted easy generalizations. A Connecticut man in South Carolina noted that "I sat down to a dinner of hog, hominy, rice and sweet potatoes, the standing fare of the South."[11] Governor Hammond of South Carolina listed corn bread and bacon, with fresh meat at times, a moderate use of fresh vegetables, and coffee as the habitual foods of the great body of Southerners.[12] But innumerable local differences existed. A stagecoach driver in Florida in the 1850s congratulated a passenger on escaping from eastern Florida, the land of "hog and hominy," and entering central Florida, the land of "sowins and chickens." Sowins was a corruption of sourings, pounded corn soured by baking in the sun.[13]

The art of cooking reached high levels in Baltimore and in some of the plantation kitchens of Maryland and eastern Virginia. In 1859 Oliver Wendell Holmes, the writer, physician, and father of the jurist, lauded Baltimore as "the gastronomic metropolis of the Union," an accolade that New Orleans might have protested.[14] Those parts of Maryland and Virginia that bordered Chesapeake Bay and the deep rivers that entered it depended heavily for their delicacies on shad, oysters, shrimp, crabs, terrapin, and wild ducks, notably the much-lauded canvasback and greenback ducks. Recipes carrying the name of Baltimore or Maryland were to spread throughout the country for planked shad, terrapin stew, beaten biscuits, hashed chicken, and fried chicken among other things.[15]

Epicures of Maryland and Virginia paid an astonishing amount of attention to the terrapin. Baltimoreans engaged in rivalry with Philadelphians on how the tortoises should be stewed. In the Baltimore black stew the terrapin was cooked in a chafing dish with salt, pepper, and Madeira, while the Philadelphians adopted the Trenton stew from an old eating club in Trenton, New Jersey, using fresh butter and cream.[16]

The cooking in the wealthy homes of Virginia and Maryland, as throughout the South, was done by slave women and occasionally by slave men. With so large a body of full-time professional cooks, it is understandable that many were highly proficient and some proved to be sensitive artists in the kitchen. The latter were greatly prized. A woman in Middleburg, Virginia, in 1849 wrote her sister about the retention of a slave named Judy during the dispersal of a family estate. "She is a fine cook," she wrote, "and there were a great many wealthy gentlemen wanting her, said they wouldn't stop at any price. If she had been put up to the highest bidder, such bidding never would have been known in this part of the world."[17]

In the coastal plantation areas of the Carolinas and Georgia, with Charleston, Beaufort, and Savannah as centers, the meals of the rice and cotton planters showed an appreciation of good cooking. Rice, a staple crop, appeared not only at breakfast with fresh butter or mixed with a soft-boiled egg, but at dinner with gravy or added to bacon and red peas to make "Hoppin' John." Rice was used in soups, pilaus, puddings, and croquettes among other forms, and rice flour went into bread, biscuits, cakes, and waffles.[18] Corn also was used in countless recipes, and in Sarah Rutledge's *The Carolina Housewife, or House and Home* of 1847, rice and corn figured in nearly 100 of the 550 recipes.[19]

Carolina and Georgia cooks, like those of Virginia and Maryland, made much use of oysters, crabs, and shrimp. In addition to terrapin, the small turtle called the cooter was also eaten. These were gathered along the streams by slaves who looked on the flesh with aversion but sold them to their masters. South Carolina meals included sweet potatoes, eggplants, and foods little known to the northward: peanuts, figs, shaddocks, palmetto cabbage, okra, and benne seeds. Outsiders did not always adjust easily. The Philadelphia-raised mother-in-law of Mary Chesnut, the diarist, could not, after sixty-five years in South Carolina, "like hominy for breakfast and rice for dinner, without a relish to give it some flavor. She cannot eat watermelons and sweet potatoes freely" or "hot cornbread at discretion and hot buttered biscuits without any."[20]

Ward McAllister, a New York social leader, remembered fondly "everyday" dishes he had known as a youth in the Savannah and Charleston areas: pilau, made of boiled chickens and a large piece of bacon laid on a bed of rice; "Hoppin' John," or cowpeas with bacon; okra soup, a constant dish; shrimp and prawn pie; crab salad; pompey head, a stuffed filet of veal; roast quail or snipe; and during the spring, shad daily — boiled, broiled, and baked. An influence of the West Indies, from which many of the early settlers had come, was evident. When McAllister visited the islands he decided that two familiar dishes, crab Creole and stuffed eggplant, which the Carolinians had considered of African origin, were instead from the West Indies. As for terrapin stew, McAllister remembered it as "a dish for the gods, and a standard party dish in days when a Charleston and Savannah party was an event to live for." Some of the fine slave cooks on plantations had been sent to Jones's, or some other of the best Charleston eating houses, for their apprenticeship.[21]

When not giving parties, the affluent of the coastal region ate much as they had during the preceding century of ham, mutton, game, seafoods, hot breads, rice, tropical fruits, and imports from the North, Europe, and the Caribbean. The hot climate limited the use of fresh meat and encouraged the importation of salt pork and corned beef from the northern states.[22] In places, game was very important. Fanny Kemble, the English actress and author who married a Georgia planter, assessed their diet there in the late 1830s as consisting largely of wild ducks, wild geese, wild turkeys, and venison.[23]

Between the southern Appalachians and the Mississippi River and from the Ohio River to the Gulf of Mexico the foods and beverages during the early nineteenth century were those of a frontier. As Virginians, Carolinians, and Georgians pushed into the wilderness they became dependent upon game, nuts, wild fruits, and wild honey. In the brief time the buffalo lasted the tongues, humps, marrow bones, and other choice parts were considered treats. The elk were also quickly killed off, but venison remained a staple for a long time, and there were wild turkeys, beavers (the tails were prized), possums, bears, rabbits, squirrels, swans, geese, and other wild fowl. Bear's fat was for long used for cooking.[24]

As quickly as possible the settlers cleared land, planted corn and truck gardens, and obtained a few hogs and chickens. As game grew scarce, pork became the principal meat. Pork and corn were the two major foods of the southern frontier, with sweet potatoes and turnips following. Those who had a cow could have fresh milk and from the surplus make butter, buttermilk, and clabber. Along the Gulf Coast the diet was different. In touch with the West Indies, with rice from both Louisiana and the Georgia-South Carolina rice mills, and with access to fish, shellfish, and tropical fruits and vegetables, the Gulf Coast in time developed a cookery, replete with pilaus and jambalayas, that resembled the Creole cuisine of lower Louisiana.

The southern trans-Appalachian region had a few unique dishes. Settlers in Mississippi adopted the Indian dish sofkee, which they renamed Tom Fuller. It was made of certain nuts added to corn, peas, dry venison, and beans. The result was a thick dish very like the succotash of northern tribes.[25] In Kentucky and Tennessee a favorite for special occasions was burgoo, a pot pie of vegetables and such game as turkey, venison, and squirrel, all highly seasoned and cooked in a large kettle.[26] But the average frontier settler was more likely to eat as one Colonel Creecy did in Mississippi during the mid-1830s: "Rusty salt pork, boiled or fried . . . and musty corn-meal dodgers, rarely a vegetable of any description, no milk, butter, eggs, or the semblance of a condiment — was my fare often for weeks at a time."[27]

Throughout this entire region corn breads were eaten without thought that there existed other kinds. Corn was ground at mills or, in more frontier regions, each family crushed its own in

174

a handmill.[28] The conversion of cornmeal into bread could be simplicity itself. An ashcake was made by mixing meal with water, adding some salt, and forming small pones which were wrapped in corn shucks and covered with hot ashes and embers in the fireplace. A hoecake was similar, except that it was toasted before the fire on a clean board, a piece of metal, or, outdoors, on a rock sloped toward the fire. What was called a corn pone was similar except that it was baked in an oven and the dough might have been raised with yeast — often a "pearl ash" from burned corncobs. When the same combination of meal, salt, and water was formed into lumps and thrown into boiling water until cooked, it was known as a corn dodger. The name, which probably came from the lively motion given the morsel by the boiling water, was retained even when the same pieces were baked.[29]

In New Orleans and its vicinity neither corn bread nor pork dominated the eating habits. Here Creole cooking was, after a century or more, attaining maturity and fame. It was a cuisine of complicated origins that used French cooking as a point of departure but did not disdain the contributions of native Indians, Spanish, slaves from Africa, West Indians, Germans, Mexicans, and immigrants from elsewhere in the United States. It was certainly the French who made New Orleans a city where food and cooking were subjects of polite conversation. Only in New Orleans would journalists notice the first strawberries, pompano, or green peas of the season.[30]

The city's location encouraged a rich and varied cookery. The semitropical climate provided a wide range of fruits and vegetables, fish, and crustaceans. Other foods were available from the West Indies, the East Coast of the United States, and Europe and by flatboats and steamboats from the continent's interior.

Lower Louisiana was a rice-growing region, and a visitor early in the century noted the "prodigious" consumption of rice. Every Creole dinner included rice which could be served simply with gravy, mixed with red beans, added to gumbo, joined with a fish or meat in jambalaya, pilaus, and croquettes, or made into hot cakes. It was the basic ingredient of a variety of desserts.[31]

Wealthy Creoles imported what they could not obtain locally. A visitor to New Orleans early in the century found that olive oil was first among the imports, followed by such things as vermicelli and other forms of pasta, vinegar, liqueurs, sausages, anchovies, pickles, fruits preserved in brandy, and dried fruits. Only the great heat discouraged the purchase of foreign cheeses.[32] As perhaps nowhere else in the country native and foreign foods joined each other on the table. A visitor to a Louisiana plantation just prior to the Civil War noticed at breakfast fish from New Orleans, potted salmon from England, preserved meats from France, and what he took to be vegetable dishes of African origin.[33]

As in most of the South, fresh meat was scarce and of poor quality in New Orleans, making the local fish and shellfish even more important. Crawfish, shrimps, crabs, oysters, turtles, and frogs were all plentiful, and the fish included the highly esteemed pompano, redfish, and rockfish. Crawfish became a major delicacy among the Creoles who as early as 1819 were making a crawfish *bisque*. Fish and shellfish were used to make *bouillabaise*, chowders, gumbos, and jambalayas.[34] The flavoring for these and other dishes was provided by onions, garlic, celery, tomatoes, bay leaves, various peppers, nutmeg, allspice, cloves, and other herbs and spices. Seasonings were often added to a *roux,* a basic part of many Creole dishes made by carefully browning flour in melted butter or lard.

North of the Ohio River between the Appalachian Mountains and the Mississippi River lay the Old Northwest. In the north this was largely settled by New Englanders and New Yorkers and in the south by immigrants from Pennsylvania, Maryland, Virginia, North Carolina, Kentucky, and Tennessee. The first settlers ate for a time the provisions they had brought with them together with wild game and foods gathered in the forest. Corn and hogs then began the move into farming and other livestock. As early as 1806 the Pittsburgh market carried beef, veal, fowls, butter, eggs, and milk, and in 1828 Frances Trollope rated the Cincinnati market equal to any place in the world "for excellence, abundance, and cheapness," though she thought the fruits, especially peaches, were inferior.[35]

Those who lived in the wilderness moved less rapidly toward a full range of foods. Pioneers in Indiana found deer plentiful for the first two decades of the century, as were wild turkeys in the southern part of the state and ducks, geese, brants, and teals in the northern part. As venison became scarce, the settlers ate more squirrels, which until about 1860 were so numerous as to be pests. Many meals were made of pork and turnips boiled together. Cucumbers were grown to make pickles, sage and red peppers to flavor meats, popcorn for the children, and watermelons for everyone. As settlements matured gardens grew in importance, and "seed swappin'" was a social pastime in February and March. On the prairies of northern Illinois, however, vegetables were largely lacking. A woman who lived there during the early 1840s found that meats — venison, quail, grouse, domestic fowl, or bacon — corn dodger, and coffee were the foods of breakfast, dinner, and supper, with fruits, sweetmeats, or pudding with dinner and a fresh baked cake for supper.[36]

As farms replaced frontier cabins, the Old Northwest revealed a different pattern of foods from that of the states below the Ohio River. Wheat began to rival, then eclipsed, corn as a bread grain. Pork receded in favor of beef and veal, and even mutton and lamb were eaten. A greater variety of vegetables was grown than in the South, and Irish potatoes became a northern, as sweet potatoes were a southern, staple. Dairy products were more plentiful than in the South, and butter, rather than pork, flavored vegetables. The more northern parts of the Old Northwest, as progeny of the New England and the Middle Atlantic states, tried to reproduce all the dishes of those regions, and usually did so without trouble. With wheat and with sweetenings provided by wild honey, maple sugar, brown sugar from Louisiana, and sorghum, even the pastries of the older regions were made. The "pie belt" took a large step westward.[37]

When once established on fertile soils that made much of the land in the East seem poor and stingy by comparison, settlers could achieve a supply of food that made them almost dizzy with self-satisfaction. Bragging and smugness alternate in the letter of one Collon Morton of Princeton, Illinois, to a friend in the East in 1842:

> there is about a hundred teems pass here dayley. wheate is worth 25 cents [per bushel] here only; corn is worth 12½ cents, oats the same; potatoes 9 cents. you must think that you could live here! we live high: buter 4 cents per pound, lard fore, chickins 6 cents, beef from one and half to two and half, pork the same. this is the land that flows with milk and honey. my boys have found fore trees of bees this fall. one

man found nineteen trees this fall. . . . I have ten grone hogs, fating six of them. it is a harde mater to give a way shotes here now. . . . grosies have ben cheep this yeare we have every cind of amusement. . . . we shal have plenty of aples and peaches here in a short time. aples were sold here this fall for twenty five cents. the fruit is all graftied fruit that we get here, the finest kind.[38]

This Old Northwest also differed from the lands to the southward in that it attracted an increasing number of immigrants from northern Europe. Large German communities grew in Cincinnati, St. Louis, Chicago, and Milwaukee, and still other Germans took up farming in such states as Illinois and Wisconsin. None of them had trouble in raising or buying the pork, veal, beef, potatoes, rye, wheat, cabbages, onions, apples, and other foods that they needed for their native cooking. In the more northern states and territories the Swedish and Norwegian immigrants missed only saltwater fish. Fredrika Bremer had excellent meals at a Swedish settlement in Wisconsin, and a Norwegian who visited countrymen in that state was served Norwegian dishes, though his hosts admitted that they found the Yankees "made fun of" their eating habits.[39] They weren't the last to suffer from a provincialism that shunted into hiding some of the rich gifts that immigrants could have given to their new country.

Throughout the South the slaves participated only slightly in the regional differences in cookery. Everywhere the slaves ate the food of the poor. They had less variety than the whites, for nearly all game was forbidden them and most other foods were doled out instead of being a matter of choice. The slaves made up a large part of the planter's wealth, and the foods they received were usually in fixed quantities and in set formulas intended to protect this investment and to keep the slaves both healthy and profitably employed. That inadequate nutrition was often the result is understandable, for the age knew little of the subject.

A "model" plantation on the Tombigbee River in Alabama in the mid-1830s gave a weekly allowance to every enslaved man, woman, and child of four pounds of bacon, a peck of cornmeal, a pint of molasses, three salted fish, a supply of fresh meat, when available, and all the vegetables they desired. Slaves could also raise pigs, poultry, and grain for themselves.[40]

Few other plantations were so generous. Throughout most of the South pork and corn were the principal slave foods. A standard weekly allowance on many plantations gave each working hand three pounds of pork, a peck of cornmeal, salt, and sometimes a small amount of molasses. In some places sweet potatoes replaced cornmeal during the winter months. In coastal areas oysters and salt or fresh fish might be partially or wholly substituted for the pork.[41]

There were planters who, like their eighteenth-century predecessors, gave their laborers little or no meat. One man, early in the century, reported that in the low countries of the Carolinas corn was the staple food of the slaves for nine months and yams for the remainder of the year, and "meat they never receive." And Frederick Law Olmsted visited a South Carolina plantation in 1853 where the allowance was a peck of meal or rice each week together with "small stores." The planter claimed that he had found meat harmful to the health of the slaves. Olmsted was not convinced: "The general impression among planters is, that the negroes work much better for being supplied with three or four pounds of bacon a week." On the plantation of Governor William Aiken of South Carolina the slave food was largely grain and vegetables, with meat being provided for only two or three meals each week. And a man who had been a slave in Georgia remembered that the slaves had received "truck that us had on the place, like greens, turnips, peas, side meat, and they sure would cut the side meat awful thin too."[42]

There were sharp differences from one plantation to another. A slave in Texas received a weekly ration of cornmeal, milk, molasses, peas, beans, and meat. Sold to another man, he found the food far better: "There plenty meat and tea and coffee, and white flour. I'd never tasted white flour and coffee, and Mammy fix some biscuits and coffee." Another slave did not forget a kind mistress in North Carolina where there was plenty to eat including sugar, rice, peas, chickens, eggs, beef, "just everything good to eat," and where the children were given johnnycake and buttermilk between meals.[43] An extraordinarily large variety of foods was issued on the Ebenezer Pettigrew plantation in North Carolina. At times collards, rutabagas, corn, tomatoes, okra, and other vegetables were given out, as well as apples, cherries, figs, peaches, berries, and grapes. The meats included chickens, geese, beef, mutton, pork, and sometimes fish. The regular rations included sugar, flour, meal, coffee, and molasses.[44]

During the working day on plantations the slave children were fed separately by an old nurse, commonly from a long trough in the yard. Into this were placed cooked vegetables, corn bread, and pot liquor or milk. The children ran to eat at the summons of a bell or horn. No slave children fed from a trough could ever doubt that they were of an inferior caste.[45]

On many plantations the slaves were allowed, encouraged, or even required to keep small gardens of their own, usually of one-half to one acre per adult male. This was most common in the rice coast plantations where the task system gave the slaves more free time. Such gardens provided fresh vegetables during the summer and fall and root vegetables, squashes, and pumpkins for the winter months. Often there were surpluses that could be sold in a nearby town. This was also true where the slaves were allowed to raise chickens and hogs for themselves. Fredrika Bremer learned that the slaves sold eggs and chickens, and every Christmas a pig as well, and thereby obtained money to buy "truck" or molasses, biscuits, and other foods. In Louisiana slaves commonly sold poultry and eggs to their masters.[46]

The dominant whites looked on slaves and firearms as a dangerous combination, so that game — other than what could be snared or taken with dogs alone — was not usually available to the blacks. Fanny Kemble regretted that the slaves on her husband's plantation in Georgia could not have firearms, for "simple traps do not do much havoc among birds — but there are many partridges, snipes, wild ducks about here — and their allowance of rice and Indian meal would not be worse for such additions."[47] Still, wildlife did find its way into the slave quarters: Children fished for catfish; rabbits were snared or caught when new ground was being cleared; and dogs were used to take opossums, highly rated as a delicacy, and raccoons. Squirrels were trapped and boiled or made into squirrel pie to be served with dumplings. "Possums?" one ex-slave remembered in Louisiana, "Sure, we ate plenty of 'em. We'd clean 'em and wash 'em, parboil 'em, then roast them on hot coals 'long side sweet potatoes. You could dry 'em too, by smokin' 'em like hams."[48]

The poverty and monotony of their diet drove slaves to maneuver as best they could within the system to obtain more and better food. Some plantations, an ex-slave in Alabama remembered, "half-starved their niggers and 'lowanced out their eating till they wasn't fitting for work. They had to slip about to niggers on other places to piece out their meals." When they could, slaves took what they were not given. This was justified by the perfect logic that since they belonged to their masters they could not steal from them — they only transferred the location of his property. Women who cooked at the big house would make large pockets under their dresses for coffee, sugar, and other things. A slave sent to the mill could carry an extra sack for some meal or flour, or slaves would take hams, lard, flour, and chickens as opportunity offered. One man recalled that a "preacher" came to the slave quarters to tell the blacks that they should not steal their master's turkeys, chickens, hogs, or meat.[49]

At times small treats were given the slaves. If the "white folks" had a camp meeting or barbecue the slaves would be given what was not eaten. On a plantation near New Orleans any leftovers in the big house were carried off by slave children to the ill and aged slaves. During hog-killing time the spareribs, backbone, jowl, feet, souse, liver, and chitterlings might be given the slaves for immediate consumption. On the Fourth of July and Christmas they might receive a barbecue or at least extra rations. A new arrival in South Carolina in 1839 saw, on Christmas Day, slaves traveling on all the roads with loads of rice, potatoes, chickens, and other foods, going from one plantation to another to spend the day with their wives, husbands, and families.[50]

Such touches of bounty could not hide the dull hunger that persisted among slaves and that revealed itself in their folktales. In these there appeared the mythical place called "Diddy-Wah-Diddy" where roast pigs and baked chickens with knives and forks stuck in their sides ran around crying "Eat Me!" or "Who'll eat me?" and there were fritter ponds of grease everywhere with fritters frying in them.

Less imaginatively an ex-slave in Louisiana remembered simply of his days in bondage that "we prayed that us niggers could have all we wanted to eat and special for fresh meat."[51]

ᎬᎥ 13 ᎦᎦᎦ
The West, 1830-1865

Our food is mush,
molasses and bacon, mixed plentifully
with dirt three times each day.

During the first third of the nineteenth century the eastern portions of the country became aware of the vast West extending
across the Great Plains, the Rocky Mountains, and on to the
Pacific coast. In 1803 the purchase of Louisiana, as the western
half of the Mississippi Valley was called, was negotiated with
France, and in the following year the Lewis and Clark expedition
began its nearly three-year exploration of the Missouri Valley and
westward to the Pacific Ocean. Soon more information on the
West trickled in. American seamen, deserting ships loading hides
off California, took up residence among the Mexicans there. Fur
traders, both independents and employees of the American Fur
Company, ranged throughout the West. During the 1820s and
early 1830s Americans settled in the Mexican province of Texas,
and others built up a trade with Mexicans in New Mexico. About
the same time missionaries went to Oregon to work among the
Indians and in denominational magazines lauded the natural
beauty and riches of the region.

Large migrations into this western world began in the 1840s.
Mormons moved to Salt Lake City in search of religious liberty;
people burning with "Oregon fever" trekked to the far Northwest;
and Forty-niners, lusting for gold, went to California. Within a
few years all these lands were incorporated into the United
States: Texas, after a revolution against Mexico and a decade as
an independent republic, was annexed in 1845; title to much of
Oregon was acquired by an 1846 treaty with England; and in the
settlement of the Mexican War in 1848, Mexico ceded California
and New Mexico and all the lands that lay between them.

The search for precious metals speeded the exploration and settlement of the West. Free gold nearly disappeared in California within a few years of its discovery there, but other "rushes" took place. In 1858 gold was found in Colorado, and the "Pike's Peak fever" raged. Soon afterward a strike in what is now Nevada opened the incredibly rich Comstock Lode. Two years later gold appeared near Lewiston, Idaho, then part of Washington Territory; in 1862 a rush occurred to the valley of the lower Colorado River; and in 1874 gold was found in the Black Hills of South Dakota. Near major rushes there were minor ones to draw miners to new sites. Most of the towns and cities created by these and other booms disappeared or became ghostly shells. Still, the mercurial movement of miners had opened new areas, where ranchers and farmers often followed.

The men, women, and children who settled this West found themselves in a far different world from that they had left. From the heavily forested and well-watered regions of the East, they entered a great American desert where both trees and water were meager or nonexistent. They saw plains stretching unbroken to the horizon and gazed in awe at mountains which made the Appalachian chain seem gentle in comparison. Of the changes in daily life that these new environments required, those involving food and drink were not the smallest.

Even most of the wild life was strange to the new arrivals. Hardly credible were the mighty herds of buffaloes on the Great Plains, black seas of them that covered the landscape as far as the eye could see. While these herds existed, the buffalo provided the most used meat on the plains. Everyone agreed that buffalo meat was both wholesome and palatable, plainsmen rating it superior to beef.[1]

So long as the herds were large only the preferred morsels — the tongue, hump, fleece fat, bone marrow, and sometimes the gall and liver — were used, but in times of scarcity nearly all the flesh was eaten fresh or jerked for future use. In time a commercial market in the East appeared for salted buffalo tongues, and thousands were killed for this delicacy alone.[2] Some hunters liked the intestines and would, after lightly cooking them, swallow yards of them without troubling to chew. There was apparently no limit to the amount of buffalo meat that could be eaten without ill effects; the American Fur Company gave each employee eight pounds daily. Buffalo meat kept well when jerked, and this added greatly to its value.[3]

The blacktail deer and the antelope were second to the buffalo as favorite and plentiful sources of food. Less common, but equally popular, were the elk.[4] In mountain areas and along wooded rivers were beavers, whose tails were a delicacy, and there were squirrels, rabbits, porcupines, several kinds of bear, and skunk, the last highly rated by those who tried it. In the Rockies the mountain sheep gave a tender, fat, and juicy meat, but these were not killed in great numbers.[5]

When hungry enough, the frontiersmen did not let food taboos or unfamiliarity stand in their way. Rattlesnakes were eaten, both happily and under duress. Horsemeat met with mixed reactions. A western expedition in 1853 lived for fifty days on horsemeat and "delectable" horse soup. But some mountaineers whom the New York journalist Horace Greeley met claimed they knew of no way to make horsemeat palatable, "though of course," they agreed, "it has to be eaten occasionally." Under compulsion, one man agreed, he had eaten wolf but "could not recommend it." Roast dog, an Indian delicacy, was tasted by many a hunter, trader, and pioneer, with varying feelings. About the panther, or "painter," there was no doubt. Many trappers rated it over even beaver tail or the best parts of the buffalo.[6] Occasionally eaten, but never highly esteemed, were the prairie dogs, or "pups," that sported by the thousands in villages dotting the Great Plains.[7]

Wild fowl on the western plains and in the mountains provided a food source that was not easily killed off. On the lower Missouri River and in the Southwest turkeys were numerous. Geese and ducks appeared on all the watercourses, and on land were prairie chickens, plover, quail, grouse, pheasants, curlew, and sage hens.[8] When fish were caught there was rejoicing. They were numerous and sometimes large on the lower Missouri River, but on the upper reaches of that river there were only small catfish. Turtles, when found, made a welcome change in the diet.[9]

More knowledgeable emigrants combed the prairies and river banks to find wild plums, grapes, cherries, and various berries. There were roots known as prairie turnips as well as wild peas, beans, and the onions which were a popular flavoring for game.[10] In some places, especially along the lower Missouri River, "bee trees" harbored wild honey and these were as important as game to some professional hunters.[11]

An early penetration of the Great Plains took place in 1821 when a group of men set out from Missouri to trade with the Mexicans in Santa Fe. So successful were this and other expeditions over the Santa Fe Trail that by 1824 the caravans of pack mules were replaced by wagon trains and with each succeeding year the number of traders and the value of their goods increased.

Independence, Missouri, became the outfitting place for these yearly expeditions. In addition to horses, mules, oxen, and wagons for the trip, each man collected food to last him on the trail. The usual supplies for an individual were fifty pounds each of flour and bacon, ten pounds of coffee, twenty of sugar, and some salt. As nonessential luxuries some beans, crackers, and a few other items might be taken. These provisions, supplemented by small game and perhaps an antelope, were expected to suffice until the travelers reached the buffalo herds 200 or 300 miles from Independence. One group recorded that it caught fish in the streams, found wild strawberries and wild goose eggs, and made soup when some turtles were caught. Then, at last, a buffalo was killed and there was great joy throughout the camp.[12] Coffee was the invariable beverage. It was, wrote Josiah Gregg in his classic account of the Trail, "an unfailing and apparently indispensable beverage, served at every meal — even under the broiling noonday sun, the wagoner will rarely fail to replenish a second time, his huge tin cup."[13]

Susan Magoffin, who accompanied her husband over the trail in 1846 and 1847, kept a diary that included her culinary adventures. She found buffalo hump soup superior to any soup served in the "best" hotels of New York and Philadelphia and the buffalo marrow superior to the best butter or most delicate oil. At Bent's Fort she ate roast duck and frijoles. As they neared the Mexican settlements she had tortillas, *chile verde* (green pepper), and then, at Santa Fe, Mexican cooking in full flower. She learned to make chocolate in the Mexican style and found Mexican cooking so delicious that she resolved to prepare a recipe book to take home with her.[14]

These foods that delighted Susan Magoffin and innumerable later immigrants were those of the Mexican Indians, little influenced by their Spanish conquerors. Before, as after, the Spanish conquest the Indians of Mexico depended heavily on corn, beans, squash, greens, tomatoes, rice, potatoes, and the young cactus leaves. Chili, in one or more of its many varieties, appeared in every meal. With no domestic animals other than turkeys or chickens, the only meats were occasional game or barnyard fowls. Fruit, eggs, veal, and pork became more common among the well-to-do after the Spanish conquest, but the poor remained heavily dependent on corn and beans, chili, and a few vegetables.[15]

When the Spanish and the Mexican Indians entered New Mexico and Arizona in the early seventeenth century they found Navajo, Apache, Hopi, Zuni, and Comanche Indians. These inhabitants of arid lands had developed a reverent attitude toward the plants and animals that nourished them. The tribes without agriculture, especially, had become both closely attuned to the seasons and highly knowledgeable about what could, or could not, be eaten. Corn was the staff of life wherever it grew, but much of the food was gathered: the roots of the wild onion and the mariposa lily provided green vegetables; seed pods were boiled and the seeds mixed with corn to make dumplings; the pine and oak nuts and the berries of a ground tomato were eaten raw. Pumpkins were cultivated and eaten uncooked or cut into strips and dried. Indians who lived in mountainous areas gathered the small, sweet nuts of the piñon tree as well as acorns and wild plums. Tea was made from a variety of plants.

On special occasions the Indians ate mountain sheep, deer, squirrel, prairie dog, mountain lion, fox, badger, and field mouse. The meat was cut into strips and sun-dried, after which it could be stored without spoiling. Fresh meat was cooked on sticks held over a bed of coals or made into a stew with vegetables. Fish were not eaten, for legend held that these were bewitched ancestors who had fallen into the river.

The Mexicans who settled in Texas, New Mexico, and Arizona brought with them a devotion to frijoles, tortillas, chilis, and their dark chocolate beverage. From the local Indian tribes they learned to use the piñon nuts and, as the Pueblo people had done for centuries, to cut up sweet pumpkins and melons in the fall and put them on stakes to dry. During the same season squashes and plums were dried on cloths spread on slate roofs, and syrup was made from cane. A favorite dish consisted of three tortillas, made from blue corn meal, layered with slices of onion and curls of yellow cheese and sprinkled with green lettuce, all soaked in cooked red chili pepper sauce.[16]

Almost simultaneous with the opening of the Santa Fe Trail was the beginning of settlement in the Mexican province of Texas. During the early 1820s settlers from the United States moved into eastern Texas, and by 1830 there were about 20,000 immigrants there, mostly from southern states. As the numbers grew a complex of difficulties with the Mexican government developed until in 1836 Texas by armed revolt won its independence from Mexico and began nearly a decade of existence as a republic. Not until 1845 was it admitted into the Union.

Although they came to know Mexican cooking, the Texas immigrants generally followed the easy and familiar diet they had grown up with. Corn was made into johnnycakes, dodgers, or hoecakes. Fried beef, venison, and black coffee became the other basic foods of most Texans, with sweet potatoes growing in importance and pork by degrees replacing beef and venison. Bear, antelope, turkeys, and other birds were shot, much wild honey was found as were wild onions, lettuce, poke greens, and watercress. Sugar was nearly unknown until sorghum cane was raised and boiled down to make molasses known as "long sweet'ng" or a black-looking sugar called "short sweet'ng." A woman who lived in Austin in 1857 found vegetables "dear and rare" except for yams, cashaws, and pumpkins. Apples, pears, or berries of any kind she never saw, but peaches, figs, and delicious melons were abundant, while the grapes, though uncultivated, were wonderful.

The river-bottom planters of coastal Texas could obtain fish from the rivers and Gulf of Mexico, grow citrus fruits, and even purchase such luxuries as wheat flour, coffee, sugar, salt, tea, and salt fish from ships or stores. Black coffee was the almost universal nonalcoholic beverage, and in some places it was thought to prevent malaria. In the river town of Brazoria some families took coffee, with brandy added, as a tonic immediately upon rising in the morning.[17]

Most Texans apparently endured meals of terrible monotony. When Frederick Law Olmsted journeyed through Texas on the eve of the Civil War he found a deadly succession of fresh or salt pork, boiled sweet potatoes, corn bread, and "revolting" coffee, a meal pattern that was only broken at times by the absence of fresh pork or sweet potatoes. Only twice outside of Austin did he meet with wheat bread, and at his Austin hotel the daily repetition of "burnt flesh of swine and bulls, decaying vegetables, and sour and mouldy farinaceous glues, all pervaded with rancid butter" was so revolting that he finally bought wheat bread from a German baker and other provisions and cooked his own meals.[18] Olmsted's adventures supported both the implication of the Texas invitation, "Sit up, stranger, take some fry!" and Horace Greeley's conclusion regarding Texans that "their prime need was a thousand good cooks." Those who had black cooks were fortunate. One woman, at least, found them "excellent in their specialties. Such coffee, cake, succotash, and fried chicken I never tasted before."[19]

The population of eastern Texas was overwhelmingly masculine, and whiskey was its favorite alcoholic drink. The early settlers of Galveston and Houston, largely bachelors, thronged to the saloons for whiskey and companionship. Not to invite all within a reasonable distance to join in a drink was a major violation of etiquette, "so that," wrote one man, "the Texans being entirely a military people, not only fought, but drank, in platoons." By the early 1840s mixed drinks were offered at Texan hotels. The great favorite was whiskey punch. As served by Galveston's Tremont House it was described by one man as "nectar of the Gods," and by another during the Christmas season as "the national drink." In addition to such common drinks as mint juleps and sherry cobblers the Galveston hotels sold a Tom and Jerry, Tip and Tym, I.O.U., "moral suasion," "vox populi," "silver top," "poor man's punch," and other fancifully named concoctions.[20]

Still another emigration into Mexican territories was undertaken by members of the Church of Jesus Christ of Latter-Day Saints, better known as the Mormons. This denomination had originated in western New York under Joseph Smith who claimed inspiration both from the Bible and the Book of Mormon, a work he said was miraculously revealed to him. Persecuted by the "gentiles," the Mormons moved to Kirkland, Ohio, from there to two different Missouri locations, and then to Nauvoo, Illinois, on the Mississippi River. Here, again, there was trouble with the non-Mormons during which Joseph Smith was killed.

Leadership now fell to Brigham Young, who decided that his

denomination could find peace only outside the United States. During the winter of 1846 – 47, an advance guard of the Mormons, knowing only that they were looking for a western site within Mexico's boundaries, stopped at a place they named Winter Quarters a few miles from Omaha. Here there was little food, and the regular diet of corn bread, salt, bacon, and a little milk brought on black scurvy. For a time death and disease hit the encampment. The following spring Brigham Young led the expedition that chose Salt Lake as the site of the Mormon settlement. The journey was so long and the vegetation for the cattle they drove so inadequate that they finally had to feed the stock with the grain, flour, and biscuits they carried for themselves. Fish and game became their own food.

For more than twenty years annual migrations to Salt Lake were to take place from sites on the Mississippi and Missouri rivers. To aid these, the Mormons built up the town of Kanesville, Iowa (later Council Bluffs) as a base. Here 4,000 acres were planted in wheat, corn, potatoes, and vegetables to provide a store of food. By 1856 great numbers of Mormons crossed the plains each year. Some traveled in companies that drove cattle and cows and had wagons to carry provisions. Others pathetically pulled handcarts which contained about 100 pounds of flour together with personal baggage and tents. Hunger was routine and death was common; one company lost a sixth of its number from cold and starvation.[21]

Due in great part to the able leadership of Brigham Young, the problem of food in Salt Lake City itself was soon solved. By ingenuity, hard work, and irrigation the desert was made to produce vegetables, fruits, and livestock. Within a few years the Mormons had a food surplus, and the gardens and orchards of their city made it a blessed oasis for those who stopped there on their way to Oregon and California.

And these emigrants to the Pacific coast needed help, for the problems involving food and drink were considerable. During a trip that could last months over arid deserts, unbridged streams and rivers, and high passes in the mountains, it was essential that the covered wagons should not be overburdened. Food had to be relatively light and compact, able to withstand time and great heat, and still be easily prepared with a minimum of cooking utensils.

At outfitting towns such as St. Joseph, Missouri, the sale of wagons, livestock, and foodstuffs to emigrants was a major business. Prices were high, and during the feverish excitement that followed the discovery of gold in California, they rose even higher. Corn jumped from fifteen cents to a dollar a bushel, and butter from eight to twenty-five cents a pound. For those with adequate funds, canned meats marked "For California" appeared which were guaranteed to keep for five years.[22]

At the beginning of a trip most of the load was food. Flour was the major item carried by those going to Oregon or California. From 125 to 200 pounds of flour per person were recommended, normally wheat flour but sometimes with some corn meal for variety. A good housewife took yeast and whenever possible would bake bread in a Dutch oven. When this was not feasible, hot biscuits were made. Sometimes crackers or hardtack were taken for ease and variety.[23]

Bacon or pork and some cattle to be slaughtered en route provided meats, and a properly stocked wagon also carried sugar, salt, coffee, dried fruit, and perhaps some beans or rice. Dried apples were eaten as a protection from scurvy, and wild onions, wild grapes, and greens were picked along the way for the same purpose. Butter could be taken if it was first boiled, skimmed, and soldered in tin cannisters — a method commonly used throughout the West. But if a cow that had recently calved was brought along, butter could be churned from fresh milk by the lurching of the wagons, being removed at night to be worked, washed, and salted. Families sometimes carried a few delicacies such as vinegar, pickles, smoked beef, maple sugar, canned sardines, bologna, or cheese. During the evening encampments women exchanged foods with each other to gain greater variety.[24]

Those who wished were able to supplement their diet with game, fish, berries, and wild greens during the trip. The meals they ate were not always poor. A man invited to eat with a friend at a camp near Fort Laramie found a feast of hot biscuits, fresh butter, honey, rich milk, cream, venison steak, green peas picked that same day from wild vines along the trail, and tea and coffee.[25] But more often bacon, beans, and coffee made up the meals. A woman who had taken the trail to Oregon wrote that "we did not seem to have time for cooking much but bacon and frying pan-bread. Then we had our everlasting sorghum molasses." A cow they were driving began to fail to give milk, "which we deplored, as we all liked bread and milk and often our evening meal was mush and milk."[26]

Cooking was not always easy. Stoves were not carried because of their size and weight and because there was no wood on the plains. A hole in the ground served as a fireplace, set in the lee of the wagon if there was a wind. Buffalo chips were the common fuel. An India-rubber poncho, used by horsemen as a protection against rain, acted as a tablecloth on the ground. At times the difficulties of cooking were compounded. A wagon trail to Oregon in 1846 suffered one evening when rain made batter out of the dough and put out the fires. An emigrant in one group paid heartfelt tribute in his journal to a young woman: "Here let me say there was one young lady which showed herself worthy of the bravest undaunted pioneer of the west for after having kneaded her dough she watched and nursed the fire and held an umbrella over the fire and her skillit with the greatest composure for near 2 hours and baked bread enough to give us a very plentifull supper and to her I offer my thanks of gratitude for our last nights repast."[27]

Whatever any meal might prove to be, it was received hungrily and gratefully. A gold seeker described the mealtime of an emigrant train:

They join their families and mess-mates with appetites that make every meal a feast. There are separate camp fires and messes with as many varying degrees of opulence and refinement; the less pretentious, particularly those that include no women, make out with a frying pan, sheet iron kettle, coffee pot and tin cup, and a butcher knife for every man. When the food is cooked they sit around it making jokes, and from greasy hands devour savory viands. Others boast more adequate culinary equipment and more civilized manners and methods of preparing and enjoying their food. But all conform to the common necessity of eating all the wholesome food required by appetites made almost voracious by outdoor life.[28]

Once the trails were clearly established and filled with emigrants there was little danger of starvation except for those caught in the mountains by early snow. This was the fate of the famous Donner party in 1846. Their food gone, the party ate the flesh of their cattle, then the hides, and finally the burned bones. Field mice and their own boots followed. Both a relief party sent to find aid and those who remained in the snowbound camp finally turned to cannibalism, though some died rather than eat the flesh of their recent companions.[29]

As the major trails became better traveled, there appeared road ranches where the moneyed could buy cold pork and corn dodgers or even beans, bacon, hominy, biscuits, sorghum, buffalo and antelope steaks, coffee, and whiskey. At times canned sardines and oysters, the most common canned goods in the West until the 1870s, could be bought. A ubiquitous luxury on the prairies was dried apple pie: a frequent passenger on the overland stage lines said it was "apple pie from Genesis to Revelation along the Platte."[30]

Whiskey was the usual alcoholic drink of the Great Plains. It went under such names as red-eye, corn juice, strychnine, tarantula juice, Jersey Lightning, leg-stretcher, and tangle leg. The last was said to consist of diluted alcohol, nitric acid, pepper, and tobacco and would tangle the legs of any consumer within the first 400 yards.[31] The trailside taverns that sold whiskey were not impressive. One was described as consisting of a ridgepole and sailcloth and large enough "to contain two whiskey-barrels, two decanters, several glasses, three or four cans of pickled oysters and two or three boxes of sardines, but nothing of the bread kind whatever."[32]

At Salt Lake City the emigrants not only rested but bought fresh fruits, vegetables, milk, buttermilk, cheese, and butter. One party that stopped there in 1849 became sick from eating an excess of fresh food. A girl, Lucy Cooke, who reached the city in July 1852, wrote to her sister how their father had given the family a treat by taking them to a boardinghouse for dinner: "And oh, when we sat down to the table I thought never did victuals look more tempting! We had roast beef, chicken, green peas, potatoes, pie, cheese, bread and butter and tea. I thought the bread and butter seemed the greatest treat; and then it all looked so clean, and the house was so trim and neat."[33]

California itself, when gold was discovered there early in 1848, was lightly settled by Mexicans, native Indians, a few Europeans, and a scattering of immigrants from the eastern United States. The Gold Rush brought a flood of adventurers, mostly from the northeastern and midwestern parts of the United States but others from Europe, Latin America, China, and Australia.

The diet of the Mexicans in California consisted of the foods of the Spanish and Indians from Mexico as modified by the contributions of the western Indians. The Mexicans brought with them beans, corn, and meats, and to these the California Indians added various seeds, nuts, roots, and wild greens. In general, corn, beans, and beef were the principal foods in California when the miners first arrived. Pigs were scarce and chickens were usually reserved for the sick.[34]

The miners could buy flour, carried by ship from the East Coast, though it was often sour and filled with long, black worms. Still, it could be used to make the flapjacks and griddle cakes that were so common in the mining camps. Pork brought from New York by ship was expensive and often bad, and the butter that came in the same fashion was brown with age. Nearly all vegetables were extremely hard to obtain during the first years, but onions could be bought as could canned sardines, canned or preserved oysters, and salt fish. Beans and dried fruits were imported from Chile, yams from the Sandwich Islands, and sea gulls' eggs selling for a dollar each from offshore Farralon Island. Turtles also came from nearby islands, and hunters brought snipe, plover, cranes, ducks, curlew, and other wild fowl to be sold, as well as elk, black-tailed deer, and grizzly bears. Salmon and salmon trout were caught in the Sacramento River.[35]

The scarcities of the early years made for strange and unhealthy meals. Miners drank bad water and got fevers. Many got scurvy from a diet of salt pork which might be fried for breakfast and boiled with beans for the midday dinner with the grease providing a sop for bread. Those arriving from the overland trip were starved for sweet and sour flavors. One man's first act was to buy vinegar and molasses, mix the two in front of the store where he purchased them, and, ignoring the throngs about him, sop them up with bread on the spot. Another miner walked eight miles to a Colma hotel when he heard it was serving a dried-apple sauce.[36] A woman wrote from Yuba in 1850: "Our fare is very plain, consisting of meat and bread, and bread and meat, with some stewed fruit, either apples or peaches, now and then (as a great delicacy) some rancid butter that has been put up in the Land of Goshen and sent around a six months cruise by Cape Horn. I have not seen an egg or a drop of milk since I have been in this country."[37] Only slowly did things improve. Vegetables appeared in the markets of a size and quality that astonished men from less fertile areas. A brewery appeared in Sacramento in 1850 and ale could be bought for twenty-five cents a glass.[38]

Restaurants, at first crude and then increasingly elaborate, came to Sacramento, San Francisco, Hangtown (later Placerville), and other mining towns. Bayard Taylor, the poet and author on a visit from the East, described an early restaurant in Sacramento. It consisted of an open, unfloored tent with plank tables and rough benches. The waiters were "rude Western boys" who had crossed the Rocky Mountains. The meals, however, could not have been bettered "for substantial richness of quality" in any part of the world:

There was every day abundance of elk steaks, unsurpassed for rich and delicate flavor; venison, which had been fattened on the mountain acorns; mutton, such as nothing but the wild pastures of California could produce; salmon and salmon-trout of astonishing size, from the Sacramento River, and now and then the solid flesh of the grizzly bear. The salmon-trout exceeded in fatness any fresh-water fish I ever saw; they were between two and three feet in length, with a layer of pure fat, quarter of an inch in thickness, over the ribs. When made into chowder or stewed in claret, they would have thrown into ecstacies the most inveterate Parisian gourmand.[39]

However good or bad the cooking might prove, most early restaurants gave only limited fare. A miner in Placer City recorded a "hearty" restaurant supper of flapjacks, bacon, stewed apples, and coffee. The same man, newly arrived as a stranger in San Francisco, was guided to an obscure hotel where he received a supper of cold beef, "sour, heavy rolls, rank butter, and an apology for lukewarm coffee."[40] And the menu at Elephant House, Sacramento, was not much better:

Hash, low grade — 75 cents
Hash, 18 karats — $1
Codfish balls, per pair — 75 cents

Beef, plain, with one potato, fair size — $1.25
Baked beans, greased — $1
Roast Grizzly — $1
A square meal — $3[41]

Even while fruit and vegetables remained luxuries and fresh butter was almost unknown, the restaurants of San Francisco multiplied and flourished to inaugurate that city's reputation as a place where "eating out" was common practice. By 1850 there was a large array of restaurants, many of them foreign. At two American restaurants on the Plaza, the United States and the California, it was possible to buy an "excellent" beefsteak "scantily" garnished with potatoes and a cup of good coffee or chocolate for a dollar. On Montgomery Street and in vacant spaces fronting the water were stands selling coffee, cakes, and sweetmeats. At the corner of Kearney Street and Jackson a basement restaurant offered two different soups, boiled salmon trout, three boiled meats, and entrées of mutton, beef, veal, lobster, venison, and ham. Macaroni, cabbage with the corned beef, and a mushroom sauce for the beefsteak were the only accompaniments for the meats.

On the Plaza and on Dupont Street were French restaurants. A large German restaurant was established on Pacific Street. Elsewhere there appeared a Fonda Peruana, an Italian confectionery, and three Chinese restaurants which were marked by long, three-cornered, yellow silk flags. The Chinese restaurants were popular with the miners and residents because of their superior cooking and low cost, one dollar for whatever one ate. "There," wrote Bayard Taylor, "the grave Celestials serve up their chow-chow and curry, besides many genuine English dishes; their tea and coffee cannot be surpassed."[42]

The opportunities to eat well increased. A resident of Sacramento City recorded his Christmas Day of 1851: "What a contrast with the last! — I dined with Dr. Austin and Major Fornet, at the Fremont House. Grizzly bear stake, Venison pie, fine vegetables, and delightful mince pie, garnished with wine."[43] One early luxury restaurant was begun by a man named Winn who in 1849 had made candies and sold them in the streets of San Francisco. Within seven years his restaurant, Winn's Fountain Head on Clay Street opposite the Plaza, became a fashionable complex consisting of an ice-cream saloon, catering establishments, and restaurants. At the latter were sold not only Winn's original candy, but "fine venison steaks, oysters, ducks, geese, partridge, snipe, teal," among other things, and in a setting of "rich Turkey carpets, costly draperies, rosewood chairs with crimson velvet cushions, sofas and Italian marble tables."[44]

In Los Angeles, where the population grew more slowly and there was not the wealth to spur on rapid change, the improvements in food and drink came slowly. A resident said that on first coming he saw strings of beef drying on fences and learned that this *carne seca* was an important article of food in southern California. In 1852 the first bakeshop opened. Until then only French bread and, presumably, tortillas were available, but the new baker introduced both German and American bread and cakes and, later, freshly baked crackers. Butter, eggs, and poultry came from San Bernardino the following year but in poor condition, especially in summer. The same year the city got a restaurant, La Rue's, with a mud floor, half a dozen cheap wooden tables, dirty tablecloths, and food that was poorly cooked but generously served. About the same time the first lager beer, imported from San Francisco, was offered for sale. Dirty water was sold by carrier in 1854 at fifty cents a bucket every day but Sunday. Prickly pears, pomegranates, quinces, and watermelons were all plenteous, the last being sold from wagons. A vendor with a loud horn peddled a few varieties of fish from San Pedro. In 1854 a hive of bees was imported from San Francisco and soon honey was for sale. Immigrants from the East by this time could try some Mexican-American restaurants where such common dishes as tamales, enchiladas, frijoles, tortillas, and *pan de huevos,* an egg bread, were served. The last two items were peddled around town by Mexican women, as was *panocha,* a dark Mexican sugar cake.[45]

Far to the north in Oregon and Washington the early settlers, largely from New England and other northern states, experienced the same lack of familiar foods during the first years of settlement. Once established, however, they grew in the rich soil all the vegetables, fruits, and grains they had known in their old homes. An early emigrant who reached Oregon in 1843 found his first years there "very quiet and uneventful. We raised wheat, oats, potatoes, peas, and all kinds of vegetables, without irrigation." The country abounded in wild berries, trout and salmon, and game. The craving for sweets led housewives to boil carrots in a sugar syrup to which ginger had been added to make a marmalade, or to make a syrup for hot cakes by boiling tomato juice with sugar until very thick and then flavoring the syrup with honey. Or whole tomatoes would be boiled in sugar syrup, dried and dusted with sugar, and eaten as a confection.[46]

Ingenuity and the riches of the country made it possible for many to approach "normal" living conditions. Mary Ellen Todd, who traveled over the Oregon Trail in 1852, described her first Christmas dinner in Oregon: "There was roasted beef and gravy, mashed potatoes, cabbage slaw, butter and old-fashioned pone bread baked in our dutch oven. Mother had made some pumpkin butter that added a spicey flavor. With all this and mother's sweetcake, and some stick [candy?] that John brought, we were amply satisfied, and all was as merry as Christmas should be."[47]

A woman who settled in the Walla Walla Valley of Washington acknowledged that there was "plenty" to eat: "The only thing lacking was variety and that was provided in summer with wild berries, fish, and prairie chickens."[48] From the Indians the settlers learned of a wild plant, the camas lily. The root of this, similar in shape and color to an onion, was very sweet when cooked. One woman said that camas-root bread was the only kind her family had in the early days.[49]

As Utah, California, and Oregon were being settled, the slower-moving frontier of farmers began to edge onto the Great Plains. During the 1850s an increasing number found farms in Kansas, Nebraska, and the Dakotas. The vast, treeless, semiarid plains, often very dry in summer and cold in winter, demanded a greater adjustment than did the Far West. The newcomers, for lack of wood, often built their houses with sod, went without fencing until barbed wire became available, farmed on dry soil, used windmills to obtain water from considerable depths for human consumption and to water livestock, and even burned dried grass or buffalo chips as fuel for cooking.

The earliest settlers on the Great Plains recorded the simplest and most monotonous diet, relieved only by occasional luxuries imported from eastern areas or, increasingly, by the produce of their own gardens. With good luck, game was shot — most commonly deer or grouse. The first years saw a deadly repetition of fat pork, hominy, hot biscuits, tea, and coffee. At times there might be corn dodgers, johnnycakes, rice, molasses, beef, apples, and chickens. From the first the settlers used all the wild greens and berries they recognized. In southwestern Kansas and eastern Colorado, for instance, the plains provided wild onions and artichokes, "lamb's quarter," which had tender leaves in the early spring, and pokeweed, which grew along many streams. There were also wild plums, black and red haws, and "possum" grapes, and in the fall walnuts, pecans, and persimmons.[50]

Still, monotony was the norm. One settler in Kansas wrote: "Our bill of fare is limited; we do not ask, 'what shall we have good for dinner?' or 'what delicacy for tea?' something to please the palate, for it is the same simple dishes, right over and over again: hominy, johnny cake, Graham pudding, *some* white bread, now and then stewed apple, a little rice, and tea occasionally for the old people."[51] Another Kansas settler, even less happily, wrote in 1854 that "Our food is mush, molasses and bacon, mixed plentifully with dirt three times each day."[52]

The duties of hospitality were hard to meet. When a prairie family went to visit another, a social act that might require a long wagon trip, it was an appreciated kindness to take along a few pounds of white flour or some butter, eggs, meat, or other delicacy.[53] A woman in Nebraska, confronted with visitors, noted the heroic efforts she was driven to:

> Having no milk, no butter, eggs or vegetables, it seemed a gloomy prospect, for those that wished to be hospitable. . . . I had a few days before found a large bush of wild gooseberries, almost large enough for use. The boys gathered them and by theirs and Ada's help they were soon picked over. I had no lard, so fried out some fat meat, made some pie crust, and baked a pie. Then made a cake using my shortening, and vinegar and saleratus to make it light, took my dry bread and dipped it in batter and fried it nice and brown, floured and fried my fat meat, had a good cup of coffee, and a dish of the stewed gooseberries.[54]

A stark simplicity was present also at Governor Mark W. Izard's inaugural ball in Nebraska Territory in 1858, where the midnight supper consisted of coffee with brown sugar, sandwiches of thick slices of bread and bacon, and dried apple pie. The coffee was passed around in a washtub, and the sandwiches were offered from a willow basket of Indian make.[55]

Slowly a greater variety of foods appeared. Horace Greeley in

1859 found the diet of Denver "decidedly limited," but he observed signs of improvement. For a time bread, bacon, and beans had formed the "staple of every meal," but then milk and eggs became reasonably priced and, even better, a man appeared in town with lettuce to sell and the promise of peas the next month.[56]

For beverages on the Great Plains, coffee — usually a rye substitute — was the overwhelming favorite over tea, and whiskey was the nearly universal alcoholic drink. Both choices reflected the overt masculinity of the frontier. An emigrant who came across a friend in Kansas City was, "after the manner of the country," instantly invited into the nearest saloon and asked his choice: "To my suggestion of lemonade, he replied with a glance at the rough crowd about us, 'That will never do in *this* country. Say Whiskey.'" For well-to-do town dwellers, champagne and oysters symbolized a festive occasion.[57]

Wherever there were enough people to make it possible, parties helped to soften the rigors and loneliness of life on the plains. Usually a special food provided a focus for the festivity and made it more exciting. In September 1855 the young men of Lawrence, Kansas, gave an entertainment with nearly 100 watermelons as refreshment. Taffy pulls were a common winter entertainment at which the young women and their escorts pulled sorghum taffy.[58] And on July 4, 1859, all the families in a Minnesota township met at a home and enjoyed music, dancing, and a dinner of ham, eggs, and rice pudding. "Quite a treat for Minnesota," commented a participant.[59]

Barbecues were very popular. For some of these the men would shoot a buffalo and the women would provide bread, pies, cakes, and preserves. A Kansas barbecue on June 13, 1850, was immense, with six cattle, twenty hogs, and over fifty sheep, pigs, and lambs roasted, to which were added over a hundred hams, several thousand loaves of bread, and hundreds of cakes.[60]

In towns the bars, symbolizing the raw frontier, provided a meeting place for the men. But during the 1850s two movements appeared: a growing number of drugstores, bakeries, and soda fountains sold ice cream,[61] and the Great Plains felt the early stirrings of a western temperance movement that would soon produce Carrie Nation and her supporters. Obviously, gentler times were coming.

❧ 14 ❧
The Civil War, 1861-1865

*Our "grub" is enough to make a mule desert,
and a hog wish he had never been born.*

When President Abraham Lincoln on April 15, 1861, issued a call
for 75,000 volunteers to put down organized resistance within the
southern states, no one could foresee that there would follow four
years of terrible death and destruction together with great dislocations in the economy and in society. Nor could Americans
imagine that their country, still largely one of farmers, would
know widespread hunger which brought suffering to both civilians and soldiers. The privations were spread unevenly, for while
the war influenced food and drink everywhere, it was in the
South that the greatest scarcities appeared.

Part of the South's trouble came because it had devoted so
much of its land to cotton that it was dependent upon the North
and Europe for grains, meats, salt, and other foods. There were
other reasons for food shortages. When the Union blockaded
southern ports there was an immediate drop in food supplies. Although there was a general, and highly successful, effort to shift
agriculture from cotton to food, the accumulated surpluses did
not always reach either the Confederate armies or the population
in general. Hoarding, speculation, and an unwillingness of the
farmers to sell for the depreciating Confederate currency all kept
foods off the markets, as did the progressive deterioration of
transportation facilities. In parts of the South military action increased the shortages. Near battle lines the land was preyed upon
by foragers from both armies, and that part of Virginia swept by
four years of war faced a food problem progressively more acute.

General William Tecumseh Sherman's army left a trail of hunger as it moved across Georgia and into the Carolinas.[1]

For a brief time Southerners gave little thought to the possibility of food shortages. A woman who lived in Richmond, Virginia, remembered that at the beginning of the war the finest oysters and terrapins were available and those with money "revelled" in canvasback and greenback ducks from Chesapeake Bay.[2] An Englishman who visited Mobile, Alabama, in 1861 found people eating oysters "as if there was no blockade, as though oysters were a specific for political indigestion and civil wars."[3]

An early worry, following secession, was that the war would deprive the southern states of ice. It did indeed do so, but this was to be only an inconvenience when compared with the scarcities of coffee, tea, sugar, and salt which quickly developed. When the saltworks in the Great Kanawha and Holston valleys were seized by Union forces and the blockade cut off outside supplies of salt, both civilians and soldiers suffered, for the lack caused the spoilage of tremendous amounts of meat and other foodstuffs. The Confederate and the state governments all made desperate efforts to find salt. Even the floors of southern smokehouses were scraped for drippings from ham and bacon sides. In some places the shortage of salt brought about near revolt, and the governments received plaintive appeals for help from the poor.[4]

The early shortage of sugar became severe after the cane-growing areas around New Orleans came under Union control in 1862. The most common replacement was sorghum which appeared on tables everywhere in the Confederacy. Honey, maple sugar, and persimmons were also employed as substitutes, and both watermelons and figs were used to make a sweet syrup. A treat was molasses pie, made of sorghum, flour, and walnuts, and another simple dessert consisted of crushed peanuts sweetened with sorghum.[5]

One man who lived through the war wrote that the coffee shortage "caused more actual discomfort among the people at large" than any other. Those lucky enough to get some real coffee were ecstatic, while others tried all the known substitutes — rye, okra seed, corn, sweet potato, acorns, dandelion roots, sugarcane, rice, cotton seed, English peas, peanuts, wheat, and beans — each parched and ground. Tea was also scarce and many replacements were used: the dried bark of the sassafras tree, the leaves of such bushes as the blackberry, raspberry, huckleberry, or currant, and of the willow tree. In coastal North Carolina the boiled leaves and twigs of the yapon shrub made a popular tea substitute.[6]

As the early scarcities of coffee, tea, salt, and sugar were joined by a growing inability of many people to obtain meats, fats, and even fruits and vegetables, a haunting fear of what might happen spread among civilians, especially those in towns and cities. "Peace alone can prevent starvation!" the Raleigh *Progress* stated in December, 1863: "It is folly to talk to us about there being enough supplies in the country."[7]

Where food had to be purchased, as in urban centers, the prospects were grimmest. Poor roads, fear of the impressment officials, and a growing unwillingness to take Confederate money all kept farmers away from city markets. Speculators and inflation often put the prices of those foods that did reach market beyond the means of the poor. One woman suggested that food should be taken from Macon and other wealthy towns: "Monopolists and misers hold enough meat and grain in their clutches to feed our army and Lincoln's!" she wrote. People in cities were seen eating from garbage cans, and a diarist labeled Richmond a clean city because food was "so cleanly consumed that no garbage or filth can accumulate." In Mobile, Alabama, placards appeared on street corners reading "Bread or Peace," and riots of women against extortioners took place there, in Atlanta, Georgia, Salisbury, North Carolina, and other cities. The largest bread riot took place in Richmond on April 2, 1863, when a crowd of over a thousand broke into shops and took meal, flour, bacon, shoes, and other articles. The government tried hard to hush up the event.[8]

Meat became ever more scarce in the South as the war continued. Much of the beef had come from the Middle West, the border states, and the trans-Mississippi West, and by mid-1863 all these sources were cut off. Even pork was in poor supply due in part to the lack of salt and because the men who had done the butchering and curing were in the Confederate armies. Fish, fowl, shellfish, and eggs were substituted, as was game when ammunition was available. For the desperate an editor in 1864 listed rats, frogs, snails, crows, snakes, locusts, earthworms, cats, and dogs as food sources. Rats were eaten by some in cities and in besieged Vicksburg, Mississippi, they brought up to $2.50 each, dressed. Some men in Savannah, Georgia, were accused of selling dog meat as lamb. All animal fats became scarce, as did butter which had largely come from the North. Sunflower seed oil was the only important replacement found.[9]

The blockade soon cut off citrus fruits, pineapples, dates, and other semitropical fruits from the Caribbean islands. In response, fruit-growing in Florida increased. Vegetables were scarce in cities, and herbs and flowers were eaten. At one time in 1863 watercress was the only fresh vegetable in the Richmond market.

Such scarcities gave free play to the ingenuity of southern housewives. Information was shared on how to raise bread without yeast, make apple pie without apples, create artificial oysters, brew beer from spruce and ginger, preserve meat and cure bacon without salt, or use egg whites and butter to create a cream substitute for coffee. To appease hunger and allay thirst "Indian Sagammite" was suggested, to be made of three parts of cornmeal and one part of brown sugar mixed with water and brewed.[10] Entertainments also bent to the times. Anyone who possessed some precious wheat flour could give a "biscuit party." One woman found biscuits at one such party were "more delicious than any eaten before or since." More common were "starvation parties" where guests were offered only water and fellowship.[11]

Not only the poor suffered from hunger. At Porcher's School in South Carolina the students had nothing but squash and hominy to eat for months. Mrs. Joseph E. Johnston, the wife of the general, had only corn bread and sorghum molasses to eat for a time. Mrs. Roger A. Pryor, the wife of a leading political figure, remembered that at Petersburg, Virginia, near the end of the war she and her children "never ate rats, mice, or mule meat," but got by on peas, bread, sorghum, and a drink made from milk mixed with roasted and ground corn.[12]

The great majority of Southerners lived in the country and suffered less than city dwellers. Although farm work was curtailed by the conscription of adult white males and hampered by the seizure of horses and mules by the military, still fruits and vegetables were abundant in season and could be dried for winter use. Common field peas, sweet potatoes, corn bread, molasses or sorghum, and some pork and game were staples normally available.[13] The well-to-do had greater luxuries. When a South

Carolina woman left Richmond for Kingsville, South Carolina, in 1865, she discovered "creature comforts of all kinds — green peas, strawberries, asparagus, spring lamb, spring chicken, fresh eggs, rich yellow butter, clean white linen for one's bed, dazzling white damask for one's table."[14]

The slaves on plantations probably suffered less decline in the quality and quantity of food because their rations were so simple and limited to begin with. The lack of salt must have reduced or eliminated their meat rations, but sweet potatoes and molasses or sorghum were increased as compensation. One scholar thinks it likely that the large-scale shift from cotton to food crops might have actually improved the diet of rural slaves during the war.[15]

The soldiers of the Confederacy rarely ate better than the civilians. Early in the war the government adopted the official ration of the United States Army for their own soldiers, and briefly some of the volunteers fared well. But real scarcities appeared as early as July 1861, and a week after the first Battle of Manassas some regiments on the Virginia front were described as "nearly starving." Beginning in the spring of 1862 general reductions of rations were authorized.

The trouble did not lie in the failure of the South to grow adequate food. Indeed, it would seem that the difficulties were more political and economic: the commissary department of the Confederacy was inexperienced and probably inefficient; the transportation system, whether of railroads or wagons, proved quite inadequate for wartime needs; the farmers were reluctant to sell their produce for anything less than gold; and incursions into the South of Union troops added chaos to uncertainty.[16]

Troop hunger was usually greater during active campaigning than during periods of quiet. After the Battle of Antietam in September, 1862, some soldiers had little but apples, green corn, and short rations of beef and flour. The worst famine was during the siege of Vicksburg when mule meat was issued officially and, when this was gone, some soldiers joined civilians in eating dogs and rats to remain alive.[17] In the trans-Mississippi West food supplies were better. In western Texas, for instance, the soldiers supplemented their corn bread and coffee with beef or venison, wild turkey, and sometimes fish from the streams.[18]

The average Confederate soldier, without adequate food,

204

learned to "make do" by other means. A woman in Richmond "heard tales" of a sudden demand for green persimmons among the soldiers, because a soldier who ate one of these "could feel his stomach draw up and at once forget that he was 'hawngry.'"[19] Or there could be other sources of food than the official issues. Relatives and friends at home sent fruits, vegetables, or even fried chicken. Soldiers bought from farmers and peddlers, although the sutlers often asked exorbitant prices for their wares. At times soldiers stole hogs and poultry and plundered gardens, orchards, smokehouses, and beehives. They also caught or seined fish and took various kinds of small game and birds. An Alabama soldier wrote proudly of a sparrow pie his mess prepared. In Texas a group of soldiers ate armadillos, some Georgians in Florida consumed an alligator, and all stationed in seacoast areas enjoyed oysters and crabs. The lack of coffee caused great unhappiness and every known substitute was employed.[20]

On the whole the soldiers of the Union army ate far better than their opponents. What was due to them by army regulations was generous. From early August 1861 to late June 1864 each Union soldier was supposed to receive twelve ounces of pork or bacon or one pound, four ounces of salt or fresh beef; one pound, six ounces of soft bread or flour, or one pound of hard bread, or one pound, four ounces of cornmeal. To every hundred men were allotted stated amounts of beans or peas, rice or hominy; green or roasted coffee, or tea; sugar, vinegar, salt, pepper, potatoes, and molasses.

Still, there was usually a conflict between theory and performance. Vegetables and fruits were rarely included in the issues, and camp fare became mainly salt pork, bread, and coffee. And since the cooking was usually done by small groups or messes, each soldier taking his turn as cook, the food was frequently unsanitary and unpalatable.[21]

As in the Confederacy, time and place made a difference. The western armies had frequent food shortages in late 1862 and 1863. In December, 1862, an Illinois soldier wrote his wife from Mississippi that "we have not been on full rations for several days."[22] But on the same day a soldier not far away wrote that "we are geting along first rait have plenty to eat of the very best we have good bread and good beef and baken and beens and homny rice potatoes dried apples molasses coffee tea shugger and crackers. We have plenty to eate and to sell too."[23] In the East the Army of the Potomac under General Ambrose B. Burnside suffered from a general food shortage. This was alleviated when General Joseph Hooker replaced Burnside. Hooker ordered the bakeries to provide soft bread, and he soon cleared the supply lines to give the soldiers more and better food than they had ever had.

The severest hunger occurred during hard campaigns. Then soldiers complained of half rations, of being "half starved," or that "our 'grub' is enough to make a mule desert, and a hog wish he had never been born. . . . Hard bread, bacon and coffee is all we draw." Men on the Goldsboro expedition of December 1862 reported that they had had only three crackers for two days. Some soldiers even admitted having robbed horse troughs of hard corn to appease their appetites.

As northern armies penetrated the South the soldiers sometimes extended their food allowances by eating, for money or as guests, at southern homes. From the blacks, especially, they received simple fare of corn bread, sweet potatoes, turnip greens, field peas, and occasionally pork. A Yankee soldier in Savannah in January 1865 wrote that "the Negroes are selling all the oysters they can get to our men. The soldier takes the tin cup and dips it into the tub or bucket of oysters, fills it full and then drinks the oysters as if he was drinking water."[24] Gifts from home, fishing and hunting, looting, and the seizure of Confederate supplies were all additional sources of food for Union soldiers.

Throughout the North and the West the Civil War had only a limited effect upon the food and drink available to civilians, at least during the war itself. Prices rose sharply for some foods, even doubling, and as a result poor families ceased buying such foods or found substitutes. Imported and luxury foods were beyond the reach of all but the very rich.[25] Still, these were but slight adjustments compared to those of the South, and in general the North enjoyed both excellent crops and considerable prosperity during the war years.

The Civil War was a major turning-point for the food industry. Earlier developments had set the scene: a great network of railroads, the multiplication of steamboats, better roads, large-scale ice-making, and improved canning techniques. The war, through government orders, served as a catalyst, providing the food industry with burgeoning military and civilian markets.

Gail Borden was one who seized the opportunity. A former teacher, surveyor, and editor, Borden had worked on the concentration of foods so that they could be kept indefinitely and during the early 1850s had created a meat biscuit that became a common ration for sailors and explorers. In 1856 he patented a means of preserving milk by adding sugar and heating it in a vacuum. By 1861 several plants were ready to supply soldiers with canned, condensed milk.

The war also aided canners. Prior to that conflict they had, in coastal locations, put up seafoods in season and fruits and vegetables at other times. Large wartime orders made it feasible to build inland packing plants for fruits and vegetables alone. Their products went to soldiers in the field, sailors on gunboats, and the wounded and sick in hospitals, and through all these canned goods became better known to the general public.[26]

Thus muscled, the American food industry was off and running in the decades after the war, following a path that would more and more substitute the factory for the home as the source of food and drink.

❧ 15 ❧

A Changing Country, 1865-1900

There is a popular prejudice against fried foods,
and a belief that abstaining from them
will cure us of our dyspepsia.

During the third of a century that followed the Civil War there appeared rapid changes in economic activity, scientific knowledge, technology, and social life — of the kind that later generations would look upon as normal. Many of these alterations grew out of the war. Government orders for food, munitions, uniforms, and other wartime necessities had greatly stimulated American industry and not only created powerful businesses but made millionaires of their owners. The legal and illegal war profits, shared by politicians and speculators, promoted an ostentatious display of the new fortunes in the form of brownstone houses lining city streets, huge hotels at such watering places as Saratoga Springs, and palaces, called cottages, at Newport. All were filled with costly displays of art and household furnishings bought in Europe, frequently at great cost but with little taste.

In the South the postwar changes were quite different. The terrible destruction done there during the war, the turmoil that accompanied the military occupation by federal troops, the ousting from power of all the section's leaders, the seizure of large amounts of property as contraband, the near ruin of southern railroads and water transportation, the social problems attendant upon the freeing of the slaves, and the impoverishment, even to great hunger, of great portions of both black and white populations, all threw into sharp relief the contrasts between the two former adversaries. Immigrants from both Europe and Asia, noting the differences, chose not to enter the South to compete in the labor market with the newly freed blacks. Thus as the North moved rapidly toward urbanism, industrialism, and a society of international origins, the South remained overwhelmingly rural, agricultural, and peopled mainly by those of Anglo-Saxon and African origins. In country areas even the diet remained a carry-over from an earlier era.

Although insulated from the outside world by oceans, which the clipper ships and steamships of the day had only slightly narrowed, Americans of the postwar period were exposed to expanding horizons through more education and greater freedom from internal problems. An ever larger part of the population went from grade school to high school and even college. The growing immigration from Europe gave native-born Americans a glimpse of other customs and cultures, and many affluent Americans journeyed abroad to see at first hand some of the world's differences. Those unable to travel so far were fascinated by the exhibits of foreign countries, as well as the wonders of scientific and industrial change, that appeared at the Philadelphia Centennial exhibit of 1876 to mark the country's first century and at the majestic Columbian World's Fair in Chicago in 1893 where the 400th anniversary of Columbus's voyage was celebrated.

Great changes took place in agriculture. In May 1862 the long-desired Homestead Bill became law, giving 160 acres of unoccupied land to anyone who would settle and work it. In the same year the Morrill Land Grant Act gave federal land to the states to support land-grant colleges, including agricultural schools. Soon, too, the government aided farmers with free seeds, farm loans, and experimental stations. In the forty years following 1860 the improved farmland increased by about 250 million acres, producing crops at a faster rate than the growth of the population. One result, of course, was to drive down the costs of food.

A profound change relative to food and drink was the growing awareness that dangerous bacteria could exist in both. Laboratory discoveries, however, reached the public only slowly. Mary Ronald, editor of an 1897 cookbook, noted that milk was a proven disease carrier and every careful mother should boil it before giving it to her children.[1] There was a heightened interest in packaging foods. Milk was bottled for the first time, and some dry foods, including bread, were wrapped to lessen contamination.[2]

Knowledge of nutrition grew. By 1840 it had been generally

agreed that proteins, fats, carbohydrates, and minerals were needed in the diet. For long it was thought that only proteins could support muscular activity, but late in the nineteenth century this idea was discarded. The composition of foods was tabulated by Karl Von Voit of the University of Munich, a task continued by his American pupil W. O. Atwater, and important work on nutrition was done by Russell Henry Chittenden as head of Yale's Sheffield Scientific School.

Popular knowledge of nutrition remained slight. For a time the public seemed aware only of the calorie, and to purchase the most of them for a given sum of money was the general goal. Not until late in the century was it widely known that the mineral elements in food were also important, and that food must contain traces of vitamins to prevent some disagreeable diseases or even death.[3]

The American housewife was given a new mantle of dignity as it became known that government bureaus were studying food and that universities were establishing departments of home economics. One cookbook editor noted that "advanced women" had been taught by higher education "to regard their domestic duties in the light of a science and an art." And Fannie Farmer, remarking the increased attention to nutrition, concluded that the study of foods and their dietetic value would soon be "an essential part of one's education."[4]

There were those who stressed the health aspect of food almost grimly. Although American writers had rarely noticed cooking as a sensuous art, this new emphasis almost excluded the role of enjoyment. Sarah Tyson Rorer, whose cookbooks were major successes, expressed the idea baldly:

> . . . the teacher or cook book (an ever present teacher) that does not teach health, body building, and economy in time and money, is short lived. There are still a few women who do elaborate cooking to please the palate and appetite, and the general habits of people. They are still in the palate stage of existence. Strive to reach a higher plane of thought — eat to live.[5]

Happily not everyone moved away from "the palate stage of existence." Mary Ronald, author of *The Century Cook Book,* while admitting that "hygiene, economy, system, and methods" were better understood and more generally practiced than in earlier times, nevertheless urged her readers to emulate the French in honoring fine cooking and to follow the great Savarin in seeking to dine rather than merely to feed.[6]

As food became an object of scientific study, the kitchen became a planned space for its preparation. The room that for three centuries had provided Americans with warmth, evening light, food, pleasant cooking odors, and an agreeable meeting place now began to lose many of these characteristics, especially in the cities, and became increasingly a laboratory presided over by a housewife-technician. The size of the kitchen shrank as its uses declined and, in urban areas, as escalating land values took their toll.

An efficient organization of the kitchen had been proposed by Catherine E. Beecher and her sister, Harriet Beecher Stowe, in their joint work *The American Woman's Home,* published in 1869. This urged a thoughtful arrangement of stove, sinks, cupboards, and storage bins to minimize waste motions. Well-lighted, waist-high working surfaces were suggested with storage space beneath for rye flour,. coarse Graham flour, and cornmeal, in addition to a flour barrel whose lid fitted flush with the other working surfaces. The range was separated from the preparation room by sliding doors to cut down on summer discomfort and to reduce kitchen odors.[7]

Other kitchen changes were useful. After the middle of the nineteenth century a kitchen might have two pumps, one for rainwater and the other for well water. The sink was made of wood with a grooved wooden drainboard. Not until the 1870s were painted iron sinks sold and not until the end of the century did enameled or porcelain sinks become common.

Experiments with the cast-iron stoves continued. Wood and coal remained the principal fuels, but coal dust, tar, sawdust, and kerosene were all tried, the last finding some favor. The gas range appeared about 1850, but for half a century it was considered both extravagant and dangerous. During the 1890s gasoline stoves had a temporary vogue that was shattered by numerous explosions. Not until late in the century was an electric stove attempted, one being included in the model electric kitchen that awed visitors to the Chicago Columbian Exposition of 1893. An innovation of real importance came by the century's end in the form of a heat indicator which could be put into the oven door of any kitchen range.[8]

There were no important improvements in the household refrigerators, or "ice boxes." Many of these were based on the principle of air circulation, but they were of poor quality and their insulation was often so bad that moisture gathered within the wall to corrode the metal lining and to promote the growth of bacteria. Often, too, the temperatures were not reduced enough to provide proper food preservation.[9]

But a wide range of new and improved appliances did appear in the kitchens. A galvanized iron boiler attached to the stove provided hot water. A hand meat grinder, or chopper, greatly speeded up the chopping of meats and other foods which had previously been done with knives. Time and trouble were also saved by eggbeaters, a farina kettle, an apple corer, a potato peeler and slicer, raisin and grape seeders, ice shredders, spice mills, and juice extractors.[10] A fuller and more sophisticated selection of kitchen knives became available, as well as measuring spoons and cups, spatulas, molds, and other small kitchen tools.[11]

Another development benefited not only the kitchen but the entire house. Until the late nineteenth century flying and crawling insects had infested houses at will, especially during the summer months when windows and doors stood open. Poison, traps, and long strips of gummed paper in the kitchen and dining room gave little relief. A revolutionary change began when, during the Civil War, a company that made wire mesh for sieves overproduced and sold its surplus to cover windows. During the next decade some screening was manufactured, but as late as the 1880s and 1890s screens remained a novelty to most people.[12]

The industrialization promoted by the Civil War did not bypass the food industry. During and following the war an ever-growing number of food items came from the large millers, processors, and manufacturers. National brands of food were not new — Baker's chocolate long antedated the war — but it was during the postwar years that they became an appreciable part of the household larder and a factor in forming popular attitudes on food and food habits. Within a few decades after the war, claims to superiority were made nationwide on behalf of Price's Baking Powder, Postum, Shredded Wheat, Grape Nuts, Foss's Flavoring

Extracts, Knox's Gelatine, Golden Cottolene Cooking Fat, Yeast Foam, Pillsbury Flour, Uneeda Biscuits, Quaker Oats, Swan's Down Flour, Lion Coffee, and Chase and Sanborn Coffee, among others. The promotion of such brands became big business. Favorable mention of products was "bought" by the placement of advertisements in cookbooks, magazines, and newspapers. Skilled lobbyists pushed for state and national legislation to protect the growing food industry.

Through every possible means the public was told that the various national brands were clean, standard in quality, reliable, delicious, and highly nutritious. The claims for cleanliness and good quality, sometimes deserved, carried weight with housewives. Although the general store, with its foods sold from boxes, crates, and barrels, was a social center and the site of fascinating odors, it also frequently sold soggy and dirty crackers, dried fruits that were mixed with pebbles, twigs, and dirt, sugar that was unclean and adulterated, flour that was uneven in quality and at times dirty, and other foods of dubious purity and uncertain origin. Reading of foods that claimed to be better, housewives brought pressure on storekeepers to stock the national brands.

Cold breakfast foods were the sharpest break from the past. About 1865 one appeared that consisted of bread crumbs.[13] Then during the 1870s a Dr. John H. Kellogg became manager of the Western Health Reform Institute in Battle Creek, Michigan, an organization founded by vegetarian Seventh-Day Adventists. Under Kellogg's direction various foods were made for the Institute's patients, including peanut butter and a flaky wheat cold breakfast food. Soon afterward Will K. Kellogg, a brother, invented Corn Flakes. About the same time Henry D. Perky, of Denver, Colorado, was creating Shredded Wheat and Charles W. Post was developing Grape Nuts and Post Toasties. New hot cereals also appeared. In 1897 Maria Parloa, compiler of popular cookbooks, wrote that the time was past when the housekeeper was limited to three or four kinds of mush: "The market is filled with many different preparations," and each was "pronounced by its maker to be the best."[14]

Both the hot and cold patented breakfast foods won huge markets. The cold ones, especially, were convenient, labor-saving, and acceptable to a generation that could forego hot mush when central heating was available. Successive generations were to eat them regularly in the firm belief that they were highly nutritious when in most cases they were not.

The food industry also made gains in commercial canning as technical advances brought lower prices. The variety of canned goods grew. A rural store in Illinois in 1865 advertised seven different canned fruits, and two years later a grocer in Flemington, New Jersey, offered canned peaches, pineapples, blackberries, whortleberries, green corn, beans, peas, asparagus, tomatoes, spiced oysters, clams, lobsters, sardines, and salmon. By then, or soon after, there were canned crab meat, beef, apricots, blueberries, and cranberry jam. Volume also rose rapidly. Where only five million cans were put up annually by 1860, a decade later the amount was six times greater.[15]

Still, in the eastern parts of the country the commercially canned foods were rarely used. They were too expensive for the poor, and the thrifty housewife preferred to do her own canning. That the commercially canned foods were sometimes unsafe also worked against them. A cookbook warned that there could be "no absolute safety" in canned goods and urged that purchases be made only from reputable houses and that the ends of the cans should not bulge, indicating the presence of spoiled food.[16] But possibly the greatest reason for the slow acceptance of canned goods was housewifely pride. Cookery was for housewives an important means of self-expression and to admit canned goods to the kitchen, except as emergency rations or as foods not otherwise obtainable, was somehow disgraceful.[17]

Through most of the West there was neither shame nor hesitancy about using canned goods, for they were often the only alternative to a diet of intolerable monotony. To the western plains came canned oysters, sardines, tomatoes, condensed milk, salmon, and various fruits and vegetables. Samuel Bowles, who accompanied the party of Schuyler Colfax, soon to be vice president in Ulysses S. Grant's administration, into the West in 1865, wrote about canned foods with seemingly heartfelt praise:

Here, too, in the mining camps of the Mountains, and along the continental pathway, — away from home orchards and gardens, and city markets, — we wonder at as we enjoy the free use of canned vegetables, fruits, fish and meats. We realize for the first time how great is the extent of the business of their preparation, — how useful and beneficent is the invention of the process. They are on every table; few New England housekeepers present such a variety of excellent vegetables and fruits, as we found everywhere here, at every hotel and station meal, and at every private dinner and supper. Corn, tomatoes and beans, pine-apple, strawberry, cherry and peach, with oysters and lobsters, are the most common; and all of these, in some form or other, you may frequently find served up at a single meal. These canned vegetables and fruits and fish are sold, too, at prices which seem cheap compared with the cost of other things out here. They range from fifty cents to one dollar a can of about two quarts. Families buy them in cases of two dozen each. And every back yard is near knee deep in old tin cans.[18]

Canned oysters from Baltimore became a staple fare in western saloons, and cowboys on the trail often used canned tomatoes to quench their thirst or as a dessert.[19]

Not only commercial but home canning increased. The home preserving of meats, fruits, and vegetables became easier during the 1850s when there appeared on the market glass jars that could be sealed. By the late 1860s the use of these had grown greatly. A popular brand was Mason's and the name "mason jar" in time was generally accepted. The glass jars were lighter, cheaper, and more sanitary than the old tin or crockery ones, and with them a housewife could not only "put up" her foods but could then admire her work. Rows of shining glass jars and the multicolored display of winter foods within them gave her pride and joy.

There were other signs of a growing interest in food and cooking. Not only were more cookbooks published than ever before, but the newspapers and periodicals gave greater attention to food than in the pre-Civil War period. Some of the new journals were addressed to household problems, including cooking: *Household, Devoted to the Interest of the American Housewife* began a thirty-five year career in 1868; the *Ladies' Home Journal* appeared in 1883 and *Good Housekeeping* two years later.[20]

Large and quickly flourishing cooking schools opened in the bigger cities. An impetus in this direction came when Pierre Blot, a Frenchman and self-proclaimed "Professor of Gastronomy," visited the United States after the Civil War and gave lectures throughout the East. He then started the New York Cooking Academy which was taken over by Juliet Corson when he returned to France. In Philadelphia, Sarah T. Rorer joined with four of her cousins to begin the Philadelphia Cooking School in 1878. Somewhat later the Boston Cooking-School was founded which soon had Mary J. Lincoln and then her pupil, Fannie Farmer, as guiding lights on the faculty. How well these schools trained their students is not clear. The Philadelphia school's course consisted of only twenty-four demonstration lectures. At some schools each student could invite "a gentleman" to share the prepared meal.[21]

The directors and faculty members of these and other schools were not backward in publishing cookbooks. Maria Parloa in Boston not only founded two cooking schools but authored a series of cookbooks. Mary J. Lincoln, of the Boston Cooking-School, was the compiler in 1886 of *Mrs. Lincoln's Boston Cook-Book*, and this was followed a decade later by the work of her pupil Fannie M. Farmer, *The Boston Cooking-School Cook Book*, a work that made its author famous. In New York, Juliet Corson prepared several popular cookbooks, and a major success was Sarah Rorer's *Mrs. Rorer's Philadelphia Cook Book* of 1886.

Some cookbooks were designed for what was thought to be a new market in the South, created by the abolition of slavery. They referred to the "change of times" in the South, or were dedicated to the young women there in this "peculiar crisis" who had only "inexperience and ignorance" of household affairs. Another mentioned the women of the "Sunny South" who had "So Bravely Faced the Difficulties Which New Social Conditions Have Imposed on Them."[22]

The Civil War's legacy of poverty and social change had hurt the eating habits of that section. The few, simply prepared foods of the poor changed least, and a great part of the South would retain a corn-pork-game diet for generations. Many planters, however, now impoverished, could no longer enjoy the meals that had given the South a reputation for fine cookery. To some extent this tradition was carried on by prosperous farmers, supply merchants, and cotton buyers of the middle class together with the new upper class of landlords, bankers, and professional men. These, as they saved or gathered wealth from the ruins, came to have gardens, livestock, and the aid of expert cooks from the reservoir of black labor.[23]

New social conditions joined with the greater interest in nutrition to create criticism of American eating habits. The editor of a housekeeper's manual noted that many people considered the "coarsest food" most healthful and avoided the "made" dishes, arguing that they, their parents, and grandparents had been healthy and that there were more important duties "than beating eggs and making pastry." Such people forgot, wrote this author, that earlier generations had used more oxygen in a day than their descendants did in three, and that the former mode of eating, including a large amount of pork, was no longer necessary.[24]

A contributor to *Harper's Magazine* in 1866 sharply attacked the country's eating habits:

As a people, we are the worst cooks and the most unwholesome feeders in the world. Hardly one in a hundred of our cooks can broil a steak or boil a potato, and not one in ten of our business men has a correct idea of feeding. Bolting down hot rolls, rendered chemically destructive of the stomach lining by preparations of soda, and swallowing hot coffee, either Mocha or rye as the case may be, is not at all a good way of breakfasting.

Like others, this author found Americans overaddicted to the frying pan:

We fry our food a great deal too much. Flour fried in fat is one of our delights. Dough-nuts, pancakes, fritters, are samples of what we do with good wheat flour. Fried ham, fried eggs, fried liver, fried steak, fried fish, fried oysters, fried potatoes, and last, not least, fried hash await us at morning, noon, and night.[25]

The new self-criticism took note of regional foibles. Mary Terhune, who edited cookbooks under the name of Marion Harland, attacked the "stereotyped" bills of fare of New England: "It is an idea which should have been exploded long ago," she wrote, "that plain roast, boiled, and fried, on Monday, Tuesday, Wednesday, and Thursday, cod-fish on Friday, with pork-and-beans every Saturday, are means of grace, because economical."[26] And the southern devotion to pork was criticized, one man stating that

217

"the southern consumption of grease — of fat in one form or another would, I am sure, astonish even an Arctic explorer." Another author estimated that the South, despite its warm climate, consumed twice as much pork as did the North.[27]

A population that was ever more urban, sedentary, and warmed by central heating, turned to simpler meals. Oscar, the maître d'hôtel at the Waldorf-Astoria in New York City, claimed, about the turn of the century, that dinners at the luxury level had declined in a generation from ten to five or six courses and that foods were served more simply than earlier, with fish being offered without sauces and salads appearing in less complicated forms. He did not know whether fear of gout or of chronic indigestion led his wealthy clients to eat less.[28] Others noticed that the primacy of the frying pan was ebbing. "There is," wrote the author of a popular cookbook, "a popular prejudice against fried foods, and a belief that abstaining from them will cure us of our dyspepsia."[29]

Table manners changed. An article in *Scribner's Magazine* in 1874 stated that eating with the knife, customary twenty or thirty years earlier, had become a "vulgarism" with the invention of the four-tined fork, though another writer fifteen years later thought that half of the lower-class Americans still followed the old custom. Discontinued as vulgar was the custom of pouring tea or coffee from the cup into a deep saucer to cool. The innovation of the butter knife also added to table politeness.[30]

Changes in the diet were credited with improvements in the American physique. Sellers of ready-to-wear clothing during the 1880s found it necessary to use a larger scale of sizes. And an Easterner who had known both New York City and Boston for half a century stated in 1895 that the men had become "more robust and more erect" and the women "greatly improved both in feature and carriage."[31]

Neither the new knowledge of nutrition nor any consequent improvement in health affected a great part of the country's population. Northern slum dwellers, southern sharecroppers, small farmers on the Great Plains, the recently freed slaves, and the underprivileged everywhere were, as always, concerned only with getting enough to eat. An appreciable portion of the country's population was regularly hungry and a larger part was badly nourished.

The poor of the rural South possibly ate less well than they had before the Civil War. A visitor to the Carolinas just after the war decided that pork made up at least half of the food of all classes outside the towns and cities. The blacks, he added, lived on corn and rice and such game as they could take. A white man admitted that "we don't give the neegurs bacon this year like we used to." Where the sharecropping system replaced the plantations, both whites and blacks were restricted to small plots of land on which they were encouraged to raise as much cotton as possible. The system sacrificed garden space to cotton and produced a diet of low nutritive value and little variety.[32]

In a country where the successful were convinced that the nation was moving inexorably toward ever greater wealth and comfort, at least for the energetic and virtuous, there were few to notice those who lived in misery. Only occasionally was the public allowed a peek into the lower levels such as that offered by an author in *Harper's Magazine*. To the peach orchards of Delaware and Maryland's eastern shore, he wrote, came the "homeless" pickers from the "back lands" of the cities and from the hospitals and almshouses. These, "generally presenting the lean ragged appearance of semi-starvation," were engaged to pick by the day with board or half board considered as part of their wages: "The experienced prefer half board, which consists of a single meal — a dinner of unlimited salt pork and johnny-cake, peaches being substituted for the other meals."[33]

Misery in the cities ballooned during the depressions that seemed to strike every twenty years. In that of 1873 – 74 tens of thousands were hungry in cities and received only meager relief at soup houses. In New York City, where Lorenzo Delmonico of the famous restaurant supervised the free meals, he reported that in one city ward alone 71,892 people had been fed between February 18 and April 7.[34]

Clearly, great changes were abroad in the land. Whereas in 1800 nearly all Americans had lived on farms and felt secure from hunger, by the late decades of the century this was no longer the case. Instead, many were boxed in cities and their welfare was tied to an economic system that chose some for prosperity but could, in the writhings of its uneven growth, consign the losers to suffering and hunger.

❧ 16 ❧
The Foods at Hand, 1865-1900

*I was obliged to own that
over a plebeian cabbage
we have had a real feast.*

New foods appeared and old ones flourished or declined in the decades after the Civil War. Spreading urbanism and the new power of industry were not solely responsible. The country's diet was touched by the vagaries of fashion, novel nutritional ideas or vogues, and the preferences of immigrant groups. Technical developments made some foods cheaper or more accessible: the ever-expanding network of railroads, improvements in cold storage and refrigerated transportation, commercial canning, and a revolution in farm machinery all played parts.

A declining portion of the food came directly from nature. Game was increasingly limited to those in near-wilderness regions or the wealthy. Wild fruits, herbs, and vegetables were neglected as cultivated ones became more accessible. The role of seafood declined in the diet as an ever-greater part of the population lived distant from the sea.

Meats still dominated meals. Anthony Trollope, the English novelist, found the United States to be one of the few countries in the world where meat was eaten two or three times daily,[1] and an American complained that his countrymen were "too carniverous" and fed "too exclusively on steaks of beef, chops of mutton, cutlets of veal, and joints of meat."[2]

The Civil War nurtured a rapid growth in the production and sale of meats. The industry centered in such cities as St. Louis, Cincinnati, and notably Chicago, all bridging the grazing lands of the Great Plains and the urban markets of the East. Large Civil War contracts fattened the Chicago stockyards during the Civil War, and soon afterward the founding of Armour and Company and Swift's helped to make the city a major meat-packing center.

The beef supply was greatly expanded by the growth of the range cattle industry in Texas and on the Great Plains. Raising cattle on the plains required a huge expanse of territory and trails which followed the pasture season northward. Cattle were driven from Texas up the Chisholm Trail to railheads in Abilene, Kansas, and other depots from which they were shipped to Chicago and other packinghouse centers.[3]

A Detroit packer, G. H. Hammond, built a meat refrigerator car in 1871, to begin a major advance in meat shipping. Now midwestern packers could send fresh meat to eastern markets, and by the early 1880s this trade was well established. The large packers set up refrigerated branches in a few leading eastern cities, from which fresh meat could be delivered to retailers as easily and more cheaply than by the local slaughterhouses. Then "peddler car" routes were established that made it possible to deliver small quantities of meat to more distant markets. To supply these new markets the midwestern packers needed mass production, and this was provided by the assembly line with the carcasses moved by power-driven machines. Soon the plants themselves were refrigerated, and this led to the manufacture of numerous by-products and meat canning.[4]

This flow of meats from the Midwest did not reach all Americans. Rural areas distant from railroads might have little meat other than salt pork. A resident of Dakota Territory complained that "hogs don't winter here," and another settler there in 1884 concluded that "*Fresh* meat is not to be thought of, if located far from a town." In towns the butcher might kill a beef once a week. A schoolteacher who "boarded round" in southern Minnesota confessed that during an entire winter she didn't once see fresh meat.[5]

As low-cost beef became available to eastern markets, some among the well-to-do began to look down on pork as rural, lower class, and inferior. Mary Terhune, a compiler of cookbooks, commented that any who had seen how pigs lived and were fed "cannot marvel at the growing prejudice against pork in all its varieties that pervades our best classes."[6] Mary J. Lincoln condemned

221

pork as an "unwholesome" meat which should never be eaten by children, those with weak digestion, "nor, indeed, by any one except in cold weather." She did admit that salt pork, bacon, and ham were less objectionable.[7]

Although pork might be snubbed at polite eastern tables, it was by no means discarded. For over two centuries it had been a mainstay of American meals and its flesh and lard had penetrated all areas of the diet. In the South and portions of the West it remained the principal meat.

Nor would any condemnation of pork have included the famous Smithfield hams of Virginia. These, to an annual output of about 20,000 hams, came largely from Surry, Southampton, and Isle of Wight counties, where the hogs ran in the woods during the summer, living on nuts, roots, and other wild foods. In the fall they were allowed to glean in the harvested fields of corn, black-eyed peas, potatoes, and peanuts. Later they were confined, kept clean, and corn-fed prior to slaughter.[8] The curing of the hams, as elsewhere in the South, was a matter of individual choice, with the virtues and drawbacks of each method being hotly disputed.

Beef did not decline in popularity. Throughout the northern states and the West, beefsteak remained a favorite dish and could appear at both breakfast and dinner.[9] Usually, beefsteak meant a thin cut of beef, fried, and with a pan gravy. For the more discriminating, beef was increasingly defined by specific cuts: sirloin steak, porterhouse steak, tenderloin steak, and filet of beef, each served plain or with dressings of onion, mushrooms, tomatoes, or in the Creole fashion.[10] Roast beef, "very undone, almost raw," was said to be the "most called for" dish in New York City restaurants.[11] Corned beef, both with cabbage and hashed, was common everywhere.[12] Beef tongue was popular, either hot or cold or as a filler for sandwiches.[13] By the 1870s the Hamburg steak had appeared, its name derived from the German city,[14] but its spectacular success lay far in the future.

While restaurant and hotel menus listed mutton and lamb chops, lamb's tongue, mutton kidneys, and lamb with mint sauce, it was only in the Northeast and Southwest that much lamb and mutton were eaten. An English visitor to New England concluded that mutton and roast beef were "the usual" meat dishes.[15] In the Southwest, lamb and mutton had been eaten by the Spanish since their first settlements. A visitor to New Mexico in the 1880s found that the inhabitants lived well on "the juiciest beef and mutton" and that mutton stew and soup were both popular. Texans, especially the Mexican-Americans, also ate both goat and kid.[16]

Turkey and chicken remained the leading fowls. Turkey was a principal Thanksgiving and Christmas dish and was usually served with cranberry sauce. Chicken was commonly boiled with a piece of pork in New England and fried throughout the South. In Maryland it was customary, after frying a chicken, to make a cream gravy in the pan to pour over the fried pieces. As early as 1878, when the Grand Union Hotel in Saratoga listed it on its menu, the dish was given the name of Maryland fried chicken.[17] The name would far outlast any memory of what it represented.

A new source of poultry appeared in 1873 when the captain of a Yankee clipper ship returned from China with some tall, white Pekin ducks. He gave some to a friend who had a farm on Long Island. There they increased and, having a fine taste, began a reputation for Long Island ducks that soon led to large-scale production.[18]

A great part of the country still took meat from the declining game of the forests, fields, and plains. Many rural dwellers could find deer and small animals to shoot or trap. Venison remained a common dish for New England Thanksgiving dinners, served roasted with currant jelly or cooked at the table over a brazier, and luxury hotels and restaurants on the eastern seaboard and in the Midwest still obtained wild fowl and venison.[19]

Some animals which had been neglected when deer, bear, and wild turkey were numerous, now became targets of hunters. In parts of New England young woodchucks were prized. There were places in South Carolina where gophers were eaten, and one unidentified southern city sold muskrats in its market. "Cooked by the old negro cooks," a woman claimed, "a stew of muskrat, or musquash, is excellent." Opossums and raccoons were eaten throughout the South, as was wild hare.[20]

In Chicago's leading hotels — the Palmer House, the Grand Pacific, and after 1890 the Auditorium — guests could order buffalo, antelope, bear, and mountain sheep, in addition to less exotic game.[21] John B. Drake of the Grand Pacific Hotel continued to give his annual game dinners, that of 1895 being served to over a thousand formally dressed guests and consisting of a lavish array of fish, shellfish, and game from all parts of the country.[22]

In the West much game was still available. General Custer's

wife at Fort Sully between Yankton and Bismarck, Dakota Territory, attended a lunch which had nine kinds, including wild goose as a special treat.[23] In Denver, antelope steak was as common as mutton or beefsteak in New England, and in the Rocky Mountains elk, mule deer, and mountain sheep were often eaten.[24] But the small game was not disdained. Jules Leclercq, the French chef at the Pacific Hotel in Kansas City, offered "ragoût de prairie dog," and throughout the West prairie dogs and rabbits were taken as larger game became scarce. Jackrabbit stew was a common dish in the Oregon country.[25]

The slaughter of the buffalo continued. When William Cody, alias Buffalo Bill, hunted to feed the crews building the western end of the Kansas Pacific Railroad in 1867, he killed twelve buffalo a day, taking only the hams and humps.[26] Other professional hunters took from their kills only buffalo tongues, which brought fifty cents apiece when salted and sent east.[27]

The wholesale shooting of wild fowl continued. In the eastern states there were still quail, snipe, woodcock, and pigeons, together with robins and other small birds. The wild turkey was found in some parts of the South and West and the pheasant had been naturalized in Ohio and Kentucky.[28] Along the southern coasts waterfowl were hunted, including cranes and herons which were "broiled, or roasted when tender, or made into high-seasoned stews."[29]

Many still rated the canvasback duck as the greatest delicacy. In early October they began to come from northern breeding grounds to winter along the shores of Long Island Sound, the Delaware and Susquehanna rivers, and especially Chesapeake Bay. Such places, wrote one man in 1870, were "fairly alive" with them, though they were slaughtered "by means of all the devices which cruelty and brutality can suggest."[30]

People not accustomed to eating the canvasbacks were sometimes horrified by the "purple meat," for it was the custom to serve them barely cooked. They were a luxury of the well-to-do, and the high prices paid for them were responsible for their rapid decline.[31] Not far behind as a rare delicacy was the redhead duck, followed by the green-winged teal, the blue-winged teal, the mallard, and the pintail, all of which brought high prices. There were also the blackhead ducks which fed along the creeks and estuaries and the swans and wild geese that sat by hundreds on the flats around Chesapeake Bay. The brant, or barnacle goose, was still seen in the 1870s along the East Coast, especially in the flats and marshes of Long Island, but their slaughter for city markets was so excessive that by the 1880s they were said to be "very rare."

Before the century ended all these wild fowl were relatively scarce. To supply city markets swivel guns had been mounted in the bows of sailboats and fired into flocks of birds with terrible effect. One writer in 1870 prayed that he might live to see the game laws of the country, "now inefficient and worthless," improved, the "wholesale, cruel, indiscriminate, and unmanly slaughter" abolished, and the time when "those miserable institutions — decoys and blinds and painted boats — shall be known no more!"[32]

The beautiful passenger pigeons, which at their height may have numbered 5 billion birds in several big flocks, were prime targets for mass killing. Throughout the nineteenth century they were shot or clubbed to be eaten fresh, dried, or pickled, to be rendered into fat or fed to the hogs. A huge demand arose for squabs to eat and for live birds for trapshooting. At a single nesting in Petoskey, Michigan, some 2,000 persons were hired to catch, kill, and process pigeons. The birds were shipped by the millions from Pennsylvania and upper New York, and in 1869 a single Michigan county sent several million baby pigeons to market.

By the 1870s public anger led individual states to ban the slaughter, but these were the states where the pigeons were no longer seen. Soon the only passenger pigeons were in cages; by 1909 two only remained alive, both in Cincinnati, and the last of these died in 1914.[33]

Seafoods still provided much of the country's food, especially in coastal areas. New Englanders remained devoted to their fish, clams, and lobsters. The last had become a delicacy, and the Union Hotel at Saratoga used over 18,000 pounds of them during its 1869 racing season. Oysters were still very popular, and it was said that in New York City alone over 3,000 people were employed in various branches of the oyster trade. By the end of the century, however, Oscar, maître d'hôtel of the Waldorf-Astoria, noticed that oysters were in progressively less demand.[34]

Chesapeake Bay remained a magnificent storehouse of seafoods. On its shores thousands worked in the herring and shad fisheries, and the great oyster beds seemed as inexhaustible as did the quantities of soft- and hard-shell crabs, shrimp, clams, codfish, mackerel, and terrapin. In coastal Maryland the soft-shell crabs were sprinkled with flour and broiled. Later came the hard-shell crabs that were either steamed and eaten from the shell or the meat combined with vegetables or eggs and then fried, stewed, or made into soups.[35] The diamond-back terrapin had become so expensive that only the rich enjoyed it, others having to be satisfied with mud turtles, snapping turtles, or the Egg Harbor terrapin from the Delaware River.[36]

Oysters were the greatest product of the Chesapeake Bay region. In the early 1840s the canning of oysters began in Baltimore, and in the course of the next fifty years about 90 percent of the country's oyster packing was done there or nearby. During the 1880s the Bay produced nearly 15 million bushels of oysters a year, and canned and pickled oysters were shipped to every part of the country. By the century's end the massive harvesting of oysters, plus the unrestricted dumping of industrial wastes into the Bay, so reduced the beds that many canners moved to new sources of supply in Mississippi, Louisiana, and elsewhere in the Deep South.[37]

Seafood was important along the Gulf Coast from Key West, Florida, to Galveston, Texas. New Orleans was the epicurean center of this coast, and its reputation depended heavily on its gumbos, jambalayas, crawfish bisques, innumerable oyster dishes, and those made with pompano, redfish, red snapper, eels, shrimp, soft-shell crabs, and terrapin.[38]

Inhabitants of Pacific coastal areas enjoyed a large variety of saltwater fish, including tuna and sardines, and from fresh waters the rainbow and other trout, salmon, catfish, and bass. Oysters, in inadequate numbers and different from eastern varieties, were taken along the coast. In 1882 a railroad passenger crossing the Great Plains noticed a strange train shunted to one side that consisted of "seventeen trucks of oysters, bound from the shores of the Atlantic to the Pacific for 'planting.'" But though San Franciscans long favored the eastern oysters, in time the tiny Olympias were also highly rated.[39]

According to legend the oyster cocktail was invented in San Francisco in the 1860s when a miner, waiting for his main order, combined oysters and tomato catsup.[40] Wherever created, it was probably inevitable that someone would join the country's favorite delicacy with its leading sauce.

Throughout the interior of the country Americans depended upon freshwater fish or seafoods that had been salted, pickled, canned, or shipped refrigerated by railroad. Canned seafoods appeared early, because the first canneries were built on the coast and marine products were the major part of their production. The canning of oysters, lobsters, and possibly sardines, began during the 1840s. Salmon was canned on the Sacramento River in California as early as 1864 and soon became a low-cost, popular food everywhere. By 1867 canned clams were also sold.[41]

The railroads took seafoods well inland. To interior parts of Virginia, where oysters and fish had been little known, "immense quantities" of shad, rockfish, and herring were shipped each March and April. And people staying at the Union Hotel in Saratoga Springs, New York, to take the waters or attend the races, could order New England lobsters, green turtle from the Florida coast or Nassau, brook trout from the Adirondack Mountains, lake trout, muskellunge, and whitefish from Lake Erie, pickled oysters from Baltimore, and pickerel from Saratoga Lake.[42]

Even greater changes came to the country's dairy industry. Within a few decades ancient and slow hand methods were swept away by fast and efficient ones. A major step was the discovery in the late 1870s that cows gave more milk when provided green feed. Soon storage bins, increasingly in the form of silos, sprouted on dairy farms everywhere. About the same time the ages-old skimming of cream off the top of the milk by hand was replaced by a Swedish invention, the DeLaval Separator, which did the work swiftly by mechanical means.

A far more important invention took place in 1890 when Dr. Stephen M. Babcock of the University of Wisconsin created a machine to test milk for butterfat value. This encouraged the improvement of dairy herds, since each cow could now be evaluated. It also made the manufacture of butter and cheese more profitable and the ancient and widespread practice of watering milk simple to detect.[43]

Still, the country's butter was generally poor. It was heavily salted, Harriet Beecher Stowe implied, because salt cost but a tenth of butter. What was worse, it often tasted of cheese, turnips, cabbages, or rancid animal fat, all due to infrequent churning and the storage of cream in unventilated cellars or dairies. Factory production made butter more uniform. This began in Orange County, New York, in the early 1860s but tended to center in Illinois, Wisconsin, and Minnesota. By the 1890s machines replaced the manual handling and working of butter. About the same time devices began to cut one-pound bricks to please city housewives.[44]

Cheese remained popular, and a form of cheddar called American cheese was widely made throughout New England, New York, and the upper Mississippi Valley. Every country store, north and south, had a large circular cheese on a platform that rotated mechanically to measure a wedge for the hinged cleaver. Cottage cheese — also called curd cheese, smearcase, or Dutch cheese — was made at home, especially by the Pennsylvania Germans, as was cream cheese, sometimes called Philadelphia cream cheese.[45]

Large-scale factory production of cheese began as early as the 1850s by farmers in Herkimer County, New York, and increased rapidly after the Civil War, stimulated by commercial rennet from Denmark. By 1880 cheese making in the home had nearly ceased. The making of cheese became a science, and new types appeared.[46] *The Century Cook Book* in 1897 listed Stilton, Cheshire, Camembert, Gorgonzola, Rocquefort, Edam, Gruyère, and Parmesan as "among the best" foreign cheeses, but added that "nearly all" of them were imitated in the United States.[47]

Much more important were changes in the eating of vegetables. Canning, improved refrigeration, and better transportation had at last freed much of the populace from the all-winter dependence upon root vegetables, squashes, cabbages, and potatoes.

But whatever the vegetables, they were still cooked to excess through custom and the ancient distrust of them in a raw state. Even half-cooked vegetables were believed able to transmit cholera.[48] A cookbook of 1869 was not unusual in asking that string beans be boiled two hours, lima beans an hour, early peas half an hour, and asparagus forty-five minutes,[49] and an 1895 cookbook stipulated three hours for string beans and two hours for carrots.[50] Juliet Corson, more enlightened, complained that "generally" Americans boiled vegetables until they became a pulp without much flavor, color, or nutriment, and that greens were rendered a brown-green mass of fiber without much taste.[51]

Following the Civil War the South increasingly grew vegetables for northern markets, an industry that developed especially near seaports and railheads.[52] Juliet Corson thought that in the decade after 1878 the railroads had lowered prices, extended the variety, and improved the quality of vegetables in northern markets. Cities near sea or rail transportation, she wrote, now had, even in winter, fresh tomatoes, radishes, cucumbers, spinach, cauliflowers, eggplants, Valencia onions, and salad greens, all but spinach from the Deep South. Some of these needed only transportation, while others depended on refrigerator cars.[53]

The eating of salsify and celeriac increased somewhat, and kohlrabi became better known as German immigrants grew and sold it. Eggplant was still expensive and rare in New York City as late as the 1870s, but despite insect infestations an increasing supply came from southern growers.[54] Artichokes were known in America since the eighteenth century and prior to the Civil War appeared often on the tables of wealthy Virginia planters. They received publicity in 1868 when they were served at a banquet at Delmonico's honoring Charles Dickens. Then in the 1880s and 1890s Italian gardeners in California raised them for shipment east.[55]

A Virginia cookbook compiler noted in 1884 that okra in her state was rarely used save in soup, carrots were generally despised but were useful in soups and stews, and cabbage had fallen into general disuse with the upper classes because of its odor. Still, she added, in cabbage served with ham, chine, or middling "you have before you the daily and favorite dish of nine-tenths of the country people, not only in Virginia, but throughout the South, with the addition of a plentiful supply of hot corn bread." In early spring, however, turnip-tops became the Virginian's favorite dish.[56]

Cauliflower grew well in only a few places and remained expensive.[57] Celery, however, was cheap and immensely popular. A French visitor listed it as a vegetable which Americans "almost incessantly nibble from the beginning to the end of their repasts," and an Englishman noted the "prodigious" amounts on the tables of New York City restaurants.[58] In homes were special celery holders of pressed glass.

Americans continued to eat mushrooms, but only vague and

inconsistent methods existed to distinguish the poisonous from the edible varieties. In 1897 *The Century Cook Book* finally provided a relatively full discussion of the leading varieties. Many people bought dried and canned mushrooms imported from Paris where they were grown in the great quarries under the city. This import had begun in 1850 and would continue until World War I.[59]

Everywhere the green and yellow vegetables were accompanied, or even replaced, by four well-established "fillers" — dried beans, rice, sweet potatoes, and white potatoes. Each of these was sold countrywide, but each also had its areas of special strength.

The traditional Saturday meal of baked beans, cooked with pork and served with brown bread, declined in New England, though less so in rural and conservative households, restaurants, and boardinghouses. In 1875 a cannery in Portland, Maine, canned some pork and beans and, as other canneries followed, the dish grew in use throughout the country. In 1891 the Van Camp Packing Company in Indianapolis added tomato sauce to their canned beans, an innovation that was copied by others.

In the lumbering camps of Maine and the upper Mississippi, beans prepared by the bean-hole method were by far the most important single food. The cooking was done in a hole in the ground protected by a small log hut. Into a huge iron pot alternate layers of salt pork and parboiled beans were placed. The pot was then sealed, put among hot coals in the hole, surrounded with live embers, and a fire was kept burning over it for up to twenty-four hours. A cook in a Minnesota pinery claimed that "nothing can swing an axe, or move a saw, or roll logs, like baked beans. No logger who has free access to that iron pot in the ashes complains of exhaustion."[60]

Beans were a low-cost and filling food for both Mexican Americans and others in Texas, the Southwest, and southern California.[61] In lower Louisiana a basic Creole dish, and often the main one, consisted of red beans cooked with onions, parsley, pepper, lard, and small bits of one or more meats, all placed on warm rice. When served with a salad this made a complete and economical meal.[62]

Rice was a staple food in coastal South Carolina and Georgia, Louisiana, and much of the Gulf Coast and lower South. Like beans and white potatoes it was cheap, but far more than either of these it mixed with, or accompanied, meats, shellfish, in some places fish, vegetables, sauces, and gravies, and went into soups, stews, stuffings, and puddings. In large parts of the South sweet potatoes played the role of filler. They were eaten not only with meat and other vegetables but were made into pies, puddings, and even bread. In Virginia a sweet potato and a glass of milk were frequently used as a "plain" dessert. By the 1880s, and probably earlier, candied sweet potatoes were known.[63] Yams, in some parts of the South, were considered "higher class" than sweet potatoes.

In the northern states, the upper South, and much of the West the white, or Irish, potato was well established. "German fried" potatoes, according to one observer, became the "indispensable" breakfast dish. For dinner, potatoes were mashed, boiled, stewed, baked, escalloped, and served as Saratoga chips. As early as 1865, wrote Harriet Beecher Stowe, the city restaurants were introducing French fried potatoes "to great acceptance."[64] No one could have guessed how popular they would become.

Like the other fillers, potatoes were important to the poor. In southern Minnesota during the 1860s the meals of indigent families might consist of potatoes cooked in their jackets and a soup made from water, browned flour, and a few small pieces of fried fat pork.[65] On the Great Plains the potato was second only to corn as a part of every meal. It was usually fried but could go into a potato pie or Mulligan stew. Settlers in Oregon counted on sliced potatoes soaked in vinegar as a "sovereign remedy" against scurvy.[66]

Although the railroads and ever-improving refrigeration increased the flow of vegetables to city people, there were places where few were seen. Through much of the South Atlantic area the collard was for many farm families the only green vegetable in winter, and consequently it was widely grown. The tender greens that appeared in the turnip patch in early spring were eagerly picked and cooked after a winter of collards and pork.[67]

Fresh vegetables were very scarce on the Great Plains. A visitor to the interior of Texas in the 1870s found that the common diet consisted of pork and corn dodgers, pork and molasses, clammy biscuits, and no vegetables at all. Soldiers stationed in the Dakota Territory sometimes got scurvy, and Elizabeth Custer wrote in the early 1870s that one forgot the taste of fresh fruits and vegetables, making it an event when they appeared. She told a visitor from the East that she gave a dinner whenever she got anything rare. When asked what she considered a rarity, "I was obliged to own that over a plebeian cabbage we have had a real feast. Once in a great while one is reluctantly sold to us in Bismarck for a dollar and a half." At times only onions were available, and it was "fried onions at breakfast and dinner, and raw onions for lunch."[68]

The eating of raw fruits increased everywhere as fear of them as a source of sickness declined and as nutritionists lauded their health value. The refrigerator car, the cold-storage warehouse, the canneries, and better transportation by land and sea all helped fruit growers reach large, nationwide markets. Mass markets in turn encouraged regional specialization: the eastern counties of Maryland and the State of Delaware were the peach centers until Georgia took the lead; strawberries became large-scale crops in the Carolinas, the Gulf states, Arkansas, Missouri, and Tennessee; Michigan and New York grew and shipped Concord grapes; and during the 1890s the refrigerator car made Rocky Ford, Colorado, a center of canteloupe production.[69]

Several tropical fruits expanded their market areas. The pineapple, which had long come to a few coastal cities from Cuba, Puerto Rico, and the Bahamas, was imported in larger amounts so that by the 1880s they sold in northern markets for from twenty-five cents to a dollar and a quarter each.[70] Toward the end of the century the avocado, or alligator pear as it was long known, also became more common in eastern cities when the Gulf states began to grow them in quantity.[71]

Bananas, which spoiled quickly, posed a greater problem. Prior to the Civil War clipper ships had made occasional deliveries to northern coastal cities, and in the decade of the 1860s one Carl Augustus Frank and his brother began a regular import of bananas from Panama to New York City. But many Americans saw their first bananas at the Philadelphia Centennial Exposition of 1876 where they were sold, foil wrapped, for ten cents apiece. As steamships became faster the coastal cities received more shipments and by 1892 Boston had bananas eight months of the year. Two years later the United Fruit Company was formed and within a few years was shipping fruit to the larger interior cities.

Still, during the same decade, over 95 percent of all bananas shipped to the United States were eaten in five port cities.[72] Most Americans still knew the fruit only as a rarity of limited uses. Cookbooks either ignored it or suggested that it be eaten with sugar, fried, or served sliced with whipped cream. One, in 1890, gave a recipe for a two-crust banana pie.[73]

Oranges kept far better than bananas, and they had long been known to northern coastal cities and much of the Deep South. Well before the Civil War it was customary to place an orange in each southern, and many a northern, child's stocking for Christmas, a custom that would long continue among all but the poor. Until the 1880s the sweet and rather dry Havana oranges were preferred in eastern cities, but after that they were more and more replaced by the less expensive mandarins and tangerines from Florida.[74]

By this time California oranges were competing for eastern markets. There, commercial growing increased after the trans-continental railroad was completed in 1869. During the 1870s large-scale tracts were put into orange groves, mainly of the seed-less Washington navel variety, and during the 1880s refrigerator cars began to make summer deliveries to the East.[75]

California's citrus fruits got great publicity in 1893 at the state's exhibit at the Columbian Exposition in Chicago. A great tower of oranges, set in a sea of lemons, was renewed every few days, and in the courtyard of the Horticultural Building was a grove of twenty lemon and thirty orange trees, blossoming and bearing.[76]

A torrent of other fruits poured eastward from California. Grapefruit culture began there in the 1880s. Table grapes and raisins, apples, peaches, pears, plums, apricots, figs, and olives were all produced for the California market and then for eastern ones. In the 1890s the date industry began and flourished, especially after someone got shoots of the Deglet Noor. To the north, Washington and Oregon came to have many pear, apple, and cherry orchards and large raspberry plantations.[77]

Fresh, cultivated fruits, except for watermelons, long remained unknown or a luxury to Great Plains dwellers. In the Dakota Territory, Elizabeth Custer ate strawberries only once in many years of frontier living. Another resident of the Territory rejoiced upon receiving some bananas from Kansas City. Oranges were so rare as to be kept for invalids.[78] It is not surprising that canned fruits were so happily received. By 1865 there were canned peaches, apricots, pineapples, strawberries, and cherries,[79] with still others to follow.

A new crop helped to satisfy the deeply entrenched yearning of Americans for sweetness. Sorghum, a coarse grass closely related to sugarcane, had been known in southern Europe for centuries. It may have been introduced to America by William R. Prince, a nurseryman of Flushing, New York, who in 1853 brought some seeds from France. The United States Patent Office publicized the Chinese sugarcane, as it was long called, and by 1859 it grew in thirty-two states. During the Civil War its use expanded rapidly in rural areas as the war cut off supplies of Louisiana sugar and molasses.[80]

In retrospect, then, the late nineteenth century anticipated many of the food changes of the following one. The foods straight from the country's forests and waters were declining, but improved transportation, refrigeration, canning, and meat-packing were making domestic meats, fruits, and vegetables available to more people and during greater parts of the year. The union of big business and the nation's foods was being sealed, a marriage surcharged with problems that as yet could only be sensed.

⚜ 17 ⚜
The Winds of Change, 1865-1900

*It is hard
for the American to rise from his winter breakfast
without his buckwheat cakes.*

Not only the foods of Americans but the ways in which they were prepared changed in the third of a century following the Civil War. As people moved from the heavy labor of farms to light work in cities, the bounteous meals and heavy dishes of a rural America had to give way. Similar adjustments were needed as labor-saving machinery increased on farms and in factories. In a different sphere the work of nutritionists, made known in schools and through the press, affected what reached the dining tables. Even some new and better kitchen tools transformed foods from old to novel forms.

New dishes and methods of cookery also came from foreign countries. Those Americans who traveled to Europe, and there were many more than formerly, felt these influences sharply. Others, throughout the country, were affected by immigrant groups.

While Americans resisted, and even mocked, unfamiliar food customs, there was no fully formed cookery to oppose all change. From the first, Americans had had to adapt to different foods as they moved to new frontiers in unfamiliar geographic regions. On each frontier there was a mingling of different races, nationalities, and classes, all momentarily deprived of their customary eating habits. A fixed pattern of eating could not harden. Rather, there took place an interchange of food customs which could occur casually through the exchange of recipes at a tea or

235

quilting party, or formally as by the marriage of an Anglo-American to a German-American.

For several decades after the Civil War the non-English influences on American food habits still came from northern and western Europe. Some were imported by wealthy Americans whose travels introduced them to foreign cooking. Mary Terhune, for one, was not impressed by the depth of their conversions:

> I know — no one better — how women who have never cared to beautify their own tables, or to study elegant variety in their bills of fare, who have railed at soups as "slops," and entrees as "trash," talk, after a year's travel in foreign lands their husband's earnings and their own pinching have gained for them. How they groan over native cookery and the bondage of native mistresses, and tell how cheaply and luxuriously one can live in *dear* Paris.

Such a "Mrs. Noveau Riche," she concluded, could dawdle all afternoon over a piece of tasteless embroidery and give the afternoon to gossip "while Bridget or Dinah prepares dinner, and serves it in accordance with her peculiar ideas of right and fitness."[1]

Less wealthy Americans who attended the Centennial Exhibition in Philadelphia during the extremely hot summer of 1876 had an opportunity to sample several exotic forms of cooking. Not only were there French, German, and American restaurants at the exhibition, but a New England kitchen which prepared dishes of that region, a southern restaurant, and a Tunisian café. Very popular was a Vienna bakery where it was possible to buy not only fine coffee but the much-admired Viennese rolls made with dazzling white flour.[2]

Although the average American remained either ignorant of French cooking or considered it somehow dishonest, not so with the rich. In 1865 the kitchen workers of New York City organized as the Société Culinaire Philanthropique, and both their name and their first president, Louis Ragot of Delmonico's, underlined the Gallic influence. The city's social leaders attended the Société's annual dinner dance.[3]

The French chefs employed by private families in New York City grew from about a dozen in 1870 to over 150 in 1880. Frenchmen presided over the kitchens of the Vanderbilts, Astors,

Goulds, Lorillards, Schuylers, and Havemeyers, among other wealthy families. Their salaries, as of those who worked in the great hotels, were very high. In 1883 the Hoffman House paid $300 a month, a great sum for the day, to Eugene Laperreque, who had been head cook for the Rothschild family in London and more recently chef of the Café d'Anglais in Paris.[4]

In far-off San Francisco French restaurants and caterers spread the French influence. Although the cooks in private homes were largely Chinese, it was said that they had learned their art from French cooks, directly or through the medium of the mistress of the house.[5]

Everywhere, cookbooks gave French-inspired recipes for soufflés, breads, soups, pastries, veal dishes, sauces, omelettes, chicken preparations, sweetbreads, and salads among other things. It became fashionable to use such words as potpourri, croûtons, potage, filet, soufflé, fricassée, ragoût, piquante, purée, croquette, consommé, and paté. Restaurant menus affected French words, though a visitor from France found fault, noting *"Hors d'noeurves"* and *"Poummie de Terre Dauphin."*[6]

French culinary practices met some resistance. A writer for *Harper's Magazine* in 1869 thought a Roman punch at dinner after the soup was a "very objectionable" practice borrowed "with many other bad fashions" from the French.[7] And a midwestern cookbook inveighed against "made-dishes," as the "horrible imitations of French cookery prevalent in America are termed," as "very unwholesome." Harriet Beecher Stowe thought that the answer to any proposal for greater culinary aesthetics would be: "O, we can't give time here in America to go into niceties and French whim-whams!"[8]

The German influence, already two centuries old, was strengthened by a large new immigration that began about 1870. Unlike the French cuisine, which appealed to the wealthy and sophisticated, German cooking affected mostly the middle and lower classes, especially in such "German" cities as Cincinnati, St. Louis, and Milwaukee. In these and other cities German beer gardens, restaurants, and saloons attracted both German immigrants and native-born. Into the country's consciousness and meals crept such things as German rolls, numerous cookies and cakes of German origin, sauerkraut, German potato salad, German fried potatoes, Hamburg steak, German noodle soup, pigs' feet and knuckles, and sauerbraten. Both potatoes and pork, already well entrenched in America, received new support. Some foods — such as the pretzel, which German immigrants to Pennsylvania had imported in the colonial period — now became known everywhere.[9]

In some places the farming of Germans was influential. An author in *The Atlantic Monthly* wrote in 1867 that "New York is indebted for its vegetable markets to the Germans, who were the first to educate the suburban soil for the growth of kitchen stuff, and who have still almost a monopoly of the market-garden business in the neighborhood of the city." Germans who settled in eastern Texas sold milk, butter, buttermilk, fresh vegetables, and salad greens to a population that normally ate only salt pork, corn bread, and sweet potatoes.[10]

Compared to the German impact, that of the Irish was slight. Their immigration began to decline after the heavy influx of the 1840s to 1860s, but for a generation Irish girls and women made up perhaps nine-tenths of the servants in homes, boarding-houses, and hotels throughout the northern states. Their background of poverty was such that it was said, cruelly, that they knew little more of cooking than how to boil and bake potatoes. One English visitor was apparently informed that in the eastern states nearly all the cooks were "raw young Irishwomen, who can boil a potato, make tolerable oyster soup, and perhaps concoct a tolerable clam chowder, but who roast badly and fry abominably."[11] The Irish certainly increased the popularity of Irish potatoes, especially since they themselves were reported to have disliked Indian corn in any form. A few Irish recipes entered cookbooks: Irish stew of mutton, potatoes, and onions, and Carrageen or Irish moss blanc-mange.[12]

The Italians had a far greater effect on American food habits. This was partly because their cooking was strange enough to interest Americans but not so different as to be unacceptable or difficult.

Although macaroni had been known in the United States since Jefferson's administration, it was through the late nineteenth-century immigration of Italians that its use became widespread. As late as 1886 it was called an upper-class "luxury," but a few years later was described as a "favorite American food, but its treatment is not as well understood as it should be." By this time Italian immigrants manufactured it in New York City, Philadelphia, and San Francisco. Macaroni with cheese and macaroni soup both gained some popularity.

Spaghetti, too, became known. Mary J. Lincoln in 1888 called it a "variety of macaroni" to be served in the same way.[13] But during the 1890s it was "discovered" in New York City. A factory on Staten Island began making it in quantity, it was featured in New York City's Italian restaurants, and cookbooks told how to prepare it.[14] Other Italian dishes were also noticed: sabayon, Italian salads, pastries, and desserts.[15]

Among the continuing immigrations from northern Europe, the arrival of Swedes in eastern cities was remarked upon. Ward McAllister, social leader and gourmet, commented in 1890 that during the preceding six years Swedish women cooks had come to the United States and were "excellent, and by some supposed to be better than chefs." They were "cleanliness itself," he added.[16]

The Chinese, though they established restaurants in major cities, remained in their eating habits as curiosities more to be marveled at than imitated. Even the chop suey that was to offer native Americans a weak conduit to the nearly infinite variety of Chinese cooking did not exist until the century's end.

New, potential sources of inspiration to American cooks came with the acquisition of Puerto Rico, the Philippines, and Hawaii, the first two following the Spanish-American War of 1898. Hawaii alone brought under the American flag native Hawaiians, Chinese, Japanese, South Sea Islanders, Koreans, and Portuguese, together with smaller groups of Samoans, English, Scots, Russians, and Germans.[17]

The first Americans who arrived in Hawaii in the early nineteenth century were given pigs, fish, yams, sweet potatoes, breadfruits, bananas, and coconuts. Missionaries discouraged the eating of roast suckling dogs which had been penned and carefully fed on coconut milk, breadfruit, and other vegetables.[18]

By the late nineteenth century the Anglo-Saxon core of American cooking was besieged from many sides. The northern European influence, including Scandinavia, continued, and from Italy, Greece and other southern and eastern European countries came surprising new tastes and ingredients. Mexican-American cooking spread from the Southwest and soon the country knew chili con carne, tamales, tacos, enchiladas, chili sauce, and, possibly a Mexican contribution, deviled eggs. And California became a funnel for foreign influences. A visitor there found it a "gourmet's sixth heaven" with unfamiliar seafoods, meats that were not factory refrigerated, and an "eclectic school of cookery" to which China, Japan, Spain, Mexico, and Hawaii had contributed.[19] As yet, however, the nation's cookbook editors scarcely noticed foreign influences. Sarah Rorer added to her work only small sections of Jewish, Spanish, and Hawaiian recipes.[20]

There was a slight, but growing, interest in American regional cooking. Southern, New England, and Creole cooking were those most noticed. But such attention was usually poorly done, as when *The Century Cook Book* stated that the distinctive and excellent dishes of the South were those made "of cornmeal, of gumbo or okra, or those seasoned with sassafras powder or twigs."[21]

Most changes in eating habits, however, came from the growing urbanism, the new food industries, food fads, and new knowledge of nutrition. Usually, the changes appeared first among urban sophisticates and then moved, if the cost was moderate, to the middle and even the lower classes.

Of the breads, those made of corn kept a strong following, especially in the South and West. Between the northern corn breads and those of the South there was a marked difference. Northern millers removed the germ which contained the fat, most of the important minerals, and much of the flavor. The result, though usually a fine, yellow, and sweet meal, was scorned by some Southerners as fit only for chickens and cattle. One southern woman admitted its sweetness, but "I have never succeeded in making really nice bread from it." The southern meal, called water-ground, was white and coarse and made a looser bread with a touch of bitterness. It had lost, in milling, only the hulls.[22]

On the Great Plains corn bread reigned alone. Settlers there, convinced that farming and corn were inseparable, long put off attempting the hard wheat that would later give the region economic strength. During the 1850s, 1860s, and 1870s corn was the staple food and corn bread usually the only bread. Children took corn bread and molasses to school for lunch and some became so tired of corn, which appeared at every meal, that in later life they refused to touch it.[23]

Wheat breads made great gains. Throughout the North white bread came into general use, while in the South wheat biscuits made with sour milk or buttermilk and soda were eaten everywhere and by nearly everybody. These biscuits could be delicious, but often they were tough, pale in color, and streaked with soda.

A revolutionary change came to wheat flours in the postwar years. When the Civil War ended, each community still had its own mill. Some areas were famous for their flours: the Genessee Valley white winter wheat of western New York was renowned, as were white winter wheat flours in Michigan, Ohio, Indiana, and Missouri. But then a technique was invented by which air currents separated flour from bran. The local grist mills, unable to afford the machinery for the new process, began to give way to larger mills. And since the new invention made successful milling of spring wheat possible, within a few years Minneapolis, in the midst of the spring wheat area, became the flour-milling center of the country.

Still another major change took place in milling. Americans visiting both Vienna's world's fair in 1873 and the Centennial Exhibition in Philadelphia three years later were delighted with the Vienna rolls of fine, white flour that they bought at each. During the same years American millers investigated in Hungary the roller-milling process that made such flours, and in 1876 the first all-roller mill in America was opened in Philadelphia.[24] Before the end of the decade Minnesota millers, aided by Hungarian engineers, built steel rolling mills that crushed wheat into fine, white, Viennese-type powder. The new flour, soon standard everywhere, was nutritionally inferior to whole wheat flour or even the less well-crushed white flours that they replaced, but the complaints of nutritionists were brushed aside.[25]

With or without the new flour, commercial bakeries faced a popular conviction that bread should be baked in the home. A British visitor in 1869 thought that nearly every family did so and that the bakers sold mainly to the poor.[26] Store bread, wrote the editor of a cookbook, was deeply suspect: "Whether on the score of health, of cleanliness, or economy, it is impossible to urge too strongly the importance of making bread at home."[27] A few years later Mary Terhune scored bakery breads as "vari-colored sponges . . . inflated with sal volatile, flavorless, and dry as chips when a day old, and too often betraying, in the dark streaks running through the interior of the loaf, want of cleanliness in the kneader."[28]

During the last third of the century there was a flowering of the sandwich. Prior to the Civil War it had been thin slices of beef, ham, or tongue, usually flavored with mustard, between thin slices of bread and used for tea, supper, picnics, or the convenience of travelers. In 1861 a sandwich of boned fish flavored with mustard or catsup was proposed, and five years later an innovative cookbook author listed cheese, cold boiled eggs, stewed fruit, jelly, and preserves as fillings. Others suggested chopped nuts, mushrooms, chicken, watercress, sardines, and jam. Inevitably this newly popular form of food used the favorite party salads in the form of both chicken and lobster salad sandwiches. From Texas came an open, toasted cheese and cracker sandwich with more orthodox ones of olives, onions, or pimientos as filling.[29]

By the 1870s the sandwich was well launched toward a prolific and varied future. It was made daintily for tea parties and in "mammoth size" for saloons and urban quick-lunch places. Its fillings, both sweet and otherwise, multiplied, and a cookbook of 1897 termed it "the chief reliance for cold lunches."[30] Recipes for "school lunch sandwiches" faced an existing fact and anticipated a remarkable future.[31]

Salads became an object of experiment more slowly. For nearly a generation after the Civil War the average American probably did not eat salads at all. But some among the middle and upper classes used lettuce salads and others made of potatoes, tomatoes, and cabbages. For balls, evening parties, or formal afternoon teas, lobster, oyster, crab, chicken, and turkey salads were highly rated.[32] Chicken salad particularly was a party favorite. An English visitor to Newport in 1869 found it always served at ball suppers there.[33] And a writer who claimed expertise on salads said it was "justly regarded as an American dainty" and one never found in perfection elsewhere and often not even in America.[34]

The well-to-do usually served green salads dressed with vinegar and olive oil. But many found olive oil too expensive, or rancid, or adulterated with cottonseed oil. Two other dressings flourished well into the twentieth century. One combined two parts of hot smoked bacon fat with one part vinegar, while the other simply combined sugar and vinegar. Few used garlic, there being a "very general prejudice" against it.[35]

During the 1880s the salad became a plaything of the adventurous. As a light dish it was suited to a population that was becoming urban and sedentary. Salads were also in harmony with the new emphasis on healthful eating. Juliet Corson, who wrote on food for both *Harper's Bazaar* and the New York *Tribune,* included lettuce or cucumber salads in many of her weekly model menus and urged her readers to use such greens as watercress, dandelions, sorrel, chicory, escarole, chives, kohlrabi, and celeriac. A visitor to California found it the "land of salads" and thought the shrimp and alligator-pear salads in San Francisco made a trip there worthwhile.[36] Cookbooks everywhere expanded their salad sections to offer recipes using hard-cooked eggs, cabbage and celery, salmon, beef, tomato and onion, apple, apricot, banana, bean, celery and walnut, cauliflower, orange, aspic of paté, and chicken with walnuts among others.[37] Mayonnaise was mixed with, or surmounted, a variety of fruits and vegetables. The word "salad" came to be used loosely, and Sarah Rorer complained that many cooks joined fruit, sugar, and alcohol and served the mixture as a salad.[38]

By the end of the century salads had found a home in many middle-class homes and restaurants. One Maximilian De Loup, in *The American Salad Book,* smugly urged Americans to cease believing that foreign countries were ahead in salad making. France had long been so, he wrote, but it no longer had the great variety of fruits and vegetables available in the United States. England was still "barbaric" in regard to salads, and the Teutonic varieties were sometimes too powerful for American tastes. Other nations were mostly imitative, as Americans had been in the past, "while we are fast learning that originality and adaptation have given us the best the world affords." De Loup admitted that Americans still ate too few green salads, but they would learn some day to prefer them to "heavy bulky materials." In the meantime, celery was used to make "the most popular and abundant" of the winter salads, fruit salads were winning converts, and the potato salad which had been served hot in the conviction that cold potatoes were unwholesome, was now being served cold.[39]

Soups lagged behind both sandwiches and salads in finding greater space on American tables. An American dinner, a foreign visitor concluded in 1869, "is usually wanting in soup — you plunge *in media*[s] *res* at once."[40] Editors of many cookbooks gave only a few soup recipes, and they omitted soup entirely from their proposed economy menus.[41]

Not everyone ignored soups. As a dish that was both economical and nutritious soup was given to men in jails, appeared in army regulations, and was included in the free lunches of saloons.[42] The Pennsylvania Germans ate soup, as did the Creoles of New Orleans, the Cajuns of the Mississippi Delta, and nearly all recent immigrants from continental Europe. Again, soup was often the first course at fashionable dinner parties,[43] and the maître d'hôtel Oscar remembered that during the 1890s it was customary for diners at both Delmonico's and the Waldorf Hotel to eat two soups, one a consommé and the other a cream soup.[44]

Coastal inhabitants found soups a good vehicle for seafoods. Terrapin, clam, oyster, crab, and lobster soups were all popular, and the chowders that had begun as stews were given increasingly greater liquid content to render them soups. New Orleans owed much of its fame as a gastronomical center to its bouillabaisses, its oyster, terrapin, crab, and crawfish soups, its clam bisque, and its gumbos of shrimp, crab, and oyster. Hot, filling, and delicious, the gumbo pleased everyone. An admirer in 1885 described it ecstatically:

> The great dish of New Orleans, and which it claims the honor of having invented, is the GOMBO. There is no dish which at the same time so tickles the palate, satisfies the appetite, furnishes the body with nutriment sufficient to carry on the physical requirements, and costs so little as a Creole gombo. It is a dinner in itself, being soup, *pièce de résistance*, entremet, and vegetables in one. Healthy, not heating to the stomach and easy of digestion, it should grace every meal.[45]

Although most Americans lived without soup, there were signs of increasing interest. It was a light dish, suited to the times, and inexpensive, a fact important in a period that saw a severe panic in 1873 and then, during the administration of Grover Cleveland, a panic in 1893 that was followed by nearly a decade of grim depression. During the last quarter of the century cookbooks began to give proportionately greater space to soups,

244

and there is evidence that in restaurants, and probably in homes, they were served more frequently.[46]

The interest in lighter foods in an increasingly sedentary country affected the size of meals. More and more the morning breakfasts of steak, ham, eggs, fried potatoes, pie, and buckwheat cakes were replaced by less formidable fare. While some Americans returned from Europe to advocate the continental breakfast of coffee and rolls, most people would have agreed with Mary Terhune that American breakfasts should be a "pleasing medium" between the "heavy cold beef and game pie of the English and the — for our climate and 'fast' habits of life — too light morning refreshment of the French."[47]

As bacon, eggs, and toast replaced steaks and pies for morning fare, the country's love of hot cakes for breakfast only grew, perhaps because they were themselves relatively light. The varieties of hot cakes were legion and had such names as rice cakes, corn cakes, griddle cakes, flannel cakes, buttermilk cakes, sourmilk cakes, flapjacks, slapjacks, hominy cakes, buckwheat cakes, and various waffles and fritters.

Of them all, buckwheat cakes were the great favorite. From their eighteenth-century centers of Pennsylvania and New Jersey these had expanded geographically until now they formed the final wintertime breakfast course through much of the country. "It is hard for the American to rise from his winter breakfast," wrote an English traveler, "without his *buckwheat cakes*. They are eaten everywhere, and nothing could be nicer."[48] The cakes were served in piles of three "because they cannot be eaten in perfection" otherwise. Butter and maple syrup were considered the proper dressing, wrote another traveler, "and it is the waiter's business at an hotel, when he sees you are finishing your breakfast, to ask 'if you will have some cakes.'" One cookbook author noted that from "time immemorial, buckwheat cakes and sausage have gone to the table side by side."[49]

On the western plains where buckwheat was unavailable, the slapjack made with wheat flour was the substitute. Slapjacks with sorghum molasses and bacon, or slapjacks "smothered in fat" often made an entire meal. A Texan in 1882 who was accused of living on bacon and slapjacks the year around denied it: "Slapjacks and molasses," he answered, "are all very well in winter, but we never touch them in summer."[50]

A major contribution to lighter meals was the invention of the hand-cranked meat and food chopper. This, doing quickly what the knife had done slowly, opened to the housewife an entire school of dishes based on chopped foods: croquettes, timbales, patties, loafs, hashes, veal birds, and Hamburg steaks, among others.

Of these, croquettes had the greatest success. These were simply minced fowl, fish, meats, or vegetables mixed with a thick white sauce, formed into a shape, and fried. Almost unknown during the 1860s — as late as 1878 being called "a sort of a mince-meat dumpling" — they grew popular during the following decades. They appealed because they gave a use for leftovers, made a dainty dish for the lunches that were increasingly replacing dinner as the midday meal, were economical, and created a whole new range of dishes in which the housewife could take pride.[51]

The Hamburg steak also won friends. Chopped beef had long been known in the Baltic states of northern Europe. Merchants from Hamburg imported it to their city as steak Tartar, often eaten raw, and in time German emigrants carried it to the United States. By the 1870s and early 1880s Hamburg steak appeared in American cookbooks just when meat grinders were beginning to replace knives for chopping purposes. It was served in lower- and middle-priced restaurants,[52] but not until the next century would it make fateful union with the roll.

The vogue for croquettes was matched by one for sweetbreads. These glands of the calf had generally been discarded until about 1870 when, possibly due to the urging of French chefs in America, they were found to be delicious, and many recipes appeared for their preparation. They were creamed, scalloped, fried, prepared with mushrooms, bacon, peas, or a tomato sauce and, joining two vogues, made into croquettes. In eastern cities, at least, sweetbreads became so popular that housewives had to order them from the butcher several days in advance.[53]

In the 1890s middle- and upper-class Americans suddenly discovered the chafing dish. This had long been known to poor and Bohemian elements as a cheap metal instrument for simple cooking. Now, however, chafing dishes moved from the low-cost and useful to the expensive and playful, and instead of tin ones for ninety cents they were made of graniteware, nickel, copper, or even silver and cost up to a hundred dollars.

The chafing dish could cook eggs, cheese, fish, shellfish, chicken, oysters, mushrooms, a Welsh rarebit, or other foods exactly to the wishes of the fastidious. Or it could provide a pleasant hot dish at lunch to replace the usual cold meat. But far more common was its use for supper parties. Then the expectancy of good fare, the pleasure of watching the preparations, and the interest of seeing something cooked over an open flame all added to the enjoyment. Only preliminary preparations should be done in the kitchen, the amateur cook was warned, "before the party assembled to assist in the cooking operation with their advice, praise, and appetite." The chafing dish, wrote one commentator, "always seems to accompany hospitality and good cheer." Fannie Farmer found it "most happily in evidence when congenial spirits meet to make glad after 'the lamps are lit,' and 'small cheer and great welcome make a merry feast.'" "With a little patience and practice," wrote another, the chafing dish "becomes a dainty accessory to my lady's charms, and many a manly heart has grown warm and tender under its gentle auspices."

The equipment could be elaborate. Wooden spoons, wooden "Russian" bowls to hold ingredients, and a Japanese tray on which to carry them were all thought necessary, with fuel flagons, skimmers, egg poachers, long-handled forks and spoons, serving dishes, spices, fuels, and wines, all making it clear that chafing-dish cookery was neither common or "Bohemian." Its principal supporters, thought Fannie Farmer, were housekeepers who did their own work and had but one maid and the society girl who through the chafing dish "first gains a taste for the art of cookery." All told it was a pleasant union of convenience and gaiety for a generation that some have labeled, not altogether wrongly, one of innocence.[54]

The desserts also moved toward lightness and were the objects of experiment. The use of heavy baked or boiled puddings declined, but did not disappear. Plum pudding remained traditional for Thanksgiving and Christmas. In Virginia, and probably elsewhere, it came to the table flaming. But the lighter puddings, such as rice pudding, bread pudding, tapioca pudding, and especially blanc mange were used more often. The gelatinous desserts were very popular, aided by a powdered gelatin which Charles Knox marketed in the 1890s.[55]

Although pies no longer appeared at several meals each day in urban areas, among farm families in northern states they were part of most meals. An English traveler decided that "pie really forms as important a factor in American civilization as the *pot-au-feu* does in France."[56] The strength of the pie tradition in New England was witnessed by Mary J. Lincoln who attempted to persuade housekeepers there to substitute fresh fruit for the "persistent pie" over which so many women toiled "for naught save the fear that they may be considered shiftless if they haven't a pie in the house."[57] She could have been addressing the Vermont farm wife whose records showed that in 1877 she had made not only 421 pies, but 152 cakes, 2,140 doughnuts, 108 puddings, and 1,038 loaves of bread.[58] A woman in Ohio, however, thought that the New England *"pie-belt"* was outranked by the Middle West where in farming areas pie was a necessity for two out of three meals.[59]

Pies, like puddings, were attacked as heavy and dangerous to the health. An author in *Harper's Magazine* in 1866 inveighed against them:

> We are fond of pies and tarts. We cry for pie when we are infants. Pie in countless varieties waits upon us through life. Pie kills us finally. We have apple-pie, peach-pie, rhubarb-pie, cherry-pie, pumpkin-pie, plum-pie, custard-pie, oyster-pie, lemon-pie, and hosts of other pies. Potatoes are diverted from their proper place as boiled or baked, and made into a nice heavy crust to these pies, rendering them as incapable of being acted upon by the gastric juice as if they were sulphate of baryta, a chemical which boiling vitriol will hardly dissolve. . . . How can a person with a pound of green apples and fat dough in his stomach feel at ease?[60]

The Pie Belt moved westward across the Great Plains. A schoolteacher in Minnesota who boarded around received mince pie in which salt pork was substituted for beef, pumpkin for apple, sorghum for sugar, and dried gooseberries for raisins.[61] Raisin or apple pies were a treat for cowboys on the Chisholm Trail in the 1870s.[62] And at stage stations on the plains pies were sold, one sufferer reported, of "sole-leather lard-soaked lower crust, half-baked, with a thin veneer of dried apples daubed with brown sugar."[63]

There were regional preferences. On Cape Cod the cranberry pie was much liked,[64] and New Englanders were devoted to squash, pumpkin, mince, and apple pies. Southerners enjoyed lemon, orange, peach, sweet potato, and pecan pies, and Texans favored the last two. Rural Ohio knew wild grape, dried apple-sauce, and green currant pies, among many others. Some varieties were novel everywhere, such as coconut, tomato, banana, cheesecake, and chocolate pies. Late in the century a vinegar pie flourished.[65]

Unlike pies, cakes were not attacked as either too heavy or unhealthy, and new recipes increased, both north and south, during this inventive period. There were pound cakes in which each principal ingredient weighed a pound, coffee cakes flavored with coffee, and sponge cakes. The ancient gingerbread cakes remained popular in the North, especially New England, and Southerners made lemon, orange, sweet potato, benne seed, and coconut cakes as well as the long-liked Sally Lunn derived from England.[66]

Cakes were frequently featured at both private parties and public occasions. At times they were given names to celebrate people, places, and major events: General Robert Lee, New Year's, Mont Blanc, Bride's, Merry Christmas, Lincoln, Union, Centennial, Phil Sheridan, Election, Thanksgiving, Tilden, Minnehaha, Kelley Island, Jenny Lind, and, a New Orleans favorite, Sarah Bernhardt.[67]

A striking development was the coming and explosion into popularity of the layer cake. The first were jelly cakes well before the Civil War.[68] After the war the variety grew, and a cookbook of 1885 listed thirty kinds.[69] This cake gave the American housewife a new way to offer, with love and pride, showy creations to her family and friends.

Another cake, a form of soufflé, appeared. Before the Civil War various cakes made with egg whites were known as white cakes, snow cakes, or silver cakes. During the 1860s some of these were named angel cake, and by the 1870s they were given the name angel food.[70]

Doughnuts remained popular throughout the North, and on Cape Cod they joined cookies and pies on the breakfast table.[71] Everywhere in New England they were a popular snack or, in the language of northern New England, a "lunch." Doughnuts were not round with a center hole until the century's end, but were instead given solid shapes.[72]

The strawberry shortcake probably emerged during the "Strawberry Fever" of the 1850s. It was possibly of New England origin with wild strawberries preferred. A Nebraska settler in 1857 mentioned "a wild strawberry shortcake" for tea but gave no other details.[73] For a decade after the Civil War the dish was usually a split biscuit, buttered, with strawberries and sugar.[74] A cookbook of 1880 mentioned it as a "great delicacy" that was eaten at tea, cut into triangles and served with sugar and cream.[75]

Pastries had to compete with fresh and canned fruits and ice creams. The last continued its huge success and was put to new uses. When Alaska was purchased from Russia in 1867, Chef Ranhofer at Delmonico's created, in celebration, a "baked Alaska," a brick of ice cream enclosed in meringue and quickly baked.[76] Near the century's end Lillian Russell, the singer, accompanying Diamond Jim Brady, the financier, to dinner at the Waldorf-Astoria Hotel, was unable to choose between ice cream and canteloupe for dessert. She finally decided to take both, whereupon the waiter returned with a half melon and a serving of vanilla ice cream in the hollow. Miss Russell was so pleased that Oscar, the maître d'hôtel, named the dish after her.[77] The combination outlasted the name.

Ice cream was given new flavors, including banana, coffee, coconut, apricot, and tutti frutti.[78] Vanilla, which had long been a favorite, temporarily lost rank. Many people considered it "injurious," reported one writer mysteriously. Highly esteemed were the Philadelphia ice creams which were made entirely of cream. When eggs were added to these they were known as Neapolitan ice creams.[79]

Two new ice-cream dishes were destined to thrive outside the home. As early as the 1870s vendors of soda water had added sweet cream to the flavored drink and this practice led naturally and easily to the invention of the ice-cream soda. The concoction, according to a relatively credible story, was created by a seller of soda water at the Semi-Centennial Exposition of the Franklin Institute in Philadelphia in 1874. Running out of sweet cream, the account goes, he obtained vanilla ice cream from a nearby vendor and served it frozen to general satisfaction.[80]

The ice-cream sundae came a quarter of a century later. Its origin may have stemmed from a ban on the Sunday sale of ice-cream sodas in some places because soda was looked on as wicked. This led to a soda-less dish which was first called a Sunday and then, to meet sabbatarian objections, a sundae. Both Evanston, Illinois, and Two Rivers, Wisconsin, claim to be the birthplace. Irrespective of which, if either, was right, by 1900 salesmen of soda-fountain supplies were offering tulip-shaped dishes to contain the new delicacy.[81] A few years later members of the Women's Lunch Club in New York City enjoyed lunches that included "ice cream overpoured with maple syrup and walnuts."[82]

A growing variety of candies met the American demand for sweet foods. There was a vogue for sugar cockles and white and green wintergreen hearts with daring mottoes: "I love you," "Be my sweetheart," or "Ever thine." There was also an active sale to children of jelly beans, cinnamon drops, seashore pebbles, chicken feed, sugar-coated nuts, and other fanciful confections.[83] Immigrants brought candy-making skills. An English traveler found "candy" and "caramels" were "institutions" in America: "Swiss *confiseurs,* German *conditorei* keepers flock over here and make fortunes."[84] In New Orleans black *marchandes* called out their wares in the streets: popcorn tictac balls made with "open kettle" brown sugar, pralines, macaroons, candied orange pieces, and nougats.[85]

Most candies were made in the home, often at parties. Taffy frequently played a role in youthful gatherings and front-porch courtings, but there were also marshmallows, caramels, nougats, peanut candy, creams, molasses candy, and candied fruits.[86]

Late in the century someone invented fudge, very possibly by simply adapting a cake-frosting recipe. Briefly, the new candy sought a name. One 1894 cookbook called each of three varieties not fudge, but "fudges," while another of the same date named the confection Ploughed Field, the instructions advising: "When cool, plow in squares with a knife." Chocolate, vanilla, and maple fudges were soon followed by coconut and divinity ones. For some years fudge-making was a countrywide fad, especially among young women. Early recipes were named Wellesley College fudge, Vassar fudge, and Smith College fudge, and an alumna of the University of Chicago remembered of the women's dormitory about 1900: "And there was fudge. Lots and lots of fudge."[87] The making of fudge, like taffy-pulling and chafing-dish efforts, was suited to the lighthearted gatherings that were one of the more pleasing aspects of the late nineteenth and early twentieth centuries.

❦ 18 ❧

Eating Out, 1865-1900

*There is scarcely a square
without several oyster-saloons;
they are aboveground and underground,
in shanties and palaces.*

By the last decades of the century there were eating places everywhere, so diverse that the country's dining habits and tastes were displayed with all that they revealed of mediocrity or excellence, of variety or monotony. There were restaurants to fit or strain any purse, to provide the familiar "home cooking" or the strange, to give fast service to the hurried or measured service to the leisured. In the largest cities those of every class, every nationality, every region, and every taste could discover places to dine that at least approximated their desires.

Americans who wished to dine in luxury might choose a large city hotel. Boston had the huge Young's Hotel and the Parker House. In New York City were the prestigious Hoffman House whose kitchen, chef, and bar all commanded immense respect, and later the Holland House, Savoy, Plaza, New Netherland, Imperial, and the Waldorf, soon through a large addition to become the Waldorf-Astoria. In Philadelphia was the Continental, in Washington the Willard, and Chicago's best were the Sherman House, the Grand Pacific, the Tremont House, the Palmer House, and the Auditorium which opened in 1890 to become a social center. The St. Charles in New Orleans was the great hotel of the South. St. Louis had the grand and comfortable Southern Hotel. In Denver the Windsor and the Brown Palace had prestige, and San Franciscans took understandable pride in their fine Palace

Hotel. Resort areas had other luxury hotels. Thus in Saratoga Springs, New York, were the Grand Union, holding nearly 2,000 guests, Congress Hall, the United States, and the Columbian.

Gone from all the larger hotels were the long tables and table d'hôte servings and from many the American Plan by which a single payment covered both room and meals. But Europeans still found grounds for complaint. When the French composer, Jacques Offenbach, stopped at the Fifth Avenue Hotel in New York, he was often seated next to a stranger, the waiter brought him a huge bill of fare, after which there was a long delay before his order was taken. Then, to his dismay, everything ordered was brought at once.[1]

This was the era, in hotels and restaurants, of small oval dishes, and what Offenbach received almost certainly came in these. A French traveler described the procedure:

Their custom is to set everything ordered, and some other dishes as well, on the table at once, forming a circle of small plates, where the meats grow cold. They concede you one empty plate, surrounded by this semi-circle of smaller plain plates, or rather small, hollow oval objects, something like a bird's bath. The real Yankee does not use this plate much, but plunges his fork at random into the little baths, fishes out something from the confused heap, or makes the most formidably-seasoned mixtures of a thousand different ingredients, after which he imagines he has dined.[2]

Anthony Trollope, never friendly to the American scene, became almost apoplectic on the subject: "How I did learn to hate those little dishes and their greasy contents!" he wrote.[3] "As a result of this mode of serving," a Polish traveler complained, "everything you eat is cold, stale, and unappetizing, even in the best restaurants."[4] By the early 1880s Americans had also begun to criticize this "medley dinner."[5]

The luxury hotels had long menus. One traveler counted fifty-two breakfast and seventy-five dinner dishes at the Fifth Avenue Hotel in New York.[6] Where the American Plan was in effect, wrote one observer, "you may see people order three or four times as much of this food as they could under any circumstances eat, and, picking at and spoiling one dish after another, send the bulk away uneaten."[7] William H. Russell, an English journalist, heard a man at the Willard in Washington order a breakfast of black tea and toast, scrambled eggs, fresh spring shad, wild pigeon, pigs' feet, two robins on toast, oysters, and a number of different breads and cakes.[8]

The disappearance of the long tables and the table d'hôte, which had led diners to compete for the food, diminished the hectic speed with which earlier generations had eaten. One tourist from Europe even denied that middle-class Americans, "who are the chief frequenters of hotels," ate any more rapidly than Europeans.[9]

Most foreign travelers, though they disliked the oval dishes and the simultaneous serving of everything, agreed that the cooking at the major hotels was good or excellent. The chefs were nearly always French, and many of the hotel owners had large farms, gardens, conservatories, and dairies near the city to provide food to their kitchens. "The American landlords," one English traveler concluded, "are very enterprising, are especially careful in the *cuisine*, and easily adopt foreign customs and inventions in the art of cookery."[10]

The great range of eating places was most evident in three American cities — New York, New Orleans, and San Francisco. Each was the major port for its coast and all were centers which had attracted people from the different regions of America and from many foreign countries.

In New York City the Waldorf-Astoria had a national reputation for sumptuous dining. It was a favorite of the after-theater crowd where such celebrities as the financier J. P. Morgan or musical-comedy queens like Lillian Russell, Anna Held, and Edna May could be seen. The hotel's use of the chafing dish to prepare specialties like chicken à la King and lobster Newburg did much to make that form of cooking a national vogue. Most housewives, too, heard of the "Waldorf salad" of chopped celery, apples, and walnuts on lettuce with a mayonnaise dressing.[11]

Delmonico's remained the most elegant, expensive, and best restaurant in the country. Its meticulously prepared French dishes aroused the admiration of all. One Frenchman wrote: *"Il est meilleur et plus somtueux, dit le New-Yorkais, que le premier restaurant de Paris, et c'est vrai* (It is better and more sumptuous, the New Yorkers say, than the best restaurant in Paris, and it's true)."[12]

Charles Ranhofer became chef at Delmonico's in 1862 and during the following thirty-four years carried the restaurant's fame to ever greater heights. Three branches were opened in New York City, and all were successful.[13] Delmonico's pleased both discriminating diners and those who enjoyed lavish expenditures and display. Stories spread of meals there where each cover cost eighty dollars, where a bouquet of rare flowers was placed before each woman, and where all guests received the menu engraved on a precious metal. But just a "first-rate" dinner at Delmonico's, wrote one man, was a "very serious affair" in cost.[14]

Soon after the Civil War Delmonico's played a part in the emancipation of women. Unescorted women were not welcomed in public restaurants. Some bought a pastry at a bakery, while others went to John Taylor's café on Broadway. He, a leading caterer, served them well-prepared food with courtesy. It was an audacious step, however, when some of the city's leading women formed the Sorosis Club and proposed luncheon meetings. Delmonico's made available a big second-floor room, and here a first meeting took place on April 20, 1868. The ensuing shock waves led some husbands to force their wives to resign, but the remainder persevered. In time a few women's restaurants appeared. One carried a large sign: "Women's Cooperative Restaurant; tables reserved for gentlemen."[15]

As Delmonico's fame grew the adjective "Delmonican" entered general use and recipes carrying the name spread. One dish became famous. In 1876 one Ben Wenberg showed Charles Delmonico a new way to cook lobster. Delmonico put it on the menu as Lobster à la Wenberg, and it so remained until, after a quarrel between Wenberg and Delmonico, the name was changed to Newberg (later modified to Newburg), by reversing the letters of the first syllable.[16]

For a brief four-year period Delmonico's only serious rival was the Maison Dorée on Fourteenth Street, founded in 1861 by a man named Martinez. Soon the Hoffman House and the old Waldorf also became competitors. Then in 1890 a greater threat appeared when Louis Sherry opened a magnificent restaurant at the corner of Fifth Avenue and Thirty-seventh Street.[17] With its elegant decor and outstanding chefs, Sherry's appealed both to the city's social set and to lovers of good cooking. Also outstanding was the French restaurant in the Brunswick Hotel which in summer had the added advantage of a large garden where meals were served under a canvas awning. The French composer Jacques Offenbach thought that Morelli's Italian restaurant and Frascati's Spanish restaurant were also excellent. He regretted that he had not found an "American" restaurant of a comparable class: "Nothing is more difficult for a foreigner than to eat an American meal in America."[18]

At quite a different level were the oyster saloons which fed the unabated appetite for oysters. A British traveler concluded that the oyster could be called "the national dish — it is at least the great dish of the Atlantic States." In New York City, he continued,

> There is scarcely a square without several oyster-saloons; they are aboveground and underground, in shanties and palaces. They are served in every imaginable style — escolloped, steamed, stewed, roasted, "on the half shell," eaten raw with pepper and salt, devilled, baked in crumbs, cooked in *patés,* put in delicious sauces on fish and boiled mutton. The English oyster is but a poor shrivelled pigmy of a fish in comparison; these are large and round, sweet and tender, and often so portly that you must divide before swallowing them. The oyster is the *sine qua non* of all dinner parties and picnics, of all night revels and festive banquets. For tenpence you may have a large dish of them, done in any style you will, and as many as you can consume. The restaurants — ostentatious and humble — are in the season crowded with oyster lovers: ladies and gentlemen, workmen and seamstresses, resort to them in multitudes, and for a trifle may have a right royal feast.[19]

Late in the century the oyster saloons were supplemented by "lobster palaces." These were more ornate and had a larger menu. The first was built by the Shanley brothers on Broadway just north of Forty-second Street and was decorated with gilding, chandeliers, elegant fittings, and fine carpets. It served not only oysters but fish, game, and chops and had an orchestra, one of the first in a New York restaurant. Even more spectacular was the Olympia, two blocks farther up, and this was followed in 1899 by that of the Chicago restaurateur, George Rector, a block above.[20]

The city had many modest foreign restaurants. On Houston and Bleecker streets were some imitative of English chophouses. These offered stewed tripe, liver and bacon, mutton chops, porterhouse steaks, pork and mutton pies, Welsh rarebit, and cuts from "joints." A favorite beverage at these was the "half-and-half," and tobies of ale were also called for. "Poached eggs and Welsh rarebits," wrote an observer, "give a sporting, noisy tone to the house, and the visits of gentlemen distinguished in the ring render a dinner exciting."[21]

A small number of unpretentious Italian restaurants offered table d'hôte dinners, each accompanied by a bottle of red wine. A sharp change took place in the 1890s when it was discovered that excellent spaghetti could be made in America. "Spaghetti joints" began to appear in many places and to flourish.[22] A plate of spaghetti and a bottle of Chianti provided innumerable Americans with a first, small introduction to the riches of Italian food and drink.

Far more numerous were the German restaurants here and there in New York City and its suburbs. Each seemed intended to provide a pleasant, nostalgic oasis for those who missed their homeland. There were German restaurants on Broadway with attached gardens where the walls might be painted with landscapes of pine trees, cascades of water, and a castle on a rocky pinnacle. Small tables were ranged about this yard "and hither crowds of Germans resort in the summer time, to feast upon *ragouts* of occult material, washed down with gallons of the ruddy malt liquor."

More characteristic than the German restaurants on Broadway, wrote one man in 1867, were the smaller ones scattered throughout the city:

> queer, dingy, rattle-trap dining-houses in which families of Teuton race — men, women, and children — appear to pass a great deal of their time. Take one as a specimen of the class. It is a small wooden house, standing in a row of similar cheap structures, close by one of the main horse-car avenues of the city. The street door opens right into the principal apartment. . . . The floor is covered with fresh sawdust. Rings of stale beer are observable on the small walnut tables, and the place reeks with the fumes of strong tobacco. The

bar, which is also a counter for the exposition — as the term now goes — of a wonderful amount and variety of pungent viands, looks like a breastwork thrown up by a regiment of gourmands to oppose the march of famine. It is piled with joints and manufactured meats adapted to the strong German stomach; — enormous fat hams, not thoroughly boiled, for the German prefers his pig underdone; rounds of cold corned beef, jostled by cold roast legs and loins of veal; pyramids of sausages of every known size and shape, and several cognate articles of manufactured swine-meat . . . baskets full of those queer, twisted, briny cakes which go variously, I believe, by the names of *Pretzel* and *Wunder;* sardine-boxes piled upon each other . . . huge glass jars of pickled oysters, flanked by huge earthen jars of caviare. Raw onions in heaps give a tone to the combined odors of all these; and through this confusion of smells come powerful whiffs of the Limburger and Sweitzer cheeses, without which the *menu* of no German restaurant would be considered complete. . . . Conspicuously posted upon the walls are the *Weinlisten,* from which documents you gather that white wine is to be had at from one dollar and a quarter to three dollars per bottle, and red wine at from one dollar to four. The inevitable keg of lager-bier lies upon its slanting trestles, behind one end of the counter.

Adjacent was a smaller room with a small fountain in the center, the walls painted with mountain scenery, the "conceptions generally being of a mixed character, comprising such anomalies as Swiss chalets shaded by tropical palms." In one corner of the room was a bust of the German writer Schiller.

Such small restaurants were busy during the daytime hours, with diners coming by twos or threes to eat and to drink lager beer. At night came a great rush, when lawyers and businessmen, small tradesmen and brokers came, many bringing their wives and children.[23]

Foreign restaurants of medium quality were in all parts of the city — French, German, Italian, Spanish, and Jewish kosher among others. These could be quite modest, like a "queer old" French one a writer mentioned in 1869. This was near Theatre Alley, downtown, where one descended steep cellar stairs into a low room with a sanded floor, hard chairs, and a small bar usually tended by a woman. At times a boy in the alcove under the side-walk played a violin. Here a soup, an entrée, a cut of roast meat with one vegetable, and cheese could be had for thirty-five cents and wine for twenty cents more, "and a very cheap and good dinner it is, with no fried dishes and no pies."[24]

For a few New Yorkers it was an adventure to go to a Chinese restaurant. It was said in the mid-1890s that sometimes two or three men might go into such a restaurant out of curiosity, but they seldom remained for long. The best method, one man wrote, was to make up a party, order dinner beforehand, and have a private room. Sometimes, he added, women were taken along to enjoy the novelty.[25] Chop suey did not yet exist to ease the way of Caucasian visitors.

To serve businessmen, artisans, and laborers the city spawned innumerable restaurants of few comforts but fast service. Some businessmen remained at work and sent out for sandwiches. A number of office buildings had their own restaurants to save their tenants time and effort, and along the streets were signs that read "Try our quick lunch." A bemused observer in the 1870s decided that nothing was "more suggestive of a piggery at swilltime" than the usual barroom or restaurant at lunchtime, for there the businessman "gulps down the slings and cobblers" and "bolts the indefinite oyster stews and clam chowders." When Offenbach saw men in saloons using their fingers to take salad from the common bowl of the free lunch, the head-waiter answered his protests: "*Time is money,* and these gentlemen are in such a hurry!"[26] At barrooms, it was noticed, men with their hats on stood in a long line beside a counter on which were cold meats, piles of sandwiches, cakes, beer, iced water, all within reach. In five minutes a man could gulp down his meal, pay, and leave.[27] One man estimated that the business people of New York City averaged only fifteen minutes for their noonday meal.[28]

For those who wanted a full meal at small cost there were modest cafés or restaurants where one could buy a plate of baked beans with ham or corned beef and bread and butter or simply coffee with biscuits soaked in butter, the original "sinkers."[29] By the early 1880s there were the "fifteen cent houses" where for that sum a cut from a hot joint with bread, butter, potatoes, and pickles could be bought.[30]

It was possible to eat even more cheaply. On the curbs of Broadway stood young girls from the slums calling out "Here's your nice hot corn, smoking hot, smoking hot, just from the pot!" There were street vendors of bananas and salted or sugared popcorn, and during the 1890s a firm called The Mexican Food Corporation filled the streets with white-clad sellers of hot tamales. These did well until the cheaper restaurants began to sell both tamales and chili con carne.[31] There were also small cafés on wheels along the streets, predecessors of the diners, and near the waterfront were tiny sidewalk restaurants no larger than five by ten or twelve feet and enclosed by glass and boards. Inside was a single counter accommodating a dozen people, and a menu limited to codfish balls, hash, coffee, doughnuts (becoming known as sinkers), and pies. To these small boxes, wrote a New Yorker, came sailors, black longshoremen, market workers, and unaccompanied women. In the same area were minute Italian basement eating houses where for five cents one could buy macaroni, toast, and coffee.[32]

New Orleans was also well endowed with restaurants and had a reputation for good cooking. A visitor there on the eve of the Civil War referred to it as "a city where Sallusts and Luculli are said to abound."[33]

The great Creole restaurants were famous. Moreau's, near the French Market under the direction of Madame Eugène, was generally considered the finest, but highly rated were Madame Venn's, Flêche's, Victor's, the St. Charles Hotel, and Antoine's, the last founded in 1840 by Antoine Alciatore who had come from Marseilles. Very popular was Begué's which had begun in 1863 as a coffeehouse. Open only for breakfast, Begué's served snails, crawfish, tripe, omelettes, halved tomatoes with parsley, beefsteaks, cheese, apples, coffee, and brandy among other offerings. Of nearly equal fame were the restaurants on Lake Pontchartrain that served fish or game meals. The Boudreaux House at Milneburg was particularly famous. This and other restaurants at Milneburg, West End, and Spanish Port were made delightful, wrote a contemporary, by "airy rooms, cool galleries, trees and flowers and walks, and a pleasant, shady, quiet, cosy, comfortable look generally."[34]

Such restaurants were not for the poor. A private dinner given by an Alabama man to twelve of his friends at the St.

Charles Hotel, using their gold service, was said to have cost $700. Leading restaurants charged about six dollars for a full dinner and less renowned ones a third as much. These were large sums for the time.

New Orleans had many eating houses for those of modest means. Generally less well furnished, these had simpler cooking and lower prices. A typical one might offer three kinds of soup and five kinds of gumbo, each at twenty-five cents; eight kinds of fish from Louisiana waters were listed at from twenty-five to sixty cents, and so on through cold dishes, broiled meats, poultry, roast meats, vegetables, entrées, dishes to order, oysters, desserts, and various wines and liquors. Such places were numerous and, one man said, "an institution" of the city.

Even less expensive were some small French restaurants on Chartres Street with names such as Les Quatre Saisons and Le Pélerin. Here an entire dinner cost only forty to fifty cents. Nearer the French Market the price fell lower, and at cheap hotels over barrooms facing the market a dinner was thirty cents, or even less for regular boarders. In the market itself were eating stands of two kinds, one being cafés where only cake, biscuits, coffee, and chocolate prepared in the Creole manner were sold. "These," wrote a resident, "are patronized by the very best people, and it is customary to take a cup of *café noir, café au lait,* or chocolate whenever you visit the market." Another group of stands were nearly restaurants, serving a limited and very cheap list of dishes, each of which cost ten cents.[35]

A boon to poor men and a pleasant convenience to all were the free lunches at the bars. This custom, which was to spread throughout the country, may have originated in New Orleans at the old St. Louis Hotel where one Alvarez was in charge of the barroom in 1837. Apparently businessmen in the French Quarter complained at having to pay restaurant prices for the small lunches they wished. To gain their patronage, Alvarez and in time all the first-class barrooms of the city — Hewlett's, Arcade, Veranda, and that at the St. Charles Hotel — began to serve free lunches. In time the offerings became large. By 1885 a saloon might, on a given day, lay out crab gumbo and rice, jambalaya, roast beef, baked beans, shallots, salads, fried tripe, fried hominy, and succotash, with a different menu each day. By ordering a glass of wine for fifteen cents the entire bill could be paid, although the average spent upon drinks would come to considerably more.[36]

In the decades following the Gold Rush, San Francisco became known as a center of fine restaurants as high wages attracted outstanding chefs from France and elsewhere and as native game was supplemented by the excellent fruits, vegetables, and seafoods from nearby valleys and waters. Many early San Franciscans adopted the European custom of living in lodgings and taking their meals in restaurants. This practice, wrote one man, produced a competition among restaurants that led them to offer good dinners with wine "after the French form" at a dollar and a half, or about a third of what an equivalent meal would have cost in New York or Boston.[37] It was estimated in 1875 that about 30,000 San Franciscans were eating in 200 or 300 restaurants.[38]

Following the Gold Rush there was a heavy demand for restaurants. The Iron House on Montgomery Street, built of sheet iron which sailing ships had brought around the Horn, was the most fashionable for a time. Also popular was the El Dorado House at Portsmouth Square which was so well patronized that its $25,000-a-month rental was not considered excessive. On Washington Street a Frenchwoman known as "Ma Tanta" established a small, neat, clean restaurant that became famous for its French peasant-style cooking.

Later, the variety of restaurants grew. Lazzuro's and Perini's each offered Italian cooking. The Anglo-American population enjoyed the Nevada which was famous for its corned beef and cabbage. Mannings was an oyster house of some fame, and The Mint was renowned in the early 1870s for its southern cooking with specialties of fried chicken, cream gravy, and corn fritters. The German restaurants included Zinkand's, a favorite site for after-theater supper parties, Techau Tavern, and the less fashionable Louvre which was German in spite of its name. Mexican restaurants were in the Latin quarter at the base of Telegraph Hill, a Japanese teahouse served the curious on Ellis Street, and there was a Turkish restaurant with appropriate hangings and rugs. The French influence was well represented with Jacques, Delmonico's, the Poodle Dog, the Pup (founded by a waiter from the Poodle Dog), Marchand's, Maison Tortoni, and later the Café Riche. Several of the French restaurants were perfectly proper on

262

their lower floors, but less so on their upper floors where men could entertain women in private rooms. More respectable women who entered the city to shop could have lunch at the Woman's Exchange where, one account said, "all is dainty and appetizing to a degree."[39]

In 1875 the Palace Hotel opened in San Francisco, having been built at a cost of $5 million, and immediately became the center for stylish entertainment. The Palace grill room was looked upon as the leading restaurant of the West Coast and its first chef, Jules Harder, as the region's authority on food. Harder had an impressive background, having been at the Grand Union Hotel in Saratoga, the Union Club in New York City, and finally at Delmonico's for ten years — in all, twenty-six years' experience in leading kitchens. In an interview in 1883 he commented on presidential eating habits: Ulysses S. Grant's habits improved after his trip around the world; Chester Arthur was the most accomplished presidential diner that Harder had known; Rutherford B. Hayes never drank wine with dinner, and such men, declared Harder, did not care very much what they ate.[40]

In 1899 Fred Mergenthaler, a chef at the Palace, described the evolution of the city's culinary habits. Many of California's builders, he said, did not care what was served them, but some of the younger generation had visited Europe, had been educated at select eastern colleges, and could order meals with discrimination. During the last twenty to thirty years, he added, San Franciscans had learned to appreciate lungs, tripe, sweetbreads, pigs' feet, and lamb's feet, all formerly thrown into the bay. Now all were expensive luxuries, as were frogs' legs. Even California oysters, he noticed, were beginning to be liked.[41]

San Franciscans of limited incomes could choose among many restaurants, including moderately priced French, German, and Italian ones. The What Cheer House, a small hotel, gave miners a good meal for fifty cents. Dinner was only forty cents at the Miner's Restaurant, and other places charged but twenty to thirty cents.[42] The Chinese restaurants, once generally popular, had receded into Chinatown where few Caucasians patronized them.[43]

New York, New Orleans, and San Francisco had no monopoly on outstanding restaurants. The Parker House in Boston was famous not only for its rolls but for its broiled lobsters,[44] and in

1875 Ober's Cafe, in time to be Locke-Ober's restaurant, began a long existence. In Philadelphia Petry's, a French restaurant, was much admired as was Pinelli's, an Italian one.[45]

In the Midwest St. Louis had the Sprague and Butler Restaurant, founded in 1859 and the most elegant dining place in the city, and Milford's Restaurant and Oyster House, begun in 1863 and expensive. There were also, in 1878, an estimated 2,500 saloons and, in summer, numerous beer gardens.

The best Chicago restaurants included Schlogl's, founded in 1879 and in time a literary center; Kuntz-Remmler's, famous for game; the Red Star Inn in the German district; Henrici's, founded in 1868 by Philip Henrici of an old Viennese family of noted restaurateurs; and Kinsley's, sometimes called the Chicago Delmonico's. After the Chicago Fire of 1871 destroyed his restaurant, H. M. Kinsley built a five-story Moorish castle on Adams Street with a Gentlemen's Restaurant, a French café, a Ladies' and Gentlemen's Restaurant, banquet rooms, and a ballroom.

Like all cities, Chicago had numerous oyster saloons, with Rector's Oyster House and the Boston Oyster House the most famous. The adventurous could go to the Chinese restaurant of Sam Moy and Hip Lung on Clark Street, and the poor could visit the five-cent "beaneries" there. Since custom frowned on unaccompanied women in most restaurants, those who came to shop in the Loop usually lunched at Marshall Field's, Mandel's, Carson Pirie's, or The Fair, the city's great department stores.[46]

New Orleans excepted, the South had few outstanding restaurants, for most well-to-do Southerners preferred eating at home or with relatives and friends. Still, a traveler concluded that the black cooks in southern hotels were "beyond comparison, the best cooks in America," especially for johnnycakes, hoecakes, hominy, and corn pones.[47] Brown's Hotel in Louisville was famed for its cooking, as was Nashville's Maxwell House from 1869 to about 1900. Baltimore had some fine German restaurants, such as Miller Brothers on Fayette Street, and in Washington, D.C., several of the eating houses were renowned for a famous local dish, waffles and catfish.[48]

Southern farmers knew an institution peculiar to their section. During the last third of the nineteenth century and well into the following one, a southern country store was likely to have, in a corner, a long counter equipped with bottles of pepper sauce, catsup, vinegar, well-worn knives and forks, cracked plates, a mechanical cheese cutter, and boxes of crackers. Here many a rural Southerner first met "bought" foods — canned oysters, sardines, salmon, or link sausages from a midwestern packing plant. A particular favorite of the farmers was sardines seasoned with pepper sauce and eaten with salt crackers.[49]

On the plains and in the mountain areas of the West the wealth from cattle ranching and mining supported some outstanding places to eat. The Windsor Hotel in Denver served such dishes as bears' paws *en gelée,* buffalo steaks, grilled antelope, elk, and innumerable game birds. At Colorado Springs the Antlers boasted that its chefs could prepare any dish known to the civilized world. The Hotel de Paris at Georgetown, Colorado, was famous for its mushroom omelettes, cassoulet Toulousain, and sweetbreads Eugénie prepared under Chef Louis Dupuy from 1875 to 1900.[50] A visitor to the Walker House in Salt Lake City found that the hotel's baker was a German, its barkeeper a Scandinavian, and so on.[51] In the Northwest, Spokane's Davenport Restaurant was regionally famous for its soups and sauces as the Rockaway Restaurant was for its steaks and oyster dishes.[52]

Outside the luxury restaurants the West offered few opportunities to eat well. In the small towns of the Great Plains the restaurant and hotel fare hardly differed from what the plains dweller could have at home. Many complained of the eternal hog meat and biscuits, the pickled cucumbers and cabbage, the dried apple sauce, and the side pork swimming in grease. Travelers arrived at one hotel to ask if they could stay the night and were told "Yes, if you can put up with darned hard fare." They got corn bread, molasses, and coffee.[53]

An uncertain fate faced anyone eating out in the West. A man in New Mexico in 1872 received a hotel meal of coffee, side meat, eggs, and *tortillas de mais.*[54] Six years later in San Antonio, Texas, a correspondent was told that at all the "un-napkin" places one could buy for twenty-five cents a "grand meal" of a steak, two vegetables, two poached eggs, a dish of stew, a dish of mutton, some stewed prunes, and bread and butter.[55] Less fortunate was a visitor to the Montana gold fields in 1869 whose dinner at a Helena restaurant was "doughnuts green and poisonous with saleratus, suspicious looking eggs fried in grease, and rusty bacon, intolerably fat."[56]

The noontime meals of innumerable Westerners who lived in the larger towns came free with a drink purchased at a saloon. For a nickel glass of beer the customer could help himself to pickled pigs' feet, slices of cold meats, hard-boiled eggs, white or rye bread, and cheese, and this sometimes in surroundings of highly polished bars, shining mirrors that reflected rows of liquor bottles, and paintings of racehorses, prizefighters, and voluptuous, lightly clad women. Some barrooms provided a "free supper" as well. A contemporary description of Bismarck, Dakota Territory, stated simply: "Many of the saloons had free lunch kitchens, from whence the poor were fed."[57]

Throughout the country dining out was rarely a glorious experience. In the late 1880s a man who had stayed at many of the better hotels of the lesser cities attempted a composite description of his meals. A waitress would appear and "gabble off" the table d'hôte menu at top speed and fling down spoon, knife, and fork for the guest to arrange properly. The entire meal was then brought in, perhaps a dozen oval dishes which were arranged around the soup: fish and sauce, a lump of nearly raw beef, a slice of roast turkey, mashed potatoes, stewed tomatoes, cranberry sauce, chicken salad, rice pudding, and a slice of apple pie with a large helping of cheese in the middle of it. The beef proved "impregnable," the turkey "obdurate," and other items hardly better.[58]

Even less happy was a diatribe sent to the *Cincinnati Commercial*. Restaurants, this correspondent complained, served coffee that was generally a "villainous compound of dandelion, burnt peas, or rye." Potatoes were "soggy, or slushy, or tough as leather" and seasoned throughout with rancid butter. As for pies, the upper crust was often a dripping compound of flour and lard, the interior a stiff compost of starch-water, sugar, and fruit dried to the consistency of glue, and the dough beneath was underdone. Particularly execrable, he thought, was the baker's habit of glossing the surface with a yellow daub of diluted molasses. Habitual restaurant eaters, wrote this irate individual, were the best patrons of patent remedies for indigestion:

You will recognize an old restaurant *habitué* by the leanness of his face, general debility, depression of spirits, and the habit of belching wind like a blacksmith's bellows. He has

266

aches and pains in his stomach, in his head, in his bowels; he takes to disease kindly, and is the first man about town to pick up the small pox, cholera, and fever.[59]

The food provided to stagecoach and railroad travelers showed an uneven improvement. During the early 1860s the traveler who arrived at western stagecoach stations tired, cramped, and dirty might find nothing but a single-roomed cabin, bare-dirt floor, milkless coffee, rancid bacon, stale beans, and green bread. There was always a large pot of mustard in the center of the table to give the "jaded victuals a false air of piquancy." All this carried a bill of two dollars. For those who protested the food the standard quip was, "Well, then, help yourself to the mustard."[60] By 1868, however, it was noticed that the meals had improved with, at times, good beef and ham, various vegetables, bread and butter, pies, canned fruits, and tea and coffee.[61]

Food provided to railroad travelers became better. Some lines, to be sure, kept the old method of eating-house depots where the service was poor and the food bad. An English woman in the early 1880s told of paying one dollar for two cups of coffee in Arizona which were unfit to drink and of train stops where the food was hard to eat and indigestible. Farther east, however, she noted, there were some stations renowned for their buffets, often attended by "bright Yankee girls."[62]

In the 1860s the dining car developed. As early as 1863 the Philadelphia, Wilmington, and Baltimore Railroad converted two day coaches into some kind of diners for use between Baltimore and Philadelphia. Other lines, probably using converted freight cars, created barrooms and "eating saloons." One part of the car was made into an "elaborate" kitchen. Next to it was a compartment arranged as a barroom with a long counter, before which were stools. Behind the counter and against the side of the car was a sideboard upon which, wrote an admirer, was "every variety of meat, hot or cold, pyramids of oysters, patés, and soups — vegetables, johnny cakes, buckwheats and a thousand species of drinks."[63]

In 1868 the Pullman Company built the first dining car to take the modern form of a restaurant on wheels. It began service on the Chicago and Alton Railroad and was named the Delmonico. A traveler from Chicago to Omaha in 1872 described

267

such a car. Expecting a greasy and untidy place, the author was delighted to find it neat, trim and clean, "as though Delmonico had furnished it." The menu was surprisingly large, the table pleasant, the food "admirably cooked," and the prices moderate. One could now eat in the wilderness at twenty-two miles an hour, the writer concluded, buffalo, elk, antelope, beefsteak, and many other things.[64] Over the years the menus grew longer and more elaborate, the diners losing money but advertising the roads that subsidized them. By 1878 there were also parlor cars where, from an end pantry, light refreshments, including alcoholic drinks, were offered.[65]

One railroad, the Santa Fe, did not choose to adopt the dining cars, though its eating-house depots were notoriously bad. But from having the poorest eating facilities the road was to develop by far the best. A young immigrant from England, Fred Harvey, was responsible. Harvey had entered the United States at the age of fourteen, had worked on railroads, and in time found an opportunity to criticize the Santa Fe's eating houses to the management. Given an opportunity to reform the system, Harvey opened his first restaurant in 1876 at Topeka, Kansas. It was an instant success and by 1883 there were seventeen in all.

The Harvey restaurants brought to the West standards that had existed there in only a few eating places. They were clean, the service was outstanding, the silverware and linen of good quality, and the waitresses, the "Harvey girls," so attractive that many of them were lost by marriage in the woman-scarce West. Most important, the food was remarkably good. Harvey took it largely from local sources that met his standards, but he had his own farms for milk, butter, and eggs. He also had a refrigerated boxcar which shuttled twice a week between Los Angeles and Kansas City to supply his restaurants with excellent California fruits and vegetables on the eastbound run and fine Kansas City meats on the return. Menus were planned and printed in Kansas City and distributed along the system so that a passenger never faced identical meals on his trip. The offerings included such delicacies as terrapin, antelope, quail, canvasback duck, bluepoint oysters, and the "Kansas City filet," a specialty.[66]

In the bitter competition for passengers during the late nineteenth and early twentieth centuries, the leading lines subsidized fine meals at modest prices. Roads became known for their specialties: the Baltimore and Ohio for its terrapin stew; the Santa Fe for broiled sage hen, Mexican quail, and charlotte of peaches with cognac sauce; the New Haven for its scrod, Cotuit oysters, and Maine lobsters; the Illinois Central for Creole dishes; and the Chicago and Northwestern for Canadian goose, rabbit stew, venison steaks, and mallard duck on its dollar dinners.[67]

As in earlier times, part of the country's "eating out" was associated with work-play gatherings. These were far fewer than earlier because the areas of rural isolation were disappearing and the simple tasks that had made cooperative effort useful were being eliminated by machinery. Still, some meetings continued. In both East and West, women met to quilt with the work being followed by a supper.[68] The Cajuns of the Mississippi Delta knew the *piocherie,* or hoeing bee, at which the hosts were expected to provide a fine dinner with gumbo, roast goose, roast pig, or chicken among other good things. The *écosserie,* or hulling bee, at which cotton was separated from the hulls, led to a similar feast.[69] In the Pacific Northwest where mechanization was slight the cooperative bees continued in full force — quilting, barn-raising, and logging bees among others. A British-born woman, Susanna Moodie, claimed that the people there had "a craze" for such bees "and run to them with as much eagerness as a peasant runs to a race-course or fair; plenty of strong drink and excitement making the chief attraction . . . noisy, riotous, drunken meetings, often terminating in violent quarrels, sometimes even in bloodshed." She herself cooked for thirty-two men her husband invited to a three-day logging bee.[70]

Throughout the country picnics remained a favorite recreation, probably increasingly so as an ever larger part of the population lived in cities. The Fourth of July was a popular day for these, and an English traveler in 1870 noted that on that day "picnics are going off in every direction — quiet little church picnics, Sunday-school picnics, social picnics, workpeople's picnics, Fenian picnics, picnics of a hundred societies and associations." And writing of a mid-America town late in the century, the novelist Edna Ferber noted that it "hummed with Foresters, Masons, Odd Fellows, Knights of Pythias, Woodmen, Knights of Columbus, Elks" who were "forever having suppers, dances, picnics," among other activities, and many had ladies' auxiliaries to organize chicken-pie suppers and cake sales.[71]

New Englanders continued their seaside chowder parties and clambakes. A favorite spot for clambakes was Rocky Point, near Providence, Rhode Island, and on moonlight nights in summer parties from Barrington or Warren would sail across the bay to that spot. All would dig clams, gather firewood, seaweed, and stones, and then bake the clams, lobsters, crabs, sweet potatoes, and ears of sweet corn, the clam steam flavoring the corn. Brown bread accompanied the feast, and watermelon made the dessert.[72]

In Newport, Rhode Island, the social leader Ward McAllister organized lavish picnics. They became, wrote a woman who lived there, *"fêtes champêtres"* with iced champagne and banquet foods. He and others soon gave costume picnics, beach picnics, picnics in the island's interior, and picnics on yachts in the harbor.[73]

McAllister's penchant for picnics may have originated in Savannah, Georgia, where he had lived earlier. The Savannah picnic he characterized as "an institution peculiar to that place." A party of about 100 people would leave Savannah on a river steamer and after half an hour's sail would reach Daufuskie Island, off the southern tip of South Carolina. The head of each family carried a large basket containing dinner, full table service, and wines for ten or twelve people. The entire company would form a group under the trees, the cloths would be laid, the champagne cooled in pails, and after dining all would dance in the open air before returning to Savannah by moonlight.[74]

Throughout the South and the West the social and public barbecues remained popular. Thus in North Carolina barbecues were served at July 4 celebrations, political rallies, and land sales. Barbecued pig was the principal dish, highly spiced, minced, and served with coleslaw and corn bread. Strong drink usually preceded the feast.[75]

Barbecues also flourished in Texas where they had appeared as early as 1836 and had become a common form of entertainment at Fourth of July celebrations, rodeos, county fairs, and almost any public gathering. In Kentucky and Tennessee, the making and serving of burgoo often replaced the barbecue. The burgoo, a thick, very well-cooked stew, could contain almost any combination of meats and vegetables. Squirrel, wild turkey, and quail were frequently among the meats, and the vegetables might include tomatoes, celery, turnips, and corn. The burgoo and the barbecue were not exclusive. In 1895, during the encampment of the Grand Army of the Republic, Gus Jaubert, a Frenchman from Lexington, Kentucky, and the leading burgoo cook of his state, prepared, overoptimistically it turned out, to serve 100,000 people. To do this he made 6,000 gallons of burgoo, using lean beef, chickens, and rabbits, and barbecued a great number of steers, sheep, and pigs.[76]

In Virginia, Georgia, North Carolina, and some other southern regions the equivalent dish was Brunswick stew. This was commonly made with chickens or one or more wild meats (squirrels were popular) together with fat bacon, green corn, tomatoes, lima beans, and sometimes other late-summer and fall vegetables. "When properly made," noted one cookbook editor, "no one is able to detect any of the ingredients."[77] It probably took its name from Brunswick County, Virginia.

To "eat out" in the late nineteenth century remained for most people an event, memorable and extraordinary. But already urbanism and faster and easier transportation were anticipating a future when to eat away from home would be commonplace.

❧ 19 ❧
Drink,
1865-1900

*I have yet to see
a cowboy who isn't a coffee drinker.*

On New Year's Day in 1863 the English traveler George Sala joined in the round of visits that New York City men customarily paid on that day and found that fine foods and rare wines, cognac, and bourbon were offered in each house. The following year an essay in *The Ladies' Repository* asked rhetorically, "Mother, sister, how many drunkards have you helped to make this New-Year's day?" In 1870 another English visitor made the same tour and discovered that eggnog, "the peculiar beverage of New Years day," was plentiful as were apple toddy, milk punch, brandy smash, and Tom and Jerry. But when Sala returned in 1880 and again spent January first in New York City, he reported that most hostesses frowned on even wine, offering instead coffee, bouillon, and chocolate. Some women, he added, served no refreshments at all, "so the custom of the day is passing." In 1893 William Dean Howells, the American novelist, pronounced this "purely American" custom "extinct as the dodo."[1]

Not only the cool breath of temperance was changing American drinking habits. Beverages, like foods, were being influenced by improved transportation, more and better refrigeration, and big business. There still remained important regional and class differences. Sala's temperance hostesses would not have been popular in many sections of New York City or any part of the American West.

Water gained importance as the temperance movement grew. It was, one man wrote, "the American national drink." At every hotel or rooming house a pitcher of ice water was placed in rooms as a matter of course, a custom that would continue into the following century. A barrel of ice water was provided passengers on trains during hot weather, and even bars had ice water at their free lunches. In restaurants "from the grandest to the humblest" foreign visitors saw with astonishment that "nothing but iced water, is the almost invariable rule at meal times."[2]

The water was frequently impure. Cities especially suffered epidemics, often with terrible death tolls, from cholera, dysentery, typhoid, and other bacterial infections caused by bad water. Sediment sometimes collected at the bottom of undisturbed glasses, especially in parts of the South.[3] In Virginia City, Nevada, the water was so grossly polluted that many people mixed it with California wines or other liquors.[4] To improve their water, city after city established water systems in the decades after the Civil War.

Sometimes purer and always more diverting than water was soda water. Not only was it a cold, refreshing beverage, but medicinal values were attributed to it. New Englanders called carbonated drinks "tonics" even into the twentieth century.[5] The simple soda fountains used before the Civil War were replaced by larger, more ornate ones. Marble fountains with silver faucets could cost $2,000 or more. At the 1876 Centennial Exposition in Philadelphia some fine ones were exhibited. One, called The Minnehaha, had a base and body of several marbles, corners finished with "beautiful pillars of burnished silver," and an arched roof of Italian marble replete with urns and topped by a "handsome" statue. A fountain in New York City was gloriously equipped with faucets for thirty-two different syrups and eight kinds of mineral water in addition to soda water.

The Centennial Exposition gave makers of soda water a tremendous boost. Not only was the summer of 1876 very hot, but the temperance forces had managed to ban the retail sale of hard liquors at the Exposition. The sellers of soda water seized the main chance. Fairgoers could not overlook a magnificent edifice that rose three stories: the bottom one, manned by attendants, contained soda water, syrups, ice, and the dispensing faucets, the second story had a beautiful fountain, and the third was illuminated from within. Throughout the fairgrounds were lesser soda-water stations where marble naiads stood over fountains that had "ingenious machines" to rinse the glasses provided for everyone's use. All the fountains did an enormous business, and those who drank at them publicized soda water throughout the country.[6]

Lemon was the most popular soda-water flavor, followed by strawberry, pineapple, vanilla, and ginger,[7] but other flavors proliferated wildly. A Boston dealer in 1890 listed Asphodel, Blood Orange, Calisays, Catawba, Ginger Ale, Kola Champaigne, and many others. Some flavors were complex: Ambrosia mixed raspberry, vanilla, and hock wine, while Clarique joined claret and lemon. There was even a mysteriously named "Don't Care" which was made of pineapple, strawberry, vanilla, port wine, and syrup. To maintain winter sales a hot soda was attempted, but with only small success.[8]

Everyone could afford soda water. In New York City gamins and newsboys surrounded stands that sold it at two cents a glass.[9] Higher on the economic scale was Delatour's soda-water stand on Wall Street. Here during summers in the 1870s Delatour dispensed a cold soda water of high quality to customers who sometimes waited in long queues.[10]

Some carbonated drinks that were destined for enormous success came after the Civil War. One of the earliest, called Herb Tea, was created by Charles E. Hires, a Philadelphia pharmacist. Challenged by some women prohibitionists because the beverage contained a small amount of yeast, Hires proved to them that it was not alcoholic. Soon afterward he changed the name to Root Beer and began a newspaper campaign urging hard drinkers to switch to it. After a few years the dry forces allowed root beer to be advertised as "The National Temperance Drink." By 1893 three million bottles of Hires root beer were being sold each year.[11] It was in the postwar period, too, that Thomas B. Welch, a dentist, learned how to sterilize the juice of New Jersey grapes and by 1870 had joined his son in the business of selling grape juice. In 1896 they moved to the Finger Lakes district of New York.[12]

Two new ingredients for soft drinks had been discovered by the 1880s. One was from the leaf of the Peruvian coca plant, and the other was an extract of the cola, or kola, nut, native to Africa and the West Indies. In 1881 an "Imperial Inca Coca" was put on the market, the first of the coca beverages.

Five years later John Styth Pemberton, an Atlanta, Georgia, pharmacist, created a syrup he called Coca-Cola. This consisted of a little caffeine, extract of cola nut, and a few other oils. For a time Pemberton mixed his syrup with an oar in the backyard and sold it to soda fountains as a headache cure. In 1891 another pharmacist bought full rights to the drink. Like root beer it met opposition. Some religious circles thought it wicked, and the owner's own church paper refused his advertisements. Despite such discouragement, Coca-Cola was bottled during the 1890s and went out to ever-widening markets,[13] as did Pepsi Cola which was begun by Caleb D. Bradham in New Bern, North Carolina, in 1896.[14]

The old trio of coffee, tea, and chocolate continued. Of the three, coffee maintained its supremacy. It was not only the country's favorite for breakfast, but many drank it with every meal.[15] Throughout the East, especially, coffee was usually taken with sugar and cream or milk.[16] During the 1870s iced coffee had some success. It was sold at the Philadelphia Exposition, and a clerk in New York City was to remember all his life the iced coffee that he bought on hot days at the counter of Delmonico's on Broad Street, made strong with cream and sugar added, then chilled in an ice-cream freezer from which it was dipped on order.[17]

Addiction to coffee was greatest in the West where it was the daily drink of virtually everyone. The coffeepot could almost stand beside the six-shooter or the covered wagon as a symbol of the Old West. To drink coffee from morning to night was normal. Coffee, hot, strong, and unadulterated by sugar or milk, was the beverage of the cowboys on ranches or on cattle drives to railroad centers. "I have yet to see a cowboy who isn't a coffee drinker," said one man who followed the Chisholm Trail in 1874. The cook on a drive would boil large pots of coffee for half an hour. Some labeled it six-shooter coffee on the theory that it was strong enough to float a revolver.[18]

Although it hardly competed with coffee, chocolate continued to have a place among American beverages. Hotels and restaurants offered it for breakfast and supper. A New York cookbook not only mentioned chocolate and cocoa as favorite luncheon beverages but said that many women, especially those who had spent much time abroad, had adopted the French custom of breakfasting upon rolls and chocolate.[19] In the Southwest chocolate was popular among Mexican Americans who had inherited the drink from their Aztec ancestors.

Tea continued to be preferred by some for breakfast and was so widely used for supper that in parts of the East that meal was called "tea."[20] Green tea was still much used; on the West Coast it was the common tea, especially among the poor. Black teas, usually taken with milk or cream in the English fashion, were at least equally in favor. Hostesses at parties often served both.[21] The rituals were not ignored. Mary Terhune noticed that the English custom of making tea at the tea table, rather than in the kitchen, was fast gaining ground.[22]

Women's tea parties known as high teas or kettledrums became a favorite recreation in cities. One woman credited their growth to a "remorseful hankering after the almost obsolete 'family tea.'"[23]

Little tea was drunk on the Great Plains. English tourists carried a supply with them, though some stage stations offered tea as an alternative to coffee.[24] At such a stop in Nebraska, Mark Twain was given a beverage called "slumgullion" by the station keeper. It pretended to be tea, wrote Twain, but "there was too much dish-rag, and sand, and old bacon-rind in it to deceive the intelligent traveller." It lacked sugar and milk and "even a spoon to stir the ingredients with." Twain thought that the man who named it had been inspired.[25]

In one form tea had a major success. In 1860 a writer for Horace Greeley's *Tribune*, Solon Robinson, published a small volume modestly titled *How to Live* which contained the sentence, "Last summer we got in the habit of taking the tea iced, and really thought it better than when hot."[26] Whoever invented it had probably been inspired by hot tea à la Russe which was very popular at the women's high teas. This was served in glasses, lacked the usual milk of hot tea, and contained the lemon slices that became a common addition to iced tea. The connection was strongly implied in cookbooks that gave recipes for "iced tea, or Russian tea," and "iced tea à la Russe."[27]

The new drink slowly gained acceptance. By 1871 it competed with iced milk and iced water on hot summer days at the Fifth Avenue Hotel in New York.[28] In the same year a writer in New Orleans commented that in "these hot climates cold tea lemonade, iced, is declared by the few who have tried it to be more fragrant and refreshing than the most liberal libations of soda-water or other effervescing liquids."[29] A traveler in 1878 found iced tea for sale on the Rock Island Railroad and a "popular" beverage in Sidney, Nebraska. In 1884 a Virginian claimed that the use of "Cold Tea" in that state was "well-nigh universal" during hot weather and, indeed, that the beverage had originated there.[30] By 1886 senators in Washington, D.C., had in their offices "large coolers of iced-tea" during summer months.[31]

Milk remained popular. Visitors from Europe were astounded at how much of it an American could drink without "getting bilious."[32] Still, there was concern about the quality. Massachusetts forbade its adulteration in 1856, and in 1882 Newark, New Jersey, began to inspect dairies. Such laws were local, inadequate, and poorly enforced. Not until the 1890s were tuberculin tests begun and pasteurizing machines introduced in some places.[33]

The strong favor shown to soda water, coffee, milk, and iced tea was no doubt owing in part to the temperance movement. Consumers of alcohol were now subjected to new attacks which struck at even wine and beer. During the 1880s and 1890s the Women's Christian Temperance Union tried to convince workers and new immigrants that abstinence would bring success and entry into the middle class. Although many immigrants were bewildered by the suggestion that wine and beer were not God-given benefits but the devil's work, by the century's end temperance workers had won the sympathy or support of nearly every progressive, radical, or conservative movement in the country.[34]

Throughout the East drinking receded from public view. Hit both by the temperance movement and by high duties and taxes, wines disappeared from the tables of many middle- and upper-class restaurants. George Sala tried to reconcile this with the large display of wines and liquors he saw in some homes. Was it hypocrisy, he asked? He decided it could be courtesy to women. Men did not smoke in their presence, and since women "as a rule are total abstainers, and look on drinking with horror," this might have led men not to drink before them.[35] Another English tourist decided that the greater expense of wines consumed outside the home might have caused the decline of public drinking.[36]

The power of the temperance lobby was revealed in various ways: The wife of President Rutherford B. Hayes stopped serving wine in the White House, thereby winning the nickname of "Lemonade Lucy"; many saloons called themselves "cafes" or "wine rooms"; and New Yorkers were forbidden to buy liquor on Sunday except in hotel rooms with a meal.[37]

The language of drinking became increasingly evasive and apologetic. One might be excused for having an "eye-opener" in the morning, preparing for meals with an "appetizer," taking a "pony" to assist one through the day, or "if you are startled at the mention of 'a drink,' you find it difficult to refuse 'at least a nip.' And who but the most morose . . . can resist the influence of 'a smile.'"[38] All, somehow, suggested the surreptitious hospitality offered from a bottle kept behind books in the parlor.

Lager beer still labored under the reputation of being a lower-class and immigrant beverage. Sala was told, not too accurately, that "'tis only the Germans and Irish . . . who drink Lager beer and whiskey in the America of to-day." Where the Germans were in strength the use of lager was common. In St. Louis, in the late 1870s, it was estimated that two-thirds of the city's women drank beer, and that lager was also consumed by the Americans, Irish, Swedes, Italians, and French.[39]

St. Louis and Milwaukee, both "German cities," became major brewing centers. At the end of the Civil War Milwaukee, with the Pabst and Schlitz companies, produced 55,000 barrels of beer; eight years later 260,000 barrels were sold.[40] All northern cities soon had beer gardens, lager beer saloons, and in the spring the colorful Bock beer signs with rampant goats. Everywhere such words as stein, lager, bock, and rathskeller came into general use.[41]

The German beer gardens became social centers not only for Germans but for native Americans and immigrants from European and even Asian countries. At the more refined ones elegantly dressed women and men came to drink beer and listen to an orchestra play Strauss or Meyerbeer. At Uhrig's in St. Louis, where the garden was located in a large wooded tract with a cave to keep the beer cold, stage shows were presented in the decade after 1876, and there were three separate music pavilions in which relays of fine orchestras played while the crowd enjoyed beer, wine, and food.[42] In New York's Bowery whole families visited the larger, more popular gardens, to eat, drink, talk, play cards or dominoes, play billiards, bowl, or shoot at targets.[43]

When New York banned the Sunday sale of liquor, the city's Germans made weekly excursions to the north and west of Hoboken, New Jersey. Here were large saloons attached to breweries, and each had a beer garden with swings and merry-go-rounds for the children and dancing platforms for adults. Large parties brought their own musicians, and it was said in 1867 that "it is pleasant to hear the strains of those bands from grove to grove on that pleasant Jersey plateau in the fine summer days."[44]

By 1870 beer-drinking Americans had clearly chosen lager beer over the English kind that one man described as "half sour, muddy and intoxicating." Americans also preferred their lager closer to the Pilsen type — pale, light-bodied, clear, and effervescent with a relatively low alcoholic content — than to the Munich type. The popularity of lager may have been due partly to its compatability, as a light-bodied brew, with the heavy consumption of meat by Americans.[45]

The expense of wines limited their use more than the temperance movement. European visitors noted how few homes had wine daily. "Wine is very expensive," wrote an Englishman, George Towle, "and it is only once in a while that it appears on the tables even of the rich — so seldom that it cannot be called a custom. Sherry, port, claret, and champagne are rare luxuries, and only appear on festive occasions, or in the houses of epicures and wealthy foreigners." Still, for important occasions champagne continued to be thought necessary, and in 1883 George Sala found that an "immense" quantity of it was consumed in Chicago.[46]

American wines had little standing in eastern markets. The Longworth vineyards in Ohio had been destroyed by mildew or rot as had been those on the islands and borders of Lake Erie and Crooked Lake in New York.[47] California wines reached the Midwest and the East after the transcontinental railroad was completed in 1869, but their quality was usually poor and they were often sold under foreign labels to gain a market.[48]

The West paid little attention to wine. Although wines were made not only in California but in Utah, New Mexico, Arizona, and Texas, only the California product had more than local markets. Even in California there was little demand, though one traveler spoke of the "invariable 'eye-opener' of California white wine, cooled with snow from the Sierras."[49]

In one part of the country, New Orleans and the Creole settlements of Louisiana, wine remained a daily beverage. "Wines were always served," wrote one Creole of the late nineteenth century, "Some families drank it at all three meals, the children receiving theirs diluted with water."[50]

The weight of the temperance movement pressed most heavily on "hard liquor," which shifted increasingly from homes into bars and saloons. Some traditional drinks maintained a domestic foothold. Many New Englanders still used their cider presses for their fall surpluses of apples and also drank locally distilled dark rums. In Delaware a peach plantation distilled 500 gallons of peach brandy a day for ready sale.[51]

Even those who drank sparingly had difficulties with temperance forces. Brand Whitlock, the Ohio Populist, remembered that moderate drinkers were particularly unpopular because they contradicted prohibitionist propaganda by suggesting that a man might use liquor and yet "not beat his wife, wreck his home, defraud his creditors, destroy himself body and soul, and fill a drunkard's grave."[52]

To guilt-ridden but determined drinkers, trying to stay afloat in the temperance storm, the bitters that had long served Southerners as a morning potion now offered an escape. Bitters, lightly disguised as medicines, were advertised in every newspaper, placarded on every shed, their names painted in large letters on trees and rocks, and sold in bottles as Red Jacket Bitters, Planter's Bitters, French, German, Mexican, and American Bitters. Hostetter's Stomach Bitters, 44 percent alcohol, made its manufacturer a millionaire. Equally famed was Dr. Ayer's Sarsaparilla which was 25 percent alcohol. A foreigner, offered Angostura bitters, discovered that it was not medicinal but rather "a better kind of whiskey a little fortified with spice." Bitters reminded another man of the story of the deacon who refused hard cider but said "call it apple-juice and I'll take a drop."[53]

Men still drank in thousands of bars and saloons, ranging from resplendent to dingy. As George Ade, the Indiana author, pointed out, the magnificent Hoffman House bar in New York had little in common with the low-browed shack near a big steel mill "with the half-naked puddlers coming in to gulp down enormous hookers of straight rye, each heroic wallop being followed by a tall glass of beer as a 'chaser.'" Nor did the Knickerbocker bar on Forty-Second Street in New York City resemble the "small-town dump where the hard nuts from the farming districts assembled to get themselves liquored 'to the key-hole' and then pull off rough-and-tumble fights, rolling around in the saw-dust." Every city, he added, had at least one expensively decorated "buffet" for the socially elect, but for each of these there were a thousand "boozing dens" that sold mainly beer and whiskey:

> Nine-tenths of all the places in which intoxicants were dished out affected a splendor which was palpably spurious and made a total failure of any attempt to seem respectable. The saloon business was furtive and ashamed of itself, hiding behind curtains, blinds and screens and providing alley entrances for those who wished to slip in without being observed.[54]

Although saloons in immigrant communities could be respectable social centers, in small towns where teetotalers were dominant they were shoved into side streets to exist as violent, even sinister, places, attracting mainly those who intended to get drunk.[55] Drinking places not endangered by local option might be confronted by bands of women holding prayer meetings outside their doors. This was the era of Carrie Nation and her followers who successfully closed Kansas saloons, sometimes by using stones and axes.[56]

In sophisticated bars mixed drinks were in demand. Many of these — sherry cobblers, planter's punches, brandy cocktails, smashes, flips, slings, and so on — had long been popular. But new ones appeared, some of which were to become famous. In Jerry Thomas's *The Bar-Tenders Guide* for 1887 there was a recipe for a Manhattan cocktail. Also listed was a Martinez cocktail made largely of gin, vermouth, and bitters. This could have been named for the Martinez who founded the Maison Dorée restaurant in New York in 1861. When the 1895 edition of Thomas's book was printed, however, the name had become Martini.[57]

The growing use of mixed drinks led to a generic name for them. There had long been gin, whiskey, brandy, and other cocktails, all containing bitters, but not until late in the century was the word cocktail extended to nearly all mixed drinks. A French visitor told of being taken to a bar where "I was not spared a single cocktail, those skilled combinations of whiskey, ice, sherry, seltzer-water and champagne."[58]

The two staples of most saloons were beer and whiskey:

"beer for the thirsty and red liquor for those who wished to induce, for at least a brief period, the sense of well-being." Scotch was nearly unknown until late in the nineties, gin was seldom demanded, and rum, said Ade, was "not a drink but merely a guaranteed remedy for bronchitis."[59]

In the West, cocktails appeared only in pretentious bars, such as that in the Grand Imperial Hotel of Silverton, Colorado, where the barkeeper was prepared to mix a Cuba Libra, Pink Lady, Texas Fizz, Stinger, Grasshopper, Salty Dog, Screwdriver, and Vodka Collins.[60] Most bars were overwhelmingly dedicated to whiskey. In Kansas, wrote one man, "the standard drink is whisky — 'stone fence,' 'forty-rod,' and 'tarantula-juice.'" He summed up the credo that helped to sustain whiskey's primacy: "Whisky and bravery are thought to be necessary for each other; 'whisky is the only drink for men,' and whoever drinks at all drinks whisky."[61]

Most whiskey came from more eastern states, but by the 1860s Mormons in Utah Territory were making a wheat whiskey. This was preferred, wrote one man, to the equal parts of water and alcohol colored with burned sugar and flavored with green tea that was sold as cognac.[62] Some Texans learned to drink mescal, a brandy made from cactus.[63]

Frontiersmen drank heavily. Montana reportedly had a saloon for every eighty inhabitants. A miner in the Black Hills of South Dakota during the gold rush there wrote: "Dealers in grub are not very plenty. Every body Seems to deal in Whiskey. You will see the glass standing on the Barrel Head in the Tent or Brush Shanty as well as the Log cabin. Every thing fluctuates here except Whiskey and Labor. Whiskey is at the top notch and labor at the lowest."[64] And a Vermonter, visiting New Mexico in the 1880s, arrived, astonished, at a sweeping conclusion: "People drink at their homes, in the stores, on the street, in the cars, everywhere, and no questions are asked."[65] Men who accumulated some wealth occasionally drank more than whiskey, as witnessed by the grubstake of a leading citizen of Deadwood, South Dakota, for a six weeks' fishing trip: a gallon of Old Crow Whiskey, a pound of beans, two dozen bottles of Bass's ale, three pounds of crackers, a bottle of bitters, a box of sardines, two gallons of sour mash, a quart of gin, ten pounds of bacon, two gallons of Whoopup Whiskey for the cook, a case of brandy, six quart bottles of whiskey, four sacks of salt, and a bottle of whiskey.[66]

Even Californians neglected their native wines in favor of whiskey. A visitor to Sacramento noted that "the custom of the country is to drink as often as possible," and that "the most common drink is whiskey 'straight.'"[67] One traveler, after discovering that whiskey was "the national drink of California," added that if one arrived at a wayside hotel during cold weather any complaint about the lack of a fire would produce the answer: "Walk right into the bar — warm you up for four bits, and heat you red hot for a dollar."[68]

~❧ 20 ❧~
The Immigrants

What kind of American consciousness
can grow in the atmosphere
of sauerkraut and Limburger cheese?

Until well after the Civil War the main stream of migration came from northern and western Europe, with the British, Germans, Irish, and Scandinavians in the forefront. Most of these caused little worry to the resident majority in the United States, because they shared a similar cultural background and outlook and, the Irish and many Germans excepted, were overwhelmingly Protestant. Although these immigrations continued, about 1880 they were joined by a different flow of refugees from economic hardship, political repression, and intolerance. The newcomers were from southern and eastern Europe and included Hungarians, Poles, Czechs, Slovaks, Russians, Greeks, Italians, and Jews among others. Even earlier the West Coast had become the goal of Chinese immigrants.

These new arrivals aroused fear and resentment because they were mostly Catholic, their customs were unfamiliar, and they threatened the jobs of others by being ready to work for low wages. Rather than settling on farms, as most earlier immigrants had done, they largely flocked to cities where they were highly visible. Huddled together in city slums they worked in sweatshops, as strikebreakers, or at the poorest paid manual work in steel plants, packing plants, and coal mines.

What to eat and drink posed problems. In Europe most had been peasants or small landowners, growing their own vegetables and obtaining fresh milk from a goat or cow. In America they were not only separated from the land but, since many migrations were largely masculine, there were too few women to cook and give continuity to the diet. They also met such novelties as iron stoves, fresh vegetables in winter, canned goods, expensive milk

284

in bottles, low-cost sugar, cheap meats, cooking utensils of agate or tin rather than copper and iron, and a confusing array of kitchen utensils.[1]

If American food habits were strange to the immigrants, so theirs were found peculiar by the Americans. During the First World War the head of a national women's patriotic organization voiced her fear: "What kind of American consciousness can grow in the atmosphere of sauerkraut and Limburger cheese?" she asked, "Or what can you expect of the Americanism of the man whose breath always reeks with garlic?"[2] While such culinary jingoism was rare, prejudice against the new food customs was common. The wealth of cooking discoveries that a sympathetic attitude would have allowed was cut off.

Of all immigrant groups the Chinese most rigidly adhered to their food habits. They were largely an agricultural people whose diet in China consisted mainly of rice, vegetables, fish, fowl, and pork. Milk was very scarce and distasteful, butter was quite unknown, and cheese caused disgust. Fish and vegetables were frequently salted to preserve them which encouraged a liking for salted foods. Certain foods, too, were credited with medicinal value: Pork liver enriched the blood and improved vision; chicken and duck were necessary for vital organs; salted fish was a good appetizer; and so on.

There were several reasons why, for about a century, Chinese cooking made barely any impression on the culinary habits of America. The quick sautéeing of vegetables over an intense heat for a matter of minutes, or even seconds, ran completely counter to the Anglo-American conviction that vegetables should be boiled for a long time. The oddity of Chinese meals was enhanced by the virtual elimination of dairy foods or sugar, by the wide range of unusual spices, herbs, vegetables, and seasonings, and by the practice of eating with chopsticks.

The Chinese had first flocked to California to find gold, or at least work. During the late 1840s and 1850s thousands of them risked their lives, for China held emigration a capital crime, and it was not until 1868 that they won full rights to leave their homeland. In the United States many were hired to construct the Central Pacific Railroad, a work they did so well that they were soon in demand as farm laborers. Again their work was outstanding.

As economic conditions worsened during the 1870s, however, demagogues led an attack on the Chinese, and for a generation they were assaulted, murdered, robbed, and driven out of their homes. Then in 1882 Congress passed the Chinese Exclusion Act, the first of a series of laws that were increasingly restrictive and humiliating to the Chinese. Not until 1943 were these laws completely repealed.[3]

The Exclusion Act did not stop the coming of the Chinese. A small legal and a larger illegal influx continued. In 1870, about 99 percent of the Chinese in the country lived on the West Coast, but soon they moved into the larger cities throughout the Middle West and along the East Coast.

Devoted to their native cookery, the Chinese, through imports from China and the produce of their own truck gardens, provided most of the herbs, vegetables, meats, and seafoods needed. The Chinese contributed greatly to California's seafood industry. An aged Chinese remembered that at Richmond, north of San Francisco, there had been thirty Chinese shrimp camps which had begun with nets imported from China. He claimed that the Chinese had been the first to take the abalone, then the crab, and to gather seaweed for soup.[4]

The Chinese also worked as cooks in private homes, restaurants, logging camps, and on railroad gangs. Chinese camp cooks may have created egg foo yong and the derivative Western, or Denver, sandwich during the late nineteenth or early twentieth century. Chinese spareribs, fried shrimps, and egg foo yong became common West Coast dishes.[5] Various legends to the contrary, chop suey was not invented in California during the Gold Rush. Americans did not know that dish until the end of the century. It probably first appeared during, or shortly after, the visit to New York City of Li Hung-chang, viceroy and foreign minister of China under the Empress Dowager. Li toured Russia in 1896 and returned to China by way of the United States. In New York City he was visited at the Waldorf-Astoria Hotel by President Grover Cleveland and other notables. An undocumented story holds that at a banquet Li spurned the hotel's cooking and ate a Chinese meal prepared by his own cook. When asked what he was eating, he replied "chop suey," meaning something chopped finely. He invited others to try the dish, they found it good, and chop suey was launched. It is more likely that some restaurateur in Chinatown, which was visited by droves during Li's visit, invented the dish, or some dish given the name, to lure Caucasians into his restaurant.

About 1900 a visitor to New York's Chinatown found chop suey was the "popular" dish there, and, if "courageously attacked," was good. It consisted of a "mess of veal, mushrooms, parsley, and a kind of macaroni, with a peculiar pungent sauce." In 1904 a cookbook suggested that a Chinese luncheon was a chance to use "more novel decorations" and gave a recipe for chop suey made with water chestnuts, bean sprouts, celery, onion, mushrooms, and chicken. Soon afterward *Lowney's Cook Book* offered a similar recipe "as a novelty, and not because we especially like it."[6] In time chop suey recipes took the form that millions would know during the second quarter of the century in Chinese restaurants, a combination of pork, celery, and onions, with a sauce of water, soy sauce, and cornstarch. The cooking time was an hour and a half, which alone suggests how far removed the dish was from Chinese tastes.[7]

Somewhat less strange were immigrants from Central Europe. Most had been tenant farmers or, if Czechs, small landowners. In either case the family had lived in a small house, kept a few livestock, and had grown nearly all their foods, of which root crops such as turnips, onions, and beets, together with potatoes, wheat, and rye were basic. The only important leafy vegetable was the cabbage which, like the root crops, could be stored throughout the winter.[8]

Polish peasants were accustomed to three meals a day of a monotonous diet in which porridges, small cakes, and potatoes figured importantly. Soup, made of a vegetable and served with sour cream, was part of every meal. Potatoes, cabbages, and beets were the leading vegetables in that order. Sour milk, sour cream, and cottage cheese were much used, and wild mushrooms were gathered whenever possible. The Poles liked beef, pork, fowl, and game, but except for smoked and cured pork, meat was eaten only at Easter, Christmas, and family festivals. Tea was a treat too expensive for daily use.

In America, many of the Poles moved into northern cities. Huge colonies grew in Chicago and Detroit, with others going to New York City and Pittsburgh as well as cities in New Jersey, Ohio, and Indiana. Many of those who wished to farm went to Connecticut, New York, and Wisconsin.

The Poles who chose city life had to change their food habits quickly. Gone were the wild mushrooms, wild honey, greens, fish, and berries. But sugar was cheap, and sweet rolls and pastries took the place of the fruits and the whole-grained bread they had known in Europe. Meat in America seemed inexpensive and the Poles bought it readily, but vegetables were thought too costly. Both coffee and tea became very popular, but citrus fruits were accepted only slowly and then mainly by the young. More eggs and veal were eaten than in Poland, and readily adopted were catsup, mustard, chili sauce, and sweet pickles. Pork remained a favorite meat, and potatoes continued in general use.[9]

The small landowners of Bohemia, the Czechs, had even less food variety than the Poles, but they were strongly attached to their ancient habits. Their long and sometimes elaborate cooking methods showed a strong German influence. The four or five daily meals were very alike, were cooked for a long time, and tended to be "heavy." Meat, potatoes, flour, and cabbage were the large items, and there were few vegetables and fruits. Rye bread and dumplings accompanied meat. Wild mushrooms and poppy seeds gave much of the flavoring. Wild plums were much eaten, and these and other fruits, poppy seeds, and cheese were used to fill the cakes and pastries.

The heaviest Czech migration was between 1870 and 1890. Many bought land or homesteaded in Wisconsin, Nebraska, Minnesota, Iowa, and Texas, while others entered skilled trades in Milwaukee, St. Louis, and later New York, Chicago, and Cleveland. The Czech neighborhoods in these cities soon had saloons where the men gathered to drink beer and bakeries where the women met for coffee and cake. Soon, too, Czech organizations acquired halls with restaurants and bars where both men and women met to eat, drink, talk, play cards, and sing.

While younger Czechs rather quickly adopted American foods, the older ones kept such traditional dishes as liver loaves, dumplings, pork with a sweet and sour sauce, and cakes. Caraway seeds, dill, and dried mushrooms continued to serve as seasonings. All ages drank both beer and coffee.

The Czechs who chose to farm in the upper Mississippi Valley were better able to retain their native cooking, including the favorite dinner dishes of roast pork, sauerkraut, and potato dumplings, or the much loved sausages and fried or baked pastries. A popular fruit-filled pastry, the kolac, or kolacky, became the basis for yearly celebrations in both Iowa and Minnesota where Czechs and non-Czechs joined to celebrate Kolacky Day in a festive mingling of music, dancing, and kolackies.[10]

Quite different were the meals of the Slovaks, who had for centuries been under Hungarian influences. Compared to the Czechs, the Slovaks ate more potatoes, fruits, vegetables, and milk, and their cooking was generally more elaborate, richer, and spicier. Staples were potatoes, cabbage, root vegetables, black bread, cornmeal, milk, and cheese, with cottage cheese being very common.

The high point of Slovak emigration was between 1885 and 1900. Many, without skills or money, became common laborers in the industrial and mining areas of Ohio, Pennsylvania, Illinois, New York, and New Jersey. Pittsburgh became a large Slovak center as did, to a lesser degree, Chicago, Cleveland, and New York.

Slovak peasants who became American city dwellers had to endure a substantial change in their eating habits. This was greatest in mining towns where the company stores sold meat, white flour, potatoes, and bread, but did not carry the less profitable fresh root vegetables and fruits, fresh buttermilk, cheese, and other foods that made part of the traditional Slovak diet. A less healthful and appealing pattern of foods resulted than the Slovaks had known in their native land.[11]

The Hungarians had the most abundant and varied food of any part of Central Europe and a cookery that was famous. When they emigrated during the last years of the nineteenth century and the early years of the twentieth, about two-thirds of Hungary's people were engaged in farming or livestock raising. On the plains were great herds of cattle, sheep, and horses, and much Hungarian cooking was influenced by the tradition of the Magyar herdsmen whose foods included the famous goulash, a rancher's stew, and *tarhonya,* a thick, dried, pulverized dough which kept for long periods and could be added to many dishes.

The Hungarian herdsmen depended heavily on meat, as the fisher folk along the rivers relied on fish. The peasantry ate grains as well as dairy products, eggs, vegetables, pork, and poultry, and in summer fruits such as plums, cherries, and apricots. Garlic and paprika were used freely in some dishes. Hungarian cooking was rather complicated. Meats were usually roasted or stewed, and common dishes joined pork with beans, veal with peas, and beef with vegetables or noodles. Bread was made of whole-wheat grain or rye flour and only in the cities were white rolls seen. Jam or dried fruit largely replaced sugar in the making of pastries, including the famous strudel. Sour milk was a popular beverage. The Hungarians ate frequently, even five or six meals a day.

Work was available for the Hungarians in the industrial and mining areas of the United States, so that few took up farming. The largest colonies grew up in Michigan, Ohio, Pennsylvania, New York, and New Jersey, with Cleveland and Detroit as the leading Hungarian urban centers. Many of the immigrants of the 1920s were professional people, largely lawyers, doctors, and engineers.

The frequent meals of Hungary were soon given up in favor of the American meal pattern, but since nearly all the foods used in Hungary could be purchased in America there was a tendency to continue the native cookery. Meat, important in Hungary, was cheap in America and took on an even larger role. The easily bought white rolls were welcomed, though the sour rye bread was kept.

Like all immigrants from Central Europe, the Hungarians found some things strange in the American diet: the eating of sweet dishes with meat; iced beverages and desserts; breakfast foods; low-priced canned goods; and all the seafoods.[12] But time, intermarriage, and the persistent, sometimes ruthless, pressures that forced minorities to surrender their own culture to that of the majority led the Hungarian-Americans toward the foods and drinks of their adopted country. At the same time Hungarian cooking was having its effect. Goulash, long an international dish, became better known, as did the strudel, the dobos torte, and other pastries. Paprika, almost unknown in America prior to the Hungarian immigration, came into wide use.

Still greater was the influence on American eating habits of the Italians who emigrated in large numbers, especially between 1900 and 1930. Most came from poverty-stricken regions of southern Italy, a land of little food and ceaseless toil. There, in millions of homes, meat was eaten only on major holidays and even spaghetti was a rare treat. A poor peasant might lunch on bread dipped in olive oil and have a supper of beans.

City dwellers and farmers with good lands ate better. Pastas, usually homemade, were common as was cornmeal used to thicken boiled beans, a favorite Neapolitan dish. Sometimes corn was mixed with rye, chestnut, or coarse wheat flour to make bread. Vegetables were very important and included lettuce, Savoy cabbage, tomatoes, eggplant, onions, asparagus, artichokes, beans of all kinds, potatoes, broccoli, celery, and peas. For seasoning there were thyme, parsley, mint, basil, garlic, and oregano. Fruits, usually raw, ended nearly every meal. Cheeses, both soft and hard, played a large role in Italian meals.

Olive oil was used everywhere, but especially in the South. Tomatoes were eaten fresh and as a major ingredient in innumerable cooked dishes. As tomato paste, *concentrato,* they joined garlic and other herbs to flavor meat and vegetable dishes at all seasons. Wine was the usual Italian beverage, but many poor southern Italians drank instead *caffe,* a coffee substitute made from any roasted and ground grain.[13]

In America, the Italians clung to their native diet with a tenacity that was exceeded only by the Chinese. Imported cheese and olive oil were bought, as were imported sausages, anchovies, herbs, pastas, wines, coffee mixtures, and other delicacies. With a stubborn insistence on freshness, the immigrants purchased many fruits and vegetables and grew still others. The small houses of Italian Americans that surrounded manufacturing towns could be identified by the fruit trees, vegetable gardens, and arbors of grape vines around them.

Though they ate their traditional foods, the Italian Americans often used their American wages to change the proportions. Meat became for many a daily food, rather than one for major holidays. Eggs and milk were consumed less than in Italy, being thought too expensive. But cakes, candy, and real coffee were all bought far more. The increased use of sugar, especially, was very great, and sweet rolls and doughnuts became regular breakfast fare. Such an increase in the eating of sugar and white flour, while the consumption of pasta remained level, resulted in a dietary imbalance.[14]

The Italian influence upon American food customs was the greater because of the active role that many took in the sale and distribution of foods. For several decades Italian Americans ran innumerable ice-cream parlors and small quick-lunch restaurants in cities until Greek immigrants began to take them over in the 1920s.[15] Italians also became very important in the wholesale and retail distribution and sale of fruits and vegetables.

By the 1920s many native American city dwellers had come to know more Italian dishes than the familiar spaghetti and macaroni: minestrone, antipasto, lasagne, cannelloni, chicken cacciatori, and spumoni ice cream, among others. By the 1930s pizza was beginning to be appreciated outside the Italian-American communities. One cookbook compiler credited the Italians in America with having "blazed the way" for the increased use of cheese, "for they serve cheese with any course, from soup through dessert."[16] Tomato paste was adopted in America as were various Italian sausages, anchovies, oregano, Chianti wine, and an increased use of zucchini squash, broccoli, and artichokes. Even garlic, which Anglo-Americans had touched only gingerly, won friends through Italian dishes.

The Greeks were another Mediterranean people with a sensuous approach to food and drink. Like the Italians, they cooked with olive oil and enjoyed wine with their meals. Most Greeks could afford meat only rarely and salt or fresh fish hardly more often. Usually the main dish of Greek farmers would be vegetables cooked in a casserole with beans, rice, peas, grain, or pasta, and well flavored with hot peppers, oregano, or some other herbs or spices. Cheese and black olives were much eaten, as were such fruits as watermelons, figs, oranges, and grapes. Only on Sundays or special occasions would fine lamb dishes be made.

The heavy meal of the day in Greece was usually at noontime with all the family present. The women of the household would prepare the long table, cutting the bread into pieces and placing wineglasses in front of each plate. A brief prayer preceded the meal and the eating followed, usually in silence, and only after the dessert of fruit would there be conversation before the afternoon siesta. Breakfasts were very light — tea, warm milk, or chocolate with bread or toast — and suppers were often the remains of dinner or a lighter version of that meal.

Although Greeks in America could buy most of their customary foods, there were some difficult adjustments. They could not find the light wines they liked, and those who worked away from home found it hard to substitute a noontime meal of cold, dry sandwiches or even a quickly served hot meal for the traditional family dinner. One young Greek could not forget either the noon-time dinners or "the memories and experiences that were associated with them."[17] A Greek woman said she "almost starved" before she became used to the "painfully tasteless" American food, the tough beef and mutton, the vegetables all cooked in water, and potatoes at every meal.[18]

Many Greek immigrants found work in the food industry. Beginning about 1895 they established stores that carried Greek wines, cheese, olive oil, black olives, currants, dried fish, sardines, figs, and so on — first in New York City and then in Chicago, Boston, and other large northern cities.[19] Some opened candy kitchens, fruit stores, ice-cream parlors, bakeries, and quick-lunch rooms. Their coffeehouses and restaurants in the Greek communities softened the lives of expatriates. Restaurants opened to the general public in northern cities and even some southern ones[20] served "American" dishes but so badly that "Greek restaurant" became a term of condemnation.[21] Only in a few large cities were there fine Greek restaurants to offer such dishes as stuffed grape leaves, moussaka, many lamb dishes, and baklava.

More international were the food and cooking of the Jews who entered the country in large numbers between about 1880 and 1914. They came from many countries, but a large proportion were refugees from the persecutions and pogroms of Czarist Russia and Poland.

Jewish cooking had arisen from a combination of national backgrounds, dietary laws, and customs relating to religious festivities. There were great differences among the Jews who poured into America, for those descended from Spanish ancestors knew dishes that were completely strange to those born in Russia. In the United States, it was the foods and cookery of Jews from eastern Germany, Russia, Poland, Rumania, and other parts of eastern Europe that came to be thought of as making up Jewish cooking.[22]

Many Jewish immigrants were Orthodox and followed strict dietary rules that few of their descendants would keep. Orthodoxy listed all foods as meat, milk, or neutral. Meat and milk were never to be eaten together, and the Orthodox ate only in their homes where separate sets of cooking and eating dishes kept the two from meeting. Meats and some other foods also had to be prepared in certain ways, and this required kosher butcher shops and food stores.

Some Jewish dishes were associated with festive meals. On Friday nights the command to celebrate the Sabbath was observed with a fine meal that might include gefilte fish (a dumpling stuffed with ground fish, onions, and spices), soup, and roast chicken or meat. On Fridays the daily black bread was replaced by challa, a white loaf baked in a long twist. Kreplach, bits of chopped meat enclosed in small, triangular pieces of dough and cooked in soup, were holiday delicacies. Latkes, or pancakes, were eaten on Chanukah at the beginning of winter. Hamantaschen, three-cornered cakes made of sweet dough filled with raisins, prunes, or poppy seed, were associated with Purim. Blintzes, apparently of Russian-Polish origin, were thin pancakes wrapped around a cheese-egg mixture and then refried, or baked, and spread with sour cream or cinnamon and sugar.[23]

The general public came to know some Jewish foods through the Jewish delicatessens, most of which were in New York City. Here in a welter of food fragrances were sold garlic pickles, potato or cabbage salads, gefilte fish, smoked salmon (lox), the bagel (a hard roll frequently eaten with cream cheese), knishes (pastries filled with meat or other things), cured beef known as pastrami, chopped chicken livers, cheesecake, a variety of sausages, braided egg breads, and sour rye and pumpernickel breads.[24]

The "new immigration" from southern and eastern Europe did not stop the continued flow of people from northern and western Europe. The German migration continued until World War I, with German restaurants and delicatessens spreading knowledge of German foods and dishes. The delicatessens sold many varieties of sausages, potato salad, herring and other fish salads, sauerkraut, smoked and spiced fish of various kinds, cold goose in meat jelly, and smoked Westphalian ham.[25] Visitors to German restaurants came to know sauerbraten, knackwurst, Thuringer and bratwurst sausages, potato dumplings, potato pancakes, and red cabbage. German settlers in the Midwest and on the Great Plains retained a great part of their culinary heritage. The band leader Lawrence Welk remembered the wedding feasts of his youth in the Strasbourg area of North Dakota where there were platters of fried chicken, ham, roast beef, sauerbraten, German wurst, big bowls of sauerkraut, many home-canned fruits and vegetables, German chocolate cakes and butter cookies, and "always" "Hockzeitkuchen" or "Kuka," a flat cookie-like sugar and cinnamon cake served in pie-shaped wedges at all German weddings, together with many glasses of *schnaps* or hot coffee.[26]

The upper Mississippi Valley attracted a great part of the Scandinavian immigrants. As early as the 1850s Norwegians settled in northern Illinois and Wisconsin, and after the Civil War they, together with Swedes, Danes, and Finns, moved into the northern Great Plains to farm while others went to northern Wisconsin and Minnesota to work in sawmills or as lumberjacks. The Swedes were especially numerous and between 1868 and 1890 nearly half a million, mostly of peasant background, emigrated to America, a great part of them going to New York, Illinois, Wisconsin, Minnesota, the Dakotas, and the Pacific Northwest.[27]

Accustomed to simple cooking in their homelands, the Scandinavians adjusted easily to American frontier fare. As quickly as possible they made the dishes they had known in Europe. A Norwegian woman in Nebraska was reported to have become less homesick when her husband raised rye for bread.[28] Non-Scandinavians adopted some foods. The lye-cured cod called *lutefisk* by Swedes and Norwegians appeared on the winter menus of Minnesota restaurants; Wisconsinites and others took over from Swedes their pickled herring, small meatballs, beet salads, and crisp rye breads; around Lake Superior the Finnish dark bread and the *piirakka* (rice-filled pasties) became popular.[29] In turn, Scandinavian housewives became expert at American baked goods, and for several generations Americans in northern states would purchase clean and appetizing breads and pastries at Swedish bakeries.

Other European immigrants added variety to American tables. Austrians brought their pastries, including the rich, many-layered tortes, Wiener schnitzel, and fine candies. Swiss made Wisconsin a major cheese-making center; Belgian communities in Wisconsin at festival time served Belgian pie composed of layers of custard, prunes, apples, and cottage cheese; Scots made their shortbreads and probably raised the quality of American soups by example; and in mining areas throughout the United States miners from Cornwall and Wales introduced their pasties, rounds of pastry filled with meat, onion, potatoes, or various vegetables. These were not only carried into the mines for lunch but were sold by bakers and restaurants in mining towns.[30]

While many immigrant culinary customs were continued in

America, the transfer had not been easy. The shock of moving into a new world, the inability to buy or grow some traditional foods, a desire to adopt American customs, and a fear of ridicule, all did damage to imported eating habits. That some foods and dishes established a footing in America was fortunate; that more did not was a loss.

⁕ 21 ⁕
The Early
Twentieth Century,
1900-1941, I

Then mothers and sisters
would spend all day on hillsides picking
maybe a bushel of wild greens.

In 1900 Americans who celebrated the start of a new century could not have guessed that the next four decades would bring one terrible war, the origins of an even more devastating one, and a depression that would plunge millions into hunger and despair.

The same time span saw less spectacular, but nevertheless important, developments. The rapid growth of industrialism and big business continued, both thriving in the warm atmosphere of government support and wartime demands. A nationwide effort was made to prohibit alcoholic beverages. The automobile ceased being a toy of the rich and became a tool of nearly everyone as concrete highways formed a countrywide network. The airplane grew from a curious invention into a mass carrier. In communication, the older telegraph and telephone were joined by radio and television, both strengthening the growing uniformity of thought and behavior.

There were important movements of people. The "new immigration" from southern and eastern Europe continued in full flood, interrupted partially by the First World War, until Warren Harding's administration when the government acted to curb this flow of the poor and persecuted. There was worry that the new immigrants were "racially" inferior, an error that academicians could have dispelled had they themselves been free from popular prejudices. Organized labor, fearful of cheap manpower from abroad, joined in opposition, as did many conservatives who were concerned about the movement of radical ideas into the country. An emergency immigration act of 1921 was followed, three years later, by the National Origins Act. This greatly limited East Asians from immigrating and set quotas on Europeans based on the 1890 census and therefore heavily weighted against the new immigration. The act also sharply reduced the total number of immigrants.

There were migrations within the country. Between 1900 and 1930 the country's farm dwellers declined from 60 percent to 45 percent of the total population, in part due to the movement during the First World War of hundreds of thousands of blacks from the South to northern cities to obtain war work. Both blacks and recent immigrants from abroad lived in slums — black ghettoes, Little Italies, and so on. Native-born whites lived in their own city islands or moved to the suburbs that sprang up around the cities.

The lives of urban women changed rapidly. More and more became stenographers, clerks, and factory workers, a process speeded up by the manpower shortage during World War I. Even housewives found their circumstances changing. As immigration was cut sharply in the 1920s the supply of cheap servants declined rapidly, and city houses and apartments reflected this with smaller kitchens and the disappearance of the "maid's room." Household appliances began to replace the maid or hired girl.

While all these changes influenced what people ate and drank, so too did the growing importance of business in the production, processing, and sale of food and drink. Among other things, the possibilities for deceiving the public grew. Aided by well-trained chemists, physicians, biologists, academicians, lawyers, and advertising men, and frequently protected by state and federal governments that identified unrestricted business growth with progress, the food industry sold the consumer foods that were impure, adulterated with dangerous chemicals, and deceptive as to their nature. Industrial chemists created food additives that prevented early decomposition, hid existing decomposition, and even restored decomposed food to a semblance of freshness. Bad eggs were deodorized with formaldehyde and sold for cake making, bad apples were made into jelly, and jams were flavored with coal tar derivatives to be sold as "currant," "blackberry," or "plum." Butchers everywhere used commercial preservatives whose effects on the human body could not be known or even guessed.[1]

The idea that laws might protect consumers from adulterated foods came slowly. Massachusetts in 1856 legislated against food adulteration, and in 1874 Illinois and then other states forbade the addition of inferior materials to food or the use of packaging and processing to conceal poor or contaminated substances. But these laws were little enforced. In 1885 Congressman A. S. Paddock of Nebraska introduced a pure-food bill in Congress that was greeted with laughter and ridicule, but the country's anger grew during the following years as evidence accumulated of fraud and abuse in food production.

The movement for food reform gained a great leader when Dr. Harvey Washington Wiley, professor of chemistry at Purdue University, became chief of the Bureau of Chemistry of the United States Department of Agriculture. In 1883 Wiley began the study of food adulteration. He dramatized his work by creating the so-called Poison Squad, a group of twelve employees of the Department of Agriculture who were given carefully controlled meals and whose health was closely watched. Wiley's reports on the progress of the Poison Squad did more than anything else to arouse public anger against the food industry's deceptions.[2]

Other strong forces pushed the federal government toward the passage of pure-food laws. About 1902 the country's leading magazines, as well as some newspapers and books, began powerful attacks on the country's ills, especially those due to big business and government corruption. Some of these "muckraker" exposés concerned filthy or adulterated foods and beverages. Samuel Hopkins Adams in *Collier's Weekly* gained thousands of new readers for that magazine with a series of articles based mainly on Wiley's researches. Additional pressure on Congress came when the General Federation of Women's Clubs organized many angry and well-informed women into the so-called Kitchen Front.[3]

By far the most inflammatory work was Upton Sinclair's *The Jungle,* a novel of 1906 that was intended to expose the unhappy lot of laborers in the Chicago stockyards, but incidentally revealed sanitary conditions so foul as to render the country rapt with horrified fascination. Clearly things were not right if deviled ham was minced tripe dyed red, much of the lamb and mutton was goat, and sausages contained rejected moldy meats dosed with chemicals, meat that had fallen on the spit-soaked and filthy floor, rats, the poisoned bread that had killed them, and rat dung. At times, too, apparently, an employee would fall into a boiling vat and would not be missed until all but his bones had gone forth as "Pure Leaf Lard."[4]

After a government commission had verified the accuracy of descriptions in The Jungle, President Theodore Roosevelt encouraged Congress to pass two pieces of legislation in June 1906. One was the Meat Inspection Act which in time did away with some animal diseases, including tuberculosis. The other was the Pure Food and Drug Act which went into effect on January 1, 1907. But within two months of its passage, Secretary of Agriculture James Wilson sided with industry when an effort was made to forbid the use of sulfur in dry fruits. In arguing that a large industry could be hurt by the ban and that there was no clear proof that the public's health was involved, Secretary Wilson could have been speaking for many of his successors. Repeatedly, the Department of Agriculture was to act on behalf of the consumer, then hear protests from the food industry, and finally either rescind or weaken the order. The later decisions were usually made behind closed doors without any consumer representatives present.[5]

Again and again Dr. Wiley's efforts to enforce the Pure Food and Drug Act were limited by President Roosevelt acting through Secretary Wilson. Four of Wiley's major efforts were against unbleached flour, Coca-Cola, saccharin, and benzoate of soda, and in each case he was prevented from taking action. President William Howard Taft later thwarted Wiley when he tried to force distillers to define and state the contents of their whiskies. Finally in 1912 Wiley resigned his post after having nearly been dismissed on trumped-up charges of having misappropriated government money.[6] Efforts to protect the consumer almost ceased; the powerful food lobbies, supported by the government, were victorious.

Although reform efforts lapsed, academic circles paid increasing attention to the nature of foods. The science of dietetics was new, and at the beginning of the century little was known about nutrition. Then, just before the First World War, scientists discovered vitamins A and B, and after the war vitamins C and D. Interest grew swiftly, and scholarly papers on vitamins rose from forty-seven in 1911 to 1,500 in 1930.

As scientific findings were publicized, many a housewife learned not to keep fresh foods too long before serving them and not to boil vegetables excessively or discard the water they had been boiled in. Milk, citrus fruits, liver, and whole-grain breads all gained prestige in a country that followed the new discoveries avidly. Although neither state nor national legislation yet existed, by 1914 about forty-five cities served school lunches, in each case finding that the student's weight, attendance, and schoolwork improved.[7]

The problem of nutrition appeared on a massive scale as part of the country's participation in the First World War when a great effort became necessary to feed its own inhabitants, to provision its army in Europe, and to supply much of the food of its Allies, both civilian and military. On the recommendation of the Council for National Defense, President Woodrow Wilson set up a Food Administration. Herbert Hoover, a mining engineer, was appointed to head it and to increase food production, cut waste, substitute plentiful for scarce foods, and protect consumers from speculators.

Aided by a cooperative public, Hoover was remarkably successful. The Food Administration used schools, the pulpit, motion pictures, posters, and the press to make food saving a national habit. An education program familiarized people with calories, vitamins, proteins, and carbohydrates, the values of fruits and vegetables, and the best means of canning, preserving, and drying foods. The public was saturated with the "gospel of the clean plate" and the slogan "Food Will Win the War." Imaginative propaganda techniques were used to promote the eating of potatoes, oatmeal, and beans among other foods.[8]

Hoover set high prices for wheat, and this led to a tremendous increase in the nation's wheat crop. He also issued frequent and specific orders to the public. On January 26, 1918, he asked for wheatless Mondays and Wednesdays, meatless Tuesdays, porkless Thursdays and Saturdays, and the use of "Victory bread" with its greater whole-wheat content in place of white bread. Later, public eating places were told to serve no bread until after the first course, only one kind of meat, no more than a half-ounce of butter per person, and not over two pounds of sugar for each ninety meals served.[9] People were also urged to raise vegetables in vacant lots or yards, the "Liberty gardens," and when Henry Ford ordered all his employees to work in such gardens or be fired, some 50,000 "shotgun gardens" resulted.[10] For many the wartime restrictions meant a more nutritious diet of whole-wheat bread, less sugar, and more fresh vegetables than usual. For those who normally had little to eat, it probably meant only that they ate less.

The war was hardly over when the country undertook a quite different crusade, the so-called Noble Experiment of prohibition. The shock was to be great to all hard and moderate drinkers, to all who enjoyed wine or beer with their meals, to those who could not dissociate good cooking from the use of liquor in the kitchen, and to those who felt the country's civil liberties were endangered.

There had been many warnings. Before the end of the nineteenth century five states had adopted prohibition, most southern states followed during the early twentieth century, and between 1916 and 1918 the majority of the midwestern and far western states fell in line. The Eighteenth Amendment to the Constitution, justified in part by the wartime need to conserve grain, was approved by the Senate and the House of Representatives in 1917. Its adoption by the states followed and it went into effect on January 16, 1920.

During the following fourteen years the country was shaken, divided, diverted, and enlivened by the legal prohibition of liquor that was over one-and-one-half percent alcohol. Many saw the ban as an effort to better man's condition; others viewed it as a naive and puritanical invasion of human rights. On the whole the measure was supported by rural areas, the Protestants, and the native-born, while in opposition were the cities, the Roman Catholics, and the more recent immigrants from Europe.

The drive to maintain prohibition had various sources. There were Southerners who wished to keep liquor out of the hands of blacks, employers who wanted sober workmen, religious persons who believed drinking was a sin, social reformers who had seen the terrible results of drunkenness, and others who wanted to cut the links between liquor and both crime and political corruption.

Millions of Americans observed the law and accepted its consequences. But it was soon clear that many would not. Much of the "color" of the 1920s came from this fact: rebellious youth of the "lost" generation, the roaring guns of gang wars, rum runners, the "stillers" of southern states, the flappers, hip flasks, speakeasies, and cocktail parties. Defiance of the law became the road to riches for some, to jail for others. For many it was only an enjoyable flouting of distasteful restrictions.

An immediate victim of prohibition was some of the best cooking that had existed in leading restaurants. Oscar of the Waldorf-Astoria complained that the ban on liquor had "ruined fine cooking and robbed America of some of its most distinctive native dishes," including both terrapin stew and lobster Newburg. Prohibition had "just killed" the art of dining, he lamented.[11] Sherry's closed in 1919 and after nearly a century of glorious history Delmonico's did the same in May 1923, both in part victims of prohibition. The overwhelming majority of Americans, of course, missed neither Delmonico's or the use of alcohol in cooking.

The country's poor looked on prohibition as class legislation which took away their beer while the middle and upper classes enjoyed their surreptitious cocktails. It was noticed that the wealthy rarely urged prohibition for themselves but did think it desirable for blacks and workingmen. One social worker commented that though he was often asked to consider the sins of the Bowery, he had never been asked to study those of Fifth Avenue.

Only the rich and farsighted stored away enough liquor to stand the siege of the dry decade. Beyond these private stores, most of the liquor of the 1920s was illegally imported or diverted from industrial alcohols. Lesser amounts came from moonshine and wine and beer illicitly made in the home.

There were some sharp changes in what liquors were consumed. A careful comparison of the preprohibition period of 1911–1914 with the prohibition years 1927–1930 showed that under national prohibition beer drinking had declined by seven-tenths, wine consumption had risen by two-thirds, and the use of spirits had increased by one-tenth. Only a quarter of the spirits were made in the home, half the beer, and three-fourths of the wine. Most Americans who drank took wine and spirits. New Jersey, through tradition, and Illinois, through the organizing abilities of Al Capone, remained beer-drinking areas. Worst was the plight of the poor who, without saloons, switched from beer to hard and bad liquors which could blind, paralyze, and even kill. In general, laborers depended on home brew, drugstore concoctions, and alley-joint alcohols.[12]

The middle and upper classes converted the trials of prohibition into diverting games. One was the cocktail party. With saloons closed, men had to find alternative sites for drinking and the home was one. There the company of women, whether wanted or not, was inevitable. For their part, many women happily accepted the new role of drinking companion.

Cocktail parties were both a defiant gesture against the prohibitionists and an exciting evasion of the law at little risk. The drinks were either the "bathtub gin" concocted from alcohol, glycerin, and essence of juniper, or a liquor of highly dubious background and vile taste purchased from bootleggers. The cocktail party even led to a new category of foods, "finger foods," or items that could be eaten with the hand that did not hold a glass.[13] Some of these would endure beyond prohibition to appear in a whole new cookbook category called "appetizers."

Speakeasies offered an even more titillating way to defy the law. During the 1920s they multiplied wildly. The New York City police commissioner estimated in 1929 that the city had 32,000 speakeasies, a number twice that of the saloons and "blind pigs" (unlicensed saloons) of preprohibition times.[14] Rather than the corner location of saloons, the speakeasies were usually in a basement, a back room, or a first-floor flat. Admission was only after scrutiny through a peephole, an unnecessary precaution that helped to maintain the air of illegality that appealed to many. Inside, the speakeasies were often dark, poorly ventilated, and frequently firetraps of inflammable decorations and inadequate exits. They catered largely to middle-class patrons and offered poor food, liquor of dubious origins, and sometimes nightclub acts. The best, like Twenty-One, had good food and imported liquor.

The nature of most liquor sold by bootleggers or speakeasies during prohibition is suggested by some of the 155 words and phrases which Edmund Wilson, the literary critic, compiled that were used during this era to indicate drunkenness. On bootleg whiskey a man might become blind, blotto, buried, cockeyed, embalmed, high, lit, oiled, ossified, owled, paralyzed, pickled, pie-eyed, polluted, shicker, soused, spifflicated, squiffy, stewed, stiff, stinko, woozy, or zozzled.[15]

Prohibition badly hurt the American wineries, and only about 100 survived in California, New York, New Jersey, Ohio, and Missouri by legally making sacramental and medicinal wines, salted cooking wines, and grape juice. Medicinal wine sold well when it was discovered that refrigerating them made the bad-tasting medicaments settle to the bottom of the bottle. Thousands of Americans made their own wines from purchased grapes.[16]

Southern mountaineers, who had long made corn whiskey for themselves and the local "fruit jar" trade, now began to distill for a nationwide underground market. Trucks carried some of this to large cities, but more went out in kegs hidden in freight cars through the connivance of railroad crewmen. Local and government agents worked to stop this trade, and thousands of mountaineers were sent to federal penitentiaries.[17]

Prohibition also promoted the soft-drink industry. There was a demand for mixers to cover the unpleasant taste of the illegal alcoholic drinks. Ginger ales moved toward dryness, with less sugar and more lemon flavor than those sold earlier.[18]

The end of prohibition came on December 5, 1933. The thirteen dry years had divided the country, had increased the wealth and power of the organized underworld, had raised a generation that made a game of illegal behavior, and had virtually ruined the American wine industry. As the prohibitionist forces had been intolerant and intransigent during their years of power, refusing all concessions to a deeply entrenched national habit, so the "wet" element would now prove uncompromising in its time of success, neither admitting error in its past ways nor acknowledging that its opponents had glimpsed any portion of truth.[19]

During the years of war and prohibition there were other changes involving food and drink, among them the means by which both reached consumers. In rural areas, when the century began, the general stores remained in control of most food sales. In southern cities the public markets still did a thriving business, but in northern cities the sale of food was increasingly divided among groceries, butcher shops, and bakeries. Village stores sent out huckster wagons to the countryside to trade groceries to farm wives for their eggs, poultry, and butter. Both farms and villages might be visited by the vegetable wagon, the baker's wagon, the ice wagon, the milk wagon, and in some places the fishmonger's white wagon. As the automobile became common many of these disappeared, though some persisted, increasingly motorized, into the 1930s.[20]

Urban groceries, the huckster wagons, country general stores, and city markets all had to face a common enemy, chain stores. These had appeared during the preceding century. The first, the Great Atlantic and Pacific Tea Company, had thirty locations in 1869 when it took that name, and three years later it had a competitor in the Jones Brother Tea Company of Brooklyn, later named the Grand Union. In 1916 the Piggly-Wiggly chain began with low prices and self-help. These and other chains grew rapidly. The Atlantic and Pacific had 1,726 stores by 1915 and 14,000 ten years later.[21]

The chain stores did not represent pure gain for the consumers. While their prices were low and their range of offerings wide, they normally dealt only in mass-produced items. This meant that locally made cheese or locally raised fresh fruits and vegetables, however good, might be ignored in favor of national brands of cheese and produce brought from distant places. Personal attention was minimal in the chain stores, and chicanery and price gouging were not unknown.

As the country's marketing conditions changed, so too did its kitchens. In cities especially they were reduced so that by 1918 some apartments had only "kitchenettes," some as small as 7½ by 2¼ feet with high shelves replacing the pantry.[22]

Whatever their size, the kitchens became more efficient. Gas stoves had existed since about 1850, but their growth was snaillike. By 1880 prejudice against them began to decline, but it was not until the 1920s that they became general in city and suburban homes. About this time they were made all white, a change that aided cleaning, the dials were elevated to a convenient level, and the oven was raised above the burners where it remained until the middle 1930s. The new stove provided clean and easy heat, quick and accurate temperature control under separate burners, and freedom from excessive kitchen warmth.[23] It marked nearly as important an upward step in the ease and efficiency of cooking and in emancipating women from kitchen drudgery as had the iron range 100 years earlier.

Although a successful electric stove remained elusive, electricity otherwise transformed the kitchen. The earliest refrigerators in 1916 consisted of the installation of the compressor, condensor, and evaporator in the purchaser's icebox. By the early 1920s some companies built complete refrigerators, and by the end of the decade this was the rule. The number in homes rose from 20,000 in 1923 to 3½ million in 1941.[24]

Smaller electric kitchen appliances grew in variety and efficiency. The few crude ones shown at the Chicago Columbian Exposition of 1893 were bettered to the point that one man, after seeing those at the New York electric exhibition of 1911, argued that the time had come for their general use in homes and hotels. The most popular were the toasters, percolators, chafing dishes, grills, and waffle irons. "Thus we see," wrote this individual, "that the housewife and the cook of the future, instead of feeling like a drudge in a smoky, smelly, overheated kitchen, will have the dignity of workers in a cool, clean laboratory for the scientific preparation of savory food and the abolition of dyspepsia."[25]

Home economists strove to design more efficient kitchens. A rational arrangement of sink, refrigerator, stove, cupboards, and other storage areas saved unnecessary steps and labor. By 1922 there were kitchen cabinets that could be arranged in various combinations, and during the 1930s the sink was patterned to fit into a complex of cupboards.[26]

Many Americans were unconcerned with these niceties, for they were victims of the Depression. Following the stock market crash of 1929 and the closing of innumerable factories, the unemployed in millions looked on hopelessly as their resources faded away and their families went hungry.

Relief measures were inadequate. When apple growers on the Pacific Coast harvested a surplus in 1930 they conceived the idea of having unemployed men sell apples on city streets. This began in New York City where 6,000 apple peddlers set up stands. Other cities followed, and while the idea was short-lived it became a pathetic symbol of the Great Depression and of the country's unreadiness to cope with human suffering on a vast scale.

Soup kitchens and emergency kitchens in cities and towns brought some relief. By January 1931 New York City had eighty-two breadlines, as they were called, serving about 85,000 meals each day. The handouts were small and simple: stew and bread; beans, bread, and coffee; bread, soup, and coffee; or cheese and meat sandwiches and coffee. The Salvation Army set up bread-lines as did hospitals, churches, fraternal orders, Tammany Hall, newspapers, individuals, and even racketeers.[27]

From 1930 to 1933 unemployment grew, and soon millions were without work for the first time in their lives. The prevalent idea was that private charity should care for the unemployed, and for several years President Hoover and state governors urged citizens to give to the Red Cross or to emergency funds. In most states the care of the poor was a county obligation, though in certain counties the poor laws were based on those of sixteenth-century England.[28] During the winter of 1931–32 some states made grants to help local authorities handle relief costs. When these proved inadequate, people turned to the national government and beginning in 1933 Congress authorized the distribution of wheat flour, salt pork, and cattle from states hit by the drought.[29]

Still, the roughly 13 million unemployed men with their families made up a third or a fourth of the country's population. That there was dire hunger and starvation was inevitable. Beggars increased on the streets, thievery rose sharply, children pleaded for food in front of grocery stores or seized food from customers as they emerged and ran off to eat it. In January 1931 there were food riots in Oklahoma and Arkansas. Pennsylvania miners were discovered who were sick and hungry, barely subsisting on dandelion leaves and wild weed roots. A committee in Chicago that investigated the city garbage dumps reported that a truck unloading garbage would be surrounded by thirty or forty men, women, and children who, as soon as the truck pulled away, would begin digging with sticks or their hands, seizing morsels of food. A man in Carlisle, Pennsylvania, suffocated his three small daughters rather than watch them starve. At least 110 deaths from starvation, mainly children, were reported in the country prior to 1934 when the Depression was still young, and far more died from diseases aggravated by hunger. A rise in rickets, scurvy, and pellagra took place as the country consumed less milk, eggs, and fresh fruit. One New York City health center reported that malnutrition among patients had risen from 18 percent of admissions in 1928 to 60 percent in 1931.[30]

The most widespread suffering came to the coal-mining areas of West Virginia and eastern Kentucky. In West Virginia about 30,000 miners were out of work, thousands of families lived in tents, many children ate only every other day, and pellagra and dysentery became common diseases. In the Cumberland plateau of eastern Kentucky perhaps half the people were hungry and some had no food at all for days at a time. In places groups of miners went to relief stations and seized bags of food.[31] A West Virginia miner looked back on the desperate scramble for food he had known during unemployment:

> I can remember carrying Red Cross flour maybe 24 pounds of it six miles over these hills. We didn't dare set it down for fear of getting it wet or a hole in it. They had a meal which was more like red dog [a slatelike road building material] than anything. But it was a blessing, even though it was probably ground up corn cobs. Then mothers and sisters would spend all day on hillsides picking maybe a bushel of wild greens. We'd have corn meal and hog lard, some greens and generally everyone had a cow and we'd have some milk. In the late fall, maybe I'd go to the garden and find an old frozen cabbage to cook.
>
> Then me and my brother we'd go work all day for some farmer for 50¢ and a meal and take the money up in beans and potatoes and apples a bushel of each and walk 3–4 miles home after 10 hours in the fields.[32]

Many more fortunate Americans still had to curtail their food spending. One man remembered the pleasures of eating two Depression treats, creamed chipped beef and canned salmon, with macaroni and cheese on less luxurious occasions. On Sundays there might be a "lucullan feast" of fried or roasted chicken with mashed potatoes, peas, and gravy.[33] This was the era when millions of Americans began what would prove a lifelong habit of eating every morsel on their plates.

Not until after Franklin D. Roosevelt's inauguration in 1933 was there a major relief program involving billions of dollars and work programs. The government had at last taken the position that justice and humanity were incompatible with hungry citizens. But unemployment, hunger, and suffering continued. Although there was an economic recovery, checked by the recession of 1937–38, there was not full employment again until the country entered World War II in 1941.

The Depression years saw the culmination of a technical development in the food industry of great importance. Although food had been frozen for shipment as early as 1876, and commercial freezing began in 1929, the process that made quantity production possible was the work of Clarence Birdseye. While fur-trapping in Labrador from 1912 to 1915, Birdseye had seen fish and game freeze solid almost instantly at forty or fifty degrees below zero. When thawed months later they had tasted remarkably fresh.

Back in the United States, Birdseye by 1926 contrived a machine that rapidly froze perishable foods by pressing them between two refrigerated metal belts. A company organized by Birdseye and others was given powerful backing when, in 1929, the Postum Company, soon renamed General Foods, purchased it. In March 1930 some frozen food was retailed, other companies began to compete, but sales did not become large until 1937.[34]

By the late 1930s home freezers began to sell rapidly. These enabled housewives to "put up" meats, fruits, vegetables, and fish or even complete meals to be taken from the freezer as needed. In 1939 the two-temperature refrigerators came on the market. These had a freezing compartment that could both quick-freeze and store small amounts of food. In succeeding decades this took up an increasingly large portion of the refrigerator.[35]

In other ways big business affected American eating habits. Publicity about malnutrition during the Depression led many people to indulge in self-dosage with vitamin concentrates. A trade journal in 1939 listed vitamin tablets as second only to laxatives among all drugstore sales. The vitamin mania reached the point where vitamins were added not only to milk, bread, and cereals, but to yeast, lipstick, and chewing gum.[36]

The quality and taste of American foods continued to decline with the introduction of new prepared, ready-to-eat items. Canned goods led the way, and by 1924 these included lobster Newburg, chicken à la King, Welsh rarebit, and plum pudding. In 1930 the first prepared biscuit mixes went on sale and then cake mixes. Soon there were also precooked hams, frozen dinners, canned gravies, bottled salad dressings, and prepared appetizers and variety foods. A cookbook editor in 1937 noted that commercially prepared pickles had superseded "to a large extent" homemade pickles.[37] Many of the prepared foods were quite ordinary ones dressed up with flavorings, including sugar, and sold at very high prices per pound or liquid measure. The taste of some, including the frozen dinners, was so poor as to limit their sale to those who disliked cooking, had no time for it, or never noticed what they ate.

The spate of processed foods, each containing preservatives and other additives, increased the demand for greater public control over the now powerful food industry. The election of Franklin D. Roosevelt marked the beginning of a new effort to limit the sale of impure and adulterated foods. The attempt was led by Rexford Guy Tugwell, appointed Assistant Secretary in the Department of Agriculture. Tugwell wanted a new law to replace the Pure Food and Drug Act of 1906 which by 1933 was "in tatters" from attacks by food-industry lobbies.[38]

There was public support for new legislation. In 1933 Arthur Kallet and F. J. Schlink published *100,000,000 Guinea Pigs*[39] which by the fall of 1935 had gone through thirty printings and had aroused great public anger with its accounts of impure, adulterated, and dishonest foods and drugs and the failure of the Food and Drug Administration to act against them. Tugwell himself approved a large display of fraudulent, dangerous, and misleading products entitled the "Chamber of Horrors," and in 1936 Ruth deForest Lamb, adopting the name, published *The American Chamber of Horrors*[40] which documented the problems the new bill was intended to solve.

Three loopholes in the 1906 Act concerned Tugwell. One allowed manufacturers to omit the list of ingredients on the labels provided they did not call their products by certain names. Thus Kraft and Borden could use low-quality, hard, and moldy cheeses to create and package something like a processed cheese without indicating the contents, and Kraft could sell a "whip" that did not have to meet the standards set for salad dressings. Second, Tugwell wished all food products rated A, B, or C according to quality. This the food industry opposed because it would have enabled consumers to buy according to quality rather than by expensively advertised brand names. Third, Tugwell wanted food products more accurately described. The industry suggested instead that the lists of ingredients should be filed with the Food and Drug

Administration where, of course, they would not be seen by the public.

In the end the bill of 1938 was so mutilated and provided with loopholes for the food industry by Senator Burton Wheeler and other like-minded senators and congressmen that it bore little resemblance to Tugwell's original plan. As finally passed, Tugwell thought, the bill was "a discredit" to everyone concerned with it. Tugwell himself had been savagely attacked by food processors and their allies among publishers and advertisers.[41] Again, as during the Theodore Roosevelt-Taft era, the interests of the industry had been given priority over the welfare of the consumers.

~❧ 22 ❧~
The Early Twentieth Century, 1900-1941, II

We have reached the point
with salads where only a few men
turn up their noses at them.

In rural parts of the South some families in the 1930s still lived on little more than pork, corn bread, greens, and coffee. But such vestigial diets faded as the Depression receded, for most Americans were adrift on the dietary currents of the new century. They ate less, saw familiar foods transformed by processing, slipped into dietary fads, and found that the usual meal patterns were breaking up. Changed living conditions and the cajolery of the food industry guided them into new eating habits.

As technology expanded, appetites shrank. Where once a farmer had eaten heavily in order to labor in the fields, now tractors and other farm machines did the work. Industrial machinery eliminated part of the toil of factory workers. The sedentary secretary ate less than the country housewife. People who had once walked now rode cars, buses, streetcars, trains, elevators, and escalators. It is understandable that by 1910 the per capita calorie consumption began to decline, including a sharp drop in the use of cereals, breads, and potatoes.[1]

The eating of meat, except in times of war or depression, did not fall off. The native-born were joined by new immigrants who hastened to satisfy a taste for meat that poverty had denied them. Werner Sombart, the German economist, credited the slow progress of socialism in America to the fact that laborers there ate

313

three times the bread and meat and four times the sugar as did German workers. "On the shoals of roast beef and apple pie," he decided, "all socialistic Utopias founder."

The quality of meats was often poor. Henry Finck, a commentator on American food, complained in 1913 that much of the "smoked" meat was made to appear so by a chemical treatment of creosote, aniline dye, and salt of iron; pork products were cured with cheap preservatives; and perhaps 85 percent to 90 percent of all poultry was kept in cold storage for months, if not years, and later sold uncleaned to increase the weight. He also found that some Americans had turned against both fresh pork and sausages (was this *The Jungle* influence?) though bacon and ham were universally relished.[2]

Game continued to fade from the American scene. By the early years of the century state game laws had largely or entirely eliminated venison and wild fowl from most restaurants and homes. The canvasback duck became nearly extinct, especially after 1917 when Army Ordnance took over some of its Chesapeake Bay feeding grounds for a proving range.[3]

Seafoods also declined. As city sewage and industrial wastes polluted coastal waters many shellfish became unsafe to eat. Oysters were normally given added weight by placing them in fresh water for a few hours before selling them, and this was nearly always done in polluted harbors or river mouths near large cities. New York City's Board of Health traced about 15 percent of the city's typhoid to the custom. Some states forbade this "soaking" of oysters, but the practice continued and, one man noticed, guests at banquets often left their oysters on the half-shell untouched.[4] The great century of the oyster was over. The joyous and uninhibited eating of oysters by rich and poor, Easterner and Westerner, Northerner and Southerner, had ended.

Fish also became less abundant and, in city markets, less varied. Salmon disappeared from New England waters, shad and sturgeon were rare in the rivers of the Atlantic coastal plain, and lake trout, sturgeon, and whitefish declined in the Great Lakes. In St. Louis, for long a city devoted to its crawfish, the quantity declined so much that in 1910 the state forbade angling for them in city waters. And though in the early nineteenth century a "great part" of the fish in New York City markets had been sold alive, by 1913 only some cod and trout were so marketed.[5]

On the positive side was the canning of fish. By the end of the nineteenth century canned salmon was available everywhere at low cost. Someone, possibly on the Pacific Coast, created the salmon loaf.[6] Then in 1903 a cannery in East San Pedro, California, put up 700 cases of albacore, and purchasers discovered to their surprise that tuna was good. By 1917 thirty-six canneries were selling all they could process, dietitians lauded the fish, and it was soon used imaginatively in many salads, sandwiches, casseroles, and creamed dishes.[7]

Unlike game and seafoods, the use of vegetables rose sharply. During the first third of the century there was a large increase in their consumption. Even more striking was the threefold rise in shipments of lettuce between 1920 and 1935.[8]

The treatment given vegetables in the kitchen changed little. Janet McKenzie Hill, a cookbook editor, complained in 1902 that few people did more than to boil and butter their vegetables: "It is safe to say that no more than one family in twenty, and perhaps not in fifty, ever cook celery, save in soup, or squash and turnip other than as plain boiled or mashed, while potatoes are either plain boiled, boiled and mashed, or fried." The novelist Theodore Dreiser wondered why it was assumed that "*all* people" preferred German fried potatoes: "If you should ask for French fried potatoes or potatoes *au gratin* or potatoes O'Brien in a small country town hotel you would be greeted with a look of uncertainty if not of resentment."[9] As late as 1927 Ida Bailey Allen could find no improvement. The United States, she wrote, was the only country where vegetables were more "accessories than real foods," nor were there more than a few housewives who knew the nutritive value of vegetables, considered them "anything more than necessary evils," or cooked them in any but "the most conservative ways."[10]

At the turn of the century a conscientious cook could not have produced more than limp beans and soggy peas if she relied for instruction on the leading cookbooks. Fannie Farmer in the 1906 edition of her *Boston Cooking-School Cook Book* was orthodox in calling for boiling string beans one to three hours and vegetables generally until "soft."[11] A study of southern farm families revealed that in many houses vegetables were put on to cook shortly after breakfast and boiled until the noon dinner.[12]

The neglect of vegetables was nationwide. A home demonstration agent in South Carolina regretted that farmers felt they were "too busy" to bother with gardens, poultry, and dairy products, and instead concentrated on cotton and other major crops.[13] And a survey of rural Ohio families for the period 1926 to 1928 showed that only potatoes, cabbages, lettuce, tomatoes, onions, corn, sweet potatoes, and string beans were widely used.[14]

That the eating of vegetables increased may have owed something to immigrations from Italy and Greece together with new nutritional knowledge. There was also a widespread belief that cereals and green and starchy vegetables were meat substitutes, leading numerous men to order vegetable luncheons.[15] Cookbooks did, however, give recipes for protein-rich vegetarian dishes, such as chestnut croquettes, peanut soufflé, and mock sausages.[16]

Some vegetables gained new popularity. Italian immigrants did not introduce but popularized broccoli,[17] which by 1920 was being grown commercially. Some "fancy" vegetables, such as artichokes and endive, had long been imported from France, but in the early twentieth century American farmers began to grow them. In 1904 a carload of artichokes was sent east from California, to begin a steady rise in their use.[18] The avocado, still called the alligator pear, also won greater favor, leading Floridians to compete with the West Indies and South America in its production.[19]

Some common vegetables became more popular. The new interest in salads and one-dish meals promoted the sweet pepper. This, stuffed with rice, meat, and other fillings, may have spread from Mexican sources in the Southwest as it certainly did from Italian influences in California and the East.[20] The eating of spinach grew when dietitians praised it and members of Congress sent free seeds to constituents. By 1900, if not earlier, it was also canned.[21] A major horticultural event took place when N. B. Keeney of Leroy, New York, developed stringless green beans. And the great demand for sweet corn led growers to develop varieties to extend the season. There were soon dozens of new kinds from the early Malakoff to the late Country Gentleman. The Golden Bantam was very popular.[22]

Canned vegetables multiplied as better machinery reduced the cost. Hominy was canned for the southern market; asparagus was canned in the 1880s; canned green peas were so popular that in 1910 a complete line of special machinery was made for them; and mushroom canning began in America in 1918 after World War I cut off those from France. When it appeared that tomato juice was rich in vitamin C it was canned in 1925 and won quick acceptance both as an appetizer and a breakfast potion.[23] The demand for pickles, which had progressively declined as fresh and canned vegetables became available throughout the year, was met largely by commercial producers. In rural areas, however, the fall rites continued of filling many jars with multicolored pickles and relishes.

The middle and upper classes inherited the custom of serving fruits at breakfast from the late nineteenth century. In 1875 Mary Terhune, a Virginian, wrote that the presence of the fruit basket at the breakfast table had recently become so common that its absence, when fruits were ripe, would be noticed and even "felt painfully" by some. "It is fashionable," she added somewhat confusedly, "and therefore considered a wise sanitary measure" to eat oranges for breakfast.[24] Thirty-five years later an English visitor decided that American breakfasts "always" included fruits — oranges, grapefruit, or small melons.[25]

In the 1920s oranges were lauded as carriers of vitamin C. Citrus growers of Florida and California, through a great advertising campaign, increased sales threefold by World War II.[26] Millions were convinced that good health depended in part on orange juice each morning, and canned and quick-frozen juices supplied the mounting demand.[27] Probably never before had a food habit been adopted so quickly by so many people.

The grapefruit, which may have originated as a seedling sport in the West Indies, was known in the United States as early as 1809, but not until the late nineteenth century did it become at all popular.[28] By 1919 it was being canned in Puerto Rico and by 1920 in Florida.

Canning made several other fruits nationally known. Figs were familiar in the lower South, and dried figs from California reached some outside that state. But when canned, California figs became an entirely different fruit for salads and desserts.[29] Similarly, the taste of canned pineapple became better known when it was processed in the Hawaiian Islands about 1910.[30]

In California it was found that the large green olives ripened, and took on a quite novel taste, if soaked for a long time in water or alkaline brine. For over a decade these ripe olives were known only to California. About 1901 some were canned and shipped eastward, but as late as 1919 Californians still ate 40 percent of them.[31]

The country's new devotion to salads led a California canner in 1913 to experiment with diced fruits for salads. Other canners competed with their own mixtures until, in 1927, the rivals agreed on a single mix.[32] This victory for uniformity affected millions of homes and innumerable restaurants where the combination was served in a glass cup as a "fruit cocktail" or was placed on a lettuce leaf and topped with a dab of mayonnaise as a salad.

During the 1930s fast-frozen fruits came on the market. Those which froze well were preferred by numerous people to fresh fruits which had to be cleaned, pared, and otherwise prepared for use. Most important to many was that fast-frozen fruits were an out-of-season alternative to canned fruits.

Grains benefited far less from the new interest in dietetics. During the first quarter of the century the use of wheat fell sharply and of corn even more.[33] Fear of starchy, high-calorie foods was partly responsible, but so too was fashion. The 1920s was the age of the "flapper" who disdained the well-rounded curves of her mother's generation and sought instead the "straight line" look.

The baking of bread moved from the home to commercial bakeries, as more women took work outside the home and families found themselves in apartments with small kitchens and little storage space. Even World War I promoted commercial baking when the government asked both bakers and the public to use flours that combined several grains, mixtures difficult for householders to obtain.

Although as early as 1895 a few bakers responded to the new awareness of bacteria by wrapping their bread in wax paper, most bakeries paid little attention to sanitation, allowing their dough to be exposed to dirt, grime, and rats. In 1912 the National Association of Master Bakers adopted a sanitary code and made an effort to cooperate with public health officials. The invention of automatic machinery soon made the wrapping of bakery bread general.[34]

The country's shift to bakery bread led to a nutritional loss, for the commercial bakers, competing for a rapidly expanding market, lowered standards to reduce prices. During the 1920s Ward Brothers, a major baker, discovered they could leave out of their loaves both wheat germ oil and milk solids.[35] Compared to sturdy homemade loaves, the mass-produced breads became an increasingly soft, airy creation of little taste. The novelist Henry Miller castigated it: "I say we make the foulest bread in all the world. We pass it off like fake diamonds. We advertise it and sterilize it and protect it from all the germs of life. We make a manure which we eat before we have had time to eliminate it."[36]

Paralleling in time the decline of homemade bread was the struggle of butter to maintain itself against margarine. It was a French chemist in 1869 who invented margarine to win a prize offered by Louis Napoleon III for a butter substitute. During the 1870s some was made in New York, and by 1881 there were fifteen plants in operation across the country. Two years later Armour and Company led a parade of meat-packers into the business.

The new product had its problems. Grocers bought it in bulk and adulterated it, leading sixteen states by 1886 to pass laws regulating its content. By this time, too, the butter producers were getting the states to prohibit the coloring of margarine to look like butter. State and national taxes on margarine also protected butter. Not until 1938 did the fortunes of margarine improve. Then vitamins A and D were added, the quality of margarine was raised, and the restrictive laws began to decrease, all adding to an immense growth in use during World War II when butter became scarce.[37]

Another innovation was a boon to parents. In 1922 a Rochester, New York, man canned some strained and puréed baby foods to be sold by prescription in drugstores. Others followed, and in 1929 a Michigan canner, Daniel F. Gerber, mass-produced such foods for grocery-store sale. Their use grew rapidly during World War II as incomes rose and help with baby care declined. In time all the major brands contained salt and sugar, added to please the taste of parents, though nutritionists believed that the sugar stimulated a lifelong craving for sweets and that the salt predisposed infants to high blood pressure later in life.[38] In 1978, to meet consumer demands, the major companies announced that both would be omitted.

The country also saw a sharp rise in soup eating, encouraged in part by nutritionists. "Up to within a few years," wrote the cookbook writer, Ida Bailey Allen, in 1927, "it [soup] has been considered an accessory — something with little or no food value, to be used either as an adjunct to an elaborate meal or when there was nothing else in the house."[39] When Gertrude Stein returned to the United States after a third of a century abroad she found that soups had increased greatly. Canned soups met much of the new demand and, since few housewives had made their own, they were little criticized. The leading canner, Campbell's, began in 1897 with five varieties and met such success that sales rose from a half million cans in 1900 to 18 million a week in the early 1920s.[40] Though not so popular as in Europe, soup had emerged from three centuries of neglect.

Salads continued their late-nineteenth-century revival, their lightness and nutritional value appealing to an urban, sedentary, and health-conscious age. Fannie Farmer told her readers in 1906 that salads had become a course at "almost every dinner," although a few years earlier they had seldom appeared.[41]

Experimentation with salads continued, as fruits, cheeses, eggs, tomatoes, cold meats, beans, potatoes, spinach, lettuce, herbs, and seafoods were combined in inspired or haphazard ways. In no other dish, wrote one cookbook editor, could so many leftovers be presented attractively.[42] In 1905 a Pennsylvania housewife won a national contest for a jellied salad that began a vogue for what were called "congealed" salads. The Caesar salad was invented in the 1920s, possibly by a restaurateur in Tijuana, Mexico, and in time it gained a following in California and elsewhere.[43] It was probably inspired in part by the "bread" salads of some European countries where small cubes of bread had been added to vegetable salads to absorb the superfluous dressing.[44]

All but the poorest Americans showed an interest in salads. According to George Rector a new salad dressing at Rector's, Delmonico's, or Sherry's in New York City could become the "talk of the town" and draw customers from its competitors.[45] And a country agent trying to improve the diet of South Carolina farmers in 1929 claimed proudly that "we have reached the point with salads where only a few men turn up their noses at them."[46]

Salad dressings posed problems. Vinegars were routinely adulterated with acetic acid, as was olive oil with cottonseed oil or, less commonly, with peanut, rape-seed, or poppy-seed oils.[47] Bottled mayonnaise and boiled dressings both grew in popularity.[48]

The creativity of the era did not bypass sandwiches. One cookbook editor called them "capable of almost infinite variety," while another thought the meat-chopper meant that fillings were limited only "by what you have at hand."[49] Sandwiches were made for wedding receptions and evening affairs, as the main lunch dish, and for schoolchildren. Sandwich fillers included such transient exotics as nasturtium petals, oranges, or pineapples and, from the Pacific Coast, dates, walnuts, and cream; peanut butter and figs; and the use of chocolate, pimiento, hot sardines, shrimp, and strawberries.[50]

Some sandwiches were destined for long-term popularity. As early as 1899 the club sandwich was known, its name of uncertain origin and its contents varying greatly.[51] By 1905 both the deviled ham sandwich and the grilled cheese sandwich existed.[52] The peanut butter sandwich was described in Atlanta, Georgia, in an 1898 recipe that concluded: "Tie with brown ribbon having the same tint as the paste."[53] Peanut butter itself had been known for about a decade, but it remained a home product until the early twentieth century when it was sold in grocery stores from wooden pails, being first stirred to distribute the oil evenly.[54]

A dinnertime change was the encroachment of casserole cooking on the old triad of meat, potatoes, and vegetable. Few Americans had used the casserole prior to the late nineteenth century, but it then increased rapidly, inspired by immigrant Italians, Greeks, Mexicans, and Hungarians. As economical dishes, casseroles were welcomed during the depression of the 1890s, the scarcities of World War I, the inflation that followed, and the Great Depression of the 1930s. A cookbook editor in 1913 thought casserole cooking could scarcely be overemphasized "in this day of high cost of living." Another writer, the following year, spoke of the "cooking in casserole craze."[55] Even during the more prosperous 1920s casserole dishes made headway,[56] possibly encouraged by the small kitchens of city dwellers and the growing scarcity of servants.

Other low-cost hot dishes were created or took on new life. Spaghetti with meat balls or a meat sauce became very popular, as did macaroni with meat or cheese, ground meat and rice, creamed chipped beef on toast, creamed codfish on mashed potatoes, corned or ·oast beef hash, meat loaf, salmon loaf, and creamed salmon. There was also a dish that combined macaroni or noodles, tomatoes, onions, ground beef, and sweet peppers. It was called German chop suey in a Chicago appearance of 1912. Anti-German feeling during World War I may have led to its being named American chop suey in a Montana recipe of 1925.[57] During the early 1980s it still was served as American chop suey or simply chop suey at church suppers in northern New England.

Among desserts, those of gelatin were a sensation. Late in the nineteenth century boxed gelatins were sold by Knox and others, and in 1895 a cough medicine maker in LeRoy, New York, made one that his wife named Jell-O. During the first years of the twentieth century this dessert, pushed by heavy advertising, caught on and sales soared dramatically.[58] Both light and cheap, it was suited to a time of spreading urbanism and recurrent economic troubles.

As yet the infiltration of American cooking by the factory was so limited and gradual that few noticed it. But there was change in the air and Sarah Tyson Rorer, an advocate of women's rights, a pioneer in domestic science, and for twenty-three years dean of the Philadelphia Cooking School, sensed it in a prophecy of 1914:

It is quite evident that we are drifting toward cooperative living. Higher prices and lack of labor are making this our only expedient. The day of personal servants is almost over; the day of community servants is at hand. Everybody specializes today, and the methods of the business world are creeping into the home. Some day we shall have central kitchens, managed by women who command big salaries because they can direct a large staff of workers. Housekeeping will be a wholesale business for a few, not retail for the many as it used to be.[59]

⟐ 23 ⟐
Eating Out,
1900-1941

There are bright lights in Chinatown
where they are preparing chop-suey
in immaculate Mongolian kitchens.

The custom of family meals, already endangered during the nineteenth century, continued to crumble in the early decades of the following one as ever more Americans ate out. Women took work in offices and factories, a movement greatly speeded by the manpower shortages of the First World War; eating at home became a chore among the well-to-do as the Immigration Law of 1942 further reduced the servant supply; and the automobile enhanced the kinetic quality of American life.

Absenteeism from the family table was also promoted by nearby golf courses, social clubs, the "movies," and other city distractions. Women's social clubs were formed that periodically held teas and luncheons. In 1905 the first Rotary Club was organized in Chicago to begin a meteoric rise of men's luncheon clubs. The Kiwanis Club began in Detroit a decade later, the Lions in 1917, and then other, similar organizations.[1]

New York City, large and cosmopolitan, shared in all the new trends in eating out. Great wealth supported luxurious restaurants; immigrants from many countries promoted variety; and the heavy concentration of people in Manhattan made the city a laboratory for space-saving and labor-saving techniques in food service.

Wealthy New Yorkers went to Delmonico's, Sherry's, the Savarin, Martin's, Robbins, or to the Waldorf-Astoria and Brevoort hotels. The first three, an account claimed, were where "multimillionaires try to force delicacies on their dyspepsias." All were large. Delmonico's reputedly served 1,500 quail each month and more than fifty gallons of their famous chocolate each afternoon. Sherry's had sixteen chefs and 200 kitchen employees, the Waldorf-Astoria claimed thirty-five chefs, while the Savarin had five or six large dining rooms, fifty men in the kitchen, and served 6,000 lunches daily.[2] In 1922 the Colony opened, a place where celebrities could see each other and enjoy outstanding cooking. About the same time Sardi's became a rendezvous of theater people.[3] During prohibition there were "speakeasy" restaurants of which the Twenty-One Club was the most famous for its meals.[4]

Among the rapidly growing foreign restaurants, those of the Chinese made the greatest gains. The Chinese-Americans did not have to face hostile labor unions as restaurateurs, and chop suey gave them a dish acceptable to Caucasians. Beginning about 1900 Chinese restaurants were opened in towns and cities across the country. For several decades these remained modest and invariably featured chop suey. Few Caucasian customers were prepared to order more than that dish, egg foo yong, egg rolls, or chow mein. "There are bright lights in Chinatown," wrote one man in 1913, "where they are preparing chop-suey in immaculate Mongolian kitchens."[5]

During World War I and continuing into the 1920s some large and elaborately decorated Chinese restaurants were opened in downtown locations of the larger cities. They offered both Chinese and American cooking, and dancing, sometimes to name bands. Their success was checked first by prohibition and the nightclubs that sprang up and then by the Depression.[6]

Anti-German feeling during the First World War hurt New York City's German restaurants, including Lüchow's on Fourteenth Street, but those who wished adventurous eating could choose among a growing number of Italian, French, and Hungarian restaurants as well as Syrian, Turkish, Swedish, Finnish, Russian, Bohemian, and many others. The Bowery was described in 1909 as having "all things for all men" from chop suey to goulash.[7] Refugees from the Russian pogroms founded Jewish restaurants such as Ratner's and Steinberg's in Manhattan or Garfield's in Brooklyn.[8]

More and more New Yorkers, especially at lunchtime, ate at a link of the proliferating restaurant chains that specialized in quick meals. Childs, founded in 1889, was one of the first and became one of the largest, with forty units by 1913. Other chains included the Baltimore, Naomi (started in Chicago), Coddington, Riker, Hartford, New Haven, and Charter Oak. Customers usually went to a buffet to choose from the soups, sandwiches, roast meats, pies, salads, fruits, and beverages and then sat at a table or in a chair with a wide arm. At some, hot cakes were made behind a large window before an admiring sidewalk audience.[9]

Self-service took another form when the cafeteria was invented in the Midwest. The first seems to have been in Chicago in 1893, and by 1895 there were four there. Soon every major city had cafeterias where the customer picked up tray, cutlery, and napkin and proceeded down a long counter, choosing food and presenting a ticket to be punched accordingly. The diner sat at a polished wood table in a tile-walled room often in full sight, through a plate-glass window, of passers-by. On leaving, the customer presented his punched ticket at the door, paid the bill, took a free toothpick, and departed.[10]

Another form of labor-saving restaurant began in the East. In 1902, Joseph V. Horn and F. Hardart, two young proprietors of a small basement lunch counter in Philadelphia, opened an automat with equipment from Germany. A decade later the first of many New York City units opened. In automats, customers used their change to open glass-fronted compartments and took out a sandwich, hot dish, piece of pie, salad, or other items.[11]

Even before Sinclair's *The Jungle* made many people queasy about eating meat, vegetarian restaurants appeared in cities. Those in New York were described in 1904 as having "bland and ladylike" titles such as The White Rose or The Laurel. Prices were low, and the offerings included vegetarian steaks, cutlets, and filets. The vegetables were "amazingly" well cooked, the same author thought, the fresh mushroom and nut dishes were outstanding, and a cream of mushroom soup was "worthy of a plutocrat."[12]

In the early twentieth century only a few restaurants made unescorted women feel at ease. A description of New York City in 1909 mentioned that women shoppers often went to the top floor of department stores where a thirty-seven or forty-nine cent luncheon was served them "with expedition and sometimes with courtesy." Some women went to the Women's Lunch Club to eat, it was said, exotic salads, sundaes, and other "innovations of endless charm."[13]

Women's emancipation was enhanced in 1920 when women won the vote. In the decade that followed, the new freedom was expressed outwardly by shorter skirts, bobbed hair, cigarette smoking, and the appearance of women in speakeasies, roadhouses, nightclubs, and restaurants that had formerly been exclusively male.

Not all women moved in step. For the more timid or less emancipated there appeared, during the 1920s, the tearooms. Run by women in great part for women, these gave their clients a polite and friendly haven. The tearooms did not, in spite of the name, specialize in afternoon tea with dainty sandwiches, but served both lunches and dinners that were often of good quality with superior pastries, though the novelist Edna Ferber considered them too devoted to the "lettuce-leaf, chopped-apple, marshmallow or cream-sauce school."[14]

Until prohibition, bars and saloons remained entirely masculine. In many the free lunch continued, but only a few of the largest and most prosperous had lavish ones. That of the Hotel Knickerbocker was famous in New York City. Lesser places offered a daily specialty, such as frankfurters on Monday, roast pork on Tuesday, and so on, or gave free bowls of soup every noon. Some bars displayed a sign promising a fried oyster, a clam, or hard-cooked egg with each drink. But, wrote George Ade, the commonest free lunch was "a stingy set-out of a few edibles which were known to give customers an immediate desire for something to drink," and included rye bread with perhaps baked beans, cheese, sausage, pigs' feet, sauerkraut, and dill pickles.[15]

For the poor there were pushcarts that sold fruits, soda water, hot dogs, and "harrowing pies and lyddite [a high explosive] doughnuts." On many large squares were lunch wagons, where for five cents one could buy small orders of food, tea, or coffee. On the street, too, were dealers in Vienna sausages, tamale men crying "All hot, all hot!" and Italian vendors who sold a penny's worth of "dubious" ice cream served on a scrap of paper. Even these curbside purchases would have seemed luxurious to slum dwellers who knew nothing better than the two-cent restaurants where for that sum a drink called "coffee" and a stale roll could be bought with the right to spend the night on a chair, a table, or in a barrel.[16]

The great Creole restaurants of New Orleans continued to give that city luster: Begué's offered its popular breakfasts until 1917, Galatoire's opened in 1905, Antoine's remained active, and Arnaud's appeared in 1918.[17] In time would come Brennan's, the Versailles, and other restaurants of note, large and small, to maintain the city's outstanding reputation for good cooking.

In San Francisco virtually all the restaurants were destroyed in the terrible earthquake and fire of April 18, 1906. But rebuilding came quickly, and soon there were many outstanding establishments, new and old, to continue the city's fame as a culinary center. There was the Tadisch Grill, renowned for seafood, Schroeder's with its hearty German fare, Jack's Restaurant, Fred Solari's on Maiden Lane, Marquard's and Tait's at the Beach, and the impressive Garden Court of the rebuilt Palace Hotel which many rated as the most beautiful public eating room in the country.[18] The old Poodle Dog, Marchand's, and Louis's Fashion Restaurant continued the city's strong French tradition. Some of the German restaurants closed during the First World War here as elsewhere in the country. In later decades San Franciscans went to Fisherman's Wharf for seafoods, including the Italian-American fish stew, cioppino, to one of the numerous "tamale parlors" for Mexican dishes, or to White Russian restaurants for shashlik or borsch. Few but the Chinese Americans went to the Chinese restaurants.[19]

Everywhere the automobile affected eating habits. By the 1920s the major highways were lined with drive-ins, some small and unpretentious, but others large and surrounded by parking lots attended by young girls in smart, brief costumes. Drive-ins of the Southwest often served tacos and chile con carne, while fried clams were made much of in New England. In 1925 the eastern seaboard saw the first of the Howard Johnson restaurants of orange-roofed Georgian-style buildings offering many flavors of ice cream and other foods. The hot meals served in these were distinguished only by being predictable.

Prohibition brought roadhouses. Small ones served beer and short orders, with a jukebox to provide dancing for a few couples. Others sold bootlegged liquors, beer, soft drinks, chili, ice cream, spaghetti, steaks, chicken, and sometimes a fish fry. The most elaborate had huge parking lots and name bands, served full meals, and displayed gaudy interiors.

Still another form of restaurant was only marginally dependent upon the automobile trade. These were the diners that evolved from the small, horse-drawn wagons that had sold simple foods in city streets since the 1880s. Called Night Owls, they were open from dusk to dawn. The first were little more than freight wagons with a griddle and icebox, but by the late 1890s some had a few stools at an inside counter. These prospered, many being bought by the Women's Christian Temperance Union to compete with the free lunches — and liquor — of the saloons.

In 1897 a new period in diner history began when Boston, New York, and Philadelphia replaced their horse-drawn trolleys with electric cars. The discarded trolleys were bought for twenty dollars each, fitted with dishes and a stove, and sold for lunch wagons. They were often dank and drafty, however, and, what was worse, attracted undesirable characters. Both Buffalo and Atlantic City banned them.

Just after World War I the P. J. Tierney and Sons Dining Car Company of New Rochelle, New York, began to make well-lighted and fully equipped wagons. Then, in the 1920s, Tierney put booths into his wagons to make them family eating places. Like his imitators, Tierney, through design and such names as "Fenway Flyer" or "Rocket Diner," tried to endow his diners with some of the glamour that attached to railroad dining cars of that time.

By the 1930s dozens of manufacturers made diners, with the great majority going to New Jersey, New York, and New England. Those in towns and villages looked to the local trade, but a few on highways catered to tourists and truckers.[20]

As the country's mobility grew, neatly packaged snacks and finger foods multiplied — popcorn, peanuts, potato chips, candy bars, among others. Some dated from the nineteenth century but now found a new popularity. When moving pictures began to talk in 1927, moviegoers were released from a rapt attention to the pantomime and could both carry on whispered conversations with their companions and consume popcorn, candy, and soft drinks.

Of the new finger foods the hot dog was the stellar performer for some decades. That the wienerwurst and the roll first met at Coney Island is not a certainty, but the combination was sold there very early at boardwalk stands to join the frozen custards, clam chowder, hot corn, cotton candy, lox, bagels, and apples on a stick. Feltman's Coney Island stand may have adopted the old Nuremberg custom of serving the sausage with a piece of bread, only substituting a roll for bread. Harry Magely Stevens, director of catering at the New York Polo Grounds, was reputedly the first, about 1900, to have heated the roll and added condiments.[21]

Nathan Handwerker did much to give the hot dog fame. Trained as a shoemaker in Poland, he emigrated to the United States and in time found work slicing rolls and making deliveries at Feltman's Coney Island stand. Feltman's charged ten cents for its hot dogs. Handwerker, after saving up 300 dollars for capital, opened a stand where the charge was five cents. Success was immediate, and Nathan's went on to become the most famous hot-dog stand in the land.[22]

The new creation had name trouble, going through frankfurter, after Frankfurt-am-Main, "sausage," "Coney Island Chicken," and "weenie," from wienerwurst. Then T. A. Dorgan, a sports cartoonist, played upon the popular suspicion that weenies contained dog meat and about 1906 published cartoons in which lively sausages made cynical remarks in talk balloons. He named his creatures "hot dogs," and the name took despite efforts by barkers to substitute the less suggestive "red hots."[23]

Equally uncertain are the origins of the hamburger sandwich. One story holds that an obscure restaurant owner ran out of bulk pork sausage for his sandwiches one day at the Summit County, Ohio, Fair in 1892 and substituted ground beef. Others have said that someone at the St. Louis Fair of 1904 began it. The hamburger, in any case, was no instant success. For the first two decades of the century it was eaten only occasionally at picnics, beaches, fairs, amusement parks, carnivals, and a few restaurants.

In the early 1920s the first major chain of hamburger stands, the White Castle, began. The original unit opened in Wichita, Kansas, in 1921, and during the next nine years the chain spread into other cities, in no place finding anyone already specializing in hamburger sandwiches. Even in 1930, when New York City got its first White Castle, it was said that one could ride all day there without seeing a hamburger sign. The White Castle's hamburgers included onion and a bun that had been cut open and placed over the patty for a time to catch the heat, juices, and aroma. Customers were urged to "buy them by the sack," and many did.[24]

A third dish to win a nationwide body of devotees also grew from nineteenth-century origins. Chili con carne may have already existed among poor Mexicans of San Antonio in the Mexican province of Texas during the 1820s. It was not until about 1880, however, that writers first mentioned the Mexican-American "chili queens" of San Antonio who came about dusk each evening to the downtown plazas with carts in which were crude tables and stools and cauldrons of cooked chili con carne. A fire was begun to keep the chili fragrantly simmering. Each chili queen had a large, ornate lamp with a brightly colored globe, and the women themselves dressed gaily.

Chili's realm expanded slowly. By 1890 a chili parlor existed in McKinney, a large town north of Dallas, and in 1893 a "San Antonio Chilley Stand" was set up on the grounds of the Columbian Exposition in Chicago.[25] Soon the dish, made with or without beans, won followers in New Orleans, St. Louis, Cincinnati, and Chicago among other places. In Cincinnati, due to some East Europeans, chili served on spaghetti became the accepted form. In 1908 a San Antonio company canned chili, and other canners followed.[26]

Another popular food began much later. During the Depression the Poor Boy sandwich — a French loaf filled with such things as sliced cold meats, tomatoes, and lettuce — flourished in New Orleans. Later, similar sandwiches, some of Italian origin, were sold throughout the country under such names as Submarine, Grinder, Hero, and Hoagie. A Creole variation in New Orleans was the Peacemaker, a French loaf scooped out, well buttered, and filled with hot oysters. It reputedly got its name from having been taken home by men who had spent a late evening out.[27] San Francisco knew a similar sandwich.

Soda fountains changed in the early twentieth century. About 1903 the drugstore fountains which stood flush against the wall began to disappear. In their place were built counters which the attendant could stand behind to use the ice-cream wells and syrup pumps to concoct sodas, sundaes, ice-cream cones, banana splits, phosphates, and at some point milk shakes, called frappes in New England, and malted milks. The first such fountain was installed at the Broad Street Pharmacy in Philadelphia,[28] and soon there were many throughout the country. Some were simple while others had backgrounds of carved wood, mirrors, marble, and stained glass.

By the 1920s the drugstore soda fountain had become a national institution, the scene of gluttonous forays by children, of hot afternoon encounters among friends, and of after-the-movie evening gatherings. Some fountains moved into another dimension by adding hot drinks, sandwiches, and even hot dishes to their repertoire.

The ice-cream cone, a principal product of the soda fountains, may have begun in Europe. Ice cream was eaten from both metal and paper cones in France during the nineteenth century, and it may first have been put into consumable containers in Dusseldorf, Germany. If, on the other hand, the edible ice-cream cone began in the United States, the most credible account has it originating at the St. Louis Fair of 1904 where there were both ice-cream and waffle stands and someone might have joined the two products. Ice-cream cones were certainly sold at the fair and were popular so quickly that before the fair ended foundries in St. Louis were making molds for the "World's Fair Cornucopia." Within a decade the ice-cream cone had become a fixture of the American scene.[29]

During the 1920s ice cream took other forms. A Danish-born schoolteacher in Onawa, Iowa, who ran a candy store on the side, noting that both chocolate candy and ice cream were popular, united them by covering a bar of ice cream with chocolate. He patented his invention in 1921 and named it "I-Scream," but changed it to "Eskimo Pie." The success was tremendous, and by the spring of 1922 sales were a million a day. The Eskimo Pie remained popular for several decades.[30]

Even greater success came to Harry Burt of Youngstown, Ohio, an ice-cream parlor owner. Burt created a chocolate-covered ice-cream bar from which a stick extended for easy handling. Named Good Humor bars, they were sold from white trucks equipped with bells and driven by a white-clad "Good Humor Man." This figure appeared during the 1930s and 1940s as the leading man in one movie and in walk-on parts in over a hundred others. The sound of the Good Humor man's bells caused excitement among children on hot summer days, and newspapers mentioned his springtime arrival as they did that of robins and crocuses.[31]

In 1923 the Popsicle — a hard-frozen ice on a stick — was invented, and later came a flow of other cold novelties: ice-cream sandwiches, prepackaged sundaes, ice-cream cakes, cake rolls, and prepackaged cones. Vanilla had become the favorite flavor for ice cream, followed by chocolate, while orange was by far the most popular sherbet with pineapple second.[32]

Other between-meal pleasures existed for the very young. Drugstores and groceries usually had glass-enclosed cases displaying confections. Many were "penny candies" — black licorice ropes, jaw-breakers which revealed a succession of colors as they were sucked upon, small wax bottles containing a sweet liquor, strips of paper on which were fastened sweet sugar drops, tiny sugar "pies" in tin cups eaten with a minute tin spoon, and innumerable other enticing morsels. By the 1920s, however, these were retreating before foil- or waxpaper-wrapped candy bars, usually sold for five cents. Sadly, during the 1930s, these became the daily lunch of many adults hard hit by the Great Depression.

⋘ 24 ⋙
World War II
and After

*More and more
the food industry shaped the country's diet.*

When Japanese planes attacked Pearl Harbor on December 7, 1941, the United States entered a third of a century of conflict as World War II was succeeded by wars in Korea and Vietnam. The era was one of social dislocations in which people were wrenched repeatedly out of customary habits and directed into new ones.

During World War II especially, over 15 million men and women entered the armed forces and over 2½ million wives were separated from their husbands. About 1,600,000 Southerners migrated to the North, and within the South some 5 million people went to industrial centers. Overall, about 27,300,000 people changed their residences during the war. Innumerable young wives lived in crowded housing at army bases and near defense plants or, after their husbands went overseas, with parents.[1]

Conscientious cooking was difficult in temporary or inadequate housing, and it was easier to eat out. Those who did cook frequently turned to processed and ready-to-eat foods. Even well-to-do housewives were affected, for between 1940 and 1944 the number of domestic servants dropped more than 20 percent because of better-paying wartime work.[2]

The great food companies gained strength as they received massive government orders for the armed forces and lend-lease programs. Sales to the government of General Foods alone rose from $1,477,000 in 1941 to $37,840,000 in 1944.[3] As during earlier wars, government contracts nudged the food industry in the direction of monopoly.

333

Huge shipments to Europe led to shortages and hoarding. Sugar rationing came early and brought a decline in home baking and fruit preserving. By the spring of 1942 steak, hamburger, and frankfurters were becoming scarce. Some people hunted game, others turned to chicken, cheese, and eggs, and a few tried horsemeat. Beginning in 1943, canned goods were rationed. The war also cut off foreign delicacies such as many spices, French and German wines, caviar, and European cheeses.[4]

Highly successful were the 20 million Victory gardens which grew 40 percent of the country's vegetables in backyards, vacant lots, or adjacent to war plants. California vegetable production was hurt, however, when the army under orders from President Franklin D. Roosevelt suddenly herded about 117,000 people of Japanese birth or ancestry, two-thirds of them United States citizens, to concentration camps in a cruel and callous violation of civil liberties. None of them had been guilty of espionage. Many of the imprisoned had been highly successful market gardeners.

Housewives turned to casseroles and food-stretchers — macaroni, potatoes, rice, dried peas, and beans — that they had used during Depression years. Fresh onions became scarce, candy nearly disappeared, long queues formed where coffee was sold, butchers were wheedled and bribed, and black markets throve in meat and other items. Consumers minded most the scarcity of meats, sugar, and butter, with few objecting to the limit on canned goods. Home canning of vegetables flourished, with about three-fourths of the country's families putting up an average of 165 jars a year. Least hurt by rationing were the nearly 3 million vegetarians.[5]

After the war Americans resumed their heavy consumption of meats. Most ate beef, with steaks popular and ground beef growing rapidly in use, partly because its convenience appealed to the expanding number of working wives. By the early 1980s the average American ate yearly about 200 pounds of red meat, fifty pounds of poultry, but only about eleven pounds of fish. Roughly a third of the fish was sold as frozen sticks or filets, much of it precooked.[6]

The varieties of seafood had changed greatly. Rivers, lakes and coastal waters became polluted everywhere, and overfishing decreased tremendously the catches of herring, yellowtail flounder, and haddock. The Atlantic salmon became scarce as did the

Chinook salmon in the Northwest. Those who enjoyed seafoods, however, could take hope in the "farming" of oysters, shrimp, pompano, clams, lobsters, mussels, and abalone. Trout and catfish were also grown in freshwater ponds.[7]

There were pronounced changes also in dairy products, fats, and oils. The eating of both cheese and ice cream rose as large-scale commercial production lowered their cost, though the quality was often poor. Cottage cheese and yogurt both became very popular. The use of lard declined as that of salad and cooking oils grew. A major event was the displacement of butter by vegetable margarine. As late as 1950 butter outsold margarine about two to one, but during the following quarter century the ratio was reversed, due in great part to President Harry Truman's signature on the Margarine Act of 1950 which ended the discriminatory taxes that the butter lobby had obtained.[8]

More and more the food industry shaped the country's diet. The eating of fresh fruits and vegetables fell as that of canned and frozen ones rose. Potatoes, after a long decline in use, came back in the decades after World War II in canned, frozen, dried, and other processed forms. Both potato chips and French fried potatoes became very popular.

Ironically, as the spate of processed foods reduced kitchen labor, the kitchen grew in efficiency. By the 1940s most kitchens had become shining and usually white rooms with gas or electric stoves, electric refrigerators, and porcelain sinks, all soon to be joined by electric blenders and mixers, electric carving knives, coffee grinders, and can openers; dishwashers and garbage-disposal units; ice crushers and food processors.

Kitchens also tended to be larger and more attractive in a partial return to the family room of earlier centuries. Dining rooms were often omitted in smaller homes, and families ate in the "breakfast nook" of the kitchen or in one end of the living room.

Meals took on new shapes. Breakfast continued its century-long decline to become for most families a slight thing of orange juice, toast, jam, and coffee — or only sweet rolls and coffee. Children were encouraged by television advertising to concentrate on cold breakfast foods. Many city dwellers ate no breakfast, and few families anywhere met together for the meal.

At lunchtime the family was most dispersed, so that dinner

became the one occasion when it might eat together, but this might be no more than a few days each week or last more than twenty minutes. By the 1950s the family dinner as a symbol of unity was disappearing. Rarely did parents and children eat together with a degree of formality, to talk, exchange thoughts, or indulge in small politenesses. The widespread use of prepared foods, often heated in microwave ovens, eliminated the premeal odors and sense of anticipation as well as the housewife's opportunity to do creative cooking.

A minority of the public reacted against the prepared foods. Aided by an ever-shortening work week and by widespread affluence, many Americans turned to food as a positive pleasure. This sensuous approach owed much to a greater appreciation of foreign cookery. The Second World War gave millions of Americans of both sexes new eating experiences in Asia and Europe where they found food treated as a serious subject and an important source of enjoyment. Millions of postwar tourists learned similar lessons. If few later tried exotic cookery, many patronized foreign restaurants in the United States, and nearly all gained tolerance of culinary differences.

For a time, the approach of some converts was naive and centered on such novelties as canned kangaroo meat or hippopotamus steaks. But Craig Claiborne, the New York *Times* food writer, wrote perhaps overoptimistically in 1961 that there had probably never been "such an absorbing interest in fine cuisine in the home as there is in this decade."[9] Clubs were formed for the mutual enjoyment of carefully prepared meals, the use of wines increased, sophisticated kitchenwares sold well, and interest grew in home-grown vegetables and imported cheeses. Oregano, basil, rosemary, and tarragon came into considerable use, as did home-ground spices — peppercorns, nutmegs, and various seeds.[10] Garlic, long suspect, and leeks grew in popularity.

A deluge of cookbooks was published, some of solid worth. Their popularity probably reflected both the new interest in cooking and the virtual disappearance of servants, forcing many women to undertake management of the kitchen. Two works sold in vast numbers: *Better Homes and Gardens Cook Book,* first published in 1930, and *Betty Crocker's Cookbook* which had appeared in 1950. Three "classics" continued to be popular: Fannie Farmer's *The Boston Cooking-School Cook Book* which dated from 1896, the *Settlement Cookbook*, first issued in Milwaukee in 1901; and Irma S. Rombauer's *Joy of Cooking*, published in 1931 and greatly enlarged in 1943.

Except for writings by Harriet Beecher Stowe and Henry T. Finck's *Food and Flavor* of 1913, American authors had largely ignored American cooking as an art. But beginning in the 1930s and 1940s M. F. K. Fisher, John and Karen Hess, James Beard, Craig Claiborne, and Mimi Sheraton all included American cooking and food habits in their writings, and a succession of magazines provided articles and an ocean of recipes: *Gourmet, Bon Appetit, Cuisine, International Review of Food and Wine, The Cook's Magazine,* and *Pleasures of Cooking.* Newspaper "food sections" ranged from the sophisticated to those that carried hand-out recipes from the food companies designed to promote their processed foods.

Cooking schools multiplied in all cities for both general and specific kinds of cookery. Television reached a larger audience. Dione Lucas, a gifted cook and cookbook compiler, was a pioneer in 1947. Then on February 11, 1963, Julia Child appeared on Boston television showing how to make *boeuf bourguignonne.* Her lessons in French cooking, given with verve but clearly and concisely, fascinated many and led some to try her recipes.

American regional cooking persisted, though weakened by the mobility of Americans, the deluge of processed foods, and the nationwide fast-food chains. Such cooking lurked out of sight in private homes, emerging only when it was general and pronounced, as in New Orleans, or in church suppers, rural benefits, and public barbecues. New England still favored beef, chicken pies, baked beans, seafoods, boiled dinners, and pies, though less traditional tastes had come with the Italians, Portuguese, French Canadians and other immigrant groups.

Westward migrations had taken New England food habits across a wide band of northern states where they vied with contributions of Slavs, Germans, Scandinavians, Italians, Greeks, Japanese, and Chinese among others. In northern cities, too, were numerous blacks who had migrated from the South during both world wars, bringing with them a liking for pigs' feet, chitlins, hog jowls, corn breads, and other foods that were called "soul foods" in the 1960s but were actually familiar to innumerable Southerners, white and black. Both north and south the blacks adjusted their diets to their economic status. To New York City came Puerto Ricans with their liking for boiled or fried rice mixed with salt pork and small pieces of tomatoes, garlic, onion, and greens. Side dishes included fried eggs, potatoes, plantains, meat, chicken, or fritters of meal flour and fried codfish.[11]

The South clung to its food habits more closely than the North. Greens, beans, and black-eyed peas were still boiled with bacon or pork, and grits flourished from the Carolinas to Texas. Corn breads kept a following as did rice in South Carolina, Georgia, and along the Gulf Coast. The southern poor, the North Carolina journalist Jonathan Daniels pointed out, depended heavily on pork, cornmeal, molasses, and moonshine — with many cups of coffee, soft drinks, and store-bought cakes. Turnips, collards, cabbages, mustard and poke greens, sweet potatoes, field peas, souse, chitlins, and buttermilk all remained in southern meals. Gardening had increased, however, and there was more milk, more fresh meat, and a great decline in rickets and pellagra.[12]

Much of Florida's native cookery was overwhelmed by the influx of sun-seekers from the North and by communities of Greeks and Cubans in several cities. Refugees from Castro's Cuba, numerous even before the mass migration of 1980, gave Miami a pronounced Cuban flavor. Many non-Cuban Floridians came to like the thick, sweet Cuban coffee as well as Cuban dishes of rice, fish, pork, black beans seasoned with lime juice, fried plantains, and roast pig.[13]

Along the Gulf Coast from Tampa to eastern Texas a Creole type of cooking continued with gumbos, jambalayas, and preparations of seafoods, sweet potatoes, yams, okra, and pastries that contained pecans, figs, and citrus fruits.[14] New Orleans kept its Creole cooking, modified in places by heavy immigrations from Cuba and Central America, especially Honduras.

Texas had several culinary regions. The upper Gulf Coast and the area north and east of Galveston as far as Nacogdoches used chili seasoning, but generally clung to the Creole, Cajun, and southern cooking of its early settlers. Rice and gravy, hominy, and pasta often replaced potatoes. Lettuce and tomato salads were common, meat was well done, pork was eaten often, and the Mexican Americans enjoyed kid.

The Rio Grande Valley along the Mexican border, including

San Antonio and Austin, fashioned Texas versions of some Mexican-American dishes — chili con carne, tacos, refried beans, enchiladas, *arroz con pollo* (rice with chicken), *cabrito* (barbecued kid), pinto beans, and chili peppers. Here and throughout central and western Texas there was a liking for hot breads, kidney beans (called pinto beans), and chicken-fried steaks, which were steaks well beaten, dredged in flour, fried, and served with a cream gravy. Throughout Texas iced tea was omnipresent.[15]

New Mexico and Arizona were both affected by the Mexican influence from the nearby hot-cooking states of Chihuahua and Sonora. Beans were important as were chili powder and corn tortillas. Fresh vegetables came from both Texas and California.[16]

The diet of cowboys and ranch hands through Texas and the Southwest, and with few differences in the northern Great Plains, continued little changed from the nineteenth century. Starches played a large role — the pinto beans, potatoes, corn, sourdough biscuits, cakes, and pies. Foods had to keep well, so sugar, coffee, jerky (dried beef), salted meats, dried fruits, evaporated milk, and canned goods were all important. For several generations the only fresh food was beef in soups, roasts, or stews. A common stew was variously known as son-of-a-gun, son-of-a-bitch, or mother-in-law and contained such "innards" as the liver, marrow gut, brains, "the melt" (a gland near the floating kidney), and heart as well as garlic and fat. Chicken-fried steak was popular, lick (syrup) with bread or biscuits was part of every meal, and jams, jellies, dried-fruit pies, and cakes were desserts. Strong black coffee was the standard beverage.

Few cowboys complained of such fare. One, in the late nineteenth century, more worldly than most, said of his fellow workers: "There's one thing I will say, you put 'em in the best hotel there is, and they'll order ham and eggs three times a day, the reason being that you can't make 'em believe there's any better food than that a-going."[17] In later decades, and especially on the larger ranches, fresh or frozen foods were often used, and to omit a salad at some ranches would cause grumbling.

California had absorbed some of the cooking of Mexico, of every part of the United States, and of the French, Germans, Italians, Japanese, Chinese, and Hawaiians, among others. The state's cookery, as M. F. K. Fisher pointed out, combined the largesse of the western soils and waters "in a free and easy way that is, as far as I know, the most thoroughly relaxed cooking of regional food anywhere and the least tainted with ethnic prejudices." A San Franciscan, she added, could shift in a day or even in one meal from traditional French to Korean dishes, or from New England style to Creole to Mexican.[18] Outdoor dining was widespread as was the eating of fruits and salads. The uniqueness of California's style struck the dramatist Lillian Hellman's father who visited her from a New Orleans background and asked, at the second night's dinner, "How can you eat salad before the soup and what kind of people eat grapefruit at dinner? What has happened to you?"[19]

In the Pacific Northwest the descendants of New Englanders, New Yorkers, and Midwesterners joined with Scandinavians and other immigrant groups in continuing as best they could their culinary traditions. In coastal areas the salmon, Alaska shrimp, Olympia oysters, various clams, Willamette crawfish, and hard-shell crabs all gave the diet variety and depth, and as in California the cooking of China, Japan, and Hawaii were influences.

Far to the north in Alaska the gold rush of 1898 brought immigrants from all the existing states as well as Swedes, Norwegians, Danes, Germans, English, Finns, and Russians. For a time all depended upon seafoods, bear, caribou, moose, reindeer, and wild fruits and a few necessaries imported from California, Oregon, and Washington. The cost of such imports declined when airplane service to Alaska began about 1935 and still more so in 1942 when the Alcan Highway, later renamed the Alaskan Highway, was opened.[20] Still, the expense of fresh fruits and vegetables remained very great, and more than elsewhere Alaska had to depend upon canned, frozen, and other processed foods.

As with foods, the nation's drinks were influenced by the food industry, the fast-food restaurants, the search for health, and the postwar interest in new taste experiences. And as the chilling impact of prohibition wore off, the country turned to its own and to foreign alcoholic drinks.

A great many Americans continued to drink milk. Nutritionists praised milk early in the century and by 1950 the average person drank 600 glasses a year. Thereafter a gradual decline began due first to fear of a gain in weight and then to concern about cholesterol. The introduction of low-fat milk in the 1960s helped to check this trend.[21]

The drinking of carbonated beverages rose swiftly, passed coffee in 1976, and became the principal between-meals drink. Sold in cans or bottles in every public place, soft drinks were the objects of massive advertising campaigns. The public ignored warnings that they often contained a possibly dangerous benzoate of soda and other untested minerals, as well as sugar. Again, many Americans did not know that some of them — including Coca-Cola, Pepsi-Cola, and Dr. Pepper — contained caffeine, an additive harmful to some people.[22]

Coffee use nearly doubled between 1909 and 1952, but then began to slip.[23] Numerous Americans, like their forebears, drank coffee both between and with meals. Easterners often added milk or cream, while Westerners tended to favor it black. Some immigrant groups — such as Scandinavians, Greeks, Turks, and Italians — were devoted to coffee while others, like the Chinese and Japanese, developed a taste for it. Iced coffee remained marginally popular. In the mid-1940s an instant coffee appeared which, during the following decades, gained mass acceptance.[24]

As the public became increasingly sedentary, many people found that the caffeine in coffee kept them awake. In 1903 technicians in Europe discovered how to remove caffeine, and in 1923 Sanka, a decaffeinated coffee, was introduced to America. By the 1970s the major coffee companies were in hot competition for a market that grew as the sale of other coffees fell. Much of the caffeine removed went into the cola drinks that were so liked by the young. Still another development took place in the 1960s when it was discovered how to freeze-dry a coffee solution into crystals that needed only hot water to become soluble.

Tea drinking fell off by two-thirds during the first half of the century, but then began a steady rise that paralleled the decline of coffee. Green teas continued in some use until World War II, after which they nearly disappeared. Many Americans still viewed hot tea as a beverage of the effete, clubwomen, the sick, or those of British or Asian origin, an attitude attacked by advertisers who pictured it as a virile brew.[25]

Iced tea remained very popular in hot weather, and spread from urban into rural areas as electric refrigerators became general. In the South it became a year-round beverage, and in Texas and the Southwest it possibly outsold both Kool-Aid and the cola drinks.[26]

As for alcoholic drinks, the years of temperance agitation and prohibition had left their mark. In Gallup Polls begun in 1939 it became clear that many forwent drink or favored a return to prohibition. In 1954 a third of the country's adults would have voted to outlaw alcoholic beverages, with prohibition sentiment strongest in the South, followed in order by the Midwest, the West, and the East. In later decades prohibitionist sentiment waned.

Drinking adults grew to 68 percent in 1974, with the gain of women drinkers in that period twice that of men. Still, in that year, 76 percent of the men drank compared to 61 percent of the women. Use decreased with age, increased with income level, was lowest in the South, and highest among professional and business people, the college trained, and Catholics. Slightly over a fourth of the men and one-tenth of the women admitted that they sometimes drank to excess, and 12 percent of all questioned stated that liquor had caused trouble in their families.[27]

Legal beer began a long, slow recovery after prohibition was repealed, for an entire generation had not known the taste of good malt drinks. As late as 1940 the per capita sale was below the preprohibition level. A greater consumption was promoted, however, by the mid-1930s innovations of putting beer into cans and short, light bottles of the "one-trip" variety, both kinds easily sold in drugstores and groceries.[28]

Wines, too, had to find a market after prohibition. Many Americans believed that only French wines were good, while others shunned wines for fear of serving the wrong kind or color or with the wrong glasses. Aside from having a glass of Chianti with spaghetti in an Italian restaurant, or a celebrative glass of sherry or port, many Americans had had no contact with wines.

Frank Schoonmaker, an American wine authority, pioneered in the 1930s in publicizing the best California wines, especially those of Napa and Sonoma counties. He urged vintners there to relinquish the French names and to call each wine after the grape variety that provided the "informing" taste. This, the varietal system, made it possible to judge each wine on its merits. Some made excellent reputations and by the 1980s competed with the best French wines as equals or superiors.

During and after World War II numerous servicemen and tourists became acquainted with European wines. In America, wine tastings multiplied and literature on the subject grew. The drinking of wines, especially table wines, rose sharply, but a Department of Agriculture study of 1978 showed that over 30 percent of the population did not drink wine at all, some for religious or personal reasons but most because they knew little about wine and were reluctant to try it.[29]

Of the distilled spirits whiskey, especially bourbon, long had the largest sale. The American preference for light-colored drinks, wrongly thought to be less intoxicating than darker ones, was partly responsible for a rising interest in Scotch whiskey. In the quarter century after 1947 imports from Great Britain rose eightfold.[30]

It is not known how much whiskey was made by moonshiners in Mississippi, Alabama, Georgia, and North Carolina. This ancient craft was long viewed with amused tolerance by all but prohibitionists and federal officers. The quality, occasionally good, worsened during prohibition when inexperienced entrepreneurs entered the business and made poor, and sometimes hazardous, corn liquor. Later the moonshiners declined in numbers due to more liberal liquor laws (Mississippi was the last state to repeal prohibition in 1969) and to highly sophisticated detection devices used by federal officers. To escape arrest many moonshiners made "scared" whiskey — speeding fermentation by the addition of battery acid, oil, or dead animals to the mash, creating a highly dangerous liquid.[31]

Bourbon's primacy was challenged by vodka which won friends in America during World War II, when gin was scarce, and which about 1960 began a swift rise in favor. Cheaper than bourbon and more versatile, vodka outsold bourbon by the late 1970s in most states. Bourbon and blended whiskies remained first in the others except New York where Scotch led.[32]

Changing fashions in foods and drinks hardly touched the poor. Until Franklin Roosevelt's New Deal their care had been largely left to private charity. In 1933 Roosevelt authorized the distribution of surplus food to destitute families, a program that ceased during the war but resumed thereafter and was supplemented in 1946 by a school lunch program.

Such aid was no panacea. In 1959, when 1,300 counties received food for the poor, a family of four was given twenty pounds of flour, ten pounds of cornmeal, nine pounds of nonfortified dried milk, two pounds of rice, and occasionally four pounds of butter and ten pounds of cheese each month. The list included no meat or vitamin C and only limited proteins and calories. Additions during the John Kennedy and Lyndon Johnson administrations still left the program nutritionally weak.

Political and economic manipulation did further damage. In some agricultural regions the aid was turned on or off to suit the labor needs of growers and planters. In cities, such as Chicago under Mayor Richard Daley, votes were garnered by the threat of withholding relief. In parts of the South the free-lunch program was provided in all-black schools but not in white ones to strengthen segregation.[33]

In 1961 President Kennedy ordered a pilot food-stamp program in seven states, an effort widened during the administration of Richard Nixon. Then in April 1968 a Citizens' Board of Inquiry into Hunger and Malnutrition issued a report entitled *Hunger, U.S.A.* This sharply pointed out that:

1. Hunger and malnutrition affected millions of Americans and was increasing in severity and extent.
2. The consequence was a toll of infant deaths, organic brain damage, retarded growth and learning rates, increased vulnerability to disease, withdrawal, apathy, alienation, frustration, and violence.
3. There was a shocking absence of knowledge in this country about the extent and severity of malnutrition.
4. Federal efforts to provide adequate nutrition for the needy had failed to reach a significant portion of the poor or to help adequately those it did reach.

Probably 10 million or more Americans were affected, the report stated.[34] A month after this report a moving CBS documentary, "Hunger in America," was shown on national television.

Government bodies and officials attacked both the report and the CBS documentary. FBI agents working for the House Appropriations Committee questioned people connected with both, and the government's Institute of Defense Analysis published a "Critical Review" of the committee's report, written by one of its employees. The Food and Drug Administration spent nearly

$200,000 and gathered 26,000 pages of testimony to prove that the country had no malnutrition problem sufficient to justify the use of vitamin supplements.[35]

For its part, the food industry discouraged measures to reduce malnutrition. Both food companies and Department of Agriculture officials opposed the use of low-cost high-protein fish concentrate and synthetic or fortified foods. A vice president of the Borden Company said that his associates did not believe that "clinical malnutrition" was a public health problem in any part of the country. The dairy lobby won a government restriction that until 1968 kept vitamins A and D out of nonfat dried milk sent to parts of the United States and to underdeveloped countries under the commodity programs. The apparent motive was fear that such milk might compete with the public sale of whole milk.[36]

The food-stamp program was expanded in the 1970s, but during that decade and into the 1980s food costs rose faster than either food-stamp allowances or welfare payments. Spurred on by inflation, some Americans learned to bypass expensive convenience foods, prepared baking mixes, and ready-to-eat snacks, while pursuing home gardening, home canning, and the brown-bagging of lunches. More families baked their own bread, working-class families gave up the weekly steak, and the casserole grew in popularity.

A pathetic effort to save on food costs appeared. The Senate Nutrition Committee found that in ghetto areas as much as a third of the cheap dog and cat foods sold was for human consumption, and that among the elderly poor the proportion was even higher.[37]

⨎ 25 ⨎

The Synthetic Era

By degrees,
food became an abstraction
divorced from its origins.

Within a few dacades after World War II shoppers could bypass fresh foods at the supermarkets in favor of processed ones that could be prepared in minutes or seconds. Whole frozen dinners were available, as were innumerable "instant" dishes packaged to catch the eye. The space given to frozen, canned, and other processed foods far outdistanced that provided for produce and fresh meats. While many remembered the delights of fresh foods, they were seduced by the convenience of packaged ones, and the young were often unaware that anything better existed.

For a time it was fast-frozen foods that grew most rapidly, as mass production lowered prices and the advantages became apparent. Although inferior to fresh foods in taste and nutritive value, frozen foods were better than canned foods in both respects. Some foods froze remarkably well, others less so, and many were damaged by thawing and refreezing during storage and shipment. But large numbers of Americans were willing to trade off taste for time.

The torrent of chemical-laden processed foods grew yearly. They were made and promoted by huge corporations whose planning, sales, and public defense were buttressed by computer technicians, lawyers, psychologists, scientists, consumer research organizations, and advertising agencies. There was growing concentration of the industry into such giants as Borden, General Foods, Beatrice Foods, General Mills, Kellogg, Kraft, Standard Brands, Nestlé, Heinz, Pillsbury, and Campbell Soup. The power of the food industry grew as great conglomerates such as Dow Chemical, Greyhound Corporation, Boeing, Tenneco, International Telephone and Telegraph, Getty Oil, R. J. Reynolds, and Philip Morris bought into it.

The use of chemicals began on the farms and ranches. Herbicides and pesticides, including arsenicals, had been used since the nineteenth century, but during the 1930s new forms appeared, and after the Second World War the revolutionary auxin type multiplied. By the 1980s all Americans carried in their bodies residues of various herbicides and pesticides. The Food and Drug Administration (FDA) was empowered in 1954 to set pesticide tolerances in foods, but in this as in other efforts it had to contend with powerful lobbies. Agribusiness pressures to increase the tolerances often prevailed.[1]

Even more difficult was the testing and control of food additives. Competition among food companies for national markets encouraged the use of additives which could pare the cost of prepared foods, or give them a long shelf life. Some aided health, such as the addition of iron to bread, but many had purely economic advantages in permitting companies to substitute cheap for expensive ingredients, such as synthetic vanilla in place of vanilla or air and thickening for cream in ice cream.[2]

Also, foods processed under severe conditions of temperature, pressure, and agitation lost natural nutrients, color, texture, and taste, and additives could repair some of the damage. Other additives heightened flavor, changed textures, clarified liquids, cured meats, and added noncaloric sweeteners.[3] In all, several thousand additives were used.

Until 1958 additives were added at will and removed only when the understaffed, slow-moving FDA could prove them dangerous. An act of 1958 accepted those already in use as presumably safe but decreed that new ones could be added only after the manufacturers had conducted safety tests. That the manufacturers, or hired laboratories, did the testing made for a built-in conflict of interest.

Of all the additives only a few have been tested and very few carefully so. Some are safe in small amounts but toxic in quantity. Some are safe by themselves but could be dangerous joined to others. Since Americans yearly take in a rich assortment of emulsifiers, coal-tar dyes, synthetic antioxidants, thickening agents, and preservatives, as well as chemicals from the air, water, drugs, and pesticides, the opportunities are great for two or more chemicals, each separately harmless, to interact and injure some organ of the body.[4] Nor can testing determine the long-range effects of additives. "We now realize," wrote a biochemist who had done research for the FDA for fifteen years, "that far more critical than acute poisoning is the subtle, long-term insidious poisoning of the body by certain chemicals that work slowly or cumulatively and whose ravages may not become evident for many years."[5]

Scientists did more than create additives, for they learned also to make reasonable facsimiles of natural foods. Or, more commonly, they created analogs — natural foods flavored and textured to be analogous to another food. Soybeans and grains were especially useful in this, and there were soon ersatz chicken, beef, tuna, bacon, nuts, sausages, "meats" in soup mixes, canned stews, chili con carne, ravioli, and hamburger patties. In 1971 the Department of Agriculture allowed schools to use up to 30 percent of soybean substitutes in meat and fish dishes in hot lunch programs.

It became increasingly clear that, against the great power of the food industries, the FDA lacked the enabling legislation, the money, the manpower, and often the will to play policeman. Even more than most regulatory agencies its decision-makers came from the industry concerned or planned to go there later in what has been called the "revolving-door" policy or the "deferred bribe." Some meetings of the FDA with industry representatives, wrote one commentator, "resemble a reunion more than a conference," and congressional auditors found that more than 150 officials of the FDA owned stock in companies regulated by that body.

In 1970 James S. Turner in *The Chemical Feast,* a study of chemical additives in food, concluded that the FDA's "meager although sometimes well-intended efforts" had been continually "neutralized" by the powerful food industries which were, together, over six times as large as General Motors. "Impotence has characterized the FDA and its predecessor agencies," he decided, "since passage of the Pure Food Act of 1906."[6]

During the late 1960s many Americans, alarmed at the growing quantity of untested chemicals in their foods, began a new, powerful phase of the long dormant food-reform movement. The plan was to eschew all processed foods with additives, together with fruits, vegetables, grains, and meats that had been grown or prepared for market with the use of chemicals.

A means to this end, organic gardening, had been advocated since 1942 by J. I. Rodale in his magazine *Organic Gardening*. In the late 1960s numerous young people, at first centered in New York and California, became converts.[7] By the early 1970s many older middle-class adults had become interested. Soon health-food stores dotted the country offering whole grains, dried fruits, nuts, herbal teas, honey, "raw" sugar, special cookies and candies, natural cheeses, tofu, yogurt, organically grown fruits and vegetables, pure juices, various granolas (a generic term for mixtures that might contain rolled oats, wheat germ, soy oil, honey, coconut, and vanilla), natural oils, seeds, beans, and numerous vitamin and mineral tablets. Then the large food companies began to produce their own granolas and protein supplement powders and to decrease or eliminate the additives in many of their products — or, by labeling or advertising with many references to nature, country, and mother's cooking, imply that they had. Both Montgomery Ward and Sears Roebuck, the country's largest mail-order firms, established health-food departments.[8]

The movement gained added strength from the writings of Adele Davis. A nutritionist and writer, her books sold by the millions and aroused concern over additives and the diseases that resulted from poor nutrition. Many of her views were acceptable to other nutritionists, but her conviction that some human ills could be prevented or cured by taking certain vitamins, sometimes in massive doses, brought angry rebuttals.[9]

Much of the public became confused. Wooed by spokesmen for the food industry and warned by advocates of health foods, repeatedly alarmed by gloomy stories of chemical-laden foods only to be reassured by industry-hired academicians, the public was driven into a fog of uncertainty.

The seemingly unlimited variety in the supermarkets increased this bewilderment. Long rows of canned, bottled, or packaged foods were offered in bright, warm colors, with striking or catchy names to stimulate sales. A chain store in a year might drop a thousand items, add more, and carry ten thousand or so in all. At times these foods changed in appearance, cost, or nutritive value, making an intelligent choice among them difficult.[10]

There was also a progressive decline in the taste, quality, and appeal of both processed and fresh foods. Processed foods were made bland in order to offend the fewest people. Government-subsidized agricultural stations developed tough, and often nearly tasteless, fruits and vegetables able to withstand machine-picking.

Since the great chains bought solely from mass producers, they ignored the minor fruits and vegetables and took only a few varieties of the major ones. By the late 1970s hardly more than a dozen varieties of apples were in important commercial production. The markets also received mass-produced meats of poor flavor and battery-raised chickens that were nearly flavorless.[11]

Most people saw their "fresh" vegetables in supermarkets where, after considerable time and handling, they arrived bedraggled, relatively tasteless, and often oversized. Such produce narrowed the quality gap between fresh vegetables and canned or frozen ones. Convenience only partly explains the greater use of processed fruits and vegetables while the consumption of fresh ones dropped.

By degrees, food became an abstraction divorced from its origins. As late as the 1930s buyers could still judge the quality of fruits and vegetables in the store by looking, feeling, smelling, tasting, squeezing, or thumping, and then in the kitchen by washing, peeling, cutting, and cooking. But increasingly foods were wrapped, boxed, frozen, canned, dried, powdered, bottled, or combined in ready-to-eat forms. Many went directly from package to the pot or oven.

Lost in a synthetic jungle where warning cries and siren songs filled the air, the consumer could only push on, alternately hopeful and despairing. Children, the object of much high-powered advertising, the aged, attracted by the convenience of processed foods, and the poor and uneducated, with less access than others to warnings, were the most vulnerable beneficiaries of the synthetic age.

Conditioned by fast-food chains and with creativity cut off by access to ready-to-eat supplies, the average family used but few of the myriad foods on supermarket shelves. There existed what Lyall Watson, the anthropologist, called "the supermarket syndrome" in which the products of the few covered the country and swept away local differences and individual preferences. A dull continuity resulted. The symptoms were "an increased unwill-

350

ingness to prepare one's own food, an ignorance of the techniques involved, a reliance on an ever-dwindling variety of foods, an offhand attitude to the whole question of eating, and a loss of curiosity about foods that had never before been tried," all leading to a loss of omnivorousness.[12]

By the last decades of the century many Americans knew only such foods as flavorless chickens, tomatoes picked green and colored with gas, hams shot up with water, or fish sticks which stood in for the wonderful variety of the oceans. Standards of taste became progressively lower as each generation was led ever further away from the earth's natural flavors and even the simplest home cooking.

Chemists who worked for agribusiness found that natural tastes were not always desired. A catsup given a "natural" taste failed on the market as did an instant coffee that was provided with a freshly ground flavor. The new norm was not the taste of nature but rather the artificial flavors that people had come to consider normal. An observer of the problem wrote, "Food manufacturers are beginning to insist that flavorists forsake their search for natural flavors in favor of imitations of imitations."[13]

As revolutionary as the growth of processed foods was the movement of diners from homes to public places. By the early 1980s Americans, on average, took one meal out of three away from home. Expenditures for meals outside the home grew more rapidly than the population, and, significantly for the future, the fastest growth came in restaurants that catered to the young.

Westerners spent most on eating out, followed in descending order by people in the Northeast, the north-central states, and the South, though the southern rate of increase was greatest. The majority of those who ate noontime meals away from home were businessmen, factory workers, students, and women shoppers. In the evening families might go out to dinner together, and there was evening trade for drive-ins, nightclubs, and fast-food restaurants. In good weather Americans picnicked; a study showed that half of the population did so one or more times a year.[14]

Many reasons led people to eat out more frequently: a great increase in the number of singles, divorced and otherwise; a scarcity of servants, leading well-to-do families to eat away from home; an ever-growing proportion of working women; and the invasion of the kitchen by prepared foods, making home cooking less attractive. Not least important, the efficiencies of mass food production and service reduced restaurant prices at a time when there was widespread affluence.

An unexpected addition to the clientele of southern lunch rooms and restaurants took place during the 1960s when, as part of the civil rights struggle, an effort was made to end segregation in eating places through "sit-ins." In Washington, D.C., Oklahoma City, Louisville, Greensboro, and other places groups of blacks and whites, or blacks alone, sat in protest at segregated lunch counters. In spite of arrests, violence, and such demagogic appeals as those of the restaurateur (later governor) Lester Maddox in Georgia, lunch rooms were increasingly opened to blacks.[15]

The country's most praised public cooking and service were found in a few dozen restaurants in cities like New York, Chicago, Cincinnati, New Orleans, Dallas, and San Francisco. Many of these restaurants were French. For devotees of such cooking it was, in retrospect, a momentous event when in 1939 a young chef, Henri Soulé, came to New York City with his kitchen aides to staff the restaurants of the French Pavillion at the World's Fair in New York City. Two years later Soulé opened Le Pavillon in Manhattan, a restaurant that was outstanding in the tradition of Delmonico's. In time a dozen or more superior restaurants were staffed by veterans of Soulé's kitchens.[16]

The mixture of ethnic restaurants was affected by the immigration reform act of 1965 which replaced the quota system that had favored northern and western Europe with one that better reflected the pressures of the world's populations and poverty. More immigrants now came from China, Thailand, Vietnam, Korea, Italy, Mexico, the Caribbean, Portugal, and Greece, each group supporting its native restaurants, old or new. By 1973 about 11 percent of the country's eating places were ethnic, the percentage having doubled in a decade. Most were in the Northeast and on the West Coast, while the South and the Middle West had relatively few.

The cooking in ethnic restaurants sometimes moved far from its original character. Greek restaurants cut down sharply on fats, Japanese ones rarely served raw fish, and the Chinese sometimes stewed rather than stir-fried, as they had long done with chop suey, to accommodate American tastes.

Unlike the earlier Chinese restaurants, overwhelmingly Cantonese, newer ones often had cooks from Peking, Szechuan, or Hunan. Some Chinese cooks had sojourned in other countries before coming to America. Thus those who had lived in Cuba offered saffron rice, fresh avocados, fried bananas, and espresso coffee along with orthodox Chinese dishes.[17]

While the country's outstanding restaurants used only the finest fresh produce and meats, others turned increasingly to processed foods. Some restaurants used only those frozen foods that could not be bought fresh. But many schools, airlines, railroads, factory restaurants, executive dining rooms, and fast-food chains relied almost completely on fast-frozen foods. Restaurants could offer, without admitting the source, shishkebab, beef Wellington, coquille St. Jacques, beef Stroganoff, and several hundred other dishes, many frozen by the country's largest food companies. The restaurants saved on kitchen labor and cost control and enjoyed a high return on sales.[18]

The multiplication of restaurants created the new profession of restaurant critic. Craig Claiborne and Mimi Sheraton in New York City, William Rice in Washington, D.C., and Jack Shelton in San Francisco were among many who wielded great power, evaluating restaurants in ways that could make the difference between success and failure.[19]

Schools for chefs also upgraded American restaurants. A leading one, The Culinary Institute of America, was founded in 1946 to help restaurant owners reorient kitchen personnel returning from the war. The institute, in Hyde Park, New York, became a full-fledged training center with an international faculty, a serious curriculum, and a yearly graduating class of well-trained chefs, bakers, and pastry cooks.[20]

Most American restaurants had neither chefs nor critical attention. Their standard fare, offered on dittoed menus, included sandwiches of ham, egg, or tunafish salads, or of hot roast beef with mashed potatoes, and whole dinners that began with vegetable soup and ended with ice cream, chocolate pudding, or pie. Some restaurants cooked with skill and pride, but in others short-order cooks had neither. A small town usually had a local eating place which was the choice of after-church Sunday diners and for the periodical luncheons of the Rotarians, the Kiwanis Club, and the Elks. Especially at noon, drugstores like Walgreens and chains such as Woolworths served lunches of milk shakes, malted milks, and Cokes, with sandwiches, hamburgers, salads, canned soups, and even hot-plate lunches. By the 1950s, however, the soda fountains began a rapid decline that would soon make them nearly extinct.

In New York City, and to a lesser degree in other cities, the delicatessen, or deli, was a center for sandwiches and salads, again most often at noon. The food served was frequently Russian or German Jewish. Many delis had begun as kosher, offering ten or fifteen salamis, rolled beef, tongue, cold pastramis, frankfurters, turkey, cole slaw, and potato salad. Mustard, stretched with pickle brine, accompanied each item. By the 1950s there were many nonkosher delis. Most were family affairs where service was informal. In time there were Italian, Greek, Puerto Rican, and West Indian delis among others.[21]

During the 1920s the fast-food chains began. White Castle hamburger stands and the Howard Johnson restaurants were among the first. In the 1950s McDonald's arrived, serving hamburgers, French fries, milk shakes, soft drinks, and a few other dishes. Other chains were founded with specialties like fried chicken, roast beef sandwiches, fish, pizzas, tacos, or doughnuts. In general the chains had clean premises, standardized menus, fast service, and the low prices that large-scale production, great efficiency, and cheap teenage labor made possible. Their offerings were found appetizing by clients whose home diets might consist largely of ready-to-eat or processed foods.

Of the quick-order foods pizza made the most sensational gains. Imported from southern Italy and Sicily, the pizza had long been a favorite of Italian Americans. After World War II and the return of veterans from Italy, pizza restaurants sprang up everywhere. Though rarely of the quality known to southern Italians, the pizza broadened the horizons of innumerable Americans, introducing them to anchovies, garlic, Italian sausages, and oregano.

The impact of the fast-food chains on the young, their most enthusiastic clientele, was immense, with all that it implied about the direction of the country's taste. In 1977 the New York City Board of Education announced that it would introduce into school lunches such fast foods as tacos, pizza, French fries, cheeseburgers, and supershakes.[22] And an advertising campaign of McDonald's was based on a study that showed that in three out of four cases it was the children, not the parents, who decided where a family would eat out.[23]

The statistics of the country's food consumption showed the influence of the fast-food chains. Between 1960 and 1976 the use of frozen potatoes rose more than five times and there were large increases in beef, chicken, fresh and frozen fish, hard cheese (mostly mozzarella used in pizzas), tomato catsup and paste, mushrooms, pickles, and ice milk. In the same time span the annual per-person sale of soda drinks rose from 192 eight-ounce servings to 493.[24]

These trends should not hide the persistence that exists in American eating and drinking habits, for devotion to fried chicken, beef, ice cream, tomato catsup, pickles, and soda water had long existed in strength. Even the fast service of the chains was in the American tradition, differing little from the quick-service restaurants of the preceding century and a half.

Epilogue

Both continuity and change mark the four centuries that passed between the first European arrivals in America, scrambling to gather a simple diet from the wilderness, and Americans of the late twentieth century who plucked their foods and beverages from supermarket shelves.

From first to last there was a striking persistence of English-inherited traits, and this despite a growing proportion of non-English in the population. For centuries most Americans ate heavily of meats, neglected vegetables, disdained any vegetable cookery other than boiling, preferred cheddarlike cheese, drank milk, shrank from garlic, cooked simply, and chose prepared condiments and sauces over other flavorings.

But uniquely American characteristics emerged as the first English landed on New World shores. For a time change was rapid as the settlers tried with varying success to transfer familiar foods to a new land, to adopt corn and other Indian-cultivated vegetables, and to become familiar with the bounty of American forests and waters.

As people moved westward from the coastal strip, their first frontier, they began a process that would be repeated for two and a half centuries across the continent. First came a period of primitive living conditions when in the forest, as later on the plains, all but essentials were discarded, delicacies and fragile foods, including most vegetables and fruits, were left behind, and the frying pan was given a major role among cooking instruments. For a time game was the principal food, but this was soon followed by pork and corn. Then, as each region emerged from frontier conditions, other foods and dishes were added, in original or modified forms, from a remembered past. At times, new foods were found in the fields and forests and new methods of preparation were adopted from Indian tribes or from among the ethnic groups that mixed on the frontier.

For long, everywhere, most foods were those raised or gathered nearby. But the tyranny of geography weakened as horse-drawn vehicles were replaced by canal boats, and as transportation was quickened or made less costly by railroads, faster ships, trucks, and airplanes. The dictates of climate and seasons, already lessened by salting, drying, smoking, and preserving in suet, vinegar, or sugar, were further curbed by ice refrigeration, canning, chemical preservatives, fast-freezing, and controlled temperatures. By degrees the ancient pattern of summer foods and winter foods was broken down.

The same time span saw the diet move from heaviness to lightness as urbanism spread and as machines lightened physical work. The change began in the early towns and cities and surfaced in the late eighteenth century when the upper classes showed an interest in French-inspired soups, salads, and omelettes. During the following century reformers censured meat-eating and the frying pan, light puddings replaced heavy ones, pork gave way to beef, corn to wheat, steak and pie disappeared from breakfast tables, light-bodied lager displaced other beers, and temperance forces made inroads on heavy drinking. Late in the century salads, sandwiches, chafing-dish preparations, croquettes, gelatin puddings, and other light and adventurous foods were embraced by the middle and upper classes. Labor-saving machinery and central heating further reduced the needs of the body for food, as would the automobile and air-conditioning in the next century. Dietitians urged more moderate eating and by the 1920s slimness became stylish. After World War II there came a fear of saturated fats.

The contributions of non-English immigrant groups to the American diet have varied greatly. Those kept in subordinate roles — the white indentured servants of the seventeenth and eighteenth centuries and the black slaves — had little chance to retain their traditional food customs. Instead, their masters or owners gave them the few simple foods of poverty. Similarly those immigrants, such as the Scotch-Irish, who moved in great numbers to the frontier were for a time tied to the game-pork-corn pattern. Those who later lived in factory towns or cities often found it impossible to buy, or afford, their accustomed foods. And, finally, all immigrants, whatever their lot, were under pressure to conform to the eating habits of the resident majority, both for the sake of convenience and to escape ridicule.

For several centuries, to be sure, most immigrants were northern and western Europeans whose foods, beverages, and cooking methods deviated only moderately from English ones. The Germans, Swiss, Dutch, Irish, Scots, and Scandinavians, in particular, cooked simply, used dairy foods, drank beer and, if necessary, water, and could easily adopt, or contribute to, the foods and dishes they found in America. The German influence was especially felt and was reinforced by successive waves of immigration for nearly three centuries. The French cuisine, less easily absorbed and unsupported by heavy immigration, reached the wealthy through outstanding restaurants and private chefs and from these sources filtered down to middle-class kitchens.

Beginning in the mid-nineteenth century more exotic foods and forms of cookery came with immigrants from other parts of the Americas, Asia, and southern and eastern Europe. The success of their native diets was uneven. The Mexican influence, in diluted form, spread slowly everywhere from Texas and the Southwest. Italian foods and dishes in time reached all levels of society and, at least superficially, all parts of the country. Some groups — notably the Italians, Greeks, Chinese, Japanese, and east-European Jews — introduced or popularized fruits, vegetables, seafoods, or traditional dishes in their adopted country as cooks, truck gardeners, fishermen, delicatessen and restaurant owners, or wholesale and retail food sellers.

In their homes, immigrants often gave up good for bad: fine homemade breads for the tasteless ones of chain stores, native cheeses for cheap processed ones, and fresh and tasteful fruits and vegetables for the offerings of the supermarkets.

Everyone saw the foods from nature taken from them. Game was decimated by the disappearance of wilderness areas and by indiscriminate slaughter. Seafoods became rare due to intensive commercial fishing and water pollution. Even oysters, once the food of all, including the poor, became a luxury.

In one respect, the ease with which foods were prepared, there was consistent and dramatic improvement. The cast-iron stove, a major step, had been succeeded by the icebox, the gas stove, the electric refrigerator, and a large array of other kitchen aids. When to these were added the time and trouble saved by commercial refrigeration and the multiplication of processed foods, all often available in a single store, the end result was revolutionary. Where a seventeenth-century housewife might have spent most of every day in the collection, preservation, storing, preparation, and serving of food, by the late twentieth century a tenth of that time might have sufficed. The rapidly growing number of meals eaten away from home saved still more time.

Yet the quality and vigor of American cooking did not keep up with improvements in kitchen efficiency. Declining culinary standards resulted in widespread use of such absurdities as bottled salad dressings and ready-made mashed potatoes. Increasingly, Americans ate and drank under the guidance of the giant food corporations, the fast-food restaurants, the powerful supermarket chains, and the advertising agencies that spoke for them all.

If such trends continue, nearly all Americans — separated from the soil and cut off from the earth's flavors, enmeshed in an industrial-urban environment and in a world of declining natural resources — may fall completely under the control of the food industries. Good cooking with fresh foods would persist only among a few, and the dichotomy would be as sharp as that in Elizabethan England between the nobility, abetted by French cooks, and the general population with its simple diet free of kickshaws.

Notes

Chapter 1: The Beginnings

1. Fynes Moryson, *An Itinerary* (Glasgow, 1908), 4:171–72; G. E. Fussell and K. R. Fussell, *The English Countrywoman: A Farmhouse Social History A. D. 1500–1900* (London, 1953, pp. 31, 56–70; C. Anne Wilson, *Food and Drink in Britain* (London, 1973), pp. 95–97; Mildred Campbell, *The English Yeoman under Elizabeth and the Early Stuarts* (New York, n.d.), pp. 246–47; Mary C. Crawford, *In the Days of the Pilgrim Fathers* (Boston, 1920), pp. 89–90; Christina Hole, *The English Housewife in the Seventeenth Century* (London, 1953), pp. 53–54.

2. Wilson, *Food and Drink in Britain*, pp. 46–49, 108, 126–28; Thomas Tusser, *Five Hundred Pointes of Good Husbandrie*, ed. W. Payne and Sidney J. Herrtage (London, 1878), pp. 27–28, 242–43; Fussell and Fussell, *English Countrywoman*, p. 31; Hole, *English Housewife*, pp. 52, 54; William Younger, *Gods, Men, and Wine* (Cleveland, 1966), p. 316; Campbell, *English Yeoman*, pp. 247–48, 311–12; Moryson, *Itinerary*, 4:171, 173.

3. For puddings see Wilson, *Food and Drink in Britain*, pp. 315–17; for pottages, *ibid.*, pp. 212, 216–17, 226.

4. Sir William Ashley, *The Bread of Our Forefathers: An Inquiry in Economic History* (Oxford, 1928), pp. 15, 42–43, 46, 136–37, 145, 153, 164; Wilson, *Food and Drink in Britain*, pp. 97, 255–59.

5. *Ibid.*, pp. 182–83.

6. Frederick J. Furnivall, ed., *Harrison's Description of England* (London, 1877), 1:144, 324; Crawford, *Days of the Pilgrim Fathers*, pp. 75–76; Campbell, *English Yeoman*, pp. 243–44; Hole, *English Housewife*, pp. 54–55; Gervase Markham, *The English House-wife* (London, 1675), pp. 51–53; Fussell and Fussell, *English Countrywoman*, p. 33; I. M., *A New Booke of Cookerie . . .* (London, 1615), p. 34; Wilson, *Food and Drink in Britain*, pp. 340, 359–62; John Evelyn, *Acetaria: A Discourse of Sallets* (London, 1699), p. 27.

7. Charles F. Mullett, *The Bubonic Plague and England* (Lexington, Ky., 1956), pp. 66, 78, 149, 216; Campbell, *English Yeoman*, p. 249; Fussell and Fussell, *English Countrywoman*, p. 34; Wilson, *Food and Drink in Britain*, pp. 342, 346–49; Christina Hole, *English Home-Life 1500 to 1800* (London, 1947), p. 13; Hole, *English Housewife*, p. 57.

8. Tobias Venner, *Via Recta Ad Vitam Longam* (London, 1628), pp. 19–20, 41; Crawford, *Days of the Pilgrim Fathers*, p. 84; J. C. Drummond and Anne Wilbraham, *The Englishman's Food: A History of Five Centuries of English Diet*

Notes

(London, 1939), pp. 44–45, 135, 138–39; André L. Simon, *Bottlescrew Days* (London, 1926), pp. 15, 27, 41; Younger, *Gods, Men, and Wine*, pp. 297–98, 309, 326; George Gascoigne, *Complete Works*, ed. John W. Cunliffe (Cambridge, 1910), 1:451–71; Markham, *English House-wife*, pp. 102–103; Campbell, *English Yeoman*, pp. 250–51; Hole, *English Housewife*, p. 58; Wilson, *Food and Drink in Britain*, p. 167.

9. Moryson, *Itinerary*, 4:173; Furnivall, *Harrison's Description*, 1:166.

10. Tusser, *Good Husbandrie*, pp. 27–28; Fussell and Fussell, *English Countrywoman*, pp. 56–70; Crawford, *Days of the Pilgrim Fathers*, pp. 89–90; Venner, *Via Recta*, p. 132.

11. Campbell, *English Yeoman*, pp. 243–51.

12. Furnivall, *Harrison's Description*, 1:144; Venner, *Via Recta*, p. 83; Fussell and Fussell, *English Countrywoman*, p. 44; Crawford, *Days of the Pilgrim Fathers*, pp. 75–76.

13. Moryson, *Itinerary*, 4:83; F. Marian McNeill, *The Scots Kitchen* (London, 1963), p. 11.

14. Marjorie Plant, *The Domestic Life of Scotland in the Eighteenth Century* (Edinburgh, 1952), p. 106; James G. Leyburn, *The Scotch-Irish* (Chapel Hill, 1962), p. 262n; F. Marian McNeill, *The Scots Cellar* (Edinburgh, 1956), p. 2; McNeill, *Scots Kitchen*, p. 13; Moryson, *Itinerary*, 4:182–85.

15. Thomas Hutchinson, *A Collection of Original Papers Relating to the History of the Colony of Massachusetts-Bay* (Boston, 1769), pp. 32–46, *passim; Records and Files of the Quarterly Courts of Essex County, Massachusetts* (Salem, Mass., 1921), 8:29–31; Karl Theodor Eben, ed., *Gottlieb Mittelberger's Journey* (Philadelphia, 1898), p. 20.

16. Alexander Young, ed., *Chronicles of the First Planters of the Colony of Massachusetts Bay* (Boston, 1846), pp. 477–78.

17. *Pennsylvania Magazine of History*, 38 (1914): 79; *Deutsche-Americanische Gesellschaft*, 18–19 (1918–19): 56–59; *Records of Essex County*, 8:29–31.

18. Frank Ried Diffenderffer, *The German Immigration into Pennsylvania*, part 2, *The Redemptioners* (Lancaster, Pa., 1900), p. 64; Eben, *Mittelberger's Journey*, p. 24; *Boston Weekly News-Journal*, October 29, 1741.

19. Hutchinson, *Papers Relating to Massachusetts-Bay*, p. 45.

20. George Chapman, Ben Jonson, and John Marston, *Eastward Hoe* (London, 1605), Act 3, Scene 2.

21. Lewis Cecil Gray, *History of Agriculture in the Southern United States to 1860* (New York, 1941), 1:3–6, 35–36; J. Franklin Jameson, ed., *Narratives of New Netherland, 1609–1664* (New York, 1909), p. 168; Daniel Denton, *A Brief Description of New-York* (New York, 1937), p. 4; Percy W. Bidwell and John I. Falconer, *History of Agriculture in the Northern United States 1620–1860* (New York, 1941), p. 5.

22. Gray, *History of Agriculture*, 1:5; Albert Cook Myers, ed., *Narratives of Early Pennsylvania, West New Jersey, Delaware* (New York, 1912), p. 229; Jameson, *Narratives of New Netherland*, p. 297; Philip Alexander Bruce, *Social Life of Virginia in the Seventeenth Century* (Lynchburg, Va., 1927), p. 171; Lyon Gardiner Tyler, ed., *Narratives of Early Virginia 1606–1625* (New York,

1907), pp. 90–91; Clayton Colman Hall, ed., *Narratives of Early Maryland 1633–1684* (New York, 1910), p. 45.

23. Albert Bushnell Hart, ed., *American History Told by Contemporaries* (New York, 1902), 1:357; Dwight B. Heath, ed., *A Journal of the Pilgrims at Plymouth: Mourt's Relation* (New York, 1963), p. 39; Gray, *History of Agriculture*, 1:5, 58–59; Bidwell and Falconer, *History of Agriculture*, p. 5; Hall, *Narratives of Early Maryland*, p. 80.

24. Sydney V. James, Jr., ed., *Three Visitors to Early Plymouth* (n.p., 1963), pp. 7, 9–10, 25; Arthur Pierce Middleton, *Tobacco Coast: A Maritime History of Chesapeake Bay* (Newport News, Va., 1953), pp. 53–54; Jameson, *Narratives of New Netherland*, pp. 295–96; Bartlett B. James and J. Franklin Jameson, eds., *Journal of Jasper Danckaerts 1679–1680* (New York, 1913), p. 53; Alice Morse Earle, *Colonial Days in Old New York* (New York, 1897), p. 134; Myers, *Narratives of Early Pennsylvania*, p. 227.

25. Jameson, *Narratives of New Netherland*, pp. 71, 168, 296; Alexander Whitaker, *Good Newes from Virginia* (London, 1613), pp. 41–42; Hall, *Narratives of Early Maryland*, pp. 44–45; Myers, *Narratives of Early Pennsylvania*, p. 227; Bidwell and Falconer, *History of Agriculture*, p. 5.

26. Bruce, *Social Life of Virginia*, p. 170; Thomas J. Wertenbaker, *The First Americans 1607–1690* (New York, 1929), pp. 39–40; Alexander S. Salley, ed., *Narratives of Early Carolina 1650–1708* (New York, 1911), p. 150; Jameson, *Narratives of New Netherland*, p. 169; Denton, *Description of New-York*, p. 41; Myers, *Narratives of Early Pennsylvania*, p. 229.

27. Harold E. Driver, *Indians of North America* (Chicago, 1961), pp. 28–29, 58–60, map 4; Denton, *Description of New-York*, p. 7.

28. Gray, *History of Agriculture*, 1:4–5, 26–28; Myers, *Narratives of Early Pennsylvania*, p. 334; Driver, *Indians of North America*, pp. 29, 38–41; Tyler, *Narratives of Early Virginia*, pp. 96–97; Eva L. Butler, "Algonkian Culture and Use of Maize in Southern New England," *Bulletin of the Archaeological Society of Connecticut*, no. 22 (December 1948), p. 28.

29. John Lawson, *A New Voyage to Carolina*, ed. Hugh Talmage Lefler (Chapel Hill, 1967), p. 82; Gray, *History of Agriculture*, 1:4–5; Driver, *Indians of North America*, pp. 42–45.

30. Charles C. Willoughby, *Antiquities of the New England Indians* (Cambridge, Mass., 1935), pp. 297–99.

Chapter 2: The Difficulties of Being First

1. Tyler, *Narratives of Early Virginia*, pp. 9–10.

2. *Ibid.*, pp. 10–11; Edward Arber and A. G. Bradley, eds., *Travels and Works of Captain John Smith* (Edinburgh, 1910), 1:lxiii, lxv, xlvii.

3. *Ibid.*, pp. lxxii, lxxiii, 95; Charles M. Andrews, *The Colonial Period of American History* (New Haven, 1934), 1:100.

4. Charles Wayland Towne and Edward Norris Wentworth, *Pigs: From Cave to Corn Belt* (Norman, Okla., 1950), pp. 78–79; Andrews, *Colonial*

Notes

Period, 1:99– 100; Gray, *History of Agriculture*, 1:15, 19– 20, 25; George R. Stewart, *American Ways of Life* (New York, 1954), pp. 83– 84.

5. Whitaker, *Good Newes*, pp. 41– 44; Arber and Bradley, *John Smith*, l:liv, lxix, 113.

6. Whitaker, *Good Newes*, pp. 41– 42; Arber and Bradley, *John Smith*, l:lxvi, cvi, 57, 59, 132; David Hawke, *The Colonial Experience* (Indianapolis, 1966), p. 95.

7. Arber and Bradley, *John Smith*, l:lxvi, 56– 58.

8. Tyler, *Narratives of Early Virginia*, pp. 130, 132, 138, 145, 158, 184– 86.

9. Andrews, *Colonial Period*, 1:108– 10.

10. *Ibid.*, pp. 112– 13.

11. George Francis Dow, *Every Day Life in the Massachusetts Bay Colony* (Boston, 1935), p. 7; Andrews, *Colonial Period*, 1:269– 71.

12. Heath, *Mourt's Relation*, pp. 20– 23, 34, 39; William Bradford, *Of Plymouth Plantation 1620– 1647*, ed. Samuel Eliot Morison (New York, 1967), pp. 65– 66.

13. Alexander Young, ed., *Chronicles of the Pilgrim Fathers of the Colony of Plymouth, from 1602 to 1625* (Boston, 1841), pp. 23– 38; Heath, *Mourt's Relation*, pp. 23, 43, 49; Arber and Bradley, *John Smith*, 1:132.

14. Bradford, *Plymouth Plantation*, pp. 77– 81, 85– 93, 127, 130– 32; Ann Leighton, *Early American Gardens "For Meate or Medicine"* (Boston, 1970), p. 91; Hawke, *Colonial Experience*, pp. 188– 90.

15. Hart, *American History*, 1:357.

16. Young, *Chronicles of the Pilgrim Fathers*, pp. 372– 73.

17. James, *Three Visitors to Early Plymouth*, pp. 7– 11, 16, 24– 25, 28– 29, 39, 79– 80.

18. Bradford, *Plymouth Plantation*, p. 116; Andrews, *Colonial Period*, 1:330.

19. Hall, *Narratives of Early Maryland*, pp. 75– 76, 78– 80, 82; Gray, *History of Agriculture*, 1:35– 38.

20. J. Franklin Jameson, ed., *Johnson's Wonder-Working Providence 1628– 1651* (New York, 1910), pp. 77, 85, 115, 210; James Kendall Hosmer, ed., *Winthrop's Journal "History of New England" 1630– 1649* (New York, 1908), 1:58– 59; Andrews, *Colonial Period*, 1:397; Young, *Chronicles of Massachusetts Bay*, p. 261.

21. Hosmer, *Winthrop's Journal*, 1:178– 81.

22. Bidwell and Falconer, *History of Agriculture*, pp. 40– 41; Jameson, *Narratives of New Netherland*, p. 132.

23. Bidwell and Falconer, *History of Agriculture*, pp. 40– 41; Peter H. Wood, *Black Majority* (New York, 1974), pp. 26– 27.

Chapter 3: The Seventeenth Century

1. Jane Carson, *Colonial Virginia Cookery* (Williamsburg, Va., 1968), pp. 17–21; Hubert G. Schmidt, *Rural Hunterdon* (New Brunswick, N.J., 1946), pp. 269–70.

2. Moryson, *Itinerary*, 4:172; Carson, *Virginia Cookery*, pp. 24–29, 41–42, 62–65, 75–79.

3. *Ibid.*, pp. 28–29, 31–32, 86–91, 94, 98, 102–105, 129; Frances Phipps, *Colonial Kitchens, Their Furnishings, and Their Gardens* (New York, 1972), pp. 23–24, 94; Peter Kalm, *Travels into North America* (London, 1772), 1:121–22.

4. Arthur Train, Jr., *The Story of Everyday Things* (New York, 1941), pp. 130–31, 150; George Francis Dow, *Domestic Life in New England in the Seventeenth Century* (Topsfield, Mass., 1925), pp. 9, 11; Hart, *American History*, 1:477–78; Alice Morse Earle, *Home Life in Colonial Days* (New York, 1898), pp. 77–78; Bruce, *Social Life of Virginia*, p. 166; Phipps, *Colonial Kitchens*, pp. 54–55.

5. Gray, *History of Agriculture*, 1:19–20; Stewart, *American Ways of Life*, pp. 78–79, 81.

6. Young, *Chronicles of Massachusetts Bay*, p. 261; Lyman Carrier, *The Beginnings of Agriculture in America* (New York, 1923), p. 148; Train, *Story of Everyday Things*, p. 136; Bidwell and Falconer, *History of Agriculture*, p. 32.

7. Gray, *History of Agriculture*, 1:19–20, 30, 38; Wertenbaker, *First Americans*, pp. 39–40; Hall, *Narratives of Early Maryland*, pp. 78, 291; Bruce, *Social Life of Virginia*, p. 170.

8. Rudolph Alexander Clemen, *The American Livestock and Meat Industry* (New York, 1923), p. 22; Bradford, *Plymouth Plantation*, pp. 174, 253; Young, *Chronicles of Massachusetts Bay*, p. 261; Hosmer, *Winthrop's Journal*, 1:53–54, 61, 81, 102, 111–12, 130–31, 152, 163, 178, 180–81, 190; Jameson, *Wonder-Working Providence*, pp. 115, 188, 209–10; Vincent Todd Harlow, *A History of Barbados 1625–1685* (Oxford, 1926), p. 270.

9. Hall, *Narratives of Early Maryland*, pp. 286, 347; James and Jameson, *Jasper Danckaerts*, p. 135.

10. Hosmer, *Winthrop's Journal*, 1:102, 130–31, 152; Jameson, *Wonder-Working Providence*, pp. 115, 210–11; Myers, *Narratives of Early Pennsylvania*, p. 252.

11. Towne and Wentworth, *Pigs*, pp. 70–74, 91; Stewart, *American Ways of Life*, pp. 83–84; Gray, *History of Agriculture*, 1:19–20; Hall, *Narratives of Early Maryland*, p. 78.

12. Hosmer, *Winthrop's Journal*, 1:53–54, 61, 111, 163; Stewart, *American Ways of Life*, p. 84; Carrier, *Beginnings of Agriculture*, p. 148; Jameson, *Narratives of New Netherland*, pp. 295–96.

13. Phipps, *Colonial Kitchens*, pp. 38–41; Carson, *Virginia Cookery*, pp. 185–89; J. C. Furnas, *The Americans: A Social History of the United States 1587–1914* (New York, 1969), p. 172.

14. Stewart, *American Ways of Life*, p. 85; Hall, *Narratives of Early Maryland*, p. 60; Gray, *History of Agriculture*, 1:30; Bruce, *Social Life of Virginia*, p.

170; John Josselyn, *New-England's Rarities*, ed. Edward Tuckerman (Boston, 1965), p. 42; A. W. Schorger, *The Wild Turkey: Its History and Domestication* (Norman, Okla., 1966), pp. 478–80.

15. Young, *Chronicles of Massachusetts Bay*, p. 246; Jameson, *Narratives of New Netherland*, p. 296; Julia Cherry Spruill, *Women's Life and Work in the Southern Colonies* (Chapel Hill, 1938), pp. 12–13.

16. John Josselyn, *An Account of Two Voyages to New-England* (London, 1675) in *Collections of the Massachusetts Historical Society*, series 3, vol. 3 (Cambridge, Mass., 1833), pp. 260–61; Hart, *American History*, 1:359; Gray, *History of Agriculture*, 1:46; Myers, *Narratives of Early Pennsylvania*, p. 264; Lawson, *Voyage to Carolina*, pp. 83–84.

17. Gray, *History of Agriculture*, 1:4; Robert Beverley, *The History and Present State of Virginia*, ed. Louis B. Wright (Chapel Hill, 1947), pp. 144–45; Hosmer, *Winthrop's Journal*, 1:176.

18. Young, *Chronicles of Massachusetts Bay*, pp. 42–43; Carrier, *Beginnings of Agriculture*, p. 85; Salley, *Narratives of Early Carolina*, pp. 145–46; James and Jameson, *Jasper Danckaerts*, p. 200; Myers, *Narratives of Early Pennsylvania*, p. 264.

19. Young, *Chronicles of Massachusetts Bay*, pp. 42–43, 156; Jameson, *Wonder-Working Providence*, pp. 69–70, 115, 210–11.

20. Alice Morse Earle, *Customs and Fashions in Old New England* (New York, 1893), pp. 155–56; Carson, *Virginia Cookery*, pp. 199–203.

21. *Old South Leaflets*, no. 69 (Boston, n.d.), 3:14–15; James and Jameson, *Jasper Danckaerts*, pp. 43–44, 47, 52, 83, 99; Harry B. Weiss, *Life in Early New-Jersey*, New Jersey Historical Series, vol. 26 (Princeton, 1964), p. 21.

22. Myers, *Narratives of Early Pennsylvania*, pp. 253, 324–25.

23. Fletcher, *Pennsylvania Agriculture*, pp. 206–207; Carrier, *Beginnings of Agriculture*, pp. 31–32.

24. Jameson, *Wonder-Working Providence*, pp. 115, 210; Hosmer, *Winthrop's Journal*, 1:159.

25. Carl Bridenbaugh, *Cities in the Wilderness* (New York, 1960), p. 51; William G. Panscher, *Baking in America* (Evanston, Ill., 1956), 1:25–26; George Lyman Kittredge, *The Old Farmer and His Almanack* (Boston, 1904), p. 328.

26. Jameson, *Narratives of New Netherland*, pp. 55, 219; Bayrd Still, *Mirror for Gotham* (New York, 1956), p. 10; Myers, *Narratives of Early Pennsylvania*, pp. 252, 327.

27. Young, *Chronicles of Massachusetts Bay*, p. 263; Tyler, *Narratives of Early Virginia*, p. 393; Stewart, *American Ways of Life*, pp. 93–94; Earle, *Customs and Fashions*, p. 150; Bidwell and Falconer, *History of Agriculture*, p. 14.

28. Gray, *History of Agriculture*, 1:17, 20, 30, 35–37; Hall, *Narratives of Early Maryland*, pp. 75, 82, 286; James and Jameson, *Jasper Danckaerts*, pp. 111, 134; Beverley, *History of Virginia*, p. 293.

29. Earle, *Customs and Fashions*, p. 150; Samuel Eliot Morison, *Vistas of History*, (New York, 1964), p. 98.

30. Jameson, *Narratives of New Netherland*, pp. 218–19; Earle, *Colonial Days*, pp. 129–30.

31. Dow, *Every Day Life*, p. 98; Still, *Mirror for Gotham*, pp. 25–26; Mary Caroline Crawford, *Social Life in Old New England* (New York, 1914), p. 249.

NOTES

32. Hosmer, *Winthrop's Journal*, 1:130–31; 2:89; Charles M. Andrews, *The Colonial Period of American History* (New Haven, 1935), 1:517; Josselyn, *Account of Two Voyages*, 3:222.

33. Alfred Goldworthy Bailey, *The Conflict of European and Eastern Algonkian Cultures 1504–1700* (Toronto, 1969), pp. 58–59; Roy L. Butterfield, "The Great Days of Maple Sugar," *National Maple Syrup Digest*, 8(July 1969): 13.

34. Noel Deerr, *The History of Sugar* (London, 1949), 1:10; James M. Usher, *History of the Town of Medford, Middlesex County, Massachusetts* (Boston, 1886), p. 38; N. B. Shurtleff, ed., *Records of the Governor and Company of the Massachusetts Bay in New England* (Boston, 1853), 2:101; Denton, *Description of New-York*, pp. 18–19; Myers, *Narratives of Early Pennsylvania*, pp. 324–25.

35. Earle, *Customs and Fashions*, p. 156; Jameson, *Wonder-Working Providence*, p. 210; Samuel Sewall, *Diary of Samuel Sewall* in *Collections of the Massachusetts Historical Society*, series 4, vol. 5 (Boston, 1878), 1:83, 239, 394; Leighton, *Early American Gardens*, pp. 97–98.

36. Myers, *Narratives of Early Pennsylvania*, p. 331; Sidney Fisher, *Men, Women and Manners in Colonial Times* (Philadelphia, 1898), 2:59; Earle, *Colonial Days*, pp. 139, 141–42.

37. Whitaker, *Good Newes*, p. 44; Gray, *History of Agriculture*, 1:25; Heath, *Mourt's Relation*, p. 39; Young, *Chronicles of Massachusetts Bay*, p. 245; Dow, *Every Day Life*, pp. 10, 42; Salley, *Narratives of Early Carolina*, p. 187; Lawson, *Voyage to Carolina*, p. 83.

38. Philip Alexander Bruce, *Economic History of Virginia in the Seventeenth Century* (New York, 1935), 2:483–86; Shurtleff, *Records of Massachusetts Bay*, 1:28; 2:5, 299; 4:41, 224, 259; Harry B. and Grace M. Weiss, *The Revolutionary Saltworks of the New Jersey Coast* (Trenton, N.J., 1959), pp. 59, 60, 66; Hosmer, *Winthrop's Journal*, 2:68, 72, 227; Andrews, *Colonial Period*, 1:517; Carson, *Virginia Cookery*, pp. 6, 184–85.

39. Hall, *Narratives of Early Maryland*, pp. 75–76; Jameson, *Narratives of New Netherland*, p. 423; Gray, *History of Agriculture*, 1:55, 58.

40. Hosmer, *Winthrop's Journal*, 2:89, 227; Andrews, *Colonial Period*, 1:517; Gray, *History of Agriculture*, 1:55, 58; Myers, *Narratives of Early Pennsylvania*, p. 253.

41. Bradford, *Plymouth Plantation*, pp. 65, 143; Jameson, *Wonder-Working Providence*, p. 77; Young, *Chronicles of Massachusetts Bay*, p. 353.

42. Beverley, *History of Virginia*, p. 293; Salley, *Narratives of Early Carolina*, p. 181; James and Jameson, *Jasper Danckaerts*, p. 111; Dow, *Domestic Life*, p. 1.

43. Jameson, *Narratives of New Netherland*, p. 219; Stanley Baron, *Brewed in America* (Boston, 1962), p. 19.

44. Young, *Chronicles of Massachusetts Bay*, p. 264; Shurtleff, *Records of Massachusetts Bay*, 1:214; Baron, *Brewed in America*, pp. 10–11; Darrett B. Rutman, *Winthrop's Boston* (Chapel Hill, 1965), p. 190.

45. Baron, *Brewed in America*, pp. 4–5, 15; Bruce, *Social Life in Virginia*, p. 172.

46. Myers, *Narratives of Early Pennsylvania*, pp. 267, 327.

47. Shurtleff, *Records of Massachusetts Bay*, 2:14; Beverley, *History of Virginia*, p. 293; Weiss, *Life in Early New-Jersey*, p. 18.

48. Charles W. Taussig. *Rum, Romance, and Rebellion* (New York, 1928), pp. 14–15; Gray, *History of Agriculture*, 1:58; Dow, *Domestic Life*, pp. 27–28; Bruce, *Economic History of Virginia*, 1:214; James and Jameson, *Jasper Danckaerts*, pp. 52, 53, 82, 135.

49. Lawson, *Voyage to Carolina*, p. 115.

50. L. H. Bailey, *Sketch of the Evolution of Our Native Fruits* (New York, 1898), pp. 2–3, 4, 8, 10–17; Earle, *Customs and Fashions*, pp. 168–69; Beverley, *History of Virginia*, pp. 133–36.

51. Hall, *Narratives of Early Maryland*, p. 97; Middleton, *Tobacco Coast*, p. 195; Bruce, *Social Life of Virginia*, pp. 172–73; Bradford, *Plymouth Plantation*, p. 373; Hosmer, *Winthrop's Journal*, 2:89–93, 154; Shurtleff, *Records of Massachusetts Bay*, 1:106; 2:100, 148, 171; Jameson, *Narratives of New Netherland*, p. 233.

52. Berton Roueché, *The Neutral Spirit* (Boston, 1960), p. 37; Alice Morse Earle, *Stage-Coach and Tavern Days* (New York, 1900), pp. 100–102; James and Jameson, *Jasper Danckaerts*, p. 52; Marcus Wilson Jernegan, *The American Colonies, 1492–1750* (New York, 1931), p. 413.

53. Roueché, *Neutral Spirit*, p. 36; Stewart, *American Ways of Life*, pp. 115–17; Myers, *Narratives of Early Pennsylvania*, p. 253; Salley, *Narratives of Early Carolina*, p. 146; Bruce, *Social Life of Virginia*, 1:172–73; Earle, *Stage-Coach and Tavern Days*, pp. 124–25; Still, *Mirror for Gotham*, pp. 25–26.

54. Earle, *Customs and Fashions*, p. 178; Earle. *Stage-Coach and Tavern Days*, pp. 125–26; Edward R. Emerson, *Beverages, Past and Present* (New York, 1908), 2:465; John Trumbull, *M'Fingal* (Hartford, 1856), p. 97.

55. Myers, *Narratives of Early Pennsylvania*, p. 267; Earle, *Stage-Coach and Tavern Days*, pp. 115–16.

56. Shurtleff, *Records of Massachuseetts Bay*, 2:97, 100–101, 111, 123, 131, 148, 171; Bradford, *Plymouth Plantation*, p. 373n; James and Jameson, *Jasper Danckaerts*, p. 135; Bruce, *Economic History of Virginia*, 1:216–20.

57. Gray, *History of Agriculture*, 1:30; James and Jameson, *Jasper Danckaerts*, p. 134; Ebenezer Cook, *The Sot-Weed Factor*, in Bernard C. Steiner, ed., *Early Maryland Poetry*, Maryland Historical Society Fund Publication no. 36 (Baltimore, 1900), p. 14.

58. Joseph B. Felt, *History of Ipswich, Essex and Hamilton* (Cambridge, Mass., 1834), p. 30; Dow, *Every Day Life*, pp. 16, 41–42, 91, 98; Earle, *Home Life*, p. 87.

59. Moryson, *Itinerary*, 4:59–60.

60. *Ibid.*, p. 24; Ashley, *Bread of Our Forefathers*, pp. 21, 145.

Chapter 4: The Eighteenth Century I

1. Bridenbaugh, *Cities in the Wilderness,* pp. 349–54; Johann David Schoepf, *Travels in the Confederation* (Philadelphia, 1911), 1:112–13, 189; J. P. Brissot de Warville, *New Travels in the United States of America, 1788,* ed. Durand Echeverria (Cambridge, Mass., 1964), pp. 199–201, 349; Kenneth and Anna M. Roberts, eds., *Moreau de St. Méry's American Journey* (Garden City, N.Y., 1947), pp. 154–55.

2. Harry J. Carman, ed., *American Husbandry* (New York, 1939), p. 37.

3. William Byrd, *The Secret Diary of William Byrd of Westover 1709–1712,* ed. L. B. Wright and M. Tinling (Richmond, Va., 1941), pp. 6, 221, 394; Ethel Armes, ed., *Nancy Shippen: Her Journal Book* (Philadelphia, 1935), p. 169; Harriette Simpson Arnow, *Seedtime on the Cumberland* (New York, 1960), p. 397; Gray, *History of Agriculture,* 1:327; J. E. Wright and Doris S. Corbett, *Pioneer Life in Western Pennsylvania* (Pittsburgh, 1940), p. 58.

4. Byrd, *Secret Diary,* p. 308; Beverley, *History of Virginia,* p. 293.

5. Thomas Anburey, *Travels through the Interior Parts of America* (London, 1789), 2:194; Arnow, *Seedtime,* pp. 394–95.

6. Hugh Jones, *The Present State of Virginia,* ed. Richard L. Morton (Chapel Hill, 1956), p. 86.

7. "Leaves from the South-West and Cuba," *The Knickerbocker or New-York Monthly Magazine,* 8(July 1836): 45; *Dictionary of Americanisms,* s.v. "hominy"; Arnow, *Seedtime,* pp. 396–97; "Journal of Lord Adam Gordon 1764–1765," in Newton D. Mereness, ed., *Travels in the American Colonies* (New York, 1916), p. 400; Schoepf, *Travels,* 2:116; Wright and Corbett, *Pioneer Life,* p. 58; Isaac Weld, *Travels through the States of North America . . . 1795, 1796 & 1797* (London, 1799), p. 105.

8. Arnow, *Seedtime,* pp. 390–91; Schoepf, *Travels,* 1:297.

9. David Ramsay, *The History of South Carolina* (Charleston, 1809), 2:202, 205–206.

10. Kalm, *Travels,* 2:88, 105; Kittredge, *Old Farmer,* p. 328; William B. Weeden, *Economic and Social History of New England 1620–1789* (New York, 1936), 2:541; Carl Bridenbaugh, ed., *Gentleman's Progress: The Itinerarium of Dr. Alexander Hamilton* (Chapel Hill, 1948), p. 105.

11. Israel Acrelius, *A History of New Sweden,* Memoirs of the Historical Society of Pennsylvania, vol. 11 (Philadelphia, 1874), p. 151.

12. Fletcher, *Pennsylvania Agriculture,* p. 227.

13. Jack P. Greene, ed., *The Diary of Colonel Landon Carter of Sabine Hall, 1752–1778* (Charlottesville, Va., 1965), 2:721.

14. Kalm, *Travels,* 2:389; Schmidt, *Rural Hunterdon,* pp. 275–78; Amelia Simmons, *American Cookery* (n.p., 1963), p. 66; Madam Knight, *The Private Journal of a Journey from Boston to New York in the Year 1704* (Albany, N.Y., 1865), pp. 61, 82.

15. U. P. Hedrick, *A History of Horticulture in America to 1860* (New York, 1950), pp. 17–18; Simmons, *American Cookery,* p. 37.

16. Kalm, *Travels,* 2:104–105; Earle, *Colonial Days,* p. 138; Johann Carl

Notes

Buettner, *Narrative of Johann Carl Buettner,* Heartman's Historical Series No. 1 (New York, [c. 1924]), p. 32.

17. Schoepf, *Travels,* 2:189.

18. Felt, *History of Ipswich,* p. 40; Byrd, *Secret Diary,* p. 38; Simmons, *American Cookery,* p. 49.

19. Schoepf, *Travels,* 2:190; Anne Grant, *Memoirs of an American Lady* (New York, 1901), p. 71; Kalm, *Travels,* 1:136; 2:118–19; Simmons, *American Cookery,* pp. 41–42; Beverley W. Bond, Jr., *The Civilization of the Old Northwest* (New York, 1934), p. 322.

20. Byrd, *Secret Diary,* pp. 78, 181; Craig Claiborne in *New York Times,* April 10, 1961, p. 34; Spruill, *Women's Life,* p. 68.

21. "Harvard Dinners," *Proceedings of the Massachusetts Historical Society, 1860–1862* (Boston, 1862), pp. 160–61.

22. Mary Tolford Wilson, "Americans Learn to Grow the Irish Potato," *New England Quarterly,* 32 (1959): 334–35.

23. *Ibid.,* p. 335; Carman, *American Husbandry,* p. 74.

24. Wilson, "Americans Grow the Potato," pp. 336–37; Kalm, *Travels,* 2:88; Carman, *American Husbandry,* p. 79; Fletcher, *Pennsylvania Agriculture,* pp. 163–65.

25. John Thomson Faris, *The Romance of Old Philadelphia* (Philadelphia, 1918), p. 63; Fredric Klees, *The Pennsylvania Dutch* (New York, 1950), pp. 339–40; Thomas J. Wertenbaker, *The Founding of American Civilization, the Middle Colonies* (New York, 1938), p. 280; Brissot de Warville, *New Travels,* pp. 81, 129; Gray, *History of Agriculture,* 1:122–23.

26. Roberts and Roberts, *Moreau de St. Méry,* p. 56; Gray, *History of Agriculture,* 1:193.

27. Kalm, *Travels,* 2:65; recipe book of Harriott Pinckney Horry, 1770, South Carolina Historical Society, Charleston, S.C.

28. Spruill, *Women's Life,* p. 68; Hedrick, *History of Horticulture,* p. 198; Anburey, *Travels,* 2:375–76; Schoepf, *Travels,* 1:94; Thomas Jefferson, *Thomas Jefferson's Garden Book 1766–1824,* annot. Edwin Morris Betts (Philadelphia, 1944), pp. 5, 21, 47, 71.

29. Brissot de Warville, *New Travels,* p. 368; Anne Hulton, *Letters of a Loyalist Lady* (Cambridge, Mass., 1927), p. 34; Jones, *Present State of Virginia,* p. 92.

30. Kalm, *Travels,* 1:58; *Dictionary of American English,* s.v. "okra."

31. Greene, *Landon Carter,* 2:737, 739; Spruill, *Women's Life,* pp. 276–77; a recipe for mushroom catsup appears in the Horry cookbook of 1770, South Carolina Historical Society, Charleston.

32. *Ibid.; Dictionary of American English,* s.v. "tomato."

33. Spruill, *Women's Life,* p. 68; Brissot de Warville, *New Travels,* pp. 368, 395; Greene, *Landon Carter,* 1:527; Schoepf, *Travels,* 2:118.

34. Beverley, *History of Virginia,* p. 146; Middleton, *Tobacco Coast,* pp. 202–203; Kalm, *Travels,* 2:114; Rev. Andrew Burnaby, *Travels through the Middle Settlements in North-America* (Ithaca, N.Y., 1960), p. 11; Grant, *Memoirs,* p. 95; Douglas Southall Freeman, *George Washington* (New York, 1951), 3:107; Schoepf, *Travels,* 1:28–29.

36. Wright and Corbett, *Pioneer Life*, pp. 58–59; Eben, *Mittelberger's Journey*, p. 79; Klees, *Pennsylvania Dutch*, p. 337.

37. Samuel Eliot Morison, *The Maritime History of Massachusetts, 1783–1860* (Boston, 1941), p. 146; François, Marquis de Barbé-Marbois, *Our Revolutionary Forefathers: The Letters of François, Marquis de Barbé-Marbois*, trans. and ed. Eugene Parker Chase (New York, 1929), p. 78.

38. Kalm, *Travels*, 1:187; Schoepf, *Travels*, 1:16.

39. Kalm, *Travels*, 1:374; Bridenbaugh, *Gentleman's Progress*, p. 39.

40. Schmidt, *Rural Hunterdon*, p. 278.

41. Lord Adam Gordon in Mereness, *Travels*, pp. 405–406.

42. Greene, *Landon Carter*, 2:861.

43. Roberts and Roberts, *Moreau de St. Méry*, p. 266.

44. Schoepf, *Travels*, 1:13–15.

45. *Ibid.*; Carman, *American Husbandry*, p. 76.

46. Burnaby, *Travels*, pp. 80–81; Roberts and Roberts, *Moreau de St. Méry*, p. 269.

47. Kalm, *Travels*, 1:228–29; Freeman, *Washington*, 3:243; Middleton, *Tobacco Coast*, pp. 202–203.

48. William Eddis, *Letters from America* (London, 1792), p. 58; Arnow, *Seedtime*, pp. 100, 126, 152–53, 165–66, 399; Francis Harper, ed., *The Travels of William Bartram* (New Haven, 1958), p. 30.

49. Edwin Valentine Mitchell, *It's an Old New England Custom* (New York, 1948), pp. 26–28; Carman, *American Husbandry*, p. 76; *A Short Description of the Province of South Carolina. . . .* (London, 1770), in B. R. Carroll, comp., *Historical Collections of South Carolina* (New York, 1836), 2:481; Duane Meyer, *The Highland Scots of North Carolina* (Chapel Hill, 1961), p. 109.

50. Harper, *William Bartram*, p. 297; Grant, *Memoirs*, pp. 93–95; Burnaby, *Travels*, pp. 93–94.

51. John Clayton to Samuel Durrant, March 21, 1739, in Freeman, *Washington*, 1:118–19; Burnaby, *Travels*, pp. 11–12; Beverley, *History of Virginia*, p. 153; *William Byrd's Natural History of Virginia*, ed. Richard Croom Beatty and William J. Mulloy (Richmond, 1940), pp. 61–70.

52. Kalm, *Travels*, 1:226–27, 367–68.

53. Beverley, *History of Virginia*, p. 153; Freeman, *Washington*, 1:118–19; *A Short Description* in Carroll, *Historical Collections*, 2:481; Kalm, *Travels*, 1:217; William Byrd, *The Prose Works of William Byrd of Westover*, ed. Louis B. Wright (Cambridge, Mass., 1966), p. 318; Meyer, *Highland Scots*, p. 109; "The Hessians in Philadelphia," *Pennsylvania Magazine of History and Biography*, 1(1877): 42–43.

54. Schoepf, *Travels*, 1:113; Roberts and Roberts, *Moreau de St. Méry*, p. 280.

55. Brissot de Warville, *New Travels*, p. 129.

56. Edmund S. Morgan, *The Gentle Puritan: A Life of Ezra Stiles, 1727–1795* (New Haven, 1962), p. 128.

57. "Journal of William Black, 1744," *Pennsylvania Magazine of History*

Notes

and Biography, 1(1877): 411; Robert Hunter, Jr., *Quebec to Carolina in 1785 – 1786,* ed. Louis B. Wright (San Marino, Cal., 1943), p. 143; Bridenbaugh, *Gentleman's Progress,* p. 48; Roberts and Roberts, *Moreau de St. Méry,* p. 318; "Extracts from the Diary of Jacob Hiltzheimer, of Philadelphia, 1768 – 1798," *Pennsylvania Magazine of History and Biography,* 16 (1892): 168.

58. Bidwell and Falconer, *History of Agriculture,* p. 110.

59. Kalm, *Travels,* 2:104 – 105; Wright and Corbett, *Pioneer Life,* pp. 62 – 63.

60. Beverley, *History of Virginia,* p. 318; Towne and Wentworth, *Pigs,* pp. 91 – 92.

61. Schoepf, *Travels,* 2:45 – 46; Burnaby, *Travels,* pp. 30 – 31.

62. Arnow, *Seedtime,* p. 397; Schoepf, *Travels,* 2:110.

63. Charles Woodmason, St. Mark's Parish, S.C., March 26, 1771, to an English friend in Charles Woodmason, *The Carolina Backcountry on the Eve of the Revolution,* ed. Richard J. Hooker (Chapel Hill, 1953), p. 196.

64. Byrd, *Secret Diary,* pp. 2, 4, 12, 23, 35, 41, 48, 58, 63, 65, 70, *passim.*

65. Schoepf, *Travels,* 2:189; Brissot de Warville, *New Travels,* pp. 116 – 17; Roberts and Roberts, *Moreau de St. Méry,* p. 56; Simmons, *American Cookery,* pp. 25 – 27; "Hessians," *Pennsylvania Magazine of History and Biography,* 1(1877): 42 – 43.

66. Esther Singleton, *Social New York under the Georges 1714 – 1776* (New York, 1902), p. 358.

67. Eben, *Mittelberger's Journey,* pp. 66 – 67; Kalm, *Travels,* 2:105; Wertenbaker, *Founding of American Civilization,* p. 280; "Memoirs of Col. Jehu Eyre," *Pennsylvania Magazine of History and Biography,* 3(1879): 298.

68. Greene, *Landon Carter,* 2:111; Anburey, *Travels,* 2:192.

69. Byrd, *Secret Diary,* pp. 3, 7, 8, 32, 41, 57, 122, 298, 354, 404.

70. Page Smith, *John Adams* (New York, 1962), 1:175.

71. Morgan, *Gentle Puritan,* p. 128; Kalm, *Travels,* 2:105.

72. Harper, *William Bartram,* pp. 13 – 14; Weeden, *History of New England,* 2:540 – 41; Bidwell and Falconer, *History of Agriculture,* p. 109.

73. Mrs. John Amory, *The Journal of Mrs. John Amory* (Boston, 1923), p. 80; Gray, *History of Agriculture,* 1:103; Spruill, *Women's Life,* p. 277; Weeden, *History of New England,* 2:540 – 41; Brissot de Warville, *New Travels,* pp. 91, 393; Simmons, *American Cookery,* p. 31.

74. Hulton, *Letters of a Loyalist,* p. 42.

75. Beverley, *History of Virginia,* p. 314; Bidwell and Falconer, *History of Agriculture,* pp. 99 – 100; Schoepf, *Travels,* 1:94; Freeman, *Washington,* 3:72; Gray, *History of Agriculture,* 1:103.

76. Kalm, *Travels,* 1:58; 2:86 – 87; Gray, *History of Agriculture,* 1:69; J. R. Magness, "Our Fruit Pioneers," *American Fruit Grower,* 81 (March, 1961), p. 9.

77. *William Byrd's Natural History,* pp. 47 – 48; Brissot de Warville, *New Travels,* pp. 116 – 17; Hulton, *Letters of a Loyalist,* p. 35; Bond, *Old Northwest,* p. 321.

78. Carman, *American Husbandry,* p. 102; Schoepf, *Travels,* 2:76.

79. Grant, *Memoirs,* pp. 71, 89; Meyer, *Highland Scots,* p. 109.

80. Gray, *History of Agriculture,* 1:69, 191; Grant, *Memoirs,* pp. 271 – 72; Simmons, *American Cookery,* pp. 67, 71 – 72; Armes, *Nancy Shippen,* p. 142.

Chapter 5: The Eighteenth Century II

1. Simmons, *American Cookery*, pp. 43, 100–101.
2. Roberts and Roberts, *Moreau de St. Méry*, p. 265.
3. Charles H. Sherrill, *French Memories of Eighteenth-Century America* (New York, 1915), p. 98.
4. Constantin Volney, quoted in Rupert Vance, *Human Geography of the South* (Chapel Hill, 1932), pp. 412–13.
5. Brissot de Warville, *New Travels*, p. 368.
6. Bidwell and Falconer, *History of Agriculture*, p. 127.
7. Greene, *Landon Carter*, 2:673.
8. Grant, *Memoirs*, pp. 271–72; Brissot de Warville, *New Travels*, pp. 391–92.
9. Knight, *Private Journal*, p. 72; Anburey, *Travels*, 2:41.
10. *Ibid.*, p. 164; Gray, *History of Agriculture*, 1:208.
11. Butterfield, "Maple Sugar," p. 13; Helen and Scott Nearing, *The Maple Sugar Book* (New York, 1950), p. 40; Eben, *Mittelberger's Journey*, p. 71.
12. Butterfield, "Maple Sugar," p. 17; Brissot de Warville, *New Travels*, pp. 246–49.
13. Nearing and Nearing, *Maple Sugar Book*, p. 19.
14. Grant, *Memoirs*, pp. 113–14.
15. Marquis de Chastellux, *Travels in North America in the Years 1780, 1781 and 1782*, ed. Howard G. Rice, Jr., (Chapel Hill, 1963), 1:109; Emily V. Mason, ed., *Journal of a Young Lady of Virginia, 1782* (Baltimore, 1871), pp. 41–42; Armes, *Nancy Shippen*, p. 169; Klees, *Pennsylvania Dutch*, pp. 417–18; Simmons, *American Cookery*, pp. 58–61, 71–72; Acrelius, *New Sweden*, p. 159n.
16. Mary Tolford Wilson, "Amelia Simmons Fills a Need: American Cookery, 1796," *William and Mary Quarterly*, 14(January 1957): 24–25; Simmons, *American Cookery*, pp. 78–83.
17. Wilson, "Amelia Simmons," pp. 25–26; Byrd, *Secret Diary*, p. 463; Greene, *Landon Carter*, 2:795.
18. John Adams, *The Works of John Adams*, ed. Charles F. Adams (Boston, 1850), 2:381; Carman, *American Husbandry*, p. 99; Schmidt, *Rural Hunterdon*, pp. 117, 277.
19. Arnow, *Seedtime*, pp. 416–17; Marie Kimball, *Thomas Jefferson's Cook Book* (Richmond, Va., 1938), p. 9.
20. Spruill, *Women's Life*, p. 73n.; Kimball, *Jefferson's Cook Book*, p. 2; Roberts and Roberts, *Moreau de St. Méry*, pp. 155, 323.
21. Bridenbaugh, *Cities in the Wilderness*, pp. 196–97.
22. Jones, *Present State of Virginia*, p. 78; Horry, recipe book of 1770; Buettner, *Narrative*, p. 36.
23. Wood, *Black Majority*, p. 233; Julian Ursyn Niemcewicz, *Vine and Fig Tree: Travels through America in 1797–1799, 1805 with some further account of life in New Jersey*, ed. Metchie J. E. Budka, Collections of the New Jersey Historical Society at Newark, vol. 14 (Elizabeth, N.J., 1965), pp. 100–101.

Notes

24. George W. Corner, ed., *The Autobiography of Benjamin Rush* (Princeton, N.J., 1948), p. 270.

25. Roberts and Roberts, *Moreau de St. Méry*, p. 325; Furnas, *Americans*, p. 163.

26. Bridenbaugh, *Gentleman's Progress*, p. 8.

27. Alexander Graydon, *Memoirs of a Life, Chiefly Passed in Pennsylvania, Within the Last Sixty Years* (Edinburgh, 1822), p. 259.

28. Sherrill, *French Memories*, p. 106.

29. Kalm, *Travels*, 1:71, 240; Weld, *Travels*, p. 184; Oscar Edward Anderson, Jr., *Refrigeration in America* (Princeton, N.J., 1953), pp. 11–12; Furnas, *Americans*, p. 163.

30. Spruill, *Women's Life*, pp. 67–68; Wilson, "Amelia Simmons," pp. 19–22.

31. *Boston Weekly News-Letter*, November 28, 1728; Crawford, *Social Life*, pp. 247–48.

32. *Ibid.*, pp. 90–91.

33. Thomas Hughes, *A Journal by Thos: Hughes for his Amusement, & Designed only for his Perusal by the time he attains the Age 50 if he lives so long (1778–1789)* (Cambridge, Mass., 1947), pp. 24–25; St. Jean de Crèvecoeur, *Letters from an American Farmer* (London, 1782), p. 210.

34. Smith, *John Adams*, 1:17.

35. Felt, *History of Ipswich*, p. 30.

36. Kalm, *Travels*, 2:88, 105.

37. Benjamin Rush, "An Account of the German Inhabitants of Pennsylvania" (1789), in the *Proceedings of the Pennsylvania-German Society*, 19 (1910): 62–63; Wertenbaker, *Founding of American Civilization*, p. 280; W. F. Dunaway, *A History of Pennsylvania* (New York, 1948), p. 269; Fletcher, *Pennsylvania Agriculture*, p. 409.

38. Acrelius, *New Sweden*, pp. 157–59.

39. Dunaway, *History of Pennsylvania*, p. 273; Joseph Doddridge, *Notes on the Settlement and Indian Wars of the Western Parts of Virginia and Pennsylvania from 1763–1783. . . .*, ed. John S. Ritenour and William T. Lindsey (Pittsburgh, 1912), p. 88; Fletcher, *Pennsylvania Agriculture*, pp. 409–10.

40. Woodmason, *Carolina Backcountry*, pp. 13, 34, 35, 36, 39, 48–49, 52, 196.

41. Gray, *History of Agriculture*, 1:327.

42. Spruill, *Women's Life*, p. 72n.; Freeman, *Washington*, 1:103–105; Burnaby, *Travels*, pp. 30–31n.

43. Grant, *Memoirs*, pp. 89–90, 115–16, 122.

44. Greene, *Landon Carter*, 2:722, 724, 900; Burnaby, *Travels*, p. 26; *Journal and Letters of Philip Vickers Fithian 1773–1774*, ed. Hunter Dickinson Farish (Charlottesville, 1968), pp. 162, 168, 172, 183.

45. Fletcher, *Pennsylvania Agriculture*, pp. 446–47; Solon J. Buck and Elizabeth Hawthorn Buck, *The Planting of Civilization in Western Pennsylvania* (Pittsburgh, 1939), p. 356; Hughes, *Journal*, pp. 88–89.

46. Faris, *Old Philadelphia*, p. 223; Roberts and Roberts, *Moreau de St. Méry*, pp. 286–87.

47. Howard Mumford Jones, *America and French Culture* (Chapel Hill, 1927), p. 305.

48. *Pennsylvania Magazine of History and Biography*, 11 (1887): 477.

49. Anburey, *Travels*, 2:290–91; Greene, *Landon Carter*, 1:344; 2:795; Byrd, *Secret Diary*, p. 459.

50. Roberts and Roberts, *Moreau de St. Méry*, pp. 98–99.

51. St. John de Crèvecoeur, *Sketches of Eighteenth Century America*, ed. Henri L. Bourdin, Ralph H. Gabriel, and Stanley T. Williams (New Haven, 1925), pp. 49, 96–97; Robert Parke to Mary Valentine Parke, Chester Township, December 1725, in Albert Cook Myers, *Immigration of the Irish Quakers into Pennsylvania 1682–1750* (Swarthmore, Pa., 1902), pp. 78–79; Arnow, *Seedtime*, pp. 418–19; Joseph Doddridge, *Settlement of Western Country* (Bowling Green, Ohio, n.d.), p. 29.

52. Buck, *Western Pennsylvania*, p. 354.

53. Ann Warder, quoted in Faris, *Old Philadelphia*, p. 63.

54. Burnaby, *Travels*, pp. 80–81; Morgan, *Gentle Puritan*, p. 121.

55. Armes, *Nancy Shippen*, p. 169; Foster Rhea Dulles, *A History of Recreation: America Learns to Play* (New York, 1965), pp. 51–52.

56. Bridenbaugh, *Cities in the Wilderness*, pp. 265, 267–68, 432.

57. Bridenbaugh, *Gentleman's Progress*, p. 175; Brissot de Warville, *New Travels*, pp. 201, 370; Jefferson Williamson, *The American Hotel* (New York, [1930]), p. 195; John Bach McMaster, *A History of the People of the United States, from the Revolution to the Civil War* (New York, 1893), 2:9; Armes, *Nancy Shippen*, p. 93; Carl Bridenbaugh, *Rebels and Gentlemen* (New York, 1942), p. 23.

58. Knight, *Private Journal*, p. 25.

59. Bridenbaugh, *Gentleman's Progress*, pp. 7, 37, 39. 90.

60. Schoepf, *Travels*, 1:166; 2:45–46, 118; McMaster, *History*, 2:9.

61. Roberts and Roberts, *Moreau de St. Méry*, p. 335.

62. Freeman, *Washington*, 4:439; 5:142, 228–29, 327.

63. Smith, *John Adams*, 1:203, 327; Wilson, "Americans Grow the Potato," pp. 343–46; Amory, *Journal*, pp. 78, 80.

64. Schoepf, *Travels*, 1:113.

65. Markham, *English House-Wife*, p. 51; Margaret Dods [Mrs. Christian Isabel Johnstone], *The Cook and Housewife's Manual* (Edinburgh, 1826), pp. 203–204; I. M., *A New Booke of Cookerie* (London, 1615), pp. 5–15; *The Housekeeper's Book* . . . ., 2d ed. (Philadelphia, 1838), p. 74. The last work, pp. 74–79, gives some "made" dishes, mainly meat pies.

66. Jones, *French Culture*, p. 305.

67. J. G. Rosengarten, *French Colonists and Exiles in the United States* (Philadelphia, 1907), p. 103; Jones, *French Culture*, pp. 137, 304–305; Williamson, *American Hotel*, pp. 213–15; Jean Anthelme Brillat-Savarin, *The Physiology of Taste* (New York, 1960), p. 285.

68. Jones, *French Culture*, p. 305.

69. Roberts and Roberts, *Moreau de St. Méry*, pp. 155, 323; J. H. Frandsen and W. S. Arbuckle, *Ice Cream and Related Products* (Westport, Conn., 1961), p. 2; Brillat-Savarin, *Physiology of Taste*, p. 286.

70. Jones, *French Culture*, p. 303.

71. *Oxford English Dictionary*, 1961 ed., s.v. "soup"; Jonathan Swift, "A Panygyric on the Dean," *The Works of Dr. Jonathan Swift* (London, 1766), 7:162; Freeman, *Washington*, 1:111; Greene, *Landon Carter*, 2:730.

72. Brillat-Savarin, *Physiology of Taste*, p. 257; Horry recipe book of 1770; Wertenbaker, *Foundations of American Civilization*, p. 280; Eben, *Mittelberger's Journey*, p. 65.

73. Williamson, *American Hotel*, p. 213; Stewart, *American Ways of Life*, p. 106; Brissot de Warville, *New Travels*, p. 303.

74. Freeman, *Washington*, 5:407.

75. Kimball, *Jefferson's Cook Book*, pp. 2–4, 7, 9, 10–13, *passim*.

Chapter 6: Eighteenth-Century Drink

1. Earle, *Stage-Coach and Tavern Days*, pp. 115–16.

2. Roberts and Roberts, *Moreau de St. Méry*, pp. 265–66.

3. Jones, *Present State of Virginia*, p. 86.

4. Freeman, *Washington*, 1:105; Eben, *Mittelberger's Journey*, p. 66.

5. *A Short Description* in Carroll, *Historical Collections*, 2:481; Kalm, *Travels*, 1:37, 196; Roberts and Roberts, *Moreau de St. Méry*, p. 147.

6. *Ibid.*, p. 323.

7. Arnow, *Seedtime*, pp. 423–24; Beverley, *History of Virginia*, pp. 316–17.

8. Crèvecoeur, *Eighteenth Century America*, 1:123.

9. Eliza Lucas Pinckney recipe, 1756, South Carolina Historical Society; Freeman, *Washington*, 1:106; Kalm, *Travels*, 1:270; Anburey, *Travels*, 2:432–33; Schoepf, *Travels*, 2:36; Earle, *Customs and Fashions*, pp. 173–74.

10. Harold L. Peterson, *The Book of the Continental Soldier* (Harrisburg, Pa., 1968), p. 146; Baron, *Brewed in America*, p. 101; Hulton, *Letters of a Loyalist*, p. 66.

11. Freeman, *Washington*, 1:106; Spruill, *Women's Life*, pp. 295–96; Jones, *Present State of Virginia*, p. 86; Singleton, *Social New York*, pp. 353–54; Ivor Noël Hume, *Here Lies Virginia* (New York, 1963), p. 130; Baron, *Brewed in America*, p. 114.

12. Smith, *John Adams*, 2:716–17; Greene, *Landon Carter*, 2:270, 273; Spruill, *Women's Life*, pp. 295–96; Baron, *Brewed in America*, p. 57; Brissot de Warville, *New Travels*, p. 91.

13. Acrelius, *New Sweden*, p. 163; Eben, *Mittelberger's Journey*, p. 66; Brissot de Warville, *New Travels*, p. 399.

14. Weeden, *History of New England*, 2:507; Rolls Milton Tryon, *Household Manufactures in the United States 1640–1860* (Chicago, 1917), pp. 229–30; Carman, *American Husbandry*, p. 115; Kalm, *Travels*, 1:184; Fletcher, *Pennsylvania Agriculture*, p. 226.

15. Tryon, *Household Manufactures*, p. 230; Gaillard Hunt, *Life in America One Hundred Years Ago* (New York, 1914), pp. 219–20; Brillat-Savarin, *Physi-*

ology of Taste, p. 58; see also Edward Field, *The Colonial Tavern* (Providence, R.I., 1897), pp. 138–41.

16. Earle, *Customs and Fashions,* p. 173; Lord Adam Gordon in Mereness, *Travels,* p. 406; Brissot de Warville, *New Travels,* p. 91; Acrelius, *New Sweden,* p. 161; Roberts and Roberts, *Moreau de St. Méry,* p. 114.

17. Earle, *Stage-Coach and Tavern Days,* pp. 118, 130; Oscar Kuhns, *The German and Swiss Settlements of Colonial Pennsylvania* (New York, 1914), p. 110.

18. Gray, *History of Agriculture,* 1:101, 114, 188, 189, 190; Bailey, *Evolution of Fruits,* pp. 16–18, 23–25, 92; Jones, *French Culture,* pp. 91, 302–303; Schoepf, *Travels,* 2:183, 185.

19. Byrd, *Secret Diary,* p. 43; Tryon, *Household Manufactures,* pp. 231–32; Kalm, *Travels,* 1:67, 100; Schoepf, *Travels,* 2:183; Acrelius, *New Sweden,* p. 160; *William Byrd's Natural History,* p. 91.

20. Kalm, *Travels,* 1:201; *A Short Description* in Carroll, *Historical Collections,* 2:231; "Bennett's History of New England," in *Proceedings of the Massachusetts Historical Society, 1860–1862* (Boston, 1862), p. 114; Singleton, *Social New York,* p. 353; Adam Smith, *An Inquiry into the Nature and Causes of the Wealth of Nations* (Edinburgh, 1870), pp. 222–23.

21. Earle, *Customs and Fashions,* pp. 168–69; Byrd, *Secret Diary,* pp. 150, 279; Jones, *Present State of Virginia,* p. 86; Schoepf, *Travels,* 2:183–84; Baron, *Brewed in America,* pp. 81–82.

22. Jones, *Present State of Virginia,* p. 86; Byrd, *Secret Diary,* pp. 188, 230, 359; Brissot de Warville, *New Travels,* pp. 91, 391n.

23. Eben, *Mittelberger's Journey,* pp. 66–67; Byrd, *Secret Diary,* p. 69.

24. Schoepf, *Travels,* 2:220; Grant, *Memoirs,* p. 116; Horry, recipe book of 1770; Earle, *Customs and Fashions,* pp. 168–71.

25. Morison, *Maritime History,* p. 19; Stewart, *American Ways of Life,* p. 117; Weeden, *History of New England,* 2:501–502; [Samuel Cooper], *The Crisis* (Boston, 1754), pp. 8–9; Freeman, *Washington,* 1:106; Emory Johnson et al., *History of Domestic and Foreign Commerce of the United States* (Washington, 1915), pp. 169–70; Hawke, *Colonial Experience,* pp. 471–72.

26. Schoepf, *Travels,* 2:220; Acrelius, *New Sweden,* p. 162; William Byrd, *William Byrd's Histories of the Dividing Line Betwixt Virginia and North Carolina,* ed. William K, Boyd (Raleigh, 1929), p. 92; Fletcher, *Pennsylvania Agriculture,* p. 447.

27. Wilson, *Food and Drink in Britain,* p. 403.

28. Wright and Corbett, *Pioneer Life,* pp. 60–61; C. F. Volney, *View of the Climate and Soil of the United States of America* (London, 1804), p. 288.

29. Robert Parke to Mary Valentine Parke, Chester Township, October 1725, in Myers, *Immigration of the Irish Quakers,* p. 74; Weeden, *History of New England,* 2:459; "A Progress to the Mines in 1732," in Wright, *Prose Works of William Byrd,* p. 374; Schoepf, *Travels,* 1:219; Acrelius, *New Sweden,* p. 161.

30. Earle, *Stage-Coach and Tavern Days,* pp. 104–105.

31. Woodmason, *Carolina Backcountry,* pp. 30, 53.

32. Roueché, *Neutral Spirit,* pp. 39–40.

33. Wright and Corbett, *Pioneer Life,* pp. 60–61; Roberts and Roberts, *Moreau de St. Méry,* pp. 279, 318; Schoepf, *Travels,* 1:219.

34. Beverley, *History of Virginia*, pp. 314–15; Kalm, *Travels*, 1:74, 270; Freeman, *Washington*, 1:106; 3:78–79, 116; Woodmason, *Carolina Backcountry*, p. 53.

35. Weld, *Travels*, p. 137.

36. Wilson, *Food and Drink in Britain*, p. 401; Earle, *Stage-Coach and Tavern Days*, pp. 117–18.

37. Knight, *Private Journal*, p. 61.

38. Schoepf, *Travels*, 2:220; Bridenbaugh, *Gentleman's Progress*, p. 5; Eben, *Mittelberger's Journey*, pp. 66–67.

39. Adams, *Works of John Adams*, 2:201; Smith, *John Adams*, 2:716–17; Kuhns, *German and Swiss Settlements*, p. 110, 111–12.

40. Earle, *Stage-Coach and Tavern Days*, p. 116.

41. Sherrill, *French Memories*, p. 86.

42. Baron, *Brewed in America*, p. 57; Grant, *Memoirs*, p. 116.

43. Richard J. Hooker, "The American Revolution Seen through a Wine Glass," *William and Mary Quarterly* 11 (January 1954): 52.

44. John Adams, "Diary," in *Works of John Adams*, 2:363.

45. Hooker, "American Revolution," p. 52.

46. *Virginia Gazette* (Purdie and Dixon), May 23, 1766.

47. J. C. Furnas, *The Life and Times of the Late Demon Rum* (New York, 1965), pp. 15–17, 38, 65, 66; Baron, *Brewed in America*, pp. 81–82, 118–19.

48. *Ibid.*, pp. 118–19; Schoepf, *Travels*, 2:219.

49. Colin Clair, *Kitchen & Table* (London, 1964), p. 134; Earle, *Customs and Fashions*, p. 180; Byrd, *Secret Diary*, p. 181; Kalm, *Travels*, 2:105; Spruill, *Women's Life*, p. 276; Benjamin Woods Labaree, *The Boston Tea Party* (New York, 1964), p. 7.

50. Crawford, *Social Life*, pp. 251–52; Kalm, *Travels*, 1:282–83; Spruill, *Women's Life*, p. 72 n.

51. Woodmason, *Carolina Backcountry*, pp. 34, 39; Doddridge, *Settlement of the Western Country*, p. 30.

52. Earle, *Customs and Fashions*, p. 168; Schoepf, *Travels*, 1:166; 2:113; "Journal of James Kenny, 1761–1763," in *Pennsylvania Magazine of History and Biography*, 37 (1913): 4, 6, 46; Anburey, *Travels*, 2:210.

53. Earle, *Customs and Fashions*, p. 181.

54. Smith, *John Adams*, 1:161.

55. Brissot de Warville, *New Travels*, p. 142; Roberts and Roberts, *Moreau de St. Méry*, p. 256; Armes, *Nancy Shippen*, p. 200.

56. Sherrill, *French Memories*, p. 78.

57. Knight, *Private Journal*, p. 33; Byrd, *Secret Diary*, pp. 1, 3, 114, 121, *passim*; Bridenbaugh, *Gentleman's Progress*, pp. 7, 96, 149, 159, 172, 187; Kalm, *Travels*, 1:289.

58. Frederick L. Wellman, *Coffee* (New York, 1961), p. 22; Clair, *Kitchen & Table*, p. 139; Bridenbaugh, *Cities in the Wilderness*, pp. 109, 267, 269, 426, 432; William Harrison Ukers, *All About Coffee* (New York, 1922), pp. 21, 36–37, 101–103, 112; Journal of John Fontaine, 1716, in Ann Maury, *Memoirs of a Huguenot Family* (New York, 1872), p. 289.

59. Chastellux, *Travels*, 1:132; 2:388; Sherrill, *French Memories*, pp. 80–81.

60. Labaree, *Boston Tea Party*, p. 266; Roberts and Roberts, *Moreau de St. Méry*, p. 165; Acrelius, *New Sweden*, p. 164.

Chapter 7: The Early Nineteenth Century, 1800 – 1860, I

1. James Rorty and N. Philip Norman, *Tomorrow's Food* (New York, 1956), p. 33.
2. Charles H. Haswell, *Reminiscences of an Octogenerian of the City of New York* (New York, 1897), p. 505.
3. Fletcher, *Pennsylvania Agriculture*, pp. 397 – 98; Mrs. Samuel Harrison Smith, *The First Forty Years of Washington Society*, ed. Gaillard Hunt (New York, 1906), p. 48; Mary Stuart Smith, *Virginia Cookery-Book* (New York, 1885), p. 83; Furnas, *The Americans*, pp. 426 – 27.
4. Schmidt, *Rural Hunterdon*. pp. 268 – 69.
5. Russell Lynes, *The Domesticated Americans* (New York, 1963), pp. 177 – 78.
6. Journal of Johannes Schweizer in Robert H. Billigmeier and Fred Altschuler Picard, eds. and trans., *The Old Land and the New* (Minneapolis, 1965), pp. 87 – 88.
7. Frances Trollope, *Domestic Manners of the Americans*, ed. Donald Smalley (New York, 1949), p. 19; John L. Hess and Karen Hess, *The Taste of America* (New York, 1977), p. 109.
8. John D. Lewis, *Across the Atlantic* (London, 1851), p. 242.
9. Frederick Marryat, *A Diary in America*, ed. Sydney Jackman (New York, 1962), p. 377.
10. A different theory on knife-fork handling is in Furnas, *The Americans*, p. 903.
11. Thomas F. De Voe, *The Market Assistant. . . .* (New York, 1867), p. 7; E. C. Wines, *A Trip to Boston* (Boston, 1838), pp. 213 – 14.
12. De Voe, *The Market Assistant*, pp. 181 – 82; Timothy Flint, *Letters from America* (Edinburgh, 1822). p. 6; Weld, *Travels*, pp. 75 – 76; [Anne Royall], *Sketches of History, Life, and Manners, in the United States* (New Haven, 1826), p. 261.
13. Flint, *Letters from America*, p. 34; Trollope, *Domestic Manners*, p. 277; Charles William Janson, *The Stranger in America 1793 – 1806* (New York, 1935), p. 185; [Royall], *Sketches of History*, p. 207.
14. *Ibid.*, pp. 196 – 97; John Woods, *Two Years' Residence in the Settlement on the English Prairie* (London, 1822), pp. 21, 25, 45, 47.
15. Virginia Clay-Clopton, *A Belle of the Fifties* (New York, 1905), p. 28.
16. [Royall], *Sketches of History*, pp. 109 – 10.
17. Charles Lanman, *Adventures in the Wilds of the United States* (Philadelphia, 1856), 1:100; Peter Neilson, *Recollections of a Six Years' Residence. . . .* (Glasgow, 1830), p. 262; Weld, *Travels*, p. 142; Bernhard, Duke of Saxe-Weimer Eisenach, *Travels through North America during the Years 1825 and 1826* (Philadelphia, 1828), 2:7.

Notes

18. Benjamin Henry Latrobe, *The Journal of Latrobe* (New York, 1905), p. 162; Sir Charles Lyell, *A Second Visit to the United States of North America* (London, 1849), 2:130; Fredrika Bremer, *The Homes of the New World* (New York, 1854), 2:213; Bernhard, *Travels*, 2:73.

19. Trollope, *Domestic Manners*, pp. 60–61; Nichols, *Forty Years*, 1:159; Charles Cist, *Cincinnati in 1851* (Cincinnati, 1851), pp. 274–75.

20. Haswell, *Reminiscences*, p. 35.

21. Richard O. Cummings, *The American Ice Harvests* (Berkeley, Calif., 1949), pp. 6, 14; Siegfried Giedion, *Mechanization Takes Command: A Contribution to Anonymous History* (New York, 1969), pp. 596–98; Basil Hall, *Travels in North America, in the Years 1827 and 1828* (Edinburgh, 1829), 2:127–28; Thomas L. Nichols, *Forty Years of American Life* (London, 1864), 1:247.

22. Hall, *Travels in North America*, 1:6; Trollope, *Domestic Manners*, p. 352.

23. Lynes, *Domesticated Americans*, p. 125; Anderson, *Refrigeration in America*, p. 3.

24. Morison, *Maritime History*, p. 308; Anderson, *Refrigeration in America*, pp. 8–10, 30–31.

25. Cummings, *Ice Harvests*, p. 62.

26. Frederick Accum, *A Treatise on Adulterations of Food, and Culinary Poisons*, 2d ed. (London, 1820), pp. 3–4.

27. Eliza Leslie, *Miss Leslie's New Cookery Book* (Philadelphia, 1857), pp. 543, 607–608.

28. Richard H. Shryock, "Sylvester Graham and the Popular Health Movement, 1830–1870," *Mississippi Valley Historical Review*, 18 (September 1931): 172–77; John R. Alden, *Pioneer America* (New York, 1966), pp. 220–21; Janet Barkas, *The Vegetable Passion* (New York, 1975), pp. 138–40; Nichols, *Forty Years*, 2:21.

29. Lyell, *Second Visit*, 1:21; Alfred Bunn, *Old England and New England* (London, 1853), pp. 269–70.

30. Kimball, *Jefferson's Cook Book*, pp. 4, 10, 13–14.

31. Ward McAllister, *Society as I Have Found It* (New York, 1890), pp. 312–13.

32. Simmons, *American Cookery*, p. 37.

33. The New York Public Library has a copy of Louis Eustache Ude, *The French Cook* (Philadelphia, 1828). Eliza Leslie's *Domestic French Cookery* was published in Philadelphia in 1832.

34. Leslie, *New Cookery Book*, pp. 35, 64–66, 183, 344.

35. Sara Josepha Hale, *The Ladies' New Book of Cookery*, 5th ed. (New York, 1852), p. xiv. A similar idea was expressed in 1817 in the *Analytic Review* in an item taken from a British journal. See Jones, *French Culture*, p. 307.

36. Leslie, *New Cookery Book*, p. 140; Eliza Leslie, *Directions for Cookery*, 20th ed. (Philadelphia, 1845), p. 14.

37. Thomas Colley Grattan, *Civilized America* (London, 1859), p. 108.

38. Johannes Schweizer in Billigmeier and Picard, *The Old Land*, p. 76.

39. Mary Caroline Crawford, *Romantic Days in Old Boston* (Boston, 1910), p. 348.

40. Mary Randolph, *The Virginia Housewife, or Methodical Cook*, 3d ed. (Washington, 1828), pp. 17–30; Leslie, *Directions for Cookery*, pp. 24–42; [Sallie Rutledge], *The Carolina Housewife, or House and Home: By a Lady of Charleston* (Charleston, S.C., 1847), pp. 38–45; [Elizabeth H. Putnam], *Mrs. Putnam's Receipt Book* (Boston, 1850), pp. 6–15.

41. Randolph B. Marcy, *Border Reminiscences* (New York, 1872), p. 218.

42. Menu of the City Hotel, New York, September 11, 1842, Misc. no. 2028, Southern Collection, University of North Carolina, Chapel Hill.

43. Robert Ernst, *Immigrant Life in New York City 1825–1865* (New York, 1949), p. 66.

44. *Ibid.*, pp. 87, 88; Mrs. Glasse, *The Art of Cookery* (Alexandria, 1812), pp. 263–64.

45. H. L. Mencken, *The American Language* (New York, 1937), pp. 112, 155.

46. Ernst, *Immigrant Life*, p. 66.

47. Marcus Lee Hansen, *The Atlantic Migration* (Cambridge, Mass., 1940), p. 202; Nichols, *Forty Years*, 2:73–74.

48. *Breakfast, Dinner, and Tea* (New York, 1860), p. 134.

49. Karl Theodore Griesinger, *Lebende Bilder aus Amerika*, in Oscar Handlin, *This Was America* (Cambridge, Mass., 1949), p. 256.

50. Hale, *Ladies' New Book*, p. iv.

51. By a Society of Gentlemen in New York, *The Universal Receipt Book* (New York, 1814), p. 128; [Maria Eliza Ketelby Rundell], *A New System of Domestic Cookery* (Exeter, 1808), p. 163; Randolph, *Virginia Housewife*, pp. 107, 109, 112–13, 118, 218.

52. Leslie, *New Cookery Book*, pp. 154, 179, 180, 197, 226, 273, 297, 299, 300, 333, 354, 525, 529, 535.

Chapter 8: The Early Nineteenth Century, 1800–1860, II

1. Marryat, *Diary*, p. 380.

2. Leslie, *New Cookery Book*, p. 252.

3. Emmett Dedmon, *Fabulous Chicago* (New York, 1953), pp. 47–48.

4. Sarah Mytton Maury, *An Englishwoman in America* (London, 1848), p. 197; Grattan, *Civilized America*, 1:107.

5. Sam Bowers Hilliard, *Hog Meat and Hoecake: Food Supply in the Old South, 1840–1860* (Carbondale, Ill., 1972), p. 47.

6. Harry Ellsworth Cole, *Stagecoach and Tavern Tales of the Old Northwest* (Cleveland, 1930), p. 211; Frederick Law Olmsted, *The Cotton Kingdom* (New York, 1861), 1:90; Billigmeier and Picard, *The Old Land*, pp. 144–45; Lanman, *Adventures in the Wilds*, 2:137.

7. Doddridge, *Settlement of Western Country*, p. 9.

8. Bessie Louise Pierce, *A History of Chicago* (New York, 1940), 2:460; Flint, *Letters from America*, p. 96; R. H. Williams, *With the Border Ruffians*

Notes

(London, 1907), p. 28; Louis C. Hunter, *Steamboats on the Western Rivers* (Cambridge, Mass., 1949), pp. 400–401; Everett Dick, *The Dixie Frontier* (New York, 1948), p. 30.

9. Williams, *Border Ruffians,* pp. 57–58; Cole, *Stagecoach and Tavern Tales,* p. 212; Maitland Edey, "Once There Were Billions, Now There are None," *Life,* December 22, 1961, pp. 169–76.

10. Charles Mackay, *Life and Liberty in America* (New York, 1859), pp. 278–79.

11. Bunn, *Old England,* pp. 26–27; Timothy Dwight, *Travels in New-England and New-York* (New Haven, 1821), 1:55; Thomas Ashe, *Travels in America* (London, 1808), p. 29; H. M. Brackenridge, *Journal of a Voyage,* in Warren S. Tryon, ed., *A Mirror for Americans* (Chicago, 1952), 3:482; Dedmon, *Fabulous Chicago,* pp. 47–48; Leslie, *New Cookery Book,* p. 304; William Howard Russell, *My Diary North and South* (Boston, 1863), pp. 18–19.

12. Trollope, *Domestic Manners,* p. 297.

13. Nichols, *Forty Years,* 2:21.

14. Anderson, *Refrigeration in America,* pp. 33–35; Bidwell and Falconer, *History of Agriculture,* p. 393.

15. F. A. Porcher, "Historical and Social Sketch of Craven County," *The Southern Quarterly Review,* 9 (April 1854): 404.

16. Fletcher, *Pennsylvania Agriculture,* p. 442.

17. John S. Wilson, M.D., in *Godey's Lady's Book and Magazine,* February, 1860, p. 178.

18. Leslie, *New Cookery Book,* pp. 221–22, 228–29.

19. Mrs. Cornelius, *The Young Housekeeper's Friend* (Boston, 1866), pp. 126–30; Leslie, *New Cookery Book,* pp. 142–44.

20. "The Diary of Robert Gilmor," *Maryland Historical Magazine,* 17 (September 1922): 264; George C. Rogers, Jr., *Charleston in the Age of the Pinckneys* (Norman, Okla., 1969), p. 83.

21. Gray, *History of Agriculture,* 2:832; Hilliard, *Hog Meat and Hoecake,* pp. 45–46; Woods, *Two Years' Residence,* p. 183.

22. Catherine E. Beecher, *Miss Beecher's Domestic Receipt Book,* 3d ed. (New York, 1851), p. 35; Bunn, *Old England,* pp. 38–39, 40; Robert Tallant, *The Romantic New Orleanians* (New York, 1950), pp. 270–71; Clara F. Bromley, *A Woman's Wanderings in the Western World* (London, 1861), pp. 29–30; Leslie, *Directions for Cookery,* pp. 85–103; Leslie, *New Cookery Book,* pp. 209–214, 593; Lydia Maria Child, *The American Frugal Housewife* (Boston, 1835), p. 43.

23. [Isaac Candler], *A Summary View of America* (London, 1824), p. 81; Clay-Clopton, *Belle of the Fifties,* p. 28.

24. Leslie, *New Cookery Book,* pp. 105–107.

25. Guion Griffis Johnson, *Ante-Bellum North Carolina* (Chapel Hill, 1937), pp. 94–95.

26. *The Book of Chowder,* ed. Richard J. Hooker (Harvard, Mass., 1978), pp. 1–3.

27. *Ibid.,* p. 4.

28. *Ibid.,* p. 27.

381

29. *Ibid.*, p. 29.

30. *Ibid.*, pp. 5–8.

31. Marryat, *Diary*, p. 157.

32. Mackay, *Life and Liberty*, p. 73.

33. Nichols, *Forty Years*, 1:268–69.

34. Williamson, *American Hotel*, p. 205; Nichols, *Forty Years*, 1:268–69; Bunn, *Old England*, p. 53.

35. Mary Livermore, *The Story of My Life* (Hartford, Conn., 1897), p. 50; Isabela Lucy Bishop, *The Englishwoman in America* 2d ed. (London, 1856), pp. 352–53.

36. Bunn, *Old England*, p. 40; Bishop, *Englishwoman in America*, pp. 352–53; Mackay, *Life and Liberty*, p. 210.

37. John F. Watson, *Annals of Philadelphia and Pennsylvania* (Philadelphia, 1857–60), 2:471.

38. Seymour Dunbar, *A History of Travel in America* (New York, 1937), p. 734; Nichols, *Forty Years*, 1:270–71.

39. Richardson Wright, *Hawkers and Walkers in Early America* (Philadelphia, 1927), pp. 65, 248.

40. Marcy, *Border Reminiscences*, pp. 216–17.

41. National Canners Association, *The Canning Industry* (Washington, 1939), p. 5; Pierce, *History of Chicago*, 1:215; Nichols, *Forty Years*, 1:159; Sara T. D. Robinson, *Kansas* (Lawrence, Kans., 1899), p. 206; Everett Dick, *The Sod House Frontier 1854–1890* (New York, 1937), p. 63; J. Milton Mackie, *From Cape Cod to Dixie*, p. 194.

42. Nichols, *Forty Years*, 1:268–69.

43. John Allen Krout and Dixon Ryan Fox, *The Completion of Independence, 1790–1830* (New York, 1944), p. 45; Canners Association, *Canning Industry*, p. 5.

44. Pierce, *History of Chicago*, 2:460–61.

45. Achille Murat, *A Moral and Political Sketch of the United States of North America* (London, 1833), p. 71; Cole, *Stagecoach and Tavern Tales*, p. 222.

46. Crawford, *Social Life*, p. 260; Schmidt, *Rural Hunterdon*, pp. 278–80; Trollope, *Domestic Manners*, p. 390; Leslie, *New Cookery Book*, p. 86.

47. Cole, *Stagecoach and Tavern Tales*, p. 112.

48. George W. Sloan, "Fifty Years in Pharmacy," *Indiana Historical Society Publications*, 3:344; Trollope, *Domestic Manners*, p. 243; E. W. Howe, *Plain People* (New York, 1929), p. 23.

49. Hilliard, *Hog Meat and Hoecake*, p. 51; Richard Osborn Cummings, *The American and His Food: A History of Food Habits in the United States*, rev. ed. (Chicago, 1940), p. 36; Daniel J. Boorstin, *The Americans: The Democratic Experience* (New York, 1973), p. 325.

50. Cummings, *The American and His Food*, p. 44; Child, *Frugal Housewife*, p. 18; William A. Alcott, *The Young Housekeeper*, 5th ed. (Boston, 1842), p. 162; Harriet Beecher Stowe, *House and Home Papers* (Boston, 1865), p. 257.

51. Leslie, *Directions for Cookery*, p. 14; Hilliard, *Hog Meat and Hoecake* p. 176; Alcott, *Young Housekeeper*, p. 150.

Notes

52. Billigmeier and Picard, *The Old Land*, p. 126; Bernhard, *Travels*, p. 65.
53. Cornelius, *Housekeeper's Friend*, pp. 171–73; Alcott, *Young Housekeeper*, p. 176; Stowe, *House and Home Papers*, p. 259.
54. Williamson, *American Hotel*, p. 219; Ishbel Ross, *Crusades and Crinolines* (New York, 1963), p. 124. Williamson gives Montgomery Hall as the hotel where the discovery was made, while Ross mentions Moon's Lake House.
55. Hedrick, *History of Horticulture*, p. 460; Society of Gentlemen, *Universal Receipt Book*, p. 45; Dwight, *Travels in New-England*, 1:44–45, 47–48; A. F. M. Willich, *The Domestic Encyclopedia* (Philadelphia, 1821), 3:178; Trollope, *Domestic Manners*, p. 61; Randolph, *Virginia Housewife*, pp. 95, 107.
56. *Ibid.*, p. 162; *Cook's Oracle; and Housekeeper's Manual* (New York, 1838), p. 239; H. L. Barnum, *Family Receipts* (Cincinnati, 1831), pp. 111, 239; Eliza Leslie, *Domestic French Cookery* (Philadelphia, 1832), p. 73; *The Cook's Own Book* (Boston, 1832), pp. 222–23; Alcott, *Young Housekeeper*, p. 180; Mrs. Henry Cust, *Wanderers: Episodes from the Travels of Lady Emmeline Stuart-Wortley . . . 1849–1855* (London, 1928), pp. 43–44.
57. Cornelius, *Housekeeper's Friend*, p. 175; Leslie, *New Cookery Book*, pp. 384–85; Mrs. E. F. Haskell, *The Housekeeper's Encyclopedia* (New York, 1861), pp. 28, 119; Hannah Widdifield, *Widdifield's New Cook Book* (Philadelphia, 1856), pp. 50, 309.
58. F. A. Buell to father, Jacksonville, Florida, December 27, 1855, manuscript letter collection of Richard J. Hooker.
59. Dwight, *Travels in New-England*, 1:49; Bremer, *Homes of the New World*, 1:522.
60. Furnas, *The Americans*, p. 461.
61. Maria Eliza Ketelby Rundell, *A New System of Domestic Cookery*, 3d ed. (New York, 1817), p. 297; Leslie, *Directions for Cookery*, p. 123.
62. Leslie, *New Cookery Book*, pp. 173, 245–46; Hale, *New Book of Cookery*, p. 55.
63. Maria Eliza Ketelby Rundell, *American Domestic Cookery* (New York, 1823), p. 18; Leslie, *New Cookery Book*, pp. 36–37, 165; Stowe, *House and Home Papers*, p. 264.
64. Leslie, *New Cookery Book*, p. 272.
65. [Rutledge], *House and Home*, pp. 78, 94; Leslie, *New Cookery Book*, pp. 171–73, 333–34; manuscript menu of the steamship *Ruth*, miscellaneous menus #2028, University of North Carolina, Chapel Hill.
66. Cornelius, *Housekeeper's Friend*, pp. 180–83; Leslie, *New Cookery Book*, pp. 568–81; [Rutledge], *House and Home*, pp. 88–94.
67. Leslie, *New Cookery Book*, p. 568.
68. Martineau, *Society in America*, 1:306.
69. Trollope, *Domestic Manners*, p. 298; Stowe, *House and Home Papers*, p. 263.
70. *Men and Manners in America* (Philadelphia, 1833), p. 70.
71. Francis F. Beirne, *The Amiable Baltimoreans* (New York, 1951), p. 342.
72. Earle, *Stage-Coach and Tavern Days*, p. 34.
73. Crawford, *Social Life*, p. 261; Earle, *Home Life*, p. 104; Joel Barlow, *The Hasty-Pudding, a Poem, in Three Cantos* (New York, 1796), p. 12.

74. Hall, *Travels*, 1:33; Esther Allen Howland, *The New England Economical Housekeeper, and Family Receipt Book* (Montpelier, Vt., 1845), pp. 32–40.

75. Leslie, *New Cookery Book*, pp. 465–66, 490.

76. *Ibid.*, pp. 520–21; Mackie, *From Cape Cod to Dixie*, p. 193; Beirne, *Amiable Baltimoreans*, p. 352.

77. Cornelius, *Housekeeper's Friend*, pp. 56–60; Widdifield, *Widdifield's New Cook Book*, pp. 281–96.

78. Leslie speaks of doughnuts as of German origin in *New Cookery Book*, pp. 443–44.

79. *Ibid.*, p. 502.

80. Clay-Clopton, *A Belle of the Fifties*, pp. 31–32.

81. [Rutledge], *House and Home*, p. 125; Glasse, *The Art of Cookery*, pp. 174, 178; [Susannah Carter], *The Frugal Housewife* (Philadelphia, 1802), p. 105; Simmons, *American Cookery*, p. 74.

82. Leslie, *New Cookery Book*, p. 496.

83. Society of Gentlemen, *Universal Receipt Book*, p. 154.

84. Haswell, *Reminiscences*, pp. 59–60.

85. Marryat, *Diary*, p. 216.

86. Nichols, *Forty Years*, 1:266–67.

87. Martineau, *Society in America*, p. 271.

88. Pierce, *History of Chicago*, 1:200–201.

89. Mackie, *From Cape Cod to Dixie*, p. 193.

90. Mrs. Basil Hall, *The Aristocratic Journey*, ed. Una Pope-Hennessy (New York, 1931), pp. 28, 66, 89; Leslie, *New Cookery Book*, p. 512.

91. Woods, *Two Years' Residence*, pp. 122, 227; Hilliard, *Hog Meat and Hoecake*, pp. 90, 180–81.

92. Cummings, *American and His Food*, pp. 43–44; Alcott, *Young Housekeeper*, pp. 213, 221, 237.

93. Hedrick, *History of Horticulture*, p. 441; S. W. Fletcher, *The Strawberry in North America* (New York, 1917), p. 42; "Diary of Robert Gilmor," *Maryland Historical Magazine*, 17 (December 1922): 340–41.

94. John McPhee, "Oranges," *The New Yorker*, May 14, 1966, pp. 160–62.

95. Bernhard, *Travels*, p. 41; Marryat, *Diary*, pp. 58, 380; Pierce, *History of Chicago*, 1:201.

96. Charles Morrow Wilson, *Empire in Green and Gold* (n.p., 1947), pp. 24–25; Cole, *Stagecoach and Tavern Tales*, p. 218.

97. Leslie, *New Cookery Book*, p. 358.

98. Fredrika Bremer, *America of the Fifties*, ed Adolph B. Benson (New York, 1924), pp. 98, 108, 147.

Chapter 9: Drink, 1800–1860

1. Joseph R. Gusfield, "Status Conflicts and the Changing Ideologies of the American Temperance Movement," in *Society, Culture, and Drinking Patterns*, ed. David J. Pittman and Charles R. Snyder (New York, 1962), pp. 104–106;

Notes

Carl Russell Fish, *The Rise of the Common Man 1830 – 1850* (New York, 1927), pp. 263 – 68; Furnas, *Americans*, pp. 511 – 12.

2. Norman Longmate, *The Waterdrinkers: A History of Temperance* (London, 1968), p. 196.

3. Capt. J. E. Alexander, *Transatlantic Sketches* (Philadelphia, 1833), pp. 250 – 51; Mackay, *Life and Liberty*, p. 139; Bishop, *Englishwoman in America*, p. 91; Marryat, *Diary*, p. 157.

4. Furnas, *Late Demon Rum*, p. 72; A. B. Grosh, *Washingtonian Pocket Companion*, 3d ed. (Utica, N.Y., 1843), p. 34.

5. Trollope, *Domestic Manners*, p. 297; Flint, *Letters from America*, p. 34; Ole Munch Raeder, *America in the Forties*, ed. Gunnar J. Malmin (Minneapolis, 1929), p. 15; Bishop, *Englishwoman in America*, pp. 152 – 53; Mary Lundie Duncan, *America As I Found It* (New York, 1852), p. 420; Bromley, *A Woman's Wanderings*, pp. 33 – 34.

6. Charles Casey, *Two Years on the Farm of Uncle Sam* (London, 1852), p. 134; Baron Klinkowströms, *America 1818 – 1820*, ed. Franklin D. Scott (Evanston, Ill., 1952), pp. 68 – 69; Haswell, *Reminiscences*, pp. 112 – 13; Philip Hone, *The Diary of Philip Hone 1828 – 1851*, ed. Bayard Tuckerman (New York, 1889), 2:150 – 51; Lately Thomas, *Delmonico's: A Century of Splendor* (Boston, 1967), p. 50.

7. Bremer, *Homes of the New World*, 1:280; Martineau, *Society in America*, p. 249; Maury, *Englishwoman in America*, p. 199; Bromley, *A Woman's Wanderings*, pp. 33 – 34.

8. Pauline Arnold and Percival White, *Food: America's Biggest Business* (New York, 1959), pp. 174 – 75, 177 – 78; John J. Dillon, *Seven Decades of Milk: A History of New York's Dairy Industry* (New York, 1941), p. 2.

9. Edwin James, *Account of an Expedition from Pittsburgh to the Rocky Mountains Performed in the Years 1819, 1820* (London, 1823), 1:77.

10. J. D. B. De Bow, *The Industrial Resources, etc., of the Southern and Western States* (New Orleans, 1853), 1:284 – 85, 288.

11. Kittredge, *Old Farmer*, pp. 184 – 85; Alexander Mackay, *The Western World* (Philadelphia, 1849), 1:99; Schmidt, *Rural Hunterdon*, pp. 279 – 80.

12. Mitchell, *Old New England Custom*, p. 15; Andrew Bell Thomason, *Men and Things in America* (London, 1838), p. 201; Paton Yoder, *Taverns and Travelers* (Bloomington, Ind., 1969), p. 145; Dick, *Dixie Frontier*, p. 292.

13. Francis Hall, *Travels in Canada, and the United States, in 1816 and 1817* (Boston, 1818), p. 38; G. G. Johnson, *Ante-Bellum North Carolina*, pp. 160 – 61; Trollope, *Domestic Manners*, p. 37.

14. John J. Riley, *A History of the American Soft Drink Industry* (Washington, D.C., 1858), pp. 2, 6 – 9, 12, 49, 112 – 14; Haswell, *Reminiscences*, p. 58; Furnas, *The Americans*, p. 459; Klinkowströms, *America*, p. 69; Marryat, *Dairy*, p. 59; J. H. Snively, "Soda-Water: What It Is, and How It Is Made," *Harper's New Monthly Magazine* 45 (August 1872): 345.

15. Ernest L. Bogart, *Peacham: The Story of a Vermont Hill Town* (Montpelier, 1948), p. 208; Klinkowströms, *America*, p. 69; Nichols, *Forty Years*, 1:88; Hall, *Travels*, p. 38; Dwight, *Travels*, 1:44; Johnson, *Ante-Bellum North Carolina*, p. 93; Billigmeier and Picard, *The Old Land*, p. 161; J. Winston

NOTES

Coleman, *Stage-Coach Days in the Bluegrass* (Louisville, Ky., 1935), p. 62; Martineau, *Society in America*, pp. 306–307.

16. Ernst, *Immigrant Life*, p. 90; Ashe, *Travels*, p. 29; Bond, *Old Northwest*, p. 410.

17. Baron, *Brewed in America*, pp. 175–76; Anderson, *Refrigeration in America*, pp. 28–29; Mackay, *Life and Liberty*, p. 73.

18. John Lewis Peyton, *Over the Alleghanies and Across the Prairies* (London, 1870), p. 79; Mackay, *Life and Liberty*, p. 204; Johnson, *Ante-Bellum North Carolina*, pp. 91–92; Gray, *History of Agriculture*, 2:827.

19. Baron, *Brewed in America*, pp. 180–81; Ernst, *Immigrant Life*, p. 125.

20. Anthony Trollope, *North America* (Philadelphia, 1863), p. 290; Bernhard, *Travels*, pp. 34, 65; George Wilson Pierson, *Tocqueville and Beaumont in America* (New York, 1938), p. 68; Martineau, *Society in America*, p. 249; Wines, *Trip to Boston*, p. 23.

21. Klinkowströms, *America*, p. 69; Ashe, *Travels*, p. 29; *Men and Manners in America*, pp. 70–71; manuscript wine book of R. F. W. Allston, South Carolina Historical Society, Charleston; Hone, *Diary*, 1:208.

22. Hall, *Aristocratic Journey*, p. 89; *Men and Manners in America*, pp. 70–71; Hone, *Diary*, 1:107; Marryat, *Diary*, p. 382; Bunn, *Old England*, p. 258; McAllister, *Society*, pp. 268–74.

23. C. C. Robin, *Voyage to Louisiana*, trans. Stuart O. Landry, Jr. (New Orleans, 1966), p. 43; Timothy Flint, *Recollections of the Last Ten Years* (Boston, 1826), p. 336; Francis and Theresa Pulszky, *White, Red, and Black* (New York, 1853), 2:95; [Candler], *A Summary View of America*, p. 78; Martineau, *Society in America*, pp. 306–307.

24. Jones, *America and French Culture*, p. 309n.; Marryat, *Diary*, pp. 381–82; Hall, *Aristocratic Journey*, p. 89; Maury, *Englishwoman in America*, p. 197; Nichols, *Forty Years*, 1:401.

25. Marryat, *Diary*, pp. 381–82; Mackay, *Western World*, 1:85.

26. Bunn, *Old England*, 1:279–80; D. R. Hundley, *Social Relations in Our Southern States* (New York, 1860), p. 227.

27. Leon D. Adams, *The Wines of America* (Boston, 1973), pp. 20–21, 74–75; Peyton, *Over the Alleghanies*, p. 78; Nichols, *Forty Years*, 1:154–57.

28. Vincent P. Carosso, *The California Wine Industry* (Berkeley, 1951), pp. 7–12, 16.

29. J. George Frederick, *Pennsylvania Dutch Cook Book* (New York, 1971), pp. 172–73; Haskell, *Housekeeper's Encyclopedia*, pp. 272–78.

30. Gerald Carson, *The Social History of Bourbon* (New York, 1963), p. 10; Roueché, *Neutral Spirit*, p. 38.

31. Bogart, *Peacham*, p. 208; Crawford, *Social Life*, p. 258; Hunt, *Life in America*, p. 171; Hall, *Travels*, p. 38; Robin, *Voyage to Louisiana*, p. 43; J. Carlyle Sitterson, *Sugar Country: The Cane Sugar Industry in the South, 1753–1950* (n.p., 1953), p. 11.

32. Younger, *Gods, Men, and Wine*, p. 417; Bogart, *Peacham*, p. 209.

33. Carson, *Bourbon*, pp. 36, 49.

34. William Cooper Howells, *Recollections of Life in Ohio from 1813 to 1840*, ed. William Dean Howells (Cincinnati, 1895), p. 125.

Notes

35. Haswell, *Reminiscences*, p. 59; Hall, *Travels*, p. 38; Bernhard, *Travels*, 1:65; 2:128; Trollope, *Domestic Manners*, pp. 116, 241; Albert A. Fossier, *New Orleans: The Glamour Period, 1800–1840* (New Orleans, 1957), p. 391; Collon Morton to Alpheus Longley, Princeton, Ill., October 25, 1842, Chicago Historical Society.
36. Ernst, *Immigrant Life*, p. 37; Russell, *Diary*, p. 158; Hundley, *Social Relations*, p. 227.
37. *Ibid.*, pp. 228–29; Wright, *Hawkers and Walkers*, p. 248.
38. Volney, *Climate and Soil of the United States*, p. 288; Flint, *Letters from America*, p. 54; Wright and Corbett, *Pioneer Life*, pp. 60–61.
39. Latrobe, *Journal*, p. 40; Richard Barksdale Harwell, *The Mint Julep* (Charlottesville, [1975]), pp. 4–5; Lyle Saxon, *Old Louisiana* (New York, 1929), p. 119; Haswell, *Reminiscences*, p. 59.
40. Trollope, *Domestic Manners*, p. 329n.
41. Marryat, *Diary*, pp. 386–87; Yoder, *Taverns and Travelers*, p. 128.
42. Marryat, *Diary*, p. 59; Lady Emmeline Stuart Wortley, *Travels in the United States* (New York, 1851), p. 39.
43. Leslie, *New Cookery Book*, pp. 609–10; Weld, *Travels*, p. 300; Grattan, *Civilized America*, 1:62; Alexander, *Transatlantic Sketches*, p. 368; Russell, *Diary*, p. 210; Jerry Thomas, *The Bar-Tenders' Guide . . .* (New York, 1862), p. 4; Clay-Clopton, *Belle of the Fifties*, p. 42.
44. *A Dictionary of Americanisms*, s.v. "cocktails;" Mencken, *American Language*, Supplement 1, pp. 256–57; Alexander, *Transatlantic Sketches*, pp. 243, 278, 368; Bunn, *Old England*, 1:108, *Dictionary of American English*, s.v. "ale-cocktail"; Thomas, *Bar-Tenders' Guide*, p. 49.
45. Haswell, *Reminiscences*, p. 379.
46. Marryat, *Diary*, p. 388.
47. William Henry Milburn, *Ten Years of Preacher-Life* (New York, 1859), p. 237; Nichols, *Forty Years*, 1:195–96; Fossier, *New Orleans*, p. 391.
48. Haswell, *Reminiscences*, p. 235; Peyton, *Over the Alleghanies*, p. 35; Alexander, *Transatlantic Sketches*, p. 278; Mackay, *Life and Liberty*, p. 109; John Lambert, *Travels through Canada and the United States of North America in the Years 1806, 1807, and 1808* (London, 1814), 2:299–300; Henry Bradshaw Fearon, *Sketches of America* (London, 1818), p. 252; Marryat, *Diary*, pp. 389–90.

Chapter 10: Dining Out, 1800–1860

1. Krout and Fox, *Completion of Independence*, pp. 90–91; Lloyd Morris, *Incredible New York* (New York, 1951), p. 4.
2. Williamson, *American Hotel*, p. 197.
3. Lewis, *Across the Atlantic*, pp. 98–99.
4. Nichols, *Forty Years*, 1:400–401.
5. Thomas, *Delmonico's*, pp. 59–60; William Chambers, *Things as They Are in America* (London, 1854), p. 189.

6. Mackay, *Life and Liberty*, p. 31; Jones, *America and French Culture*, pp. 308 – 309; Nichols, *Forty Years*, 2:11 – 12; menu from the Parker House, Boston, January 4, 1858, New York Public Library; *Men and Manners in America*, p. 348; Tallant, *New Orleanians*, pp. 98 – 100.

7. Menus from: Lake House, Chicago, June 11, 1854; Congress Hall, Saratoga Springs, September 8, 1856; International House, Niagara Falls, June 17, 1857; Parker House, Boston, January 4, 1858, New York Public Library.

8. Bunn, *Old England*, pp. 38 – 39.

9. Bishop, *Englishwoman in America*, p. 353; Bromley, *A Woman's Wanderings*, p. 73; William Hancock, *An Emigrant's Five Years in the Free States of America* (London, 1860), p. 77.

10. Thomas, *Delmonico's*, pp. 8 – 9, 12, 14; Marryat, *Diary*, p. 376n.; Ernst, *Immigrant Life*, p. 88.

11. Haswell, *Reminiscences*, pp. 53, 388; Ernst, *Immigrant Life*, pp. 88 – 89; Meryle R. Evans, "Knickerbocker Hotels and Restaurants 1800 – 1850," *New-York Historical Society Quarterly*, 36 (October 1952): 398, 402.

12. Clay-Clopton, *Belle of the Fifties*, p. 31; Grace King, *New Orleans: The Place and the People* (New York, 1895), p. 292; *Men and Manners in America*, pp. 348 – 49.

13. Hall, *Travels*, 1:31 – 32.

14. Michael and Ariane Batterberry, *On the Town in New York from 1776 to the Present* (New York, 1973), p. 98; Marryat, *Diary*, p. 422.

15. Bunn, *Old England*, p. 53; Bishop, *Englishwoman in America*, pp. 352 – 53.

16. Evans, "Knickerbocker Hotels," p. 400; Nichols, *Forty Years*, 1:268 – 70; James Boardman, *America, and The Americans* (London, 1833), pp. 87 – 88; Weld, *Travels*, p. 142.

17. Hall, *Travels*, p. 38; Nichols, *Forty Years*, 2:11 – 12.

18. Alexander, *Transatlantic Sketches*, p. 269.

19. *Men and Manners in America*, p. 297; W. E. Baxter, *America and the Americans* (London, 1855), pp. 92 – 93; Bromley, *A Woman's Wanderings*, p. 39.

20. Flint, *Letters from America*, pp. 135 – 36; Marryat, *Diary*, p. 377.

21. Yoder, *Taverns and Travelers*, p. 135.

22. Bishop, *Englishwoman in America*, p. 144.

23. Marryat, *Diary*, pp. 215, 380; Dick, *Dixie Frontier*, p. 214; Peyton, *Over the Alleghanies*, p. 124; Frederick Law Olmsted, *A Journey through Texas. . . .* (New York, 1857), p. 15.

24. Yoder, *Taverns and Travelers*, pp. 138 – 39; Milburn, *Preacher-Life*, p. 193.

25. James R. Creecy, *Scenes in the South* (Philadelphia, 1860), pp. 90 – 91.

26. Nichols, *Forty Years*, 1:119; Dunbar, *Travel in America*, pp. 854, 858 – 59, 862, 870; Alvin F. Harlow, *Old Towpaths* (Port Washington, N.Y., 1964), p. 345.

27. Benjamin Henry Latrobe, *Impressions Respecting New Orleans: Diary and Sketches, 1818 – 1820*, ed. Samuel Wilson, Jr. (New York, 1951), p. 174.

28. Milburn, *Preacher-Life*, p. 192.

29. Tallant, *New Orleanians*, pp. 268 – 69.

30. Hall, *Aristocratic Journey*, p. 35.
31. Peyton, *Over the Alleghanies*, p. 43; menus in Hunter, *Steamboats on Western Rivers*, pp. 400–401; Miriam Davis Colt, *Went to Kansas* (Watertown, N.Y., 1862), pp. 33–34; Nichols, *Forty Years*, 1:117; 2:4; Alexander, *Transatlantic Sketches*, p. 243.
32. Hunter, *Steamboats on Western Rivers*, pp. 400, 402.
33. *Ibid.*, pp. 424–25.
34. Marryat, *Diary*, p. 360; Russell, *Diary*, p. 16.
35. C. C. Andrews, *Minnesota and Dacotah*, 4th ed. (Washington, 1857), pp. 21–22.

Chapter 11: Parties, Frolics, Bees, and Celebrations, 1800–1860

1. Evans, "Knickerbocker Hotels," pp. 381–82.
2. Hunt, *Life in America*, pp. 222–23.
3. Pierson, *Tocqueville and Beaumont*, p. 364.
4. Bremer, *Homes of the New World*, 1:100.
5. Henry Barnard, "The South Atlantic States in 1833, As Seen By a New Englander," ed. Bernard C. Steiner, *Maryland Historical Magazine* 13 (December 1918): 317–18; Ashe, *Travels*, p. 316.
6. Bernard, *Travels*, 1:64.
7. Saxon, *Old Louisiana*, pp. 148–49.
8. Beirne, *Amiable Baltimoreans*, pp. 342–43.
9. Hone, *Diary*, 1:8; Grattan, *Civilized America*, 1:106–107 discusses the use of hired cooks for parties.
10. Morris, *Incredible New York*, p. 28.
11. Hone, *Diary*, 2:27–28.
12. Trollope, *Domestic Manners*, p. 59.
13. Mrs. Roger A. Pryor, *My Day: Reminiscences of a Long Life* (New York, 1909), p. 55; Johnson, *Ante-Bellum North Carolina*, pp. 160–61; F. A. Buell to father, Jacksonville, Florida, December 27, 1855, manuscript letter collection of Richard J. Hooker.
14. Singleton, *Social New York*, pp. 350–51.
15. Earle, *Stage-Coach and Tavern Days*, p. 90.
16. Bunn, *Old England*, pp. 24–27.
17. Mackay, *Western World*, 1:242; Bremer, *Homes of the New World*, 1:273–74; Earle, *Stage-Coach and Tavern Days*, pp. 90–91; Trollope, *Domestic Manners*, p. 177.
18. Lanman, *Adventures in the Wilds*, 1:256–58.
19. [Salomon de Rothschild], *A Casual View of America: The Home Letters of Salomon de Rothschild 1859–1861*, trans, and ed. Sigmund Diamond (Stanford, Calif., 1961), p. 70 and n.
20. Hooker, *Book of Chowder*, p. 6.
21. *Dictionary of American English*, s.v. "chowder."

22. Howells, *Recollections*, pp. 148–51; Dick, *Dixie Frontier*, pp. 128–29; Johnson, *Ante-Bellum North Carolina*, p. 92.

23. John W. Blassingame, *The Slave Community: Plantation Life in the Antebellum South* (New York, 1972), p. 52.

24. Lanman, *Adventures in the Wilds*, 1:276–79.

25. Woods, *Two Years' Residence*, p. 213; Nichols, *Forty Years*, 1:27; Johnson, *Ante-Bellum North Carolina*, p. 92; Earnest Elmo Calkins, *They Broke the Prairie* (New York, 1937), p. 96; Dick, *Dixie Frontier*, pp. 128–30; Mackie, *From Cape Cod to Dixie*, p. 411; Fletcher, *Pennsylvania Agriculture*, p. 444.

26. Duncan, *America As I Found It*, p. 161; Henry Bradshaw Fearon, *Sketches of America* (London, 1819), p. 223.

27. Nichols, *Forty Years*, 1:28.

28. Lanman, *Adventures in the Wilds*, 1:226–27.

29. Haswell, *Reminiscences*, pp. 69–70.

30. Fletcher, *Pennsylvania Agriculture*, p. 449.

31. Johnson, *Ante-Bellum North Carolina*, pp. 91–92, 93.

32. Robin, *Voyage to Louisiana*, p. 115.

33. Smith, *First Forty Years*, p. 1; Leslie, *New Cookery Book*, p. 521; *The Housekeeper's Book* (Philadelphia, 1837), p. 140; Child, *Frugal Housewife*, p. 72; Bernhard, *Travels*, p. 51.

34. R. Carlyle Buley, *The Old Northwest: Pioneer Period 1815–1840* (Indianapolis, 1950), 1:330–31, 332.

35. Transcript of the diary of John Hamilton Cornish, December 23, 1843, 5:189, Southern Historical Collection, University of North Carolina, Chapel Hill.

36. Harriet Beecher Stowe, *Oldtown Folks* (Boston, 1894), p. 337; Imogene Wolcott, *The Yankee Cook Book* (New York, 1963), p. 252.

37. Clay-Clopton, *Belle of the Fifties*, p. 217; Livermore, *Story of My Life*, p. 80; Wortley, *Travels*, p. 39.

38. Marryat, *Diary*, pp. 58–59.

39. Weld, *Travels*, p. 111.

40. *Men and Manners in America*, p. 15; see also Rev. Isaac Fidler, *Observations on Professions, Literature, Manners, and Emigration in the United States and Canada* (New York, 1833), p. 85; Leslie, *New Cookery Book*, p. 605; Mrs. John King Van Rensselaer, *The Social Ladder* (New York, 1924), pp. 43–44.

41. [Rothschild], *Casual View of America*, p. 87.

42. Harnett T. Kane, *The Southern Christmas Book* (New York, 1958), pp. 47–48, 121, 152, 155, 177; Bremer, *Homes of the New World*, 2:201; Julia Cooley Altrocchi, *The Spectacular San Franciscans* (New York, 1949), p. 97.

43. Livermore, *Story of My Life*, p. 77.

44. Klees, *Pennsylvania Dutch*, pp. 418–23.

45. Wilson, *Food and Drink in Britain*, pp. 136–37; Leslie, *New Cookery Book*, pp. 276–77.

46. Diary of John Hamilton Cornish, 5:189.

47. F. Garvin Davenport, *Ante-Bellum Kentucky: A Social History, 1800–1860* (Oxford, Ohio, 1943), p. 29.

48. Blassingame, *Slave Community*, pp. 42–43.

49. Bremer, *Homes of the New World,* 1:112.

50. Ulysses Prentiss Hedrick, *A History of Agriculture in the State of New York* (New York, [1966]), p. 217.

51. Bremer, *Homes of the New World,* 1:112 – 13.

52. Stowe, *Oldtown Folks,* pp. 337 – 41; Edward Everett Hale, "How Dear to My Heart," in Barrows Mussey, ed., *Yankee Life by Those Who Lived It* (New York, 1947), p. 38.

Chapter 12: The Regions, 1800 – 1860

1. Mackie, *From Cape Cod to Dixie,* p. 411.

2. Mary J. Lincoln, *Mrs. Lincoln's Cook Book* (Boston, 1896), pp. 284 – 85, 287 – 88; Leslie, *New Cookery Book,* p. 229.

3. Stowe, *Oldtown Folks,* p. 265.

4. Dwight, *Travels in New England,* 1:377.

5. Alcott, *Young Housekeeper,* pp. 137 – 39; Dwight, *Travels in New England,* 1:377.

6. Frederick, *Pennsylvania Dutch Cook Book,* p. 6.

7. *Ibid.,* pp. 9, 37, 63, 105, 119, 129, 169, 173 – 74; Klees, *Pennsylvania Dutch,* p. 415; Jesse Leonard Rosenberger, *The Pennsylvania Germans* (Chicago, [1923]), pp. 50, 59.

8. Johannes Schweizer in Billigmeier and Picard, *The Old Land,* pp. 104, 113; Elizabeth H. Lea, *Domestic Cookery,* 3d ed. (Baltimore, 1859), pp. 182 – 83; Klees, *Pennsylvania Dutch,* pp. 428 – 29.

9. Frederick, *Pennsylvania Dutch Cook Book,* pp. 105, 149; Klees, *Pennsylvania Dutch,* pp. 426 – 27.

10. Mrs. Johannes Schweizer to her parents, in Billigmeier and Picard, *The Old Land,* p. 157.

11. Diary of John Hamilton Cornish, 5:54.

12. Vance, *Human Geography,* p. 414.

13. Lanman, *Adventures in the Wilds,* 2:136 – 37.

14. Oliver Wendell Holmes, *The Professor at the Breakfast-Table* (Boston, 1892), p. 84.

15. Celestine Eustis, *Cookery in the Old Creole Days* (New York, 1904), p. 24; Annie E. Dennis, *The New Annie Dennis Cook Book* (Atlanta, 1905), pp. 82, 117; *Knoxville Cook Book* (Knoxville, 1907), pp. 71, 74, 158.

16. McAllister, *Society As I Have Found It,* p. 261.

17. E. N. Noland to Ella Mackenzie, Glen Ora, Middleburg, Va., November 14, 1849, Ella Noland Mackenzie Papers, University of North Carolina, Chapel Hill.

18. Robert Malloy, *Charleston* (New York, 1947), pp. 252 – 53; Robert Wilson, *Half Forgotten By-Ways* (Columbia, S.C., 1928), p. 151; cookbook, c. 1840, Gibbes-McGilchrist Collection, South Carolina Historical Society, Charleston.

19. [Rutledge], *Carolina Housewife,* p. v.

20. Mackay, *Life and Liberty,* p. 204; [Rutledge], *Carolina Housewife,* pp.

99, 101–102, 117, 128, 161; Mary Boykin Chesnut, *A Diary from Dixie*, ed. Ben Ames Williams (Cambridge, Mass., 1980), p. 229.

21. McAllister, *Society As I Have Found It*, pp. 260–61, 312, 314; Chesnut, *Diary from Dixie*, p. 226.

22. Weld, *Travels*, p. 142; Lanman, *Adventures in the Wilds*, 1:100; [Candler], *Summary View of America*, p. 79.

23. Frances Anne Kemble, *Journal of a Residence on a Georgian Plantation in 1838–1839* (New York, 1863), p. 20.

24. Dick, *Dixie Frontier*, pp. 287–88; Gray, *History of Agriculture*, p. 867.

25. Dick, *Dixie Frontier*, p. 291.

26. *Ibid.*, p. 127. See also Jesse E. Harbison, "Food and Drink in Kentucky and Tennessee 1780–1820," M.A. thesis, Roosevelt University, 1966.

27. Creecy, *Scenes in the South*, p. 106.

28. Tryon, *Household Manufactures*, pp. 218–21; Alexander, *Transatlantic Sketches*, p. 260; Calkins, *They Broke the Prairie*, pp. 94–95.

29. Hundley, *Social Relations*, pp. 86–87; Mackay, *Western World*, 1:259–60.

30. Mackie, *From Cape Cod to Dixie*, p. 165.

31. Robin, *Voyage to Louisiana*, p. 112; *Louisiana, A Guide to the State*, comp. workers of the Writer's Program of the Works Projects Administration, American Guide Series (New York, 1941), p. 227.

32. Robin, *Voyage to Louisiana*, pp. 44, 112.

33. Russell, *Diary*, p. 149.

34. Tallant, *New Orleanians*, p. 98; Harnett T. Kane, *Queen New Orleans* (New York, 1949), pp. 305–17; Latrobe, *Impressions*, p. 84; *Men and Manners in America*, p. 349; Latrobe, *Journal*, p. 162.

35. Doddridge, *Settlement of the Western Country*, p. 10; Ashe, *Travels*, p. 29; Trollope, *Domestic Manners*, pp. 60–61.

36. Logan Esarey, *The Indiana Home* (Crawfordsville, Ind., 1947), pp. 33–35, 37, 64, 66; Eliza W. Farnham, *Life in Prairie Land* (New York, 1846), pp. 332–33.

37. Marryat, *Diary*, p. 107; Calkins, *They Broke the Prairie*, p. 96; Cole, *Stagecoach and Tavern Tales*, p. 218.

38. Collon Morton to Alpheus Longley, Princeton, Ill., October 25, 1842, Chicago Historical Society. All punctuation supplied by the author.

39. Bremer, *America of the Fifties*, p. 218; Handlin, *This Was America*, pp. 206–207.

40. Lanman, *Adventures in the Wilds*, 1:185–86.

41. Vance, *Human Geography*, pp. 416–17; U. B. Phillips, *American Negro Slavery* (New York, 1952), pp. 239–40, 265; Dick, *Dixie Frontier*, p. 83; Gray, *History of Agriculture*, 2:836; Frederick Law Olmsted, *A Journey in the Seaboard Slave States* (New York, 1856), p. 432; Guion Griffis Johnson, *A Social History of the Sea Islands* (Chapel Hill, 1930), pp. 135–36; Robert Howard Taylor, *Slaveholding in North Carolina: An Economic View*, James Sprunt Historical Publications, 18, nos. 1–2 (Chapel Hill, 1926), p. 89.

42. F. A. Michaux, 1802, in Handlin, *This Was America*, p. 122; Olmsted, *Seaboard Slave States*, p. 432; Bremer, *America in the Fifties*, pp. 107–108;

William Dosite Postell, *The Health of Slaves on Southern Plantations* (Baton Rouge, 1951), p. 32; B.A. Botkin, ed., *Lay My Burden Down: A Folk History of Slavery* (Chicago, 1945), p. 71.

43. *Ibid.*, pp. 61, 160.
44. Postell, *Health of the Slaves*, pp. 34–35.
45. Eugene D. Genovese, *Roll, Jordan, Roll: The World the Slaves Made* (New York, 1974), p. 62.
46. Hilliard, *Hog Meat and Hoecake*, pp. 182–83; Bremer, *Homes of the New World*, 1:297; Pulszky and Pulszky, *White, Red, and Black*, 2:104; De Bow, *Industrial Resources*, 2:331.
47. Kemble, *Journal of a Residence*, p. 20.
48. Russell, *Diary*, p. 132; Botkin, *Lay My Burden Down*, pp. 53, 84, 90; West Chapman, quoted in Writer's Project, Louisiana, *Gumbo Ya-Ya*, Lyle Saxon and Edward Dryer, comps., (Boston, 1945) pp. 238–39; Genovese, *Roll, Jordan, Roll*, pp. 546–47.
49. Botkin, *Lay My Burden Down*, pp. 25, 26, 90. Genovese, *Roll, Jordan, Roll*, p. 620, points out the slave logic that distinguished between stealing and "taking" from their masters and shows how the same argument appeared in Brazil and other places where slavery existed. Olmsted, *Cotton Kingdom*, p. 106, states a similar idea.
50. Eliza Ripley, *Social Life in Old New Orleans* (New York, 1912), p. 194; Botkin, *Lay My Burden Down*, pp. 144–45; Taylor, *Slaveholding in North Carolina*, p. 90; Phillips, *American Negro Slavery*, pp. 238–39, 503; Clay-Clopton, *Belle of the Fifties*, p. 217; diary of John Hamilton Cornish, December 26, 1839.
51. Botkin, *Lay My Burden Down*, pp. 10, 121.

Chapter 13: The West, 1830–1865

1. George Frederick Augustus Ruxton, *Life in the Far West*, ed. Le Roy R. Hafen (Norman, Okla., 1951), p. 267; Hiram Martin Chittenden, *The American Fur Trade of the Far West* (New York, 1936), 2:801–802; Josiah Gregg, *Commerce of the Prairies*, ed. Max L. Moorhead (Norman, Okla., 1954), p. 237; Horace Greeley, *An Overland Journey from New York to San Francisco in the Summer of 1859* (New York, 1860), p. 170.
2. Chittenden, *American Fur Trade*, 2:801, 805; E. Douglas Branch, *The Hunting of the Buffalo* (New York, 1929), p. 110.
3. George Frederick Augustus Ruxton, *Adventures in Mexico and the Rocky Mountains* (London, 1847), pp. 267–68; Albert D. Richardson, *Beyond the Mississippi: From the Great River to the Great Ocean* (New York, 1867), p. 175; Chittenden, *American Fur Trade*, 2:802; Colt, *Went to Kansas*, p. 125; Rudolph Friederick Kurz, *Journal of Rudolph Friederick Kurz*, ed. J. M. B. Hewitt, Bureau of American Ethnology Bulletin 115 (Washington, 1937), pp. 242–43.
4. Chittenden, *American Fur Trade*, 2:816–17; F. A. Root and W. E. Con-

nelley, *The Overland Stage to California, Personal Reminiscences and Authentic History of the Great Overland Stage Line*. . . . (Topeka, 1901), p. 85; Greeley, *Overland Journey*, pp. 102, 170–71; Thaddeus A. Culbertson, *Journal of an Expedition to the Mauvaises Terres and the Upper Missouri in 1850 by Thaddeus A. Culbertson*, ed. John Francis McDermott, Bureau of American Ethnology Bulletin 147 (Washington, 1952), p. 94.

5. Chittenden, *American Fur Trade*, 2:810–11, 818; Stanley Vestal, *The Missouri* (New York, 1945), p. 74; Franklin Langworthy, *Scenery of the Plains, Mountains and Mines* (Ogdensburgh, N.Y., 1855), p. 106; Evan Jefferson Jenkins, *The Northern Tier; or Life among the Homestead Settlers* (Topeka, 1880), p. 46; Alexander Majors, *Seventy Years on the Frontier* (Chicago, 1893), pp. 201, 227; [P. A. Tabeau], *Tabeau's Narrative of Loisel's Expedition to the Upper Missouri*, ed. A. H. Abel (Norman, Okla., 1939), p. 82; James, *Expedition from Pittsburgh*, 1:102; Washington Irving, *The Western Journals of Washington Irving*, ed. John Francis McDermott (Norman, Okla., 1944), p. 149.

6. Chittenden, *American Fur Trade*, 2:820, 823, 827; Solomon Nunes Carvalho, *Incidents of Travel and Adventure in the Far West*, ed. Bertram Wallace Korn (Philadelphia, 1954), p. 191; Greeley, *Overland Journey*, p. 171; Kurz, *Journal*, p. 72.

7. Richardson, *Beyond the Mississippi*, p. 171; Culbertson, *Journal*, p. 59; Irene D. Paden, *The Wake of the Prairie Schooner* (New York, 1943), p. 89.

8. [Tabeau], *Tabeau's Narrative*, p. 88; Chittenden, *American Fur Trade*, 2:824; Robinson, *Kansas*, p. 206; William Ransom Hogan, *The Texas Republic: A Social and Economic History* (Norman, Okla., 1947), p. 33; Dick, *Sod House Frontier*, pp. 60, 272–73; Root and Connelley, *Overland Stage*, p. 85; Elizabeth B. Custer, *Boots and Saddles or Life in Dakota with General Custer* (New York, 1885), pp. 37–38; Jenkins, *Northern Tier*, pp. 68–75.

9. [Tabeau], *Tabeau's Narrative*, p. 9; Custer, *Boots and Saddles*, p. 82; Hogan, *Texas Republic*, p. 33; Everett Dick, *Vanguards of the Frontier* (New York, 1941), p. 201.

10. [Tabeau], *Tabeau's Narrative*, pp. 93–94, 96–97, 98; Mollie Dorsey Sanford, *Mollie: The Journal of Mollie Dorsey Sanford in Nebraska and Colorado Territories, 1857–1866*, ed. Donald F. Danker, (Lincoln, Nebr., 1959), pp. 44, 51; Chittenden, *American Fur Trade*, 2:796–97; H. M. Brackenridge, *Journal of a Voyage up the River Missouri; Performed in Eighteen Hundred and Eleven* (Baltimore, 1816), pp. 116–17, 140; Colt, *Went to Kansas*, p. 66; Mari Sandoz, *Love Song to the Plains* (New York, 1961), pp. 59, 66–67; Paden, *Wake of the Prairie Schooner*, p. 269.

11. Chittenden, *American Fur Trade*, 2:828; Irving, *Western Journals*, p. 92.

12. Dick, *Vanguards*, pp. 190–91, 192, 201.

13. Gregg, *Commerce*, p. 39.

14. Susan Magoffin, *Down the Santa Fe Trail* (New Haven, 1926), pp. 43, 56, 75, 89, 93–94, 107, 135, 164–65, 208–209.

15. Manuel Gamil, *Mexican Immigration to the United States* (New York, 1969), pp. 140–42.

16. Carolyn Niethammer, *American Indian Food and Lore* (New York, 1974), pp. xix–xxi; Paul Horgan, *The Heroic Triad* (New York, 1954), pp. 62–63, 127–28.

Notes

17. Hogan, *Texas Republic*, pp. 31—35, 38; Amelia A. Barr, "Housekeeping in Texas," *Here and There in Our Own Country* (Philadelphia, [1885]), p. 182; [John Marvin Hunter], *Cooking Recipes of the Pioneers* (Bandera, Tex., 1948), pp. 8—9.

18. Olmsted, *Journey through Texas*, pp. 15, 60—62, 112; Olmsted, *Cotton Kingdom*, 1:369.

19. *Ibid.*, 1:361; Vance, *Human Geography*, p. 415; Barr, "Housekeeping in Texas," p. 182.

20. Hogan, *Texas Republic*, pp. 40—41.

21. Dick, *Vanguards*, pp. 212—27.

22. *Ibid.*, pp. 235, 236.

23. Lorenzo Sawyer, *Way Sketches containing Incidents of Travel Across the Plains*. . . . (New York, 1926), p. 108.

24. Randolph B. Marcy, *The Prairie Traveler: A Hand-Book for Overland Expeditions* (New York, 1859), p. 33; George R. Stewart, *The California Trail* (New York, 1962), p. 120; Sawyer, *Way Sketches*, p. 108; Dee Brown, *The Gentle Tamers: Women of the Old West* (London, 1973), p. 113.

25. Stewart, *California Trail*, p. 121.

26. Adrietta Applegate Hixon, *On to Oregon* (Fairfield, Wash., 1971), p. 21.

27. Clyman's journal, quoted in Paden, *Wake of the Prairie Schooner*, p. 45; Brown, *Gentle Tamers*, pp. 104—105.

28. R. B. Marcy, *Marcy and the Gold Seekers: The Journal of Captain R. B. Marcy*, ed. Grant Foreman (Norman, Okla., 1939), p. 57.

29. Paden, *Wake of the Prairie Schooner*, pp. 462 ff.

30. Dick, *Sod House Frontier*, pp. 102—107; Brown, *Gentle Tamers*, p. 125.

31. Richard F. Burton, *The City of the Saints, and Across the Rocky Mountains to California* (New York, 1862), p. 24.

32. Greeley, *Overland Journey*, p. 74.

33. Glen Chesney Quiett, *Pay Dirt: A Panorama of American Gold-Rushes* (New York, 1936), p. 33; Paden, *Wake of the Prairie Schooner*, p. 299.

34. Walter Colton, *Three Years in California* (New York, 1850), p. 40; Ana Bégué Packman, *Early California Hospitality* (Glendale, Calif., 1938), p. 13.

35. Paden, *Wake of the Prairie Schooner*, p. 474; Bayard Taylor, *Eldorado: Or, Adventures in the Path of Empire*, 2d ed. (New York, 1850), 1:116.

36. Paden, *Wake of the Prairie Schooner*, p. 474; Quiett, *Pay Dirt*, p. 79.

37. Brown, *Gentle Tamers*, p. 194.

38. Joseph Goldsborough Bruff, *Gold Rush* (New York, 1944), p. 466.

39. Taylor, *Eldorado*, 1:222.

40. Bruff, *Gold Rush*, pp. 460, 470.

41. Quiett, *Pay Dirt*, p. 66.

42. Taylor, *Eldorado*, 1:113, 116—17; Altrocchi, *Spectacular San Franciscans*, p. 44.

43. Bruff, *Gold Rush*, p. 469.

44. Altrocchi, *Spectacular San Franciscans*, pp. 24, 28, 40, 48, 77, 88, 116, 126—27.

45. Harris Newmark, *Sixty Years in Southern California*, ed. Maurice H.

Newmark and Marco R. Newmark, 3d ed., rev. (Boston, 1930), pp. 24–25, 133, 134, 216, 247, 363, 370.

46. Sidney Warren, *Farthest Frontier: The Pacific Northwest* (New York, 1949), p. 61; Edward Henry Lenox, *Overland to Oregon* (Fairfield, Wash., 1970), p. 59.

47. Hixon, *On to Oregon*, p. 21.

48. Margaret Griffin, "Pioneer Life in the Pacific Northwest," typescript in the Eastern Washington State Historical Society, Spokane.

49. Brown, *Gentle Tamers*, p. 196.

50. Carl Coke Rister, *Southern Plainsmen* (Norman, Okla., 1938), p. 76; Mrs. Orpen, *Memories of the Old Emigrant Days in Kansas, 1862–1865* (Edinburgh, 1926), p. 74; Edna Florig, "Food and Drink in Four Great Plains States to 1890," M.A. thesis, Roosevelt University, 1965, pp. 34–37.

51. Colt, *Went to Kansas*, p. 49.

52. Lela Barnes, ed., "Letters of Cyrus Kurtz Holliday, 1854–1859," *Kansas Historical Quarterly* 6 (August 1937): 246.

53. Dick, *Sod House Frontier*, p. 364.

54. Sanford, *Mollie*, p. 36.

55. Sandoz, *Love Song*, p. 157.

56. Greeley, *Overland Journey*, pp. 164–65.

57. Richardson, *Beyond the Mississippi*, pp. 27, 106, 147.

58. Dick, *Sod House Frontier*, p. 379.

59. J. H. Beadle, *The Undeveloped West: Or, Five Years in the Territories.* . . . (Philadelphia, 1873), p. 713.

60. Root and Connelley, *Overland Stage*, p. 417.

61. Dick, *Sod House Frontier*, p. 63.

Chapter 14: The Civil War, 1861–1865

1. Mary Elizabeth Massey, "The Food and Drink Shortage on the Confederate Homefront," *North Carolina Historical Review* 26 (1949): 307.

2. Clay-Clopton, *Belle of the Fifties*, p. 168.

3. Russell, *Diary*, p. 108.

4. *Ibid.*, pp. 139, 167; Arthur M. Schlesinger, *Paths to the Present* (New York, 1949), pp. 249–50; Clay-Clopton, *Belle of the Fifties*, p. 223; Henry William Ravenel, *The Private Journal of Henry William Ravenel 1859–1887*, ed. Arney Robinson Childs (Columbia, S.C., 1947), p. 210; Ella Lonn, *Salt as a Factor in the Confederacy* (New York, 1933), pp. 14 ff.

5. Massey, "Food and Drink Shortage," pp. 318–21.

6. *Ibid.*, pp. 326–29.

7. Cited in Arthur Charles Cole, *The Irrepressible Conflict 1850–1865* (New York, 1934), p. 402.

8. Bell Irvin Wiley, *The Plain People of the Confederacy* (Baton Rouge, 1943), pp. 41, 49; Clay-Clopton, *Belle of the Fifties*, p. 194; Massey, "Food and Drink Shortage," p. 308; James Ford Rhodes, *History of the United States*, 5 (New York, 1907): 363–65.

9. Massey, "Food and Drink Shortage," pp. 313–16; Phoebe Yates Pember, *A Southern Woman's Story: Life in Confederate Richmond,* ed. Bell Irvin Wiley (Jackson, Tenn., 1959), pp. 83–84, 86.

10. *Confederate Receipt Book* (Richmond, Va., 1863; reprint ed., Athens, Ga., 1960), pp. 7–9, 13–18, 24–26.

11. Massey, "Food and Drink Shortage," pp. 321, 333.

12. *Ibid,.* pp. 309, 332; Pryor, *Reminiscences of a Long Life,* p. 204.

13. Wiley, *Plain People,* pp. 34–40.

14. Charles H. Wesley, *The Collapse of the Confederacy* (Washington, 1937), p. 15.

15. Wiley, *Plain People,* p. 90.

16. Wesley, *Collapse of the Confederacy,* pp. 10–15.

17. Bell Irvin Wiley, *The Life of Johnny Reb, the Common Soldier of the Confederacy* (Indianapolis, 1943), pp. 90–93.

18. Williams, *With the Border Ruffians,* p. 323.

19. Clay-Clopton, *Belle of the Fifties,* p. 79.

20. Wiley, *Life of Johnny Reb.* pp. 99–103; Wiley, *Plain People,* pp. 21–22.

21. Bell Irvin Wiley, *The Life of Billy Yank* (Indianapolis, 1951), pp. 127–28.

22. *Ibid.,* p. 227.

23. To Sinna from her husband, Camp Defiance, December 7, 1862, manuscript collection of Richard J. Hooker.

24. Wiley, *Life of Billy Yank,* pp. 225–27, 232–33.

25. Pierce, *History of Chicago,* 2:463–64.

26. Earl Chapin May, *The Canning Clan* (New York, 1937), pp. 177, 212–13, 224–25; Emerson David Fite, *Social and Industrial Conditions in the North during the Civil War* (New York, 1910), p. 82; John W. Oliver, *History of American Technology* (New York, 1956), p. 231; James H. Collins, *The Story of Canned Foods* (New York, 1924), pp. 16–17; Cummings, *American and His Food,* p. 67.

Chapter 15: A Changing Country, 1865–1900

1. Mary Ronald, *The Century Cook Book* (New York, 1897), p. 257.

2. H. D. Renner, *The Origin of Food Habits* (London, 1944), pp. 228–29.

3. C. C. Furnas and S. M. Furnas, *The Story of Man and His Food* (New York, 1937), pp. 33–34.

4. Ronald, *Century Cook Book,* p. 28; Fannie Merritt Farmer, *The Boston Cooking-School Cook Book* (Boston, 1906), preface.

5. Sarah T. Rorer, *Mrs. Rorer's New Cook Book* (Philadelphia, 1898), preface.

6. Ronald, *Century Cook Book,* p. ix.

7. Giedion, *Mechanization Takes Command,* pp. 516–19; Lynes, *Domesticated Americans,* pp. 133–34.

8. *Ibid.*, pp. 120–21.

9. Anderson, *Refrigeration in America*, pp. 113–14.

10. Marion Harland, *Common Sense in the Household: A Manual of Practical Housewifery* (New York, 1880), p. 9; Helen Louise Johnson, *The Enterprising Housekeeper* (Philadelphia, 1906), pp. 7–9, 60–79.

11. Ronald, *Century Cook Book*, pp. 82–83 and pictures facing pp. 92, 292, 386.

12. Lynes, *Domesticated Americans*, pp. 129–32.

13. Gerald Carson, *Cornflake Crusade* (New York, 1957), p. 67.

14. Furnas, *The Americans*, p. 900; Maria Parloa, *Miss Parloa's Young Housekeeper* (Boston, 1897), p. 209.

15. Schmidt, *Rural Hunterdon*, p. 280; Bitting, *Appertizing*, pp. 151, 159, 166, 729, 791; Cummings, *American and His Food*, p. 69.

16. Juliet Corson, *Family Living on $500 a Year* (New York, 1888), p. 46.

17. Calkins, *They Broke the Prairie*, p. 345.

18. Samuel Bowles, *Our New West.* . . . (Hartford, Conn., 1869), pp. 199–200.

19. Samuel Bowles, *Across the Continent* (Springfield, Mass., 1866), pp. 6, 21; Wayne Gard, *The Chisholm Trail* (Norman, Okla., 1954), pp. 120–21, 123–24; Beadle, *Undeveloped West*, p. 786; Bowles, *Our New West*, p. 38; Furnas, *Americans*, pp. 690–91.

20. Cummings, *American and His Food*, pp. 70–71.

21. C. C. Furnas and S. M. Furnas, *Man, Bread and Destiny: The Story of Man and His Food* (New York, 1937), pp. 274–75; George Sala, *America Revisited.* . . . (London, 1882), 1:177.

22. Sarah A. Elliott, *Mrs. Elliott's Housewife.* . . . (New York, 1870), p. v; A. P. Hill, *Mrs. Hill's New Cook Book* (New York, 1870), p. 12; *The Dixie Cook-Book*, rev. ed. (Atlanta, 1883), preface; Mary Mason, *The Young Housewife's Counsellor and Friend* (Philadelphia, 1871), preface.

23. See Emily Stevens Maclachlon, "The Diet Pattern of the South: a Study in Regional Sociology," M.A. thesis, University of North Carolina, 1932.

24. Haskell, *Housekeeper's Encyclopedia*, pp. iv–v.

25. C.W. Gesner, "Concerning Restaurants," *Harper's New Monthly Magazine*, 32 (April 1866): 591–92.

26. Harland, *Common Sense*, p. 12.

27. Sidney Andrews, *The South Since the War* (Boston, 1866), p. 182; Harland, *Common Sense*, p. 114.

28. James Remington McCarthy, *Peacock Alley: The Romance of the Waldorf-Astoria* (New York, 1931), pp. 100–101.

29. Ronald, *Century Cook Book*, p. 36.

30. Lynes, *Domesticated Americans*, pp. 182–83; Max O'Rell and Jack Allyn, *Jonathan and His Continent* (New York, 1889), p. 286.

31. Schlesinger, *Paths to the Present*, p. 243.

32. Andrews, *South Since the War*, pp. 182, 204; Hilliard, *Hog Meat and Hoecake*, p. 66.

33. William C. Lodge, "Among the Peaches," *Harper's New Monthly Magazine* 41 (September 1870): 515.

34. Thomas, *Delmonico's*, pp. 153–54.

Chapter 16: The Foods at Hand, 1865 – 1900

1. Trollope, *North America*, p. 277.
2. [Robert Tomes], *The Bazar Book of Decorum* (New York, 1870), p. 184.
3. See Clemen, *Livestock and Meat Industry*, pp. 218 – 220.
4. Allan Nevins, *The Emergence of Modern America 1865 – 1877* (New York, 1928), pp. 36 – 38; Anderson, *Refrigeration in America*, pp. 49, 51, 57, 59; Oliver, *American Technology*, pp. 385 – 86; Clemen, *Livestock and Meat Industry*, p. 220.
5. Dick, *Sod House Frontier*, pp. 275, 400; Mary Dodge Woodward, *The Checkered Years: Excerpts from the Diary of Mary Dodge Woodward written while Living on a Bonanza Farm in Dakota Territory During the Years 1884 to 1889*, ed. Mary Boynton Cowdrey (Caldwell, Idaho, 1937), p. 101; Francis Jameson Rowbotham, *A Trip to Prairie-Land being A Glance at the Shady Side of Emigration* (London, 1885), p. 220; Anna T. Lincoln manuscript, 1860, given in Theodore C. Blegen and Philip D. Jordan, *With Various Voices* (Saint Paul, Minn., 1949), p. 275.
6. Harland, *Common Sense*, p. 116.
7. Lincoln, *Boston Cook Book*, p. 245.
8. *Knoxville Cook Book*, p. 50.
9. Paul de Rousiers, *American Life* (New York, 1892), p. 314; T. S. Hudson, *Scamper Through America. . . .* (New York, 1882), p. 83; Sir John Leng, *America in 1876* (Dundee, Scotland, 1877), p. 266; Walter Gore Marshall, *Through America* (London, 1882), pp. 56 – 57.
10. James Fullarton Muirhead, *The Land of Contrasts: A Briton's View of His American Kin* (Boston, 1898), p. 268; Furnas, *Americans*, p. 693; Stewart, *American Ways*, p. 105; Leng, *America in 1876*, pp. 266 – 67; Hudson, *Scamper*, pp. 83 – 84; Tallant, *Romantic New Orleanians*, pp. 270 – 71.
11. Marshall, *Through America*, p. 40; "Concerning Restaurants," *Harper's Magazine* 32 (April 1866): 592.
12. Marshall, *Through America*, pp. 108 – 109.
13. *Ibid.*; Joseph Husband, *The Story of the Pullman Car* (Chicago, 1917), pp. 49 – 50.
14. *Dictionary of American English*, s.v. "hamburg"; *Dictionary of Americanisms*, s.v. "hamburg"; Grace Townsend, *Dining Room and Kitchen* (Chicago, 1891), p. 102.
15. George Makepeace Towle, *American Society* (London, 1870), 1:270; Marshall, *Through America*, pp. 56 – 57, 108 – 109; Husband, *Story of the Pullman Car*, pp. 49 – 50, 80; Leng, *America in 1876*, pp. 266 – 67; Muirhead, *Land of Contrasts*, p. 268; *Historical Sketch Book and Guide to New Orleans and Environs* (New York, 1885), pp. 85, 90.
16. C. M. Chase, *The Editor's Run in New Mexico and Colorado* (Montpelier, Vt., 1882), p. 215; Thomas Hughes, ed., *G. T. T. Gone to Texas* (New York, 1884), pp. 23 – 24, 26.
17. Menu of the Grand Union Hotel, 1878, Saratoga, N.Y., Buttolf Collection, New York Public Library. In B. C. Howard, *Fifty Years in a Maryland*

Kitchen (Baltimore, 1873), p. 52, the only fried chicken recipe calls for a sauce made of butter, cream, parsley, salt, and pepper. See also Frederick Philip Stieff, comp., *Eat, Drink & Be Merry in Maryland* (New York, 1932), p. 86.

18. *Wall Street Journal*, July 13, 1972, pp. 1, 33.

19. E. Catherine Bates, *A Year in the Great Republic* (London, 1887), 1:74–75; Corson, *Family Living*, p. 408; Towle, *American Society*, 1:323; F. Barham Zincke, *Last Winter in the United States* (London, 1868), pp. 8–9.

20. Russell, *Diary*, p. 88; Corson, *Family Living*, pp. 219–20, 221, 253; Harland, *Common Sense*, pp. 155, 159–60.

21. Pierce, *History of Chicago*, 2:470.

22. John Drury, *Rare and Well Done: Some Historical Notes on Meats and Meatmen* (Chicago, 1966), pp. 138–42.

23. Custer, *Boots and Saddles*, p. 71.

24. William Peirce Randel, *Centennial: American Life in 1876* (Philadelphia, 1969), p. 37; Ernest Ingersoll, "Rocky Mountain Cookery," *Scribner's* 20 (May 1880): 125–26.

25. Randel, *Centennial*, p. 56; *The Web-Foot Cook Book* (Portland, Oreg., 1885), pp. 34, 35, 45; Colonel W. F. Cody, *An Autobiography of Buffalo Bill* (New York, 1924), p. 223; W. F. Rae, *Westward by Rail* (London, 1871), p. 84; Howard Ruede, *Sod-House Days* (New York, 1937), pp. 40, 110, 111, 113, 135; Custer, *Boots and Saddles*, pp. 109, 271–73, 275.

26. Cody, *Autobiography*, p. 117.

27. Dick, *Sod House Frontier*, p. 159.

28. Zincke, *Last Winter*, pp. 81–82; Ronald, *Century Cook Book*, pp. 196–99; *New Orleans As It Is* (Cleveland, [1885]), p. 56; Harland, *Common Sense*, pp. 167–69.

29. Corson, *Family Living*, p. 221.

30. "The Game Water-Fowl of America," *Harper's* 40 (February 1870): 434.

31. *Ibid.*, p. 435; O'Rell and Allyn, *Jonathan and His Continent*, p. 62; Corson, *Family Living*, pp. 226–27.

32. Wilson, *Half Forgotten By-Ways*, p. 238; "Game Water-Fowl," pp. 435, 437.

33. Maitland Edey, "Once There Were Billions, Now There Are None," *Life*, December 22, 1961, pp. 169–76.

34. T. B. Thorpe, "A Modern Bill of Fare," *Harper's New Monthly Magazine* 41 (September 1870): 607; Joseph Hatton, *To-day in America* (London, 1881), 1:92; McCarthy, *Peacock Alley*, p. 100.

35. Howard, *Fifty Years*, pp. 17–18, 29, 48; Francis F. Beirne, *The Amiable Baltimoreans* (New York, 1951), pp. 350–51.

36. Wilson, *Half Forgotten By-Ways*, p. 226.

37. *Ibid.*, pp. 243, 254; Bitting, *Appertizing*, p. 800.

38. *New Orleans As It Is*, p. 57; *La Cuisine Creole*, 2d ed. (New Orleans, 1885), pp. 26–31; Russell, *Diary*, p. 131.

39. Helen Evans Brown, *West Coast Cook Book* (reprint ed., 1952), pp. 119, 143; Hudson, *Scamper*, p. 98.

40. *Hotel Gazette*, June 22, 1889, cited in Williamson, *American Hotel*, p. 221

41. Oysters were apparently first canned during the 1840s and sardines during the 1850s. Clams may not have been canned until the 1860s. See also Bitting, *Appertizing*, pp. 784, 791, 796, 800, 805, 817; Schmidt, *Rural Hunterdon*, p. 280; Thorpe, "A Modern Bill of Fare," pp. 606–10; May, *Canning Clan*, pp. 150–58.

42. Smith, *Virginia Cookery-Book*, p. 58; Thorpe, "A Modern Bill of Fare," pp. 606–10.

43. Oliver, *American Technology*, pp. 386–89.

44. *Ibid.*, pp. 388–89; Stowe, *House and Home Papers*, pp. 241–42.

45. Lewis Atherton, *Main Street on the Middle Border* (Bloomington, 1954), p. 46; Calkins, *They Broke the Prairies*, p. 345; Thomas C. Clark, *Pills, Petticoats and Plows* (New York, 1944), pp. 44–45; Marion Harland, *Breakfast, Luncheon and Tea* (New York, 1875), pp. 158–59; Howard, *Fifty Years*, pp. 357, 359; Haskell, *Housekeeper's Encyclopedia*, pp. 364–66; Laura Trowbridge, *Excelsior Cook Book* (New York, 1870), pp. 212–14; Ronald, *Century Cook Book*, pp. 369–70; Lea, *Domestic Cookery*, pp. 182–83; Marion Cabell Tyree, *Housekeeping in Old Virginia* (Louisville, Ky., 1879; reprint ed., Louisville, Ky., 1965), p. 68.

46. Oliver, *American Technology*, p. 389.

47. Ronald, *Century Cook Book*, p. 370.

48. Ladies of Detroit and Other Cities, *The American Home Cook Book* (Detroit and Chicago, 1878), p. 2; Cummings, *American and His Food*, pp. 43–44.

49. Lea, *Domestic Cookery*, pp. 53–54.

50. Mrs. Henry Lumkin Wilson, *Tested Recipe Cook Book* (Atlanta, 1895), p. 29.

51. Corson, *Family Living*, p. 117.

52. A. Oemler, *Truck-Farming at the South* (New York, 1900), p. 5.

53. Corson, *Family Living*, pp. 26–31; Anderson, *Refrigeration*, p. 157.

54. Oemler, *Truck-Farming*, p. 176.

55. Smith, *Virginia Cookery-Book*, p. 120; Corson, *Family Living*, pp. 127–28; Thomas, *Delmonico's*, p. 117; Bitting, *Appertizing*, p. 355.

56. Smith, *Virginia Cookery-Book*, pp. 123, 130, 269.

57. Oemler, *Truck-Farming*, pp. 163–64.

58. Sala, *America Revisited*, 1:97; Marshall, *Through America*, p. 40.

59. Townsend, *Dining Room*, p. 187; Corson, *Family Living*, p. 123; Ronald, *Century Cook Book*, pp. 45–46, 314–20; *Historical Sketch Book*, p. 87; Bitting, *Appertizing*, p. 536.

60. Randel, *Centennial*, p. 69; Dick, *Vanguards*, pp. 396, 400–401; Bitting, *Appertizing*, pp. 405–406; U.S. Department of Agriculture, Office of Experiment Stations, C. C. Woods and E. R. Mansfield, "Studies of the Food of Maine Lumbermen," *Bulletin*, 149 (1904), pp. 9, 18; J. M. Tuttle, "The Minnesota Pineries," *Harper's New Monthly Magazine* 36 (March 1868): 414.

61. Jerry Bryan, *An Illinois Gold Hunter in the Black Hills: The Diary of Jerry Bryan March 13 to August 20, 1876* (Springfield, Ill., 1960), p. 14; Chase, *Editor's Run*, p. 215; Martha Summerhayes, *Vanished Arizona* (Philadelphia, 1908), pp. 168–69.

62. Kane, *Queen New Orleans*, pp. 315, 318; *Gumbo Ya-Ya*, p. 61.

63. Olmsted, *Journey through Texas,* pp. 15–16, 60–61, 115; Smith, *Virginia Cookery-Book,* p. 135; E. R. Tennent, *House-Keeping in the Sunny South* (Atlanta, 1885), p. 79.

64. Emily Faithful, *Three Visits to America* (Edinburgh, 1884), pp. 49–50; Towle, *American Society,* 1:267; Leng, *America in 1876,* pp. 266–67; O'Rell and Allyn, *Jonathan,* p. 290; Hudson, *Scamper,* pp. 83–84; *Historical Sketch Book,* pp. 88–90; Stowe, *House and Home Papers,* p. 259.

65. Jessie Marsh Bowen, *A Chronicle of Claremont Township and Village* (Claremont, 1937), as reprinted in Blegen and Jordan, *With Various Voices,* pp. 256–57.

66. Isabella L. Bird, *A Lady's Life in the Rocky Mountains* (Norman, Okla., 1960), pp. 73, 111; Custer, *Boots and Saddles,* pp. 105, 309; Bryan, *Diary,* p. 39; Marshall, *Through America,* pp. 129–30; Dick, *Vanguards,* p. 484; Nancy Wilson Ross, *Westward the Women* (New York, 1944), pp. 179–80.

67. Rosser Howard Taylor, *Carolina Crossroads: A Study of Rural Life at the End of the Horse-and-Buggy Era* (Murfreesboro, N.C., 1966), p. 33.

68. Edward King, *The Great South* (Hartford, 1875), pp. 183–85; Custer, *Boots and Saddles,* pp. 171, 172, 305.

69. Lodge, "Among the Peaches," pp. 511–18; Anderson, *Refrigeration,* pp. 149–50, 155, 156–67.

70. Bitting, *Appertizing,* p. 304; Corson, *Family Living,* p. 162.

71. Maximilian De Loup, *The American Salad Book* (New York, 1900), p. 110.

72. Wilson, *Empire in Green,* pp. 25–28, 70–72, 82, 92, 99, 107, 170.

73. *Buckeye Cookery* (Minneapolis, 1890), p. 162; Ronald, *Century Cook Book,* p. 531; Frances Willey, *The Model Cook Book* (Philadelphia, 1890), p. 279.

74. Corson, *Family Living,* p. 171.

75. Ralph J. Roske, *Everyman's Eden: A History of California* (New York, 1968), p. 399.

76. Furnas, *Americans,* p. 707.

77. Roske, *Everyman's Eden,* pp. 400–406; Bowles, *Our New West,* p. 348; Brown, *West Coast Cook Book,* p. 197.

78. Custer, *Boots and Saddles,* p. 172; Woodward, *Checkered Years,* pp. 53, 57–58.

79. Bowles, *Our New West,* pp. 199–200; Bitting, *Appertizing,* pp. 151, 202.

80. *Ibid.,* p. 715; Bidwell and Falconer, *History of Agriculture,* p. 382; Dick, *Sod House Frontier,* pp. 85–87, 274; Schmidt, *Rural Hunterdon,* p. 123.

Chapter 17: The Winds of Change, 1865–1900

1. Harland, *Breakfast, Luncheon and Tea,* pp. 11–12.
2. W. Fraser Rae, *Columbia and Canada* (London, 1877), pp. 105–106.
3. Williamson, *American Hotel,* pp. 215–16.

4. Faithful, *Three Visits*, pp. 353–54; Williamson, *American Hotel*, pp. 214–15.

5. Altrocchi, *Spectacular San Franciscans*, p. 202; Julian Ralph, "San Francisco's Rich Fare," *Harper's Weekly* 40 (March 21, 1896): 275.

6. De Rousiers, *American Life*, p. 317.

7. Alfred L. Carroll, "On Digestion and Food," *Harper's New Monthly Magazine* 39 (November 1869): 894.

8. Ladies of Detroit, *American Home Cook Book*, p. 2; Stowe, *House and Home Papers*, p. 246.

9. Nevins, *Emergence of Modern America*, p. 46; King, *The Great South*, pp. 224–25; Helen Campbell, *Darkness and Daylight: Lights and Shadows of New York Life* (Hartford, Conn., 1896), pp. 469–70; McCarthy, *Peacock Alley*, p. 101; Atherton, *Main Street*, pp. 58–59; Russell, *Diary*, p. 34.

10. "Germany in New York," *Atlantic Monthly* 19 (May 1867): 555–56; Olmsted, *Journey through Texas*, pp. 15–16, 61, 84, 115, 144, 187, 254, 280–81.

11. Sala, *America Revisited*, 2:293–94.

12. Towle, *American Society*, 1:263–64; Campbell, *Darkness and Daylight*, p. 376; Ladies of Detroit, *American Home Cook Book*, p. 93; Sala, *America Revisited*, 2:293–94; Hill, *New Cook Book*, p. 315.

13. Janet McKenzie Hill, *Practical Cooking and Serving* (New York, 1902), p. 335; Marshall, *Through America*, pp. 108–109; Haskell, *Housekeeper's Encyclopedia*, pp. 67, 419; Corson, *Family Living*, p. 37; Howard, *Fifty Years*, p. 17; D. A. Lincoln, *Boston Cook Book* (Boston, 1888), pp. 308–309. See also Ronald, *Century Cook Book*, p. 225.

14. Brown, *Golden Nineties*, p. 383; Janet McKenzie Hill, *Salads, Sandwiches and Chafing-Dish Dainties* (Boston, 1899), p. 229. In 1886 Sarah T. Rorer wrote that "Spighetti [*sic*] is the most delicate form of macaroni that comes to this country." Sarah T. Rorer, *Mrs. Rorer's Philadelphia Cook Book* (Philadelphia, 1886), p. 358.

15. Ronald, *Century Cook Book*, pp. 401, 418, 446, 498; Ladies of Detroit, *American Home Cook Book*, pp. 295–96; De Loup, *American Salad Book*, p. 127; Howard, *Fifty Years*, pp. 191, 200.

16. McAllister, *Society As I Have Found It*, pp. 305–306.

17. Katherine Bazore, *Hawaiian and Pacific Foods* (New York, 1940), pp. xi, xxvii.

18. Maili Yardley, *Hawaii Cooks* (Rutland, Vt., 1970), pp. 10–12.

19. E. G. Myers, comp., *The Capitol Cook Book* (Austin, Tex., 1899; facsimile ed., Austin, Tex., 1966), p. 14; *The Texas "Four Hundred" (Put to Service) Cook Book*, 3d. ed. (Dallas, 1909), pp. 12–13; Julian Ralph, *Our Great West* (New York, 1893), p. 441.

20. Rorer, *Mrs. Rorer's New Cook Book*, pp. 670–79, 680–84, 691–702.

21. Ronald, *Century Cook Book*, pp. 228–49; Rorer, *Mrs. Rorer's New Cook Book*, pp. 685–90; Annie Clarke, *Mrs. Clarke's Cook Book* (Washington, 1899), pp. 41–42, 52, 130.

22. Edward Everett Dale, "The Food of the Frontier," *Journal of the Illinois State Historical Society*, XL (1947), 45; Henry T. Finck, *Food and Flavor: A*

NOTES

Gastronomic Guide to Health and Good Living (New York, 1913), pp. 457–58; Harland, *Common Sense*, p. 283.

23. Furnas, *Americans*, p. 169; Dick, *Sod House Frontier*, pp. 270–72; Olmsted, *Journey through Texas*, pp. 61, 84, 112.

24. Rae, *Columbia and Canada*, p. 105; Clarke, *Clarke's Cook Book*, p. 129; Herman Steen, *Flour Milling in America* (Westport, Conn., 1973), p. 46.

25. Rorty and Norman, *Tomorrow's Food*, pp. 59–64.

26. Towle, *American Society*, 1:271.

27. Ladies of Detroit, *American Home Cook Book*, pp. 249–50.

28. Harland, *Common Sense*, pp. 282–83.

29. T. J. Crowen, *Mrs. Crowen's American Lady's Cooking Book* (New York, 1866), pp. 329, 405; Haskell, *Housekeeper's Encyclopedia*, pp. 81–82; *Texas "Four Hundred,"* p. 19; Ladies' Auxiliary of the Y.M.C.A., *The El Paso Cook Book* (El Paso, Tex., 1898), pp. 88–89.

30. Townsend, *Dining Room*, pp. 403–404; Marshall, *Through America*, p. 40; De Rousiers, *American Life*, p. 314; Ronald, *Century Cook Book*, pp. 364–67.

31. [Milon W. Ellsworth], *The Successful Housekeeper* (Detroit, 1887), p. 39.

32. [A. Rivington and W. A. Harris], *Reminiscences of America in 1869* (London, 1870), p. 66; Lea, *Domestic Cookery*, pp. 30, 51–52; Howard, *Fifty Years*, pp. 98–100; Harland, *Breakfast, Lunch or Tea*, pp. 146–63; Tyree, *Housekeeping*, pp. 191–200; Harland, *Common Sense*, pp. 187–97; *The Ladies' Hand-Book and Household Assistant* (Claremont, N.H., 1886), pp. 39–40.

33. [Rivington and Harris], *Reminiscences*, p. 66.

34. De Loup, *American Salad Book*, p. 56.

35. Lincoln, *Boston Cook Book*, p. 310; De Loup, *American Salad Book*, pp. 10, 28; Calkins, *They Broke the Prairie*, p. 346; [Ellsworth], *Successful Housekeeper*, p. 225.

36. Corson, *Family Living*, pp. 123–29, 387–89; Ralph, *Our Great West*, p. 441.

37. C. S. Richardson and M. E. McClary, *A Collection of Tried Recipes Contributed by Various Malone Housekeepers. . . .* (Malone, N.Y., 1882), pp. 20–21; *Ladies' Handbook*, p. 40; Willey, *Model Cook Book*, pp. 145–50; Townsend, *Dining Room*, pp. 198–99; Ronald, *Century Cook Book*, pp. 374–85; The Ladies of the Presbyterian Church, Paris, Kentucky, *Housekeeping in the Blue Grass: A New and Practical Cook Book* (Cincinnati, 1878), pp. 42–43.

38. Rorer, *Mrs. Rorer's New Cook Book*, p. 439.

39. De Loup, *American Salad Book*, pp. 9, 56, 76–77, 98, 106, 110.

40. Towle, *American Society*, 1:270.

41. Corson, *Family Living*, pp. 387–89; Howland, *Economical Housekeeper*, p. 71; Cornelius, *Housekeeper's Friend*, pp. 147–51; Lea, *Domestic Cookery*, pp. 31–34; Trowbridge, *Excelsior Cook Book*, pp. 64–69.

42. Paul Bourget, *Outre-Mer* (New York, 1895), p. 210; *Historical Sketch Book*, pp. 88–89.

43. "On Digestion and Food," p. 894.

404

44. Karl Schiftgiesser, *Oscar of the Waldorf* (New York, 1943), p. 197.

45. *Historical Sketch Book*, pp. 86–91; Russell, *Diary*, pp. 131, 232; Hodding Carter, *Lower Mississippi* (New York, 1942), p. 418; *New Orleans As It Is*, p. 56.

46. Howard, *Fifty Years*, pp. 1–27; Rorer, *Mrs. Rorer's Philadelphia Cook Book*, pp. 2–36; Tyree, *Housekeeping*, pp. 69–84; Bourget, *Outre-Mer*, p. 353; Willey, *Model Cook Book*, pp. 13–24; Marshall, *Through America*, p. 40.

47. Harland, *Breakfast, Luncheon and Tea*, p. 66.

48. Towle, *American Society*, 1:269.

49. Zincke, *Last Winter*, pp. 80–81; Clarke, *Clarke's Cook Book*, p. 143.

50. Zincke, *Last Winter*, pp. 81, 228–29; Bryan, *Illinois Gold Hunter*, pp. 14, 25, 29; Dick, *Sod House Frontier*, p. 275; Hughes, *Gone to Texas*, pp. 23–24, 164, 181.

51. See "Croquettes" in Harland, *Breakfast, Luncheon and Tea*, pp. 75–77; The Ladies of the Seventh Presbyterian Church of Cincinnati, *Practical Receipts of Experienced Housekeepers*, 2d ed. (Cincinnati, 1878), p. 167.

52. *Dictionary of American English*, s.v. "hamburg"; Townsend, *Dining Room*, p. 102; Ronald, *Century Cook Book*, pp. 151–52.

53. Harland, *Breakfast, Luncheon and Tea*, pp. 86–92; Lincoln, *Mrs. Lincoln's Boston Cook Book*, pp. 242–44.

54. Ronald, *Century Cook Book*, pp. 329–37; Farmer, *Boston Cooking-School Cook Book*, pp. 464–72; Linda Hull Larned, *The Hostess of To-Day* (New York, 1907), p. 259; *Gourmet* 17 (October 1957): 18–19; Fannie Merritt Farmer, *Chafing Dish Possibilities* (Boston, 1900), p. 20.

55. Harland, *Common Sense*, pp. 371–403; Smith, *Virginia Cookery-Book*, p. 167; S. G. Knight, *Tit-Bits* (Boston, 1865), pp. 54–60; Ronald, *Century Cook Book*, pp. 429–43.

56. Sala, *America Revisited*, 1:109.

57. Lincoln, *Mrs. Lincoln's Boston Cook Book*, p. 391.

58. *Harper's Bazar* 11 (December 7, 1878): 783.

59. Mrs. F. D. Bergen in *Journal of American Folklore* 13 (January 1900): 66.

60. C. W. Gesner, "Concerning Restaurants," *Harper's New Monthly Magazine* 32 (April 1866): 591–92.

61. Anna T. Lincoln manuscript, 1860, in Blegen and Jordan, *With Various Voices*, p. 275.

62. Gard, *Chisholm Trail*, p. 124.

63. Ross, *Westward the Women*, p. 181.

64. Joseph Crosby Lincoln, *Cape Cod Yesterdays* (Garden City, N.Y., [c. 1935]), pp. 88–89.

65. Knight, *Tit-Bits*, pp. 62–67, 109; *K.K.K. Cook Book by the "Kute Kooking Klub,"* Honey Grove, Texas (Cincinnati, 1894), p. 71; *Journal of American Folklore* 13 (1900): 66; Bates, *Great Republic*, 1:74–75; Clarke, *Clarke's Cook Book*, p. 152; *Capitol Cook Book*, pp. 86–88; The Ladies' Association of the First Presbyterian Church, eds., *The First Texas Cook Book* (Houston, Tex., 1883; reissue, Austin, Tex., 1963), pp. 98–100.

66. Tyree, *Housekeeping*, pp. 320–21, 324; Howard, *Fifty Years*, pp.

260–61, 270; T. J. Kirkpatrick, *The Housekeepers New Cook Book* (Springfield, Ohio, 1883), pp. 192–93; Trowbridge, *Excelsior Cook Book*, pp. 103–104, 116, 118, 120; Ladies of the Centenary M. E. Church, New Bern, N.C., *The Elm City Cook Book* (New Bern, N.C., 1896), p. 23.

67. Howard, *Fifty Years*, pp. 258, 260, 262; Tyree, *Housekeeping*, pp. 309–10, 312, 320; Trowbridge, *Excelsior Cook Book*, pp. 113, 118; *The Farm and Household Encyclopedia* (New York, 1888), p. 340; *Buckeye Cook Book*, pp. 45, 53, 60–61, 68–69; Knight, *Tit-Bits*, p. 81; *Gumbo Ya-Ya*, p. 162.

68. Leslie, *New Cookery Book*, pp. 535–36; Howard, *Fifty Years*, pp. 258–60.

69. "The Saratoga Favorite," Published by the Young Women's Mission Circle of the First Baptist Church, Saratoga Springs, N.Y., 1885 (Saratoga Springs, N.Y., 1885), pp. 110–18.

70. James Beard, *James Beard's American Cookery* (Boston, 1972), p. 642; Trowbridge, *Excelsior Cook Book*, pp. 104, 110, 116; *Buckeye Cook Book*, pp. 60–62; Willey, *Model Cook Book*, p. 282; *Housekeeping in the Bluegrass*, ed. by Ladies of the Presbyterian Church, Paris, Kentucky (Cincinnati, [1874]), p. 169; Ronald, *Century Cook Book*, p. 467.

71. Lincoln, *Cape Cod Yesterdays*, p. 90.

72. Knight, *Tit-Bits*, pp. 76, 81; Harland, *Common Sense*, p. 330; Parloa, *Young Housekeeper*, p. 250.

73. Sara T. Paul, *The Economical Cook Book* (New York, 1905), p. 226; Haskell, *Housekeeper's Encyclopedia*, p. 181; Sanford, *Mollie*, p. 44.

74. Trowbridge, *Excelsior Cook Book*, p. 157; Maria Parloa, *Miss Parloa's Original Appledore Cook Book* (Boston, 1881), p. 206.

75. Harland, *Common Sense*, pp. 296–97.

76. Thomas, *Delmonico's*, p. 191.

77. Schriftgeisser, *Oscar of the Waldorf*, pp. 128–29.

78. *Housekeeping in the Bluegrass*, pp. 130–31.

79. Ronald, *Century Cook Book*, pp. 389–90; Rorer, *Mrs. Rorer's Philadelphia Cook Book*, pp. 445–454.

80. Riley, *American Soft Drink Industry*, pp. 10–11, 114; Paul Dickson, *The Great American Ice Cream Book* (New York, 1972), pp. 61–62.

81. *Ibid.*, pp. 64–66.

82. Rubert Hughes, *The Real New York* (New York, 1904), p. 263.

83. Louis Untermeyer, *A Century of Candymaking, 1847–1947* (Boston, 1947), pp. 11, 21, 26.

84. Sala, *America Revisited*, 1:107.

85. Ripley, *Social Life*, p. 25.

86. Ronald, *Century Cook Book*, pp. 517–28.

87. *Milwaukee Cook Book*, ed. Mrs. J. Magie (Milwaukee, 1894), p. 326; *Cookery Craft: As Practised in 1894 by the Women of South Church, St. Johnsbury, Vt.*, ed. Mrs. C. H. Merrill (St. Johnsbury, 1894), p. 145; Ladies' Missionary Society of the Central Presbyterian Church, Atlanta, Georgia, *The Southern Housekeeper* (Atlanta, 1898), p. 133; Farmer, *Chafing Dish*, p. 145; Hedwig Loeb in *The University of Chicago Magazine*, 70 (fall 1977): 42.

Chapter 18: Eating Out, 1865–1900

1. Randel, *Centennial*, p. 25.
2. De Rousiers, *American Life*, p. 316.
3. Trollope, *North America*, pp. 291–92.
4. Henry Sienkiewicz, *Portrait of America: Letters of Henry Sienkiewicz*, ed. Charles Morley (New York, 1959), p. 4.
5. Sala, *America Revisited*, 1:177.
6. Zincke, *Last Winter*, pp. 8–9.
7. "Reminiscences of American Hotels," *North American Review* 152 (January 1891): 89.
8. Russell, *Diary*, p. 34.
9. Zincke, *Last Winter*, p. 62.
10. Towle, *American Society*, 1:323.
11. Morris, *Incredible New York*, pp. 238–39, 242.
12. G. Sauvin, *Autour de Chicago* (Paris, 1893), pp. 16–17.
13. Thomas, *Delmonico's*, pp. 85–86, 122.
14. De Rousiers, *American Life*, pp. 317–18; Sala, *America Revisited*, 1:92.
15. Ross, *Crusades and Crinolines*, pp. 37–38, 95; Muirhead, *Land of Contrasts*, p. 268.
16. Thomas, *Delmonico's*, pp. 149, 221–22.
17. *Ibid.*, pp. 86, 226.
18. Randel, *Centennial*, p. 25; Sala, *America Revisited*, 1:92; Morris, *Incredible New York*, p. 111.
19. Towle, *American Society*, 1:272–73.
20. Brown, *Golden Nineties*, pp. 321–22.
21. Gesner, "Concerning Restaurants," p. 593; Charles Townsend Harris, *Memories of Manhattan in the Sixties and Seventies* (New York, 1928), p. 24.
22. Brown, *Golden Nineties*, p. 383.
23. "Germany in New York," *Atlantic Monthly* 19 (May 1867): 556–58.
24. William Dean Howells, *Letters of an Altrurian Traveller* (1893–94; Scholars' Facsimiles and Reprints, Gainesville, Fla., 1961), p. 108; Towle, *American Society*, 1:328.
25. Campbell, *Darkness and Daylight*, pp. 562–64.
26. [Tomes], *Bazar Book of Decorum*, pp. 186, 203; Randel, *Centennial*, p. 25.
27. De Rousiers, *American Life*, pp. 314–15.
28. "Childs: The Quick Lunch Business in New York," *Caterer Monthly* (February 1898), quoted in Grace M. Mayer, *Once Upon a City* (New York, 1958), p. 391; Howells, *Letters of an Altrurian*, p. 108.
29. Harris, *Memories of Manhattan*, p. 25.
30. Sala, *America Revisited*, 1:92.
31. Brown, *Golden Nineties*, pp. 154–55; Morris, *Incredible New York*, p. 32; Sigmund Kransz, *Street Types of Great American Cities* (Chicago, 1896), pp. 90, 134, 142.

32. Willard Glazier, *Peculiarities of American Cities* (Philadelphia, 1885), p. 34; Campbell, *Darkness and Daylight*, pp. 215– 16.

33. Russell, *Diary*, p. 232.

34. *Historical Sketch Book*, p. 86; Sala, *America Revisited*, 2:122; Deirdre Stanforth, *The New Orleans Restaurant Cookbook* (New York, 1967), pp. 12– 13.

35. *Historical Sketch Book*, pp. 87– 88; *New Orleans As It Is*, p. 55.

36. *Ibid.*, p. 56; *Historical Sketch Book*, pp. 88– 90.

37. Williamson, *American Hotel*, p. 222; Bowles, *Our New West*, pp. 345– 46.

38. Samuel Williams, "The City of the Golden Gate," *Scribner's Magazine* 10 (July 1875): 274.

39. Clarence E. Edwords, *Bohemian San Francisco* (San Francisco, 1914), pp. 10– 16; Lucius Beebe, "Dining Out," *The American Heritage Cookbook* (n.p., 1964), pp. 333– 34; Julian Ralph, "San Francisco's Rich Fare," *Harper's Weekly* 40 (1896): 275; Charles Keeler, *San Francisco and Thereabout* (San Francisco, 1903), pp. 45– 47.

40. Oscar Lewis and Carrol D. Hall, *Bonanza Inn* (New York, 1939), pp. 4, 11, 67, 69, 70– 72.

41. *Ibid.*, pp. 73– 75.

42. Bowles, *Our New West*, p. 346; "The City of the Golden Gate," p. 274.

43. Gunther Barth, *Bitter Strength: A History of the Chinese in the United States 1850– 1870* (Cambridge, Mass., 1964), p. 43.

44. Bates, *Great Republic*, 1:56.

45. Randel, *Centennial*, p. 25.

46. J. A. Dacus and James W. Buel, *A Tour of St. Louis. . . .* (St. Louis, 1878), pp. 294, 296, 297, 478, 481; Dedmon, *Fabulous Chicago*, pp. 116– 17; *Rand McNally & Co's Handy Guide to Chicago* (Chicago, 1893), pp. 43, 45, 107.

47. Towle, *American Society*, 1:324.

48. Alfred Leland Crab, *Nashville: Personality of a City* (Indianapolis, 1960), p. 101, Beirne, *Amiable Baltimoreans*, pp. 354– 55; Clarke, *Mrs. Clarke's Cookbook*, p. 140.

49. Clark, *Pills, Petticoats and Plows*, pp. 44– 45.

50. Beebe, "Dining Out," *American Heritage Cookbook*, pp. 331– 33.

51. Sala, *America Revisited*, 2:294.

52. Jay J. Kalez, *Saga of a Western Town. . . Spokane* (Spokane, Wash., 1972), p. 83.

53. Dick, *Sod House Frontier*, p. 404.

54. Beadle, *Undeveloped West*, p. 482.

55. Hughes, *Gone to Texas*, p. 15.

56. Harold E. Briggs, *Frontiers of the Northwest: A History of the Upper Missouri Valley* (New York, 1940), p. 52. See also Richard A. Van Orman, *A Room for the Night: Hotels of the Old West* (Bloomington, Ind., 1966), pp. 110, 113– 14.

57. Atherton, *Main Street*, pp. 58– 59; Rae, *Westward by Rail*, pp. 231– 32; Jessamine Burgum, *Zezula or Pioneer Days in Smoky Water Country* (Valley City, N.D., 1937), p. 98.

58. O'Rell and Allyn, *Jonathan*, pp. 288–91.
59. *Cincinnati Commercial*, July 16, 1864.
60. Samuel Bowles, *The Switzerland of America: A Summer Vacation in the Parks and Mountains of Colorado* (Springfield, Mass., 1869), p. 31; Ross, *Westward the Women*, p. 181.
61. George W. Pine, *Beyond the West* (Utica, N.Y., 1871), pp. 176–77; Bowles, *Our New West*, p. 38; Bowles, *Switzerland of America*, pp. 31–33.
62. James David Henderson, "*Meals by Fred Harvey*": A Phenomenon of the American West (Fort Worth, Tex., 1969), p. 1; Faithful, *Three Visits*, p. 48; Towle, *American Society*, 2:184–85.
63. John F. Stover, *American Railroads* (Chicago, 1961), p. 166; John W. Starr, *One Hundred Years of American Railroading* (New York, 1929), pp. 284–87; Towle, *American Society*, 2:178–79; Husband, *Story of the Pullman Car*, pp. 49–50; Rae, *Westward by Rail*, pp. 29–30.
64. Charles Nordhoff, "California," *Harper's New Monthly Magazine* 44 (May 1872): 872.
65. Marshall, *Through America*, pp. 67, 108–109; Mark Twain, *Roughing It* (New York, 1871), pp. 19–20; Hudson, *Scamper*, pp. 83–84.
66. Henderson, "*Meals by Fred Harvey*," pp. 1, 5, 11–15. See, also, Finck, *Food and Flavor*, pp. 6–8.
67. Lucius Beebe, "Dining Out," *American Heritage Cookbook* (n.p., 1964), pp. 329–30.
68. Taylor, *Carolina Crossroads*, p. 26; Harry Hansen, ed., *Texas: A Guide to the Lone Star State*, American Guide Series (New York, 1940), p. 113.
69. Lauren C. Post, *Cajun Sketches* (n.p., 1962), pp. 137–39.
70. Brown, *Gentle Tamers*, p. 156.
71. Edna Ferber, *A Peculiar Treasure* (New York, 1939), p. 106; Towle, *American Society*, 2:61.
72. Glazier, *Peculiarities of American Cities*, pp. 402–403; Lincoln, *Mrs. Lincoln's Cook Book*, pp. 180–81.
73. James Laver, *Manners and Morals in The Age of Optimism 1848–1914* (New York, 1966), p. 210.
74. McAllister, *Society As I Have Found It*, pp. 102–103.
75. Taylor, *Carolina Crossroads*, pp. 80–81.
76. B. A. Botkin, ed., *The Treasury of American Folklore* (New York, 1944), pp. 579–80. For burgoo and the somewhat similar Kentucky gumbo see Corson, *Family Living*, pp. 221–22.
77. Harland, *Common Sense*, pp. 155, 159–60; Tyree, *Housekeeping*, pp. 211–12; *Housekeeping in the Bluegrass*, p. 168.

Chapter 19: Drink, 1865–1900

1. Sala, *America Revisited*, 1:184, 190–92; Towle, *American Society*, 2:53–54; Mrs. N. M. 'Conaughy, "New-Year's Calls," *Ladies' Repository* 24 (April 1864): 224; Howells, *Letters of an Altrurian*, p. 103.

2. Henri Kowalski, À Travers l'Amérique: Impressions d'un Musicien (Paris, 1872), p. 31; Zincke, Last Winter, p. 66; Faithful, Three Visits, pp. 49–50; Sienkiewicz, Portrait of America, p. 4; Hudson, Scamper, pp. 45–46; De Rousiers, American Life, pp. 303, 314, 318; Baxter, America and the Americans, p. 44.

3. O'Rell and Allyn, Jonathan, p. 287.

4. Sienkiewicz, Portrait of America, p. 233.

5. Riley, American Soft Drink Industry, p. 12.

6. J. S. Ingram, The Centennial Exposition (Philadelphia, 1876), pp. 288–89; Snively, "Soda Water," p. 346; Riley, American Soft Drink Industry, pp. 64, 66, 72; M. G. de Molinari, Lettres sur Les États-Unis et Le Canada (Paris, 1876), pp. 47, 57; Randel, Centennial, p. 289.

7. Snively, "Soda Water," p. 345.

8. Riley, American Soft Drink Industry, pp. 10–11, 114; Snively, "Soda Water," p. 344; Lucy Kavaler, Freezing Point: Cold as a Matter of Life and Death (New York, 1970), p. 297.

9. Campbell, Darkness and Daylight, p. 624.

10. Riley, American Soft Drink Industry, pp. 62–63.

11. James J. Nagle in New York Times, July 3, 1960, Financial Section 3, p. 9.

12. Adams, Wines of America, p. 67.

13. Milward W. Martin, Twelve Full Ounces (New York, 1969), pp. 11–12, 19; Ely Jacques Kahn, Jr., The Big Drink (New York, 1960), pp. 55–56; Riley, American Soft Drink Industry, p. 118.

14. Ibid., pp. 117–18.

15. Muirhead, Land of Contrasts, p. 271; Smith, Virginia Cookery-Book, p. 35.

16. Leslie, New Cookery Book, p. 595.

17. De Molinari, Lettres sur Les États-Unis, p. 47; Thomas, Delmonico's, p. 123.

18. Hughes, Gone to Texas, pp. 23–24; Gard, Chisholm Trail, p. 122.

19. Harland, Breakfast, Luncheon and Tea, p. 364.

20. Muirhead, Land of Contrasts, p. 271; Towle, American Society, 1:271.

21. Haskell, Housekeeper's Encyclopedia, p. 207.

22. Harland, Common Sense, p. 483.

23. Harland, Breakfast, Luncheon and Tea, pp. 360–61.

24. Bird, Lady's Life, pp. 73, 84, 111; Bowles, Across the Continent, pp. 6, 21.

25. Twain, Roughing It, p. 18.

26. Solon Robinson, How to Live (New York, 1860), p. 157.

27. Harland, Breakfast, Luncheon and Tea, pp. 360–61; Lincoln, Mrs. Lincoln's Boston Cook Book, p. 112; Robert Somers, The Southern States Since the War (New York, 1871), p. 235.

28. Kowalski, À Travers l'Amérique, p. 31.

29. Somers, Southern States, p. 235.

30. Marshall, Through America, pp. 108–109, 130; Smith, Virginia Cookery-Book, pp. 41–42.

31. *Dictionary of American English,* s.v. "iced tea."

32. Marshall, *Through America,* p. 98; Faithful, *Three Visits,* p. 354.

33. Arnold and White, *Food,* pp. 174–76; Schlesinger, *Paths to the Present,* p. 248.

34. Gusfield, "Status Conflicts," *Society, Culture, and Drinking Patterns,* pp. 105–11.

35. Sala, *America Revisited,* 1:278.

36. Towle, *American Society,* 1:270.

37. Brown, *Golden Nineties,* pp. 320–21, 323; Adams, *Wines of America,* p. 30.

38. John Francis Maguire, *The Irish in America* (London, 1868), p. 283.

39. Sala, *America Revisited,* 1:100; Dacus and Buel, *A Tour of St. Louis,* p. 478.

40. Nevins, *Emergence of Modern America,* p. 46.

41. Mencken, *American Language,* p. 155; Brown, *Golden Nineties,* p. 125.

42. Ernst, *Immigrant Life,* p. 125; King, *Great South,* p. 224; "The Summer Beer Gardens of St. Louis," *Bulletin of the Missouri Historical Society* 9, no. 4, pt. 1 (July 1953): 391–92.

43. Matthew Hale Smith, *Sunshine and Shadow in New York* (Hartford, Conn., 1869), pp. 216–17; Campbell, *Darkness and Daylight,* pp. 469–70; "Germany in New York," p. 559.

44. *Ibid.,* p. 560.

45. Baron, *Brewed in America,* p. 228.

46. Towle, *American Society,* 1:270; [Rivington and Harris], *Reminiscences,* p. 55; Sala, *America Revisited,* 2:122.

47. William J. Flagg, "Wine in America and American Wine," *Harper's New Monthly Magazine* 41 (June 1870): 111–14.

48. Carosso, *California Wine Industry,* pp. 38, 43, 96; Muirhead, *Land of Contrasts,* pp. 270–71; Adams, *Wines of America,* p. 22.

49. Beadle, *Undeveloped West,* pp. 270, 486, 660–61, 747; Hughes, *Gone to Texas,* p. 80; Carosso, *California Wine Industry,* p. 96.

50. *Gumbo Ya-Ya,* p. 172.

51. Lodge, "Among the Peaches," p. 516.

52. Quoted in Furnas, *Late Demon Rum,* p. 80.

53. Zincke, *Last Winter,* pp. 77–78; Furnas, *Americans,* pp. 904–905; David Macrae, *The Americans at Home* (Edinburgh, 1870), 2:306–307.

54. George Ade, *The Old-Time Saloon* (New York, 1931), pp. 26–28.

55. Atherton, *Main Street,* pp. 58–59.

56. Brown, *Gentle Tamers,* pp. 272–77.

57. See Sections on "Cocktails" in Jerry Thomas, *The Bar-Tender's Guide* (New York, 1887 and 1895). In Charles Ranhofer, *The Epicurean* (New York, 1908), p. 1066, the cocktail is given as a "Martine Cocktail."

58. De Rousiers, *American Life,* p. 318.

59. Ade, *Old-Time Saloon,* pp. 52–59.

60. Lucius Beebe and Charles Clegg, *Narrow Gauge in the Rockies* (Berkeley, Calif., 1958), p. 30.

61. Beadle, *Undeveloped West,* p. 227.

62. Burton, *City of Saints*, p. 320.
63. Hughes, *Gone to Texas*, p. 37.
64. Ralph, *Our New West*, p. 205; Bryan, *Illinois Gold Hunter*, p. 28.
65. Chase, *Editor's Run*, p. 216.
66. Quiett, *Pay Dirt*, p. 251.
67. Rae, *Westward by Rail*, p. 231.
68. Beadle, *Undeveloped West*, p. 747.

Chapter 20: The Immigrants

1. Ely Jacques Kahn, Jr., *The American People: The Findings of the 1970 Census* (New York, 1973), p. 179; Frederick Lewis Allen, *The Big Change: America Transforms Itself 1900 – 1950* (New York, 1952), p. 60; Michael M. Davis, Jr., *Immigrant Health and the Community*, ed. William S. Bernard, Americanization Studies no. 5 (1921; reprint ed., Montclair, N.J., 1971), pp. 246 – 47.
2. Maurice R. Davis, *World Immigration* (New York, 1936), p. 496.
3. David Te-Chao Cheng, *Acculturation of the Chinese in the United States: A Philadelphia Study* (Philadelphia, 1948), pp. 228 – 29; Betty Lee Sung, *Mountain of Gold: The Story of the Chinese in America* (New York, 1967), pp. 10, 30 – 36, 43 – 45, 50 – 57, 80.
4. Interview with Leland Chin as given in Victor G. and Brett de Bary Nee, *Longtime California: A Documentary Study of an American Chinatown* (New York, 1973), p. 77.
5. Beard, *American Cookery*, p. 110; Brown, *West Coast Cook Book*, p. 177.
6. *Seen by the Spectator. . . .* (New York, 1902), pp. 202 – 204; *The Good Housekeeping Hostess* (New York, 1904), pp. 72, 74; Maria Willett Howard, *Lowney's Cook Book* (Boston, 1908), pp. 153 – 54; Ivan Light, "From Vice District to Tourist Attraction: The Moral Career of American Chinatowns, 1880 – 1940," *Pacific Historical Review* 43 (August 1947): 384; Sung, *Mountain of Gold*, p. 202; Cheng, *Acculteration of the Chinese*, p. 90.
7. *Pictorial Review Standard Cook Book* (New York, 1932), pp. 216 – 17.
8. The National Research Council, Committee on Food Habits, *Some Central European Food Patterns and Their Relationship to Wartime Programs of Food and Nutrition*, misc. pub. 1943, p. ii.
9. Sula M. Benet and Natalie Joffe, "Polish Food Patterns," in *ibid.*, pp. 1 – 9; Bertha M. Wood, *Foods of the Foreign-Born in Relation to Health* (Boston, 1922), p. 49; Paul Fox, *The Poles in America* (New York, 1922), pp. 48 – 49.
10. Svatava Pirkova-Jakobson and Natalie Joffe, "Czech and Slovak Food Patterns," *Some Central European Food Patterns*, pp. 2 – 3, 5 – 8; *Minneapolis Star*, March 24, 1971, p. 19C.
11. Pirkova-Jakobson and Joffe, "Czech and Slovak Food Patterns," *Some Central European Food Patterns*, pp. 5 – 7, 10 – 12.
12. Natalie Joffe, "Hungarian Food Patterns," *Some Central European Food Patterns*, pp. 1 – 9. Mr. Robert Diamant of Highland Park, Ill., provided me the list of foods strange to Hungarian immigrants.

13. Erik Amfitheatrof, *The Children of Columbus: An Informal History of the Italians in the New World* (Boston, 1973), pp. 156, 240–41; Phyllis H. Williams, *South Italian Folkways in Europe and America* (New Haven, 1938), 55–61; Peter H. Rossi, *Progress Report: Study of the Bases for Changing Food Attitudes* (Chicago, 1958), p. 10; Waverly Root, "The Italian Table," *Holiday* 48 (July–August 1970): 31; Davie, *World Immigration,* p. 114.

14. Williams, *South Italian Folkways,* pp. 61–64; Natalie F. Joffe, "Food Habits of Selected Subcultures in the United States," National Research Council, Report of the Committee on Food Habits, 1941–1943, *Bulletin of the National Research Council,* no. 108 (October 1943), pp. 98–99.

15. Konrad Bercovici, *Around the World in New York* (New York, [1924]), p. 62.

16. Ida Bailey Allen, *Ida Bailey Allen's Modern Cook Book* (Garden City, N.Y., 1927), p. 310.

17. Panos Anagnostopoulos, "Greek vs. American Eating Habits," unpublished essay of May 11, 1961, in possession of Richard J. Hooker.

18. Demetra Vaka Brown, *A Child of the Orient* (New York, 1914), p. 271.

19. Thomas Burgess, *Greeks in America* (Boston, 1913), p. 34.

20. Henry Pratt Fairchild, *Greek Immigration to the United States* (New Haven, 1911), p. 127; Burgess, *Greeks in America,* pp. 34–38; Bercovici, *Around the World,* p. 62.

21. Henry Miller, *Remember to Remember* (London, 1952), p. 73. Miller castigated such restaurants and compared what they served to the "damned good" cuisine in Greek-American homes.

22. Harry Golden, *The Greatest Jewish City in the World* (New York, 1972), pp. 106–107.

23. Davis, *Immigrant Health,* pp. 258–59; Golden, *Greatest Jewish City,* pp. 107–108.

24. Dale Brown, *American Cooking* (New York, 1968), p. 74; Leonard Levinson, "Cosmopolitan Tastes," *American Heritage Cookbook,* p. 248.

25. Finck, *Food and Flavor,* pp. 341, 343–46.

26. Lawrence Welk with Bernice McGeehan, *Wunnerful, Wunnerful* (Englewood Cliffs, N.J., 1971), p. 26.

27. Furnas, *Americans,* p. 696.

28. Smith, *Americans in the Making,* p. 211.

29. Dale Brown, *American Cooking: The Northwest* (New York, 1970), pp. 145–46, 148, 152.

30. Fred L. Holmes, *Old World Wisconsin* (Eau Claire, Wis., 1944), pp. 103, 139–41, 164; Brown, *American Cooking: The Northwest,* p. 148; Beard, *American Cookery,* pp. 329–30.

Chapter 21: The Early Twentieth Century, 1900–1941, I

1. Mark Sullivan, *Our Times* (New York, 1927), 2:501–508.

2. Oscar E. Anderson, Jr.,, *The Health of a Nation: Harvey W. Wiley and the Fight for Pure Food* (Chicago, 1968), pp. 71–74, 120; Rorty and Norman, *Tomorrow's Food*, p. 36; James S. Turner, *The Chemical Feast* (New York, 1970), pp. 107–108.

3. Anderson, *The Health of a Nation*, p. 128; Rorty and Norman, *Tomorrow's Food*, pp. 188–89.

4. Furnass, *Americans*, p. 872; Sullivan, *Our Times*, 2:476, 481.

5. Turner, *Chemical Feast*, pp. 109–10.

6. *Ibid.*, pp. 111, 116; Rorty and Norman, *Tomorrow's Food*, p. 191.

7. Fred Harvey, "The Case of Jack the Dullard," *Good Housekeeping Magazine*, 58 (February 1914): 226; Dixon Wecter, *Age of the Great Depression* (New York, 1948), pp. 282–83.

8. Margaret Cussler and Mary L. De Give, *'Twixt the Cup and the Lip* (New York, 1952), p. 166; Maxey Robson Dickson, *The Food Front in World War I* (Washington, 1944), pp. 43, 63, 184.

9. Mark Sullivan, *Our Times* (New York, 1933), 5:419–22; Schlesinger, *Paths to the Present*, pp. 250–51.

10. Caroline Bird, *The Invisible Scar* (New York, 1966), pp. 243–44; Wecter, *Age of the Great Depression*, p. 39.

11. Schriftgeisser, *Oscar of the Waldorf*, p. 198.

12. Andrew Sinclair, *Era of Excess: A Social History of the Prohibition Movement* (New York, 1964), pp. 174, 197, 234–35, 237, 239.

13. Stephen Birmingham, *The Right People: A Portrait of the American Social Establishment* (Boston, 1968), pp. 241–42; Beard, *American Cookery*, p. 8.

14. Sinclair, *Era of Excess*, p. 230.

15. *Ibid.*, pp. 236–37.

16. Adams, *Wines of America*, pp. 25–26.

17. Harry M. Caudill, *Night Comes to the Cumberlands* (Boston, 1962), pp. 153–54.

18. Riley, *American Soft Drink Industry*, p. 139.

19. Sinclair, *Era of Excess*, pp. 413–14.

20. Lynes, *Domesticated Americans*, p. 129; Schmidt, *Rural Hunterdon*, pp. 203–204.

21. Randel, *Centennial*, p. 316; Atherton, *Main Street*, pp. 222–29, 240; Edwin P. Hoyt, *That Wonderful A. & P.* (New York, 1969), p. 113.

22. Anna Merritt East, *Kitchenette Cookery* (Boston, 1918), pp. 1, 27.

23. Giedion, *Mechanization Takes Command*, pp. 537–39; Lynes, *Domesticated Americans*, p. 121; Ronald, *Century Cook Book*, p. 39.

24. Anderson, *Refrigeration in America*, pp. 195–97; Giedion, *Mechanization Takes Command*, p. 602.

25. Finck, *Food and Flavor*, pp. 200–201, 204–205.

26. Lynes, *Domesticated Americans*, pp. 134–35.

27. Edward Robb Ellis, *A Nation in Torment: The Great American Depression, 1929–1939* (New York, 1970), pp. 125–27, 129–31.
28. T. Harry Williams, Richard N. Current, and Frank Freidel, *A History of the United States Since 1865*, 2d ed., rev. (New York, 1965), p. 506.
29. Wecter, *Age of the Great Depression*, pp. 47, 142.
30. Schlesinger, *Paths to the Present*, pp. 252–53; Ellis, *Nation in Torment*, pp. 149, 241–44, 247; Wecter, *Age of the Great Depression*, p. 39. A good discussion of hunger during the depression is in Bird, *Invisible Scar*.
31. "No One Has Starved," *Fortune* 6 (September 1932): 28; Broadus Mitchell, *Depression Decade: From New Era through New Deal, 1929–1941* (New York, 1947), pp. 104–105; Caudill, *Night Comes to the Cumberlands*, pp. 184–85.
32. Taped interview with William Linkous, May 25, 1972, in Tams, W. Va., conducted by William Mares of Burlington, Vt.
33. Russell Baker, "Red Meat Decadence," *New York Times*, April 3, 1973, p. 41.
34. *Time*, December 7, 1959, p. 94; Anderson, *Refrigeration in America*, pp. 298–300; General Foods, "Quick Frozen Foods — The Beginning," dittoed release, April 1959; E. W. Williams, *Frozen Foods: Biography of an Industry* (Boston, n.d.), pp. 2–3.
35. Collins, *Story of Canned Foods*, pp. 192, 196; Anderson, *Refrigeration in America*, pp. 287–88, 298–300.
36. Wecter, *Age of the Great Depression*, pp. 282–83.
37. Helen Robertson, *Merry Mixer Cook Book* (New York, 1937), p. 458.
38. Sidney Margolius, *The Great American Food Hoax* (New York, 1971), p. 15.
39. Published in New York.
40. New York, 1936.
41. Turner, *Chemical Feast*, pp. 125–35.

Chapter 22: The Early Twentieth Century, 1900–1941, II

1. Frederick J. Stare and Martha F. Trulson, "The Implementation of Preference," *Food and Civilization: A Symposium*, ed. Seymour M. Farber *et al.* (Springfield, Ill., 1966), p. 230.
2. Sombart is quoted in Schlesinger, *Paths to the Present*, p. 252; Finck, *Food and Flavor*, pp. 66, 70, 97, 100, 486.
3. Thomas, *Delmonico's*, p. 329.
4. Finck, *Food and Flavor*, pp. 87–90, 96. A German visitor to the United States in 1913 still found that the oyster cocktail — four to six cold Blue Points in a little wine glass — was the "first delicacy" of the country. Julius Menschl, *Eine Kulinarische Weltreise* (Leipzig, Germany, 1913), p. 21.
5. Finck, *Food and Flavor*, p. 490.
6. Ladies' Aid Society of the First Presbyterian Church, *Coos Bay's Cook*

415

Book (North Bend, Oreg., 1907), p. 11; Mary J. Lincoln and Anna Barrows, *The Home Science Cook Book* (Boston, 1910), pp. 86–87.

7. May, *Canning Clan,* pp. 114–17, 190–92; Newmark, *Sixty Years in Southern California,* pp. 628–29; Bitting, *Appertizing,* p. 842. There is a reference to "tunny fish" in Henrietta Sowle, *I Go A-Marketing* (Boston, 1900), p. 70, which could refer to either canned or fresh tuna.

8. Vance, *Human Geography,* p. 422; Louella G. Shouer, "How America Eats," *How America Lives,* ed. J. C. Furnas (New York, 1941), p. 292.

9. Hill, *Practical Cooking,* p. 285; Theodore Dreiser, *A Hoosier Holiday* (New York, 1916), p. 81.

10. Allen, *Modern Cook Book,* p. 447.

11. Farmer, *Boston Cook Book,* pp. 252, 256.

12. Vance, *Human Geography,* p. 427.

13. *Ibid.,* p. 432.

14. Hughina McKay and Mary Ann Brown, "Foods Used by Rural Families in Ohio During a Three-Year Period," Ohio Agricultural Experiment Station *Bulletin* no. 492 (October 1931), pp. 1–37.

15. Allen, *Modern Cook Book,* p. 319.

16. *New Delineator Recipes* (Chicago, 1929), pp. 82–87; Jessie Marie De-Both, *Modernistic Recipe-Menu Book* (Chicago, 1929), pp. 257–66.

17. *Pictorial Review Standard Cook Book,* p. 154; DeBoth, *Modernistic Recipe-Menu Book,* pp. 52, 63.

18. George Rector, *The Girl from Rector's* (New York, 1927), p. 157; Finck, *Food and Flavor,* p. 237.

19. *Ibid.,* pp. 239–40; Rector, *The Girl from Rector's,* p. 156.

20. *El Paso Cook Book,* p. 149; St. Mary's Guild, comp., *Cookery Recipes* (Mill Valley, Calif., 1902), p. 88; *The First Presbyterian Cook Book* (Spokane, Wash., c. 1906), pp. 32–33; Howells, *Letters of an Altrurian,* p. 100.

21. Bitting, *Appertizing,* pp. 613–14.

22. Finck, *Food and Flavor,* pp. 456–57, 491–92.

23. Bitting, *Appertizing,* pp. 528, 536, 551, 643, 678.

24. Harland, *Breakfast, Luncheon and Tea,* p. 308. A similar remark was made in 1902 in Hill, *Practical Cooking,* p. 559.

25. Katherine G. Busbey, *Home Life in America* (London, 1910), p. 137.

26. Rorty and Norman, *Tomorrow's Food,* p. 121.

27. Bitting, *Appertizing,* pp. 216, 265; F. J. Schlink, *Eat, Drink and Be Wary* (New York, 1935), pp. 128–29.

28. Hedrick, *History of Horticulture,* pp. 298–99.

29. Collins, *Story of Canned Foods,* p. 205.

30. Bitting, *Appertizing,* p. 304.

31. Collins, *Story of Canned Foods,* pp. 176–83.

32. Schlink, *Eat, Drink,* pp. 166, 209–10, 304.

33. Vance, *Human Geography,* p. 422.

34. Panscher, *Baking in America,* 1:93–99, 109, 188.

35. Rorty and Norman, *Tomorrow's Food,* p. 65.

36. Miller, *Remember to Remember,* p. 64.

37. S. F. Riepma, *The Story of Margarine* (Washington, 1970), pp. iii, 1–2, 110–16, 124–25.

38. Bitting, *Appertizing*, p. 691; "The Fabulous Market for Food," *Fortune*, 48 (October 1953): 272; *New York Times*, March 18, 1974, p. 30; *Consumer Reports*, 40 (September 1975): 529.

39. Allen, *Modern Cook Book*, p. 119.

40. James R. Mellow, *Charmed Circle: Gertrude Stein and Company* (New York, 1975), p. 494; Collins, *Story of Canned Foods*, p. 187.

41. Farmer, *Boston Cook Book*, p. 287.

42. Helen Cramp, *The Institute Cook Book* (n.p., c. 1910), p. 193.

43. Beard, *American Cookery*, pp. 33–34, 39, 67.

44. De Loup, *American Salad Book*, p. 128.

45. George Rector, *À La Rector* (New York, 1933), p. 83.

46. Vance, *Human Geography*, p. 436.

47. Finck, *Food and Flavor*, pp. 228, 232–33, 243.

48. Caroline B. King, *Caroline King's Cook Book* (Boston, 1929), p. 88.

49. Cramp, *Institute Cook Book*, p. 329; Sidney Morse, *Household Discoveries* (Petersburg, N.Y., 1908), p. 44.

50. *First Presbyterian Cook Book*, p. 49; *The Mission Cook Book* (Tucson, Ariz., 1909), p. 23; *The Artistic Needle Worker's Cook Book* (Marshfield, Oreg., 1905), pp. 73–74; *Corona Club Cook Book* (San Francisco, 1910), pp. 144–45.

51. Howard, *Lowney's Cook Book*, p. 199.

52. Dennis, *Dennis Cook Book*, p. 164; *Needle Worker's Cook Book*, p. 73.

53. Ladies' Missionary Society, *Southern Housekeeper*, p. 89.

54. Rorer, *Mrs. Rorer's New Cook Book*, p. 535; *New York Times*, May 9, 1965, p. 21.

55. Cramp, *Institute Cook Book*, p. 475; *Two Hundred Recipes For Cooking in Casseroles*, ed. Olive M. Hulse (Chicago, 1914), p. vii.

56. *Good Housekeeping's Book of Recipes and Household Discoveries* (New York, 1920), p. 103; *New Delineator Recipes*, pp. 185–96.

57. The Woman's Society of Bethany Union Church, Chicago, *The Bethany Union Cook Book* (Chicago, 1912), p. 39; *The Bozeman Woman's Club Cook Book* (n.p., 1925), p. 162.

58. *General Foods Family Album* (n.p., n.d.), p. 6.

59. Elise Biesel, "The First Cook in the Land," *Good Housekeeping Magazine*, 58 (March 1914): 421.

Chapter 23: Eating Out, 1900–1941

1. Jesse Frederick Steiner, *Americans at Play* (New York, 1970), pp. 131–32.

2. Hughes, *Real New York*, pp. 260–61; Carol Truax, *Father Was a Gourmet: An Epic of Good Eating at the Turn of the Century* (New York, 1965), p. 17.

3. Iles Brody, *The Colony* (New York, 1945), pp. 11–14; Vincent Sardi, Sr., and Richard Gehman, *Sardi's* (New York, 1953), p. 1.

4. Morris, *Incredible New York*, p. 326.

NOTES

5. Edward Hungerford, *The Personality of American Cities* (New York, 1913), p. 49.
6. Calvin Lee, *Chinatown, U.S.A.* (New York, 1965), p. 71; Rose Hum Lee, *The Chinese in the United States of America* (Hong Kong, 1960), p. 261.
7. John C. Van Dyke, *The New New York* (New York, 1909), p. 247.
8. Golden, *Greatest Jewish City*, pp. 57, 109–10.
9. Menschl, *Eine Kulinarische Weltreise*, pp. 43–47; Hungerford, *Personality of American Cities*, p. 31; Hughes, *Real New York*, pp. 258, 268; Mayer, *Once Upon a City*, p. 391; Brody, *The Colony*, p. 24.
10. Mencken, *American Language, Supplement I*, pp. 352–53; Ilya Ilf and Eugene Petrov, *Little Golden America* (London, [1946]), pp. 24–27.
11. Mary Bralove in the *Wall Street Journal*, May 2, 1973, p. 38; Peter Hart in the *New York Times*, May 20, 1961, pp. 26, 30.
12. Hughes, *Real New York*, pp. 257–58.
13. Van Dyke, *New New York*, p. 191.
14. John L. Hess in the *New York Times*, August 3, 1973, p. 14; Ferber, *A Peculiar Treasure*, p. 188.
15. Ade, *Old-Time Saloon*, pp. 34–47.
16. Menschl, *Eine Kulinarische Weltreise*, p. 53; Hughes, *Real New York*, pp. 71, 256; Jacob A. Riis, *How the Other Half Lives* (New York, 1914), p. 74.
17. Stanforth, *New Orleans Restaurant Cookbook*, pp. 12–13, 21, 31, 47.
18. Jonathan Norton Leonard, *American Cooking: The Great West* (New York, 1971), p. 119; James Beard, *Delights and Prejudices* (New York, 1964), pp. 184–86.
19. Helen Throop Purdy, *San Francisco, As It Was, As It Is, And How to See It* (San Francisco, 1912), pp. 148–52; Charles Caldwell Dobie, *San Francisco: A Pageant* (New York, 1939), pp. 287, 289–93.
20. Richard J. S. Gutman and Peter Ames Richards, "A Guide to Dining Out . . . Way Out," *New York Times*, September 15, 1974, Travel Section, p. 1.
21. Oliver Pilat and Jo Ranson, *Sodom by the Sea* (Garden City, N.Y., 1943), p. 239; "Famous Nathan," *New York Times*, August 3, 1966, p. 25; Mencken, *American Language*, p. 186n.
22. "Famous Nathan," p. 25.
23. Pilat and Ranson, *Sodom by the Sea*, p. 241; *Dictionary of Americanisms*, s.v. "hot dog."
24. E. W. Ingram, Sr., *"All This from a 5-cent Hamburger!"* (New York, 1964), pp. 8–9; James Beard remembered hamburgers and hamburger stands at beach resorts in California from as early as 1911–12. Beard, *American Cookery*, p. 312.
25. Frank X. Tolbert, *A Bowl of Red* (New York, 1966), pp. 39–40.
26. *Ibid.*, p. 62.
27. Eleanor Early, *New Orleans Holiday* (New York, 1947), p. 97.
28. Dickson, *Great American Ice Cream Book*, p. 92.
29. *Ibid.*, pp. 67–70.
30. *Ibid.*, pp. 73–74; Arnold and White, *Food*, p. 185.
31. Dickson, *Great American Ice Cream Book*, pp. 77–81.
32. *Ibid.*, p. 83; Kavaler, *Freezing Point*, pp. 298–99.

Chapter 24: World War II and After

1. Williams, Current, and Freidel, *United States since 1865,* pp. 605 – 606.
2. Richard R. Lingeman, *Don't You Know There's a War On?* (New York, 1970), p. 165.
3. General Foods, *Annual Report 1945,* p. 17.
4. Lingeman, *Don't You Know There's a War On?,* pp. 254 – 63; John Morton Blum, *V Was for Victory: Politics and American Culture during World War II* (New York [1976]), pp. 98 – 99.
5. George Horace Gallup, *The Gallup Poll: Public Opinion, 1935 – 1971* (New York, [c. 1972]), 1:410, 415, 488.
6. *Wall Street Journal,* January 9, 1973, p. 1; *Consumer Reports,* 38 (March 1973): 187.
7. *Wall Street Journal,* January 9, 1973, p. 1; H. E. Crowther, "The Water's Harvest: Fish of All Kinds for Our Tables," U.S. Congress, House, *Food for Us All: The Yearbook of Agriculture 1969,* 91st Cong., 1st sess., pp. 15 – 17; *New York Times,* September 27, 1972, p. 49.
8. U.S. Department of Agriculture, *Consumption of Food in the United States, 1909 – 1952,* Agricultural Handbook no. 62, pp. 109 – 110, 137; U.S. Congress, House, *Food for Us All,* p. 52; *New York Times,* August 6, 1978, p. 24; Riepma, *Story of Margarine,* pp. 124 – 26.
9. Craig Claiborne, ed., *The New York Times Cook Book* (New York, 1961), p. ix.
10. Craig Claiborne, "Guided Tour in the 'World of Spice,'" *New York Times Magazine,* March 13, 1960, p. 66.
11. Elena Padilla, *Up from Puerto Rico* (New York, 1964), pp. 154 – 57.
12. Emily Stevens Maclachlan, "The Diet Pattern of the South: A Study in Regional Sociology," M.A. thesis, University of North Carolina, 1932, pp. 7, 9 – 10; Jonathan Daniels, *Tar Heels: A Portrait of North Carolina* (New York, 1941), pp. 258, 262.
13. Elizabeth Alston, "Florida: the Natives Swing to Cuban Cooking," *Look,* April 6, 1971, pp. 47 – 49.
14. Hodding Carter and Anthony Ragusin, *Gulf Coast Country* (New York, 1961), pp. 151 – 53; *New York Times,* August 2, 1975, p. 32.
15. Morton Gill Clark, *The Wide, Wide World of Texas Cooking* (New York, 1970), pp. 4, 10, 58, 95, 107, 191 – 92, 251, 259; Leonard, *American Cooking: The Great West,* pp. 34, 37; Ann Criswell, "Is There Really an American Cuisine," *Saturday Review World,* 1 (November 20, 1973): 34.
16. Richard Wormser, *Southwest Cookery, or At Home on the Range* (Garden City, N.Y., 1969), pp. xi – xiii, 38, 45 – 46.
17. Bonnie and Ed Peplow, *Roundup Recipes* (Cleveland, 1951), pp. 3 – 4, 8 – 15, 41; Ralph, *Our Great West,* p. 387.
18. As given in Leonard, *American Cooking: The Great West,* p. 7.
19. Lillian Hellman, *An Unfinished Woman* (Middlesex, England, 1972), p. 48.
20. Bess A. Cleveland, *Alaskan Cookbook* (Berkeley, Calif., 1960), pp. 7, 8, 142.

21. Sylvia Porter in *Sarasota Herald-Tribune,* December 31, 1970, p. 10.

22. Turner, *Chemical Feast,* pp. 51–57.

23. U.S. Department of Agriculture, *Consumption of Food 1909–1952,* p. 143; Gallup, *Gallup Poll,* 2:1220; Leslie Maitland in *New York Times,* March 15, 1975, p. 12.

24. Packard, *Hidden Persuaders,* pp. 141–43.

25. *Ibid.,* pp. 143–45.

26. Clark, *Wide, Wide World of Texas Cooking,* p. 21.

27. Gallup, *Gallup Poll,* 2:1296; Gallup Poll Release, June 9, 1974, pp. 1–5.

28. Baron, *Brewed in America,* pp. 327–28, 331; *New York Times,* February 19, 1975, p. 22.

29. *Ibid;* Adams, *Wines of America,* pp. 29–30, 32–33, 36–39; *New York Times,* January 7, 1976, p. 44; *ibid.,* March 17, 1976, p. 44; *ibid.,* July 7, 1976, p. 20; *ibid.,* Jan. 24, 1979, p. C12.

30. David Daiches, *Scotch Whiskey* (n.p., 1970), pp. 121–22; the figures on Scotch imports were given the author by the Scotch Whiskey Association in London.

31. *New York Times,* December 1, 1970, pp. 45, 51; *ibid.,* June 3, 1973, p. 3.

32. *Ibid.,* January 13, 1975, pp. 43, 47.

33. Nick Kotz, *Let Them Eat Promises: The Politics of Hunger in America* (Englewood Cliffs, N.J., 1969), pp. 19, 23.

34. *Hunger, U.S.A.: A Report by the Citizens' Board of Inquiry into Hunger and Malnutrition in the United States* (Boston, 1968), pp. 10, 32.

35. Kotz, *Let Them Eat Promises,* pp. 115–17; Turner, *Chemical Feast,* p. 72.

36. Kotz, *Let Them Eat Promises,* pp. 132–36.

37. William Robbins in *New York Times,* June 20, 1974, pp. 1, 17; Joseph M. Winski in *Wall Street Journal,* May 29, 1975, pp. 1, 25; Jack Anderson, "Merry-Go-Round," *Caledonian-Record* (St. Johnsbury, Vt.), June 21, 1974, p. 4.

Chapter 25: The Synthetic Era

1. Ruth Mulvey Harmer, *Unfit for Human Consumption* (Englewood Cliffs, N.J., 1971), pp. 12, 66–67; *New York Times,* August 13, 1975, p. 20; William Robbins in *ibid.,* June 12, 1980, pp. C1, C6.

2. Michael F. Jacobson, *Eater's Digest: The Consumer's Factbook of Food Additives* (Garden City, N.Y., 1972), pp. 7–9.

3. Jacqueline Verrett and Jean Carper, *Eating May Be Hazardous to Your Health* (New York, 1974), pp. 24–27.

4. Jacobson, *Eater's Digest,* pp. 17, 23–24, 37; Sidney Margolius, *Health Foods: Facts and Fakes* (New York, 1973), p. 5.

5. Verrett and Carper, *Eating May Be Hazardous,* p. 43; *Sarasota Herald-Tribune,* February 22, 1976, p. 13E.

6. Verrett and Carper, *Eating May Be Hazardous,* pp. 94–95; Turner, *Chemical Feast,* pp. 3–4.

7. Wade Greene, "Guru of the Organic Food Cult," *New York Times Magazine,* June 6, 1971, pp. 30–31, 54, 56, 58, 60, 65, 68, 70.

8. Harmer, *Unfit for Human Consumption,* pp. 182–83; *New York Times,* October 15, 1972, p. 10; John Keats, *What Ever Happened to Mom's Apple Pie?* (Boston, 1976), p. 141.

9. Daniel Yergin, "'Let's Get Adelle Davis Right' Supernutritionist," *New York Times Magazine,* May 20, 1973, pp. 32–33, 57–66, 71.

10. Ruth Winter, *Poisons in Your Food* (New York, 1969), pp. 2, 185–86.

11. Waverley Root, "Taste is Falling! Taste is Falling!" *New York Times Magazine,* February 16, 1975, pp. 18, 48; Berton Roueché, "One Hundred Thousand Varieties," *The New Yorker,* August 11, 1975, p. 39; Hess and Hess, *Taste of America,* p. 42.

12. Lyall Watson, *The Omnivorous Ape* (New York, 1971), pp. 54–55.

13. Mary Bralove, in *Wall Street Journal,* April 30, 1974, p. 41.

14. Philip H. Dougherty in *New York Times,* February 5, 1975, p. 54; Eileen F. Taylor, "100 Million Times a Day, Americans Eat Out," *Food for Us All,* pp. 62, 64; *Sarasota Herald-Tribune,* March 10, 1974, p. 5.

15. Merrill Proudfoot, *Diary of a Sit-In* (Chapel Hill, 1962), pp. xi, 189.

16. Raymond A. Sokolov in *New York Times,* September 23, 1971, p. 70; Joseph Wechsberg, *Dining at The Pavillon* (Boston, 1962), pp. 28, 30, 34.

17. Horace Sutton, "The Food Fraternity," *Saturday Review World* November 20, 1973: p. 37; Ralph Blumenthal in *New York Times,* July 27, 1972, p. 29.

18. *Newsweek,* January 14, 1974, p. 53; David A. Andelman in *New York Times,* July 31, 1974, p. 38; *ibid.,* August 18, 1974, p. 11.

19. Sutton, "Food Fraternity," p. 37; Peggy J. Murrell in *Wall Street Journal,* November 2, 1974, pp. 1, 23.

20. Craig Claiborne in *New York Times,* January 28, 1971, p. 41; *ibid.,* January 28, 1973, p. 37.

21. Judy Klemesrud, "Pastrami City: A Day in the Life of a Delicatessen," *New York Times,* October 9, 1972, p. 26; Ruth Glazer, "The Jewish Delicatessen," in *Commentary on the American Scene,* ed. Elliott E. Cohen (New York, 1953), pp. 191–92, 194–97.

22. *Wall Street Journal,* June 28, 1977, p. 1.

23. Anthony Lukas, "As American as a McDonald's Hamburger on the Fourth of July," *New York Times Magazine,* July 4, 1971, p. 26.

24. Letitia Brewster and Michael F. Jacobson, *The Changing American Diet* (Washington, D.C., [1978]), p. 78.

Index

Index

Index